English Drama:
A Critical
Introduction

Gāmini Salgādo

ST. MARTIN'S PRESS   **NEW YORK**

ISBN 0–312–25429–6

Library of Congress Cataloging in Publication Data

Salgādo, Ramsay Gāmini Norton, 1929-
   English drama, a critical introduction.

  Bibliography: p.
  Includes index.
  1. English drama—History and criticism. I. Title.
PR625.S2 1981   822'.009   80-22444
ISBN 0–312–25429–6

Contents

Preface		v
1.	Medieval Drama	1
2.	The Emergence of the Secular Drama	25
3.	Elizabethan Drama	37
4.	Varieties of Comedy	51
5.	Jacobean and Caroline Tragedy	85
6.	The Restoration Theatre and its Drama	133
7.	Sentiment and Melodrama: The Eighteenth and Nineteenth Centuries	162
8.	The Twentieth Century	177
Chronological Table		210
Selective Bibliography		221
Index		227

We transport you into a world of intrigue and illusion . . .clowns, if you like, murderers — we can do you ghosts and battles, on the skirmish level, heroes, villains, tormented lovers — set pieces in the poetic vein; we can do you rapiers or rape or both, by all means, faithless wives and ravished virgins — flagrante delicto at a price, but that comes under realism for which there are special terms. Getting warm, am I ?

Tom Stoppard: Rosencrantz and Guildenstern are Dead.

Preface

This book tries to give an account of drama in England from its medieval beginnings to the early nineteen-seventies. The emphasis is mainly on dramatic texts, for several reasons. The physical conditions of the English theatre in its greatest period called upon language to serve functions discharged by other means in later theatres — settings, lighting, the use of actresses as well as actors and so on. Hence many dramatic texts are immensely rich in their verbal texture. The text is also the most stable element in that transient whole which is our experience of a play. And finally, texts lend themselves more easily to written commentary because in most cases they, rather than performances, form the common experience shared by reader and writer.

I have however, constantly tried to bear in mind that dramatic texts are not very usefully discussed outside the context of performance. In talking of individaul plays I have made some attempt to relate them not only to that imagined theatre of the mind without which no rewarding reading of a play is possible, but also to the specific theatres for which they were designed. And because theatre, the most social of art forms, has a peculiarly intimate relation to the society within which it flowers or fades, I have paid attention to that society, usually in the specific form of particular audiences.

The discussion of individual plays has been made as detailed as space allowed and plot summary conscientiously pared down to the intelligible minimum, as my intention has been to direct or redirect attention to the plays rather than provide a substitute for them. I have been guided by the principle that plays chosen for discussion should be of intrinsic rather than historical interest, though the distinction is not always as clear as it ought to be. Shakespeare has not received extended discussion for fairly obvious reasons, though the reader will sense his presence everywhere in the book, as it is everywhere in English drama, being not so much a figure in that drama as one of its conditions.

Perhaps it needs to be added that I have no particular theory about the relationship of theatre to society except that it has been demonstrably different at different periods. Nor have I a general theory of the development of drama or other magic key to unlock all mysteries.

A book taking in as wide a span as this one and attempting to touch on several different related topics is even more indebted to the work of others than is usually the case. It would be quite hopeless to attempt acknowledgement of all debts, even if I were consciously aware of them. Specific references are given in footnotes, which I have used sparingly. The very selective bibliography records my principal sources of information, ideas and productive disagreement.

Sarah Cohen was cheerfully encouraging when I first began work on this book and her subsequent characteristic blend of quiet patience and gentle prodding was one of the chief factors in its completion. Another was the speed, efficiency and conscientiousness with which Melba Chapman transformed a messy manuscript into an intelligible typescript. To both my heartfelt thanks.

Exeter, 18 January, 1980

1

Medieval Drama

We have a natural tendency to flatten out the past, and the further we move back in time the flatter we make it. We imagine the past as less chaotic than the present, its people and their activities as less various and surprising than our own. Naturally, because no matter how great our imaginative awareness may be, *we* can only fully respond to the present; only the here and now can be 'felt in the blood and felt along the heart' by *us*. But two points are worth making here, both shatteringly obvious and therefore often forgotten. The first is that every bit of the past was the present to a large group of people and with knowledge, sympathy and imagination we can still have access to it, if only a limited access — the limits being set by the accidents of history and our individual capacities. The second point is that such informed frequentation of the past is, or can be, an important part of our response to the present, can quite literally be part of our own sense of what it is to be alive here and now. Just as each of us would be immeasurably poorer and more confused without our individual memories, so we are diminished to the extent that we are cut off, or cut ourselves off, from the richness and variety of the past.

With these considerations in mind, we may begin our study of English drama by noting the variety of dramatic forms which go under the general rubric of 'medieval drama' and the scope and extent of the theatrical traditions within which it flourished. Too often medieval drama is either the subject of specialized scholarly study or tends to be discussed in relation to the Elizabethan drama which followed it, as if the importance of the earlier drama is solely due to its fore-shadowing of greater things to come. As we shall see, the Elizabethan and Jacobean drama is full of splendour and spectacle and its greatest achievements have never been surpassed before or since. But it is as well to state here simply and clearly that this chapter is based on the conviction that if the Elizabethan and Jacobean drama had never existed, the drama of the medieval period would still be what it undoubtedly is, one of the great achievements of the European theatre.

Drama and Liturgy

But it is time we made some necessary distinctions and provided some sort of framework within which generalizations can find substance and support. As noted above, many different kinds of theatrical and quasi-theatrical offering are loosely labelled 'medieval drama'. Like everything else in the Middle Ages, all these dramatic forms were related to the Church and its activities, but the nature and extent of the relation varied according to the forms in question. Logically as well as chronologically, the earliest form of medieval 'drama' was that of the church ritual

1

itself. Up till about the last quarter of the tenth century, the only dramatic spectacles generally seen in England (apart from the pre-Christian folk rituals and the
folk plays derived from them such as the mummers' play of St. George) were
connected with the services of the various festivals of the Christian year. Before the
Reformation England was of course part of the universal Catholic Church, sharing
with the rest of European Christendom a common creed, ritual and language. The
Catholic Mass was inherently dramatic in the ordinary sense of the word, incor-
porating many elements associated with theatrical representation — a set text,
'distancing' from everyday discourse through chant and the use of a 'sacred'
language, stylized movement, costumes and properties and so on. An influential
work by a German bishop of the early ninth century explicitly interpreted the
Mass as a symbolic drama of salvation centred on the crucifixion and resurrection
of Christ. Even more 'dramatic' were the gospel stories associated with the various
seasons of the Church's year, notably the great festivals of Easter and Christmas.
These gave rise to the so-called *tropes* or embellishments of the liturgical text
through mime, chant and music. The earliest and most celebrated of these is the
Quem Quaeritis ('whom do you seek?') trope performed at Eastertide, of which
over 400 versions from all over Europe are extant. It tells the story of the meeting
between the angels and the three Marys at the empty tomb on Easter morning.
The English version, dating from the last quarter of the tenth century is found in
the *Regularis Concordia* of Ethelwold, Bishop of Winchester. It is worth quoting at
some length not only for its historical interest but because of the clearly defined
impulse towards dramatic representation behind it. While the third lesson is being
chanted,

> let four brothers vest themselves. Let one of them, vested in an alb (a long
> white robe) enter as if to take part in the service and approach the place
> where the sepulchre is and sit there quietly with a palm in his hand. While
> the third respond is chanted, let the other three follow bearing censers with
> incense in their hands and, with hesitating steps as if seeking something, let
> them come to the place of the sepulchre. *These things are done in imitation* of
> the angel seated within the tomb and the women coming with spices to
> anoint the body of Jesus. (my italics)

The words I have emphasized make the mimetic intention quite plain. The
emotion of the Congregation is heightened by this dramatic enhancement of the
liturgical occasion. We note that the priests take on the roles of the women and the
angels, and that the vestments function as theatrical costumes in the same way that
the palm becomes a theatrical property. There is not much dialogue for this little
play (none at all in the gospels) and all of it is in Latin, but the occasion and the
dramatic action would doubtless have made it moving even for the large majority
of the audience of all classes who were ignorant of Latin. 'Whom seek ye in the the
tomb, O followers of Christ?' asks the angel, to whom the women reply 'Jesus of
Nazareth the crucified, O dweller in heaven'. The angel tells them: 'He is not here,
he has risen, even as he foretold. Go, announce that he has risen from the dead'. At
this the three women turn to the choir and chant 'Alleluia, the Lord has risen'. The
angel, still seated, recalls the women to show that the cross, standing for Christ

himself, is missing leaving only the cloth in which it was wrapped. 'Come and see the place where the Lord was laid' he chants. The women spread out the cloth to show the world that Christ is risen and sing 'The Lord has risen from the tomb' and lay the cloth on the altar. The priest then leads the choir and congregation in the *Te Deum* to the triumphant peal of the church bells.

The Easter trope is a representative specimen of the liturgical drama. Clearly recognizable as a piece of Church ritual shaped into dramatic form it is still, as the ending shows, closely linked to the over-arching religious occasion within which it occurs and in terms of which it acquires significance in the minds of the congregation. As time went on the dramatic elements of the episode were developed and elaborated through the addition of fresh characters and scenes. The apostles Peter and John also come to the tomb and the Marys buy ointment from a spice-vendor, a total stranger to the Biblical version. There are also, as we might expect, similar playlets associated with other Church festivals such as the Nativity plays at Christmas. But while the liturgical drama undoubtedly catered to the taste for dramatic spectacle in the congregation, it is unlikely that it developed into the great cyclical dramas, sometimes called mystery or miracle plays whose span of action covered nothing less than all human time, from the Creation to the Last Judgement. There are several reasons for doubting that the mystery cycles developed by some process of accumulation from the liturgical drama just described.[1]

The Miracle Plays

The liturgical drama eventually came to be performed in the vernacular, often outside the church itself. But neither of these factors could have helped to expand that drama into the mystery cycles because the liturgical drama *always* remained tied to the specific festivals with which it was associated, being, as we have seen, a heightening of the Church ritual, not an integral part of it, and deriving its significance entirely from that ritual. This means first that particular playlets would have been performed *only* at those periods of the Church year appropriate to them and second that the number of such playlets would be comparatively small. And the surviving body of liturgical drama (fairly full where the Continent is concerned though depleted in England by Reformation ardour) suggest that most communities possessed only one or two such 'occasional' plays, certainly nothing approaching the breadth and grandeur of the cycle drama. We must look elsewhere for the origin of the latter.

In 1215 the Fourth Lateran Council approved the doctrine of Transubstantiation whereby Christ in His Real Presence was believed to be in the consecrated bread and wine of the Holy Sacrament. Fifty years later in 1264, Pope Urban IV instituted the feast of Corpus Christi as a public celebration of God's greatest gift, the blood and body of his son to redeem man's sins. Though the Church commemorated the Holy Sacrament on the day of the Last Supper (Maundy

---

[1] What follows is mainly a summary of the argument developed and substantiated with skill, insight and scholarship by V.A. Kolve in *The Play called Corpus Christi* (London, 1966).

Thursday), the date set aside for the public celebrations of the feast of Corpus Christi varied from 23 May to 24 June. Thus, from the very beginning, the feast of Corpus Christi was not tied to the Church's calendar in the sense that other great religious occasions were; and we may note that the time of year chosen was well suited to outdoor celebrations in Europe.

Urban IV's death prevented the implementation of the feast until 1311, when Clement V ordered its adoption. One of the principal features of the feast was the procession of the Host, still commemorated in some parts of Catholic Europe. This was a visible demonstration of the community's faith in the capacity of the Eucharist to perform miracles and reached its climax when the priest held the Blessed Sacrament on high so that all the people could see it. There were probably dramatic renderings of various miracles associated with the Eucharist.

But the blood and body of Christ was not simply the instrument of local and temporal miracles, however spectacular. It was also, as the Church repeatedly stressed, the supreme and eternal gift of God to man. It put the faithful in mind of the Last Supper and the Crucifixion. In themselves these were events to be contemplated with shame and sorrow rather than rejoicing *unless* they could be linked with the Resurrection which in turn looked forward to the Last Judgement and back to the Creation and the Fall. Thus the injunction to *celebrate* the feast of Corpus Christi led naturally to a consideration of the whole nature and testing of man and the impulse to do this in dramatic terms probably lies behind the creation of the cyclical drama which is the crowning glory of the medieval theatre. The fact that it took all creation as theme and subject meant that this drama could develop almost indefinitely and absorb almost anything; but the fact that its shape and structure were determined by a clearly defined pattern of significance (in which the passion of Christ was central) made it capable of handling this vast and heterogeneous body of material with coherence and authority.

Neither of the two terms by which the medieval cycle drama is known are particularly appropriate. The term 'miracle' was originally applied to plays dealing with the lives of saints while any play with a Biblical subject was called a 'mystère', a sense which the English term can retain only with difficulty, in competition with the more usual meanings of the word. We need to bear in mind constantly that while individual plays or scenes from the cycles can be and have been performed with great success, this drama was always conceived as an all-encompassing whole and attains its true stature and significance only in relation to the cyclic structure which informs it. This does not of course mean that any given cycle sprang up whole and complete from the beginning, but that it was always capable of accommodating additions within the overall structure.

The English cycle drama

The ravages of reforming zeal saw to it that most of the Corpus Christi plays in England (they continued to be called by this name even when they were performed at other times, such as Whitsun) were destroyed. It is probable that every community of any size in medieval England had its own Corpus Christi play. Though there is no firm documentary evidence for the existence of such plays in England before 1375, references to the plays as well-established suggest that this drama may have existed from fifty years or so earlier. Four complete English cycle-texts have survived, as well as a complete list of 36 or 38 plays constituting yet another cycle. The Chester cycle, dating from about 1375, contains 24 plays, the York cycle has twice that number, the Wakefield cycle (sometimes called the Towneley cycle after a former owner of the unique surviving manuscript) 32 plays and the N-town cycle 42 plays. 'N' may stand for *nomen* or name. The banns for the play contain the following words:

> A-Sunday next if that us may
> At six of the bell we 'gin our play
> In N-town

— the actual name of the town would have been filled in according to the locality. One play each survives from the cycles of Norwich and Newcastle-upon-Tyne and there are also some single plays which may or may not have been part of cycles. There is also a trilogy in Cornish dealing with the Creation, the Passion and the Resurrection. Most of the texts are in single manuscripts often much later than the period when the plays were originally performed. This is all that has survived of a drama which was popular throughout England and Scotland for two centuries and more.

All the surviving cycles contain plays dealing with the central myths of the Christian view of man and human history within its cosmic setting. Beginning with the fall of Lucifer we move from the Creation to the primal murder of Abel by Cain and Noah's Flood. Then there is the story of Abraham and Isaac, the Nativity and the raising of Lazarus. The cycles come to one kind of climax with the Passion and the Resurrection and reach their triumphant close with Doomsday.

Some of the cycles also contain plays dealing with the story of Moses, the baptism of Christ, the temptation in the wilderness and the assumption and coronation of the Virgin Mary. Though certain plays (such as those in the Towneley cycle attributed to the so-called Wakefield Master) have the hallmark of a single author, the cycles are generally of composite authorship over a period of time which may have been as much as fifty years. Like the great medieval cathedrals, the cycle drama has a vaster business in hand than the expression of an individual personality and it looks on human time under the aspect of eternity.

The authors of this drama are unknown to us, though they were members of the clergy. In creating this drama their selection from the vast body of material provided by the Old and New Testaments was guided not so much by individual preference for the most obviously dramatic material as by a tradition of commentary and interpretation by the early fathers of the Church which was the received orthodoxy, shared by the clergy and congregation alike. Central to this received teaching was the conception of the three visitations of God, the first as creator of man, then as redeemer and finally as judge of man. The many parallels between Adam and Christ (the second Adam as St Paul termed him) provided links between the Creation, the Fall and the Incarnation, while the Fall itself presupposed some inveterate malice towards God and his Creation on the part of the serpent which in turns suggested the revolt and fall of Lucifer. Thus we can discern the basic shape of the cycle drama as given and available to the men who wrote and witnessed it; the drama derives its authority from an independent tradition of significance.

Within this basic structure, the choice of episodes from the Old Testament (relatively few common to all the surviving cycles, considering the wealth of material available) was governed by the well established tradition of figural interpretation. Incidents from the Old Testament were seen as both true in themselves *and* as prefiguring later events recorded in the New Testament. The tradition had the powerful sanction of Christ's own practice of referring to his own situation in terms of parallels drawn from the earlier scriptures. Since the central focus of the Corpus Christi feast was Christ's sacrifice, the drama chose those events from the Old Testament which particularly related to that sacrifice. Thus the blood of Abel prefigured the blood of Christ, Noah saving his family from the flood was an image of Christ saving the whole human family from the destruction of hell, Abraham offering Isaac as a sacrifice imaged the greater sacrifice of himself by Christ. But the later event was not merely a repetition of the earlier but a further development of it. Abel's blood cried out for vengeance, Christ's was offered for mercy, Abraham did not finally have to lose his son but the Son of Man was sacrificed, and so on. The significance of the dramatic enactment lies in a relationship between an event and its analogue. Both were believed in as true and important but in the difference between them lay the meaning of the drama. The relationships are not always made explicit in the plays themselves, nor need they have been, since they were part of the common outlook behind medieval sermons, stained glass windows and sculpture. They dramatized the movement from justice to mercy, from Law to Love.

It is evident therefore that this drama is not a collection of miscellaneous bits and pieces haphazardly put together by enthusiastic but inept or unsophisticated amateurs. We may note its stark realism, or its earthy humour, its occasional lyric beauty and poignant austerity of utterance. All these are present and have been justly praised. But we should never forget that they exist within a structure as solid, shapely and spectacular as that of the great medieval cathedrals. We should no more think of being patronizing or condescending about the cycle drama of the Middle Ages than we would about Salisbury spire.

The cycle drama as theatre

Modern revivals, now a regular part of the theatrical scene in many parts of England, have demonstrated that the medieval drama still has the power to interest and move large numbers of people most of whom no longer share the world outlook which gave rise to it. The power and authority of the drama is most fully revealed when it is played in conditions as near as may be to those for which it was originally produced.

As has been suggested, the cycle drama was intended from the outset for outdoor performance. The staging of different plays within the cycle became the responsibility of one or other of the great craft guilds, each of which had its own patron-saint. Sometimes, though not invariably, a particular guild would choose a play especially appropriate to it, as when the Shipwrights undertook the story of the ark or the Butchers staged the crucifixion. The ties between the guilds and the Church were very close (some guilds were not craft guilds but purely religious associations) but only the guilds had the personnel, resources and organization capable of handling the complicated and expensive business of performing these plays regularly.

There were two main styles of presentation, both of them with an extensive tradition of European development behind them by the time they arrived in England late in the fourteenth century. They are referred to under different names by various scholars. Here, they will be called 'place-and-scaffold' and 'pageant waggon' staging.

'Place-and-scaffold' staging was the more ambitious and elaborate of the two. Basically it consists of raised scaffolds arranged round a bare area or 'place' (*platea*). Each of the scaffolds represented a particular locality — Paradise, the Mount of Olives, the house of Simon the Leper, or whatever the particular action required — and had a suitably decorated stage. The locations could be symbolic — the abode of Lust for instance, or the World itself — as well as realistic. The action took place between these particular locations and the unlocalized 'place' in front of them. The audience stood, or occupied specially erected stands in the surrounding area. Actors in the unlocalized area were never far from the audience and would sometimes move among them, as when the Messenger in the N-Town Trial of Christ is instructed by stage directions to

come into the place running and crying 'Tidings! Tidings!' and so round about the place, 'Jesus of Nazareth is taken! Jesus of Nazareth is taken!'

There were many dramatic opportunities offered by place-and-scaffold staging and surviving texts show that they were often exploited with skill and tact. In the first place the movement from one location to another or from scaffold to place had great dramatic potential, as when God descends to address Noah in the Wakefield play. It also offered the possibility of movement on a larger scale than pageant-waggon staging, as when Christ is dragged to and fro between the courts of Herod and Pilate in the N-town play already referred to. The scene illustrates yet another dramatic possibility, that of the sudden revelation, by drawing wide the curtain of a particular scaffold, of a striking tableau:

Here they take Jesus and lead him in great haste to [the] Herod; and the Herod's scaffold shall unclose, showing Herod in state, all the Jews kneeling, except Annas and Caiphas, they shall stand.

The presence of several scaffolds as well as the neutral place also provided the possibility of dramatic juxtaposition, where a scene in one scaffold could be contrasted with that in another, violent movement in the central place with a still tableau in a scaffold or vice versa. One such juxtaposition occurs in the scene, again from the N-town cycle, where Jesus and his disciples are seen partaking of the Passover feast in accordance with the Old Law, while in another the Jewish priests are planning His punishment for allegedly breaking that Law.

In a theatre with so much emphasis on physical movement and so many opportunities for it, the danger is of course that mere to-ing and fro-ing for its own sake would be resorted to whenever inspiration flagged, especially if it could be decked out as some kind of procession and embellished with an elaborate stage property; if you had gone to the trouble and expense of constructing a ship that actually moved or a devil breathing smoke and crepitating fire, the temptation to use these expensive items oftener than called for by strict dramatic necessity would be a natural one. It would be surprising if medieval playmakers never succumbed to it; but a newcomer to this drama is likely to be more surprised at how often the creators of these plays imaginatively exploit the possibilities of their stages rather than become enslaved by them.

The second main variety of medieval stage was on a more compact scale. It consisted of stages erected on 'pageants' which were moved from one place to another. The word 'pageant' is likely to cause some confusion because it was used indifferently to signify either the vehicles on which the plays were performed or the plays themselves. It is easy to understand how this method of staging came about if we recall that the feast of Corpus Christi originally began not as a dramatic festival but as a communal procession. Much as in a Lord Mayor's Show or Carnival procession of today, the Procession of the Host would have had floats depicting tableaux associated with the occasion, showing either particular miracles of the Host or scenes taken from the entire panorama of the Christian view of man and the world. It is reasonable to suppose that the cycle drama grew by the elaboration of the latter from silent tableaux to plays with words and action. This is certainly more plausible than the notion that the cycle drama developed out of the liturgical variety. To begin with, the pageants would be simply part of the procession and seen by those who followed it and by bystanders. The long-established practice of performing allegorical tableaux on specially constructed stages on the route of a royal entry doubtless influenced the technique of the pageant waggons. But in comparison to the former, the mechanical and other effects possible on a movable waggon must have been severely limited, though for their play of the Last Judgement the drapers of Coventry paid, among other things, for a hell-mouth complete with fire, a windlass and three fathoms of cord, pulpits for angels and a torch to set the world on fire. The only surviving description of a waggon stage in England is by David Rogers and is based on his father's manuscript notes which date from the sixteenth century. 'These pageants or carriage[s]' writes Rogers

> was a high place made like a house with two rooms, being open at the top; the lower rooms they apparelled and dressed themselves, and in the higher room they played: and they stood upon six wheels. And when they had done with one carriage in one place, they wheeled the same from one street to another . . .

As Rogers indicates, the pageant waggons adopted a routine where each would stop at a specified point, perform its play and move on to the next point, while the spot it had vacated would be occupied by the next pageant and its play, and so on to the end of the cycle. In theory, therefore, all a spectator had to do was wait in one particular spot from dawn (at York the procession assembled at 4.30 a.m.) till sunset and he could see the entire cycle. But in York at least, as a recent scholar has shown,[1] this would not have been possible; there would not have been time to do all the plays at all twelve (or sixteen) stations. Other places such as Chester took three days to perform a shorter cycle of plays, or, like Coventry, had very few stations. It is possible that at York and perhaps elsewhere, the pageant waggons started out in a single close procession, miming their play till all the stations were occupied and then acted their plays at the same time, moving on to allow the waggons which had not yet performed to do so.[2]

But how, if at all, the complete programme was managed is of less importance from our present standpoint than what pageant-waggon staging might have been like, what limitations it imposed on playwright and players and what advantages, if any, it had. The limitations are more immediately striking than any possible opportunities. The restrictions on stage machinery have already been noted, though we should not exaggerate this (the great age of theatrical machines was yet to come). More serious perhaps was the restriction of the acting space and the fact that the action was further removed from the audience than in the place-and-scaffold staging (though one of the N-town plays has the stage direction: 'Here Herod rages on the pageant and in the street also'). Finally, there would not have been a great deal of scope in this type of staging for violent or expansive movement or striking juxtapositions or contrasts of grouping.

It is not always possible to say definitely whether a play was written for one or other type of staging, partly because the texts of the cycles as we have them are conglomerates from different sources and not prompt copies and partly because such stage directions as do occur are often consistent with either type of staging. It is also worth noting that if one or more waggons were ranged round an open playing space (as seems occasionally to have happened once the theatrical part of the Corpus Christi celebrations was separated, probably some time early in the fifteenth century, from the procession proper), the ensuing performance was indistinguishable from place-and-scaffold staging. It is nevertheless possible to suggest that pageant-waggon staging did offer certain dramatic possibilities, mainly the inverse of its limitations. Thus the very smallness of the space enabled the dramatist to sharpen his focus and achieve moments of great intimacy and intensity, and the impracticability of much movement on a large scale provides the opportunity for concentration on a simple action or situation. The nativity play performed by the thatchers of York is as good an example as any of the creative use of pageant-waggon staging. With great economy of movement and language the play brings out at one and the same time the homeliness, the dignity and the mystery of the Virgin birth.

It would be a mistake to think that the costumes and properties used in these plays, in whatever style of staging, were drab or amateurish. There is plenty of pictorial evidence from the Continent and documentary evidence (such as inventories and statements of expenditure incurred) from English records to suggest otherwise. We may best imagine these stage spectacles as magnified versions of

---

[1] Alan Nelson, 'Principles of Processional Staging: York Cycle,' *Modern Philology* 67 (1969-70)
[2] see Stanley J. Kahrl, *Traditions of Medieval English Drama* (London, 1974).

medieval illuminated manuscripts — all that glittering splendour of gold and crimson and radiant blue with the added dimensions of voice and movement. Costumes were either symbolic, as when Eve wore a close-fitting white garment to symbolize naked innocence, or contemporary — the two priests in the N-town play wore the scarlet robes of medieval bishops.

Neither should we over-emphasize the fact that these plays were performed by amateurs rather than professionals. The members of a particular guild charged by the civil authorities with the production of a play were, it is true, not professional men of the theatre but butchers, tanners, cordwainers, and so on. But we know that the guilds took their responsibilities seriously, and the elaborateness, even lavishness of the presentations must have taken up a good deal of the time of all those concerned. In short, those involved in these productions, whether as actors, stage managers, designers or whatever, must have spent so much of the year at these duties that the distinction between amateur and professional is likely to have been blurred if not entirely obliterated. It is no accident that modern theatre directors and stage designers are turning increasingly to the techniques and conventions of the medieval theatre for their inspiration.

We have considered the cycle drama as a series of presented spectacles because that is how it was conceived by its creators and first experienced by its audience. But, while these plays are probably performed more often today than at any time in the intervening centuries, it is still probably true that most people first encounter them as printed texts. In this form they are less immediately accessible to the modern reader. The vagaries of medieval spelling and grammar occasionally get in the way of understanding and enjoyment, though the extent of this can very easily be exaggerated. Modernized editions, of which several good ones exist, offer one way out of the difficulty, but something more than 'quaintness' (a thoroughly expendable quality anyway) is inevitably lost — nuances of meaning, metrical effects and so on. A further difficulty arises from the fact that there is still a good deal of confusion and uncertainty as to the exact nature of the surviving texts, their relation to each other and to the performances which were based on them. None of the texts of the complete cycles are the original working manuscripts but only copies of these. The 48 plays of the York cycle exist in a manuscript which modern scholarship assigns to some period in the mid-fifteenth century, although the cycle is known to have existed in some form in the last quarter of the fourteenth century. There are five manuscript versions of the Chester cycle of 25 plays of various dates from 1591 to 1607. The 32 plays of the Wakefield (Towneley) cycle include five borrowed from the earlier York cycle surviving in a unique manuscript of the second half of the fifteenth century. The date 1468 appears at the end of a play in the N-Town cycle, in the same hand as that of most of the manuscript. Some of the manuscripts, such as those of the York (and possibly the Wakefield) cycle are 'registers' or official copies of each individual play made for the civic authorities. Others would have been the property of individual guilds. Many individual plays exist in a form which shows signs of evident revision of earlier texts.

The establishment of definitive texts of these plays is probably an impossible task. Nevertheless the texts as they stand, however imperfect or doubtful in provenance, are still in many cases very rewarding to read, provided we use our imagination to stage them as they were intended to be staged. And the best of them have far more to offer then the humour and realism for which they are often somewhat condescendingly praised. Indeed, we are likely to miss the main impact of this drama if we insist on seeing it in these terms. For while there are vivid flashes of humour, earthy, sardonic or simply obscene, none of the plays as a whole can honestly be called wildly funny, nor of course were any of them intended to be. As for realism, we should distinguish clearly between the occasional telling detail from everyday life that brings a character or situation into sharp dramatic focus and an overall commitment to the portrayal of external reality (the world as perceived by our senses) as a dramatic objective. Instances of the former abound, but medieval drama had no concern whatever with the latter. Though the cycle drama was not a religious ritual in any sense (it was presented and received as 'play' or 'game' rather than 'earnest' to use the medieval terms) it was concerned with the same reality, the reality of man's eternal destiny, for which his life here and now was seen as no more than a rehearsal. As such, the details of material life were strictly subordinated to this overall purpose, which was to render the eternal Christian verities — man's proneness to evil, the hope offered by Christ's sacrifice, the certainty of the Last Judgement — in terms that would go home to men's business and bosoms.

These points are well illustrated by one of the best of the plays, *The Crucifixion* from the York cycle. This play, presented jointly by the painters and pinners (pin makers) has often been singled out for the brutal realism of detail with which the physical business of nailing Christ on the cross and then setting the cross with its burden upright are handled. No doubt the pinners took a grim relish in their expert attention to matters such as getting the right nail in the right place:

> Yes, here is a stub (nail) will stiffly stand;
> Through bones and sinews it shall be sought.
> This work is well, I will warrant.

Throughout the play there is a single-minded concentration on the mechanics of the crucifixion, so that it may appear that the dramatist's chief interest lay in rendering the whole business as realistically as he could. But the effect of this concentration on realistic detail is not merely to make us say to ourselves, 'Yes, that's just how it must have been'. That is only part of the intention, and not the principal part. We are more powerfully aware of many other elements in the drama. The most obvious of these is the contrast between the professional garrulity of the four soldiers and the resounding silence of Jesus, who speaks only twice during the entire scene, and each time addresses his heavenly Father. But the two speeches of Jesus are not mere repetitions one of another. In the first the *general* significance of the activity we are all witnessing is expressed in an idiom starkly contrasting with the matter-of-fact brutality of the soldiers:

> Almighty God, my Father free,
> Let these matters be marked in mind:
> Thou bade that I should buxom (ready) be,
> For Adam's plight to be pined. (tortured)

Here to death I oblige me,
From that sin to save mankind,
And sovereignly beseech I thee
That they for me may favour find;
And from the fiend them fend, (protect)
So that their souls be safe
In wealth withouten end;
I keep not else to crave.

The mocking incomprehension of the soldiers only serves to heighten the poignancy of Jesus words:

Weh! Hark, sir knights, for (by) Mahound's blood!
Of Adam's kind is all his thought.

The meekness with which Jesus lies down on the cross also gains its real meaning from the words he has spoken; he obeys not out of fear but because of a pledge given earlier to die for mankind.

The first speech of Jesus occurs early on in the play, before the actual business of nailing him to the cross has begun. The bulk of the play is now taken up by the physical process itself. At one level, the preoccupation in their task of men at work may recall to the modern playgoer such a play as David Storey's *The Contractor*, where the dramatic action is framed by the putting up and taking down of a marquee. But this is not one physical action among others, it is the most horrible and the most hopeful of all actions that have ever taken place, the action which gives point and purpose to all other human actions. The modern reader, who is daily made aware of the prevalence of physical torture in the world and the way it is often justified by its perpetrators on the ground that they were only doing their job, is unlikely to miss the point of the soldiers' professional dissatisfaction with holes that have been made at too great a distance for the arms and legs, and the ensuing discussion of how best to make the victim's body fit the cross:

His limbs on length then shall I lead,
And even unto the bore (hole) them bring.

But the detail about stretching the hand till it reaches the hole in the wood is not there merely to horrify (like most of the other physical details, it is not an invention of the dramatist but has an established history in medieval scriptural commentary and visual art). It leads quite naturally to the taunting questions which the soldiers feel entitled on the successful completion of a tricky task, to ask of Jesus:

I Soldier: Say, sir, how likes you now
              This work that we have wrought?
IV Soldier: We pray you say us how
              You feel, or faint you aright.

It is as the shattering reply to this that the dramatist gives Jesus his second and final speech — it too begins as a general blessing:

All men that walk by way or street,

Take tent ye shall no travail fine;
(Take care that you waste none of my travail)
If any mourning may be meet,
Or mischief measured unto mine.

But it closes in to become a prayer for those whom we have just witnessed putting Jesus on the cross from which he prays:

My Father, that all bales (evil) may bate,
Forgive these men that do me pine,
What they work wot they naught;
Therefore my Father, I crave,
Let never their sins be sought, (looked into)
But see their souls to save.

Once again, the effect is not of the words of Jesus alone, but of those words and the mocking response they evoke coming so close together:

I Soldier:	Weh! Hark! He jangles like a jay.
II Soldier:	Methink he patters like a pie.
III Soldier:	He has been doing so all day,
	And made great moving of mercy.
IV Soldier:	Is this the same that gan us say
	That he was God's Son almighty?

The audience is made aware not only how it might have been, but of how it would be if it were to happen all over again. These men have done the job they were ordered to do 'as Pilate deemed' and their satisfaction, and the sheer physical effort they have engaged in, finds expression in savage banter, but they are not monsters, merely nailmakers representing soldiers. The Crucifixion is shown as a permanent possibility of human nature as all-embracing love and forgiveness are shown as part of the divine; to praise this drama for its realism seems a huge irrelevance. As for humour, no doubt there is some kind of humour here and there in the language and stage business, but it is of a kind that an audience accustomed to black comedy will easily be able to distinguish from ordinary humour; it exists not to make us laugh and relax but to make us laugh and feel shame or sorrow or at least discomfort.

Before we turn our attention to another variety of medieval drama we may look briefly at one more cycle play, the N-Town version of *The Woman Taken in Adultery*. The N-Town cycle probably belonged to a touring group (though there are problems yet unsolved as to how such a large and elaborate organization as would be required for the staging of the cycle operated on tour). As part of the preliminary publicity, banns for the play would be proclaimed in outlying areas. The banns for this play locate the principal point of dramatic interest, the trap laid for Christ:

They conceived this subtlety:
If Christ this woman did damn truly,
Against this preaching then did he,

> Which was of pity and of mercy;
> And if he did her save,
> Then were he against Moses' law,
> That biddeth with stones she should be slaw, (slain)
> Thus they thought under their awe (power)
> Christ Jesus for to have.

Either Christ would have to contravene Mosaic law or his own teaching. No doubt most of the audience knew how he escaped the dilemma, just as most of the Greek audience knew in broad outline the myths used by the Greek dramatists; but, as Nabokov remarked, detail is always welcome. Here the playwright begins with forty lines of a sermon by Christ opening with the rolling Latin syllables:

> Nolo mortem peccatoris
> (I do not want the death of the sinner)

Though Christ addresses the audience directly, much as a priest would address his congregation, the formal dignity of the Latin opening is kept up to a large extent in the stylized simplicity of the sermon. The themes of the play we are about to see — the certainty of God's mercy to the repentant sinner and the necessity for men to show mercy towards each other — are propounded with strength and clarity of utterance:

> Each man to other be merciable,
> And mercy he shall have at need;
> What man of mercy is not treatable (inclined to)
> When he asketh mercy he shall not speed.
> Mercy to grant I come indeed:
> Whoso ask mercy he shall have grace;
> Let no man doubt for his misdeed,
> But ever ask mercy while he hath space.

This could very easily have been a sermon from the pulpit. But coming as it does at the beginning of a play on a known subject, its effect is to heighten the audience's expectation of the action to follow. Without, however, immediately satisfying that expectation by bringing on the woman herself, the dramatist now shifts the scene to the scribe and the Pharisee bewailing the fact that Jesus's daily increasing following is a threat to their authority and pondering how to bring down this low-born rabble-rouser:

> A false quarrel if we could feign,
> That hypocrite to put in blame,
> All his preaching should soon distain
> And then his worship should turn to shame.

There is no intention here of expressing individual character through language. The aim is to make clear to the audience the sustained malice of officialdom, though the sense of outraged dignity is real enough:

All our laws he doth defame —
That stinking beggar is wondrous bold!

The contrast with the speech of Christ is unmistakable.

Hard on the heels of the priest's discussion comes a character known simply as the Accuser. He offers to provide just what they are looking for, a chance to discredit Jesus. (To consider this a convenient coincidence is to miss the point entirely. The dramatist chooses and orders his incidents in order to clarify his chosen theme; the story he tells has an authority far greater than his own, so plausibility is not his primary concern.) He knows where a woman and a man are fornicating and can take them there. At this very moment they are at their filthy game. The Scribe and the Pharisee consider this offer while the Accuser urges them to make haste if they are not to lose this opportunity. At the woman's house they are met by a young man who comes running out 'with shoes untied and holding up his breeches with his hand' (another 'realistic touch') who threatens to kill whoever tries to stop him leaving. The Pharisee prudently lets him pass with a curse which the young man promptly returns, adding a curse to the audience for good measure. This is a scene which obviously has some humorous potential, but the dramatist's main emphasis is on the seizing of the woman and the implacable determination of the priests to bring down on her the full weight of the Mosaic law. Even her request to be killed then and there instead of being publicly stoned is refused with sanctimonious malice:

Fie on thee, scout! (slut) the devil thee quell!
Against the law shall we thee kill?
First shall hang thee the devil of hell,
Ere we such follies should fulfil.
Though it like thee never so ill,
Before the prophet thou shalt have law:
Like as Moses doth charge us till,
With great stones thou shalt be slaw.

The Scribe, the Pharisee and the Accuser each in turn refuse the woman's appeals for mercy; the dramatic effect is to make us feel that we are in a world where love is a matter of cowardly intrigue and adamantine law the only reality.

The final scene takes place when the woman is brought to Jesus at the temple. The silence of Jesus while the three accusers keep on baiting him as to what verdict he will pronounce is as strikingly effective here as his opening sermon. A stage direction says:

Here Jesus, while they are accusing the woman, shall all the time write on the ground with his finger.

Even when the woman appeals to him, Jesus is silent. Only when the question has been asked several times over and the brutality of the intended punishment repeatedly stressed does he reply, in words that have much of the strength and authority of their Biblical original:

> Look which of you that never sin wrought,
> But is of life cleaner than she;
> Cast at her stones and spare her nought,
> Clean out of sin if that ye be.

That is all his reply, but it is enough to send his accusers back to their 'three separate places' with their heads hung low in shame. But their soliloquies make it clear that they are only ashamed at being forced publicly to acknowledge that they have sinned (presumably Jesus has been writing of their sins on the ground), not genuinely contrite. Only the woman is truly penitent and Jesus sends her away with his blessing and his charge:

> For me thou shalt not condemned be;
> Go home again and walk at large:
> Look that thou live in honesty,
> And will no more to sin, I thee charge.

The play ends with Jesus once more returning to the general theme of God's mercy, after the particular instance of it has been dramatized. But this time the role of Jesus dissolves into that of the priest blessing the congregation and becomes finally that of a sinner asking for God's blessing for himself and his fellow-sinners, the audience:

> Now God, that died for all mankind,
> Save all these people both night and day;
> And of our sins he us unbind,
> High Lord of heaven that best may. Amen.

For all that what we have witnessed is a play and not a religious service, it is part of the strength of this dramatic tradition that both its action and its language could fall back so easily on those of religion. Only a very naive reader or spectator would consider the dramatic effect achieved by the actor playing Jesus referring to himself in the third person ('Now God, that died for all mankind') as itself naive. It is no more naive than Prospero's epilogue at the end of *The Tempest* which also embraces god-like mage, actor and finally mere human being.

Morality Plays

In the play of *The Woman Taken in Adultery* we noted a character called, simply, the Accuser. Very occasionally other miracle plays have characters defined not simply by their role but by some abstract quality or attribute of character. Thus we have Backbiter and Raise Slander, the detractors of the Virgin Mary in the N-Town play of *The Trial of Joseph and Mary* and Contemplation who acts as commentator in the group of plays to which *The Trial* belongs. This kind of symbolic characterization becomes a central feature of a type of drama that seems to have grown side by side with the cycle plays. It is commonly called the Morality play and we first hear of it in England in the fourteenth century when Wycliff refers to a lost play which dramatized the Lord's Prayer. The earliest complete example of a morality play in English, however, is *The Castle of Perseverance* (c.1425).

The miracle plays, as we have seen, took their characters and incidents from the scriptures and sacred legends, fleshed out as necessary with situations and personages taken from contemporary life. Their setting was the entire created world and their time-span the whole of human history cradled between the Creation and the Day of Judgement. The time-span of the morality play on the other hand was that of the individual life on earth, considered not realistically but allegorically. Its central character was always the generalized image of humanity, whether he was called Mankind or Humanum genus, or, as in the best of the moralities, Everyman. Given such a protagonist, we should not be surprised to find that the events of these plays are also similarly generalized. Man is surrounded by the personified figures of the various temptations by which mortal life is beset and by other figures embodying the choices open to him. The action of each play shows him moving through these temptations and possibilities, at first choosing ill, but finally, with the aid of knowledge and grace, making the choice that will ensure his eternal bliss.

Put in this summary fashion, morality drama may sound as if all of it consisted of one worthy, earnest and deadly boring play with only minor variations. Certainly what has survived of it in English is less varied and immediately exciting, and considered purely as literary texts has far less to offer than the cycle drama. But even here there are distinctions to be made, and what needs to be constantly emphasized is first, the variety even within the morality plays that have come down to us, and secondly that the language of many of the plays comes truly alive only when embodied in performance. The nature and variety of morality drama can be appreciated by taking a closer look at three of its best known examples, but a brief general consideration of the allegorical drama and its ancestry may be helpful.

The use of allegorical representation was a well established habit of the medieval mind by the time it came to be employed in the drama. Painting, sculpture and poetry such as Langland's *Piers Plowman* had made allegory a fairly familiar technique. Allegory differs from what has been called the figural mode in that, while both seek to point to a significance beyond what is represented, in *figura* both the thing depicted and the thing which it signifies are taken to be real and important. In allegory what is represented exists for the sake of that which is signified by it; it has no independent authority or validity.

The practice of allegorizing the basic teachings of Christianity is quite common in medieval sermons, as one would expect, considering that the greater part of the congregation would be quite unused to abstract thinking. The literary forerunner of the medieval morality drama is perhaps to be found in the work of the fourth-century Christian writer Prudentius. Prudentius wrote two allegorical works, both of which have fairly obvious similarities to the later drama. In the first, *Psychomachia* or The Battle for the Soul, the Soul is the arena on which a series of combats between the personified Vices and Virtues takes place. The lost English Paternoster play may well have stemmed from the tradition inaugurated by Prudentius since we learn from the description of another such play given at

Beverley that the protagonist was sinful man and the other characters represented the seven deadly sins and, presumably, the grace of God. (Each clause of the Paternoster was believed to be especially efficacious against one of the deadly sins).

The other allegory written by Prudentius was the *Hamartigenia* or The Origin of Sin. Here the Soul is seen as a fortress beseiged and finally taken by the Devil and a host of Vices. This pattern of action bears a striking general resemblance to that of the earliest extant English morality, *The Castle of Perseverance.* This play is also noteworthy in that the unique manuscript of it contains the earliest English illustration of a theatrical setting.

The plan shows a circular area surrounded by a ditch full of water. In the middle of this 'place' stood the castle itself, while ranged around the other side of the ditch were five scaffolds, those of Flesh, World, Belial, Covetousness and God. Beneath the Castle on a bed lay the protagonist, Humanum Genus or Mankind. The manuscript text begins with the banns announcing that the play is to be performed a week hence in N-. The play itself opens with the speeches of the World, the Flesh and the Devil, each boasting Herod-like of his might. Man then rises from his bed, a new born soul for whom Good and Bad Angels contend. Predictably he takes the advice of the Bad Angel, and mounts the scaffold of the World. Here the Good Angel saves him from the Vices and leads him, through Confession, Shrift and Penitence, to the Castle of Perseverance. Perseverance is to be understood here as a kind of Christian patience and long-suffering in the face of temptation, disappointment and failure. At the Castle, Satan and his cohorts attack Mankind, a scene which must have had considerable drawing power to judge by the stage direction in the manuscript drawing:

> He that shall play Belial, look that he have gunpowder burning in his hands and in his ears and in his arse when he goeth to battle.

Though the forces of Hell are repulsed by the Virtues hurling showers of roses emblematic of Christ's redeeming blood, Mankind is betrayed by Covetousness who leads him once more towards wordly riches. These prove transitory and Death comes to him, followed by judgement at the throne of God. Justice and Mercy battle for him and at the end God admits him to Heaven. The play ends with a Te Deum preceded by a warning quatrain:

> Thus endeth our games!
> To save you from sinning;
> Ever at the beginning
> Think on your last ending!

The Castle of Perseverance is a very long play (the banns refer to the performance commencing at nine in the morning , and it must have taken all day to perform the full text) and much of its didactic intent is expressed in a language that has not enough life in it to sustain the modern reader's interest. The stanza form in which most of it is written soon becomes monotonous in reading; its staple can be fairly represented by the Bad Angel's initial temptation of Mankind:

> Come on, man! Whereof has thou care,
> Go we to the World, I rede (advise) thee bleve (quickly)

For there thou shalt mow (be able to) right well fare,
In case if thou think for to thrive;
No lord shall be thee like.
Take the World to thine intent
And let thy love be thereon lent;
With gold and silver and rich rent,
Anon thou shalt be rich.

Nevertheless, the occasional modern revival shows that, suitably abridged, the play can still capture the audience. The attack on the castle by Satan's army is one of the few moments in the action with comic possibilities, but to stress these at the expense of the overall didactic effect would clearly be a distortion of the play's intention. That intention is plainly brought out in much of the physical action involved. Thus when Mankind makes the wrong choice and decides to throw in his lot with the forces of evil in the World, the decision is dramatized by his crossing from the place to the World's scaffold on the other side of the ditch.[1] This constant movement from the central place to the various scaffolds keeps the action flowing smoothly, while confusion is avoided by the essentially symbolic nature of the action as well as by the use of a rudimentary colour symbolism for the costumes. The manuscript drawing contains the following instructions:

> The four daughters [of God; Mercy, Peace, Truth and Righteousness] shall
> be clad in mantles, Mercy in white, Righteousness in red altogether, Truth
> in sad (sober) green and peace in black . . .

Thus, while the play may be overlong its single-minded seriousness gives it an authority which is still capable of being transmitted.

The manuscript of *The Castle of Perseverance* (now in the Folger Library, Washington) is bound up with two other morality plays in different hands. (The trio is collectively referred to as the Macro plays after an eighteenth-century bibliophile, the Rev. Cox Macro, who owned the manuscripts. All three originate from East Anglia.) One of these plays is called *Mankind* and, while it has obvious similarities to the *Castle*, the differences too are instructive and serve to illustrate the variety already referred to within this dramatic form.

Both plays are in the allegorical tradition but where the *Castle* calls for some 35 characters with hardly any room for doubling, *Mankind* has just seven speaking parts, with the possibility of doubling between Mercy, represented as a pious old man and Titivillus, the devil appointed by Satan to catch in a net and store in a bag man's sinful and blasphemous thoughts and words (he also appears in one of the Wakefield plays). Where the *Castle* is clearly intended for place-and-scaffold performance, the text of *Mankind* includes a reference to the 'goodman of this house' which indicates that it was intended for performance in an inn by a travelling troupe; the compactness of the cast and the absence of any but the

[1] Richard Southern in *The Mediaeval Theatre in the Round* (London, 1957) has suggested that the scaffolds, contrary to what is shown in the manuscript drawing, were within the circular space bounded by the ditch (which, in his view was intended to keep out non-paying spectators), but I do not find this theory convincing.

simplest of properties reinforce this view. As we shall see, short plays intended for performance indoors, in banqueting halls, inns or guild halls became increasingly common in Tudor times. *Mankind* makes full use of the possibilities of this method of staging.

Perhaps the most striking differences between the two plays lies in the contrast between the didactic seriousness of the earlier play and what appears to be chaotic head-on collision between serious moral purpose allegorically expressed and a series of ribald and often explicitly obscene farcical episodes which seem to delight in the physical aspects of defecation for their own sake. Mankind, the hero, is aware from the beginning of the body's imperfection and the soul's continuing struggle within it. At first he takes Mercy's advice to heart and lives a life of temperance — 'Measure is treasure' — and honest toil. The spade with which he beats off his tempters would link him as a dramatic figure in the medieval audience's mind with the Abel and Adam of the miracle plays; digging the soil was the traditional Biblical symbol for man's labour, the opposite of the deadly sin of sloth.

His tempters all typify this sin as well as others, such as intemperance and lechery. They are three gallants called New-guise, Nowadays (the modern equivalents would perhaps be Trendy and With-it) and Nought, aided and abetted by Mischief and the devil Titivillus. Where the three human tempters fail, the devil, working 'invisibly', succeeds by attacking man through the weakness of his flesh and through false suggestion. A board put underneath the ground makes Mankind give up his digging and when he lies down to rest, Titivillus suggests in a dream that Mercy, his spiritual guide, has been hanged for horse-stealing. This is enough to send Mankind to the ale-house where he carouses with his late enemies New-guise and the others and resolves to lead a life of crime, in a scene where his long coat is progressively cut down to a short jerkin allegedly more suited to the man of fashion. Mankind loses all he has, despairs and resolves to commit suicide, an enterprise in which his companions willingly but ineptly assist him. At the last moment he is saved by Mercy who finds him truly penitent.

The trouble is that the scenes involving New-guise and the other evil characters take on a life of their own which threatens to cancel out the impact of the moral lesson. It would be easy to stage the play as a boisterous farce whose real dramatic force lies in its mockery of the orthodox Christian morality. When Mischief taunts Mercy by turning one of her own utterances to Mankind on its head ('The corn shall be saved, the chaff shall be brent') Mercy has nothing very much to say in reply, and the vigorous buffoonery of Mischief's lines stays in the mind:

> For a winter corn-thresher, sir, I have hired,
> And ye said: the corn shall be saved and the chaff should be fired;
> And he proveth nay, as it showeth by this verse:
> 'Corn serveth breadibus, chaff horsibus, straw firibusque.'
> This is as much to say, to your lewd understanding,
> As: the corn shall serve to bread at the next baking:
> 'Chaff horsibus et reliquid',
> The chaff to horse shall be good provender;

When a man is for-cold the straw may be brent;
And so forth, etc.

What is worse, the language and gestures of Titivillus and the rest have a relentless emphasis on excrement and excrementation (occasionally varied by references to damaged genitals) which only the most dedicated coprophile could relish for long.

On consideration, however, more can be claimed for the play of *Mankind* than that it is an obscene anti-religious farce paying lip service to morality or an earnest didactic drama clumsily nailed on to scenes of ribald horseplay. The very contrast between the dignified formal language of Mercy and the obscenities of the devil and gallants dramatizes one of the play's leading ideas — that bad language is one form of intemperance and one that is closely connected with sloth. The particular form of bad language used here, with its emphasis on the physical processes of the body underlines by contrast Mankind's forgetfulness of his soul's welfare. It is noteworthy that Mankind's language takes on its colouring first from the idiom of Mercy and then from that of his lewd companions, to return at the end to the speech-style of his spiritual guide.[1] The pattern of the play's moral is thus enacted at the linguistic level as well as at the level of allegorical action.

Perhaps the term 'allegorical action' is slightly misleading here, for it is not allegorical in quite the sense in which the hero's visits to the various scaffolds or the defeat of the devils by the Virtues wielding red roses in *The Castle of Perseverance* are. As presented in performance, the action of *Mankind* would not strike the audience as allegorical. If, as is probable, the play was intended to be performed in an inn, the actions of the tempters in drinking, dancing and making obscene jokes would seem quite appropriate to such a place, and the tempters would be dressed as young men about town of the day rather than in symbolic costumes. Even the scene where Mankind's coat is progressively shortened would strike the audience as farcical rather than allegorical. In fact the dramatist uses a good deal of cunning in so arranging matters that the audience itself is trapped into joining in the singing of an obscene parody of a carol, thus falling into the same temptation as Mankind. The action of digging the ground, though its traditional significance has been noted, could hardly strike a predominantly agrarian community as especially allegorical. It is clear, therefore, that in many ways *Mankind*, while sharing a common ancestry in medieval art and the sermon with *The Castle of Perseverance* is a very different descendant.

The last of the morality plays we shall consider is the most straightforwardly allegorical of the three; it is also incomparably the finest. The moral play of *Everyman* exists in four printed copies, each of a different edition printed between 1508 and 1537. It is very similar to a Flemish play called *Elckerlyc* printed in 1595. The English version was probably written late in the fifteenth century and may derive from the Flemish one. At a further remove it is related to an old Buddhist parable about a man summoned by a judge, before whom only one of his three friends, symbolizing his good deeds, will consent to accompany him. The central character, Everyman, is shown in the full pride of his manhood, being

[1] Compare the way Othello's language takes on Iago's idiom as the latter's poison works within him.

commanded by Death to prepare for his last journey. His sometime companions — Fellowship, Kindred, Wealth — all forsake him and he turns in despair to Good Deeds, who is too weak to help him. But Knowledge appears unbidden and renews his faculties (Five Wits) so that he is ready to undertake his journey to the grave, where only Good Deeds may accompany him. Everyman receives from Confession the precious jewel of penance, puts on the garment of contrition and descends into the grave with Good Deeds. The moral of the play is then drawn by an expositor (Doctor) who comes on to speak the Epilogue.

Once again it would be easy to fasten on incidental qualities such as humour (of which there is, in all honesty, very little) or realism in this play because these are the qualities immediately accessible to us today. But the dramatic vitality of the play lies elsewhere. The boldness of the unknown dramatist's approach to his material is immediately striking and is echoed in many a later play.

> I pray you all give your audience,
> And hear this matter with reverence,

begins the Messenger, making no attempt to conceal the fact that this is a play and inviting the audience to respond in an appropriate frame of mind to the unfolding drama. He gives a brief but telling summary of the action returning at the end to the point of dramatic departure, a device which Marlowe remembered when he came to write the opening of *Dr Faustus*. The long speech of God to Death which follows gives us, the audience, a vantage point superior to that of Everyman. We see his struggles — to bribe, to delay, to evade, to retreat — as futile and therefore sympathize with him.

There is no need and therefore no attempt to provide naturalistic entrances and exits for the characters; when they are needed, they appear. The scene is unlocalized because this stage is literally all the world, just as Everyman is every man.

The simple but starkly dramatic contrast between the verbal protestations of Everyman's erstwhile companions and their eventual behaviour is exemplified in Fellowship's

> In faith, an thou go to hell,
> I will not forsake thee by the way.

followed by his immediate desertion. Thus the characters are condemned out of their own mouths. As we follow Everyman he grows to full awareness of his true nature and condition. The first lesson he learns is that the journey to which he is called is immediate and inescapable. The momentous finality of the situation generates powerful dramatic ironies, as in Fellowship's last farewell — 'Yea, by my faith! To God I betake thee!'

Though in the human scale the ties of kinship may be stronger than those of mere companionship — 'For over his kin a man may be bold' — this counts for nothing in Everyman's encounter with Kindred and Cousin. The sudden personal detail which is Cousin's excuse for not accompanying Everyman — 'No, by our Lady! I have the cramp in my toe,' is startlingly effective in its austere context, but it is not so much its humour we are meant to respond to as the desolating contrast between the issues involved and the literal lameness of the excuse.

The dramatic interest is now centred on the question of who can and will help Everyman — 'what friend were best me of to provide?' But even as we become aware of the question we are sure that Everyman's answer, Riches, is the wrong one. (We have already seen that Riches is of no avail as a bribe offered to death.) The contrast is the familiar one between the worldly influence of Riches and its ineffectualness in man's real need. The point is becoming ominously clear that worldly possessions are not merely no help but a positive hindrance on Everyman's last journey — 'for my love is contrary to the love everlasting' in Goods' own words. But for the first time there is a hint that the proper use of worldly Goods may have helped:

Goods: But if thou had loved me moderately during,
As to the poor to give part of me,
Then shouldst thou not in this dolour be,
Nor in this great sorrow and care.

Clearly the play, though it speaks for the poor, addresses itself to all men, rich and poor alike. Goods' gaily casual 'Therefore farewell, and have good day' like Fellowship's earlier leavetaking, strikes a chilling note as it implicates the audience. In Goods' words too we can see the emergence of a new aspect of the theme, one which the cycle drama, by the nature of its interests and emphasis, tended to obscure or underplay. This is the aspect of individual responsibility which is to become an obsessive concern in later tragedy. We are left in no doubt that the various worldly lures are not simply pitfalls into which Everyman cannot help stumbling — 'Marry, thou brought thyself in care'. He has freedom of choice.

The reversal of the dramatic action comes when Everyman turns to his Good Deeds — significantly the only character who knows without being told that Everyman has been summoned before God; it is as if Good Deeds had all along been prepared and waiting for this. All the others were able but unwilling; Good Deeds is willing but unable. The question now is how she can be made capable of accompanying Everyman. She turns for succour to her sister Knowledge (i.e. of religious truth) whose resonantly simple promise to Everyman stands in memorable contrast to the smooth prevarications of his earlier associates:

Everyman, I will go with thee and be thy guide,
In thy most need to go by thy side.

Knowledge is the first to offer, unconditionally and without being asked, to accompany Everyman. Thus begins the second and positive phase of the hero's pilgrimage, led by Knowledge through Confession to penance, and prayer. We may note that Everyman does not need to be told about God and Christ — he knows perfectly well already. It is simply that other things have distracted him and obscured this knowledge; Everyman is perhaps the supreme example of *memento mori* in an age much given to remembrance of the four last things.

The play proceeds with the simplest of physical actions. Apart from a series of encounters and the final descent into the grave, the only proper actions are those of Everyman scourging himself and putting on the robe of contrition. They are charged with meaning, imitating as they do the real life observances of penitence and purification. But if this is 'realism' it is something very different from what is normally meant by the term, for its end is as far removed as possible from the creation of a naturalistic illusion.

The triumphant forward movement continues, assisted now by Beauty, Strength, Discretion and Five Wits (Five Senses). The panegyric on the clergy is balanced by an attack on priestly corruption and both are doubtless indications of clerical authorship. But they ae not to be seen as extraneous intrusions of the author's private interests; in the medieval context the question of whether the priest was a good shepherd or an evil one is literally a matter of life and death, far more relevant to the theme of *Everyman* than it is, say, to that of Milton's *Lycidas*.

In sharp contrast to the character who begged piteously to delay his journey at the play's beginning the transfigured Everyman who has received the last sacraments is eager to be on his way — 'and our friends let us go without longer respite'. In the final phase of the drama the initial pattern of forsaking Everyman is repeated, but with a difference. Everyman still has the last lesson to learn that not even his new companions are steadfast to the end. First Beauty, then Strength, then Discretion and Five Wits abandon him (the order roughly corresponding to that of physical decay). This is a genuinely surprising dramatic twist, more perhaps for the modern than the medieval audience, insofar as we have been tempted into believing that in his second choice Everyman has chosen aright. Our superior vantage point has now disappeared; we see no better, know no more than Everyman himself. The last lesson is thus the true answer to the first question — who is Everyman's real friend and guide? The one he least valued, Good Deeds.

The play concludes as it began, with a direct address to the audience:

This moral men may have in mind.
Ye hearers, take it of worth, old and young

ending with a prayer 'that we may live body and soul together' to which the audience is invited to say Amen. We would have to be totally insensitive to the play's power and subtlety to think of this as artistic naiveté. On stage, radio and screen in innumerable adaptations, *Everyman* continues to show the enduring vitality of the very greatest drama. Part of the impact is doubtless due to our sense that it deals with fundamental human concerns; but we would not respond as we do if the dramatist had dealt with these questions in a trivial, sentimental or irresponsible fashion.

Whether in the form of the vast cycle drama or the more compact moralities, medieval drama grew out of a unified vision of man in his relation to God, to time and eternity. Within its generous framework it was able to accommodate episodes ranging from the farcical to the near-tragic with their corresponding emotional effects. If tragedy sees man as an isolated creature battling against an implacably hostile universe, then the truly tragic note could not occur within this drama, which was that of the divine comedy of man's providential salvation. When this unity was fragmented and man came increasingly to be seen as a stranger alone if unafraid in a world where ideas of order were threateningly undercut by intimations of chaos, Elizabethan tragedy was born; but in that haunted and disordered world we shall often hear echoes of the vanished wholeness.

2

The Emergence of the Secular Drama

In some ways the title of this chapter can be misleading. There was an independent tradition of secular theatre from the beginning, developing alongside the Church-sponsored miracle and morality drama. Furthermore, the latter was also secular in at least two senses, first that it probably always existed for performance outside the church, in secular time and place, rather than growing out of the liturgical drama, and second in that from the beginning it was able to accommodate characters, incidents and language which were part of the waking and working life of its audience. Nevertheless it remains true that we can only speak in any real detail of English secular drama from about the end of the fifteenth century. This is largely due to the historical accident that the first complete text of a secular drama to have survived dates from that time. But it is worth reminding ourselves that a fragment of such a drama, *The Interlude of the Student and the Girl* is at least a hundred years older, and that there are allusions to plays based on popular romances dating from roughly the same time as the great age of the cycle drama.

It is only sixty years since the full text of *Fulgens and Lucrece* by Henry Medwall was rediscovered. It is based on a *novella* written in Latin some seventy years before the play was first performed, and printed by Caxton in an English trans-lation in 1481. Its theme was a commonplace of medieval discussion, namely whether true nobility is a matter of being well born or of integrity of character. The form in which Medwall presents his play also owes something to the medieval *debat* or formal disputation on a set topic. But it also owes a good deal to other kinds of entertainment current in Tudor times, such as Christmas games, songs, jousts and mummings. Indeed, a brief consideration of the circumstances under which *Fulgens and Lucrece* was first produced is as revealing as an examination of the text itself, for it tells us much about Tudor drama in the upper reaches of society.

We know very little about Medwall's life but we do know that he was Chaplain to Henry VII's great Cardinal, John Morton, Archbishop of Canterbury. As Lord President of the Privy Council, Morton was as much a prince of the state as of the Church and entertained foreign ambassadors at his residence, Lambeth Palace. Lavish banquets often lasting several hours were one of the features of Tudor hospitality and it was during the intervals between courses at such a banquet that *Fulgens and Lucrece* was performed, and from which the term 'Interlude' used to describe the characteristic dramatic form of the early Tudor period probably derived.

The very shape of the play is determined by its original occasion, for it consists of two parts separated by courses of the banquet and is designed for performance in the great hall of a Tudor mansion, in the presence of guests seated at tables with drink at their side and a blazing fire in the great fireplace. One end of such a hall usually had two doors leading into the kitchen and often a minstrel gallery above. It was in the space before these doors that the play was performed so that, with the exception of those sitting at the high table at the far end the spectators would be on the same level and in the same light as the players, and not very far from them. Some of them would probably sit or stand among the performers themselves. This proximity and the ensuing intimacy is ingeniously exploited in Medwall's play and many others of its kind.

The story of the play proper is set in classical Rome, but it begins with immediacy when one of two servants (identified simply as A and B) who, according to the Latin stage direction 'enters speaking':

> For Goddes will
> What mean ye, sirs, to stand so still?
> Have not ye eaten and your fill
> And paid nothing therefor? . . . .
> I trow your dishes be not bare
> Nor yet ye do the wine spare;
> Therefore be merry as ye fare,
> Ye are welcome each one
> Unto this house without feigning.

A rebukes the audience for sitting in serious contemplation after all the good cheer they have had, whereupon B tells him that a play is just about to begin and that he has learned its plot from one of the players. He then helpfully summarizes the main plot, which tells of Fulgentius, a Roman senator, and his daughter Lucrece. The latter has two suitors, Flaminius, a wise plebian who has done good service to the state and risen to high office, and the idle and dissolute patrician Cornelius. In his source, a question mark hangs over which of the two Lucrece should choose but Medwall ends his play by having his heroine choose the worthy but low-born Flaminius. This conclusion would not have displeased the host, Cardinal Morton who had himself risen from modest beginnings to the highest office in the land through loyal and devoted service, nor the recently crowned Henry himself, who preferred to elevate personally men like Morton and create an upper class beholden to him, rather than rely on the uncertain loyalty of the ancient nobility. Thus though the topic was traditional, its contemporary relevance would hardly have been missed by its audience.

What is even more striking than the 'message' is the way Medwall manoeuvres the two 'servants' A and B into the play itself. A is sure B must be one of the players, which B denies, claiming that he is only a servant. (They were probably both.) Eventually they each become a servant to one of the suitors, making the transition from Tudor England to ancient Rome with breathtaking nonchalance. Medwall had ample precedent for this in the deliberate use of anachronistic detail in the cycle plays which has been noted earlier. From that drama too, he may have got the idea of introducing a comic underplot in which the courting of Lucrece's maid by A and B highlights by way of parody the concerns of the main plot (much as, in the Second Shepherd's Play of the Towneley cycle the Nativity is high-lighted by the misdemeanours of Mak the sheep stealer and the attempted disguising of the stolen sheep as a new-born babe). Whatever its origin, the underplot, comic, ironic or otherwise, was an important part of the Elizabethan inheritance from the earlier drama. In *Fulgens and Lucrece* it enabled Medwall to introduce contests of song, wrestling and jousting to provide 'solace' or enter-tainment value to the 'sentence' or high seriousness of the tale he dramatized.

Morality and Interlude

Medwall's play shows a deliberate and highly sophisticated use of the convivial atmosphere of a banquet and the inevitable pauses between courses are skilfully worked into the structure of the play. Because the audience is not primarily there to see a play but to take part in a banquet and because the surroundings are the permanent architectural features of the banqueting hall, the opportunities for the creation of dramatic illusion are limited. The audience are not in a theatre which, with their willing cooperation, can be imagined as Rome but in a great hall of a Tudor mansion. Instead of evading this situation or apologizing for it, Medwall exploits it with a boldness and virtuosity which may remind a twentieth-century playgoer of Pirandello's experiments with theatrical illusion. In shape and atmos-phere *Fulgens and Lucrece* is worlds away from *Everyman,* yet Medwall himself, and the circle in which he moved, may serve to remind us that we must not draw too sharp a distinction between the morality play and the secular interlude. The only other play certainly known to be by Medwall is called *Nature* and has many of the concerns of *Everyman* though lacking anything like its dramatic impact.

Nature has the familiar allegorical figures and symbolic action of the earlier morality plays such as *Mankind* and *The Castle of Perseverance.* It depicts Man's life as a battle between the virtues and the vices in which man first yields to tempta-tion and gives way to sensuality but finally repents. The Nature of the title is the organizing principle behind the scheme of things, the laws ordained by God which give order and coherence to the world. It is, however, not quite as tedious as this summary makes it sound, mainly because of Medwall's sure sense of the dramatic occasion and the energy with which the vices are presented. When we reflect that both *Fulgens and Lucrece* and *Nature,* with all their boisterous fun and bawdy innuendo enlivening the serious themes, were presented in the residence of the Archbishop of Canterbury, probably by his household servants assisted by profes-sional actors, we can get some idea of the range of drama in the early Tudor period.

Medwall's patron has another interest for the student of drama because, through the figure of Sir Thomas More he provides a link with the other pioneers of the secular interlude. More was a page in Morton's household and evidently an enthusiastic amateur of the drama, for his son-in-law and biographer William Roper reports that when a play was in progress More would 'suddenly sometimes step in among the players, and never studying for the matter, make a part of his own there presently among them'. In the play of *Sir Thomas More* (c.1595) in which Shakespeare had a hand, More himself is shown giving a banquet to which the troupe of Cardinal Wolsey arrives to offer a choice of plays for the entertainment and edification of the guests. The host selects the interlude of *The Marriage of Wit and Wisdom*(c.1579).

According to a contemporary More himself wrote comedies though it is not possible to say definitely whether any of the interludes which have survived from the period are his work. But he is connected with the three men who can be identified as the first begetters of the Tudor interlude, Medwall himself, John Rastell and John Heywood. Rastell not only printed *Fulgens and Lucrece* but was himself the author of *The Nature of the Four Elements* and possibly also of *Gentleness and Nobility* on a theme similar to that of Medwall's play and *Calisto and Melibea,* all probably composed in the 1520s. He married More's sister Elizabeth. Their daughter Joan married John Heywood who is in many ways the most important figure in the history of the Tudor interlude.

Heywood lived to be over 80 and when he died in exile some time after 1578, the first public playhouse in England was already open. But his surviving plays belong to the second decade of the sixteenth century and his career as singer, musician, deviser and presenter of pageants and dramatist once again reminds us of the versatility of Tudor aristocratic and royal entertainment, for Heywood worked at the court of the Catholic Queen Mary as well as that of the Protestant Edward VI. Of the six interludes generally attributed to him, four are debates rather than plays proper, though they are debates conducted with great verbal energy and irrepressible high spirits (in one of them, *A Play of Love*(c.1525) a character is instructed to run about the audience wearing a sugar-loaf hat stuck full of lighted squibs shouting 'Water, water! Fire, fire!') The best of these is *The Play of the Weather*(c. 1527), on the surface a slight fable derived from a Latin dialogue about various members of society who appear before Jupiter to plead for the weather that suits them best. But not very far below this surface is a firm though by no means uncritical endorsement of a social order where each knows his place and keeps it under the benevolent supervision of an enlightened monarch. When Merry Report acts as mediator between Jupiter and the petitioners, the distinctions of social rank are carefully preserved. The Gentleman and the Merchant have no difficulty in obtaining a direct meeting with Jupiter, but the Ranger (keeper of the royal parks) being lower down the social scale cannot do so, nor can the millers, despite the declared intention of one of them to 'go even boldly' to the deity's presence (in accordance with the widespread folktale tradition of the humble subject who takes his plaint direct to the monarch, bypassing high office holders). And Jupiter the monarch reconciles sectional interests by a wise passiveness to which not only the petitioners but the audience itself is invited to assent; he decides to let the weather stay exactly as it is. The need for tolerance and mutual understanding and obedience to the sovereign at a time when national dissension threatens is wittily and tactfully presented to the ruling elite — superfluously perhaps, but satisfyingly.

Though Heywood's play *The Four Ps* has professional religious men for two of its four characters (the palmer and the pardoner; the other two are the 'pothecary and the peddler) and even tells of a descent into hell and has a spasm of orthodox piety at the close (Heywood was a devout Catholic), it is unremittingly worldly in its tone as the pardoner's allusion to one of the lesser devils he meets at hell gate illustrates:

> And first to the devil that kept the gate
> I came, and spake after this rate:
> All hail, sir devil and made low curtsey.
> Welcome, quoth he, thus smilingly.
> He knew me well, and I at last
> Remembered him since long time past.
> For, as good hap would have it chance,
> This devil and I were of old acquaintance:
> For oft, in the play of Corpus Christi,
> He hath played the devil at Coventry.

The description of the arch-fiend perhaps harks back to a performance Heywood himself may have witnessed of a miracle play but it is its grotesque humour in which Heywood delights:

> . . .then low as well I could
> I kneeled, which he so well allowed,
> That thus he becked, and by St Anthony,
> He smiled on me so well-favouredly,
> Bending his brows as broad as barn-doors,
> Shaking his ears as rugged as burrs,
> Rolling his eyes as round as two bushels,
> Flashing the fire out of his nostrils,
> Gnashing his teeth so vaingloriously,
> That methought time to fall to flattery.

The dispute which gives the interlude such meagre plot as it has turns on who can tell the biggest lie; the palmer wins hands down by his solemn remark that in all his travels he has never met an ill-tempered woman. But the simple and fairly predictable tale is enlivened not only by the vigour of Heywood's language but also by the numerous opportunities for gesture and mimicry, instances of which are found in both the extracts quoted.

In addition to these four plays (the one not yet mentioned is *Witty and Witless*) full of speechifying and no plot to speak of, Heywood is also credited with two lively farces *The Pardoner and the Friar* and *Johan Johan* (both written about 1529). These two plays, anti-clerical in temper though not fiercely so, have no perceptible moral intent and are none the worse for that. What they do have are plots that move along at a great pace to reach a satisfying farcical climax. The malefactors escape punishment in *The Pardoner and the Friar,* while the cuckolded husband in *Johan Johan* mutters under his breath as he sits mending a bucket while his wife is at supper with her lecherous lover, the priest Sir John ('Sir' was a common title for a priest at this time), though he finally summons up the courage to drive them out of doors. Though it is very closely based on a French farce, Heywood's play remains in its own right one of the few early comedies which are still genuinely funny to read as well as to watch.

In the work of men like Medwall, Rastell and Heywood we can see the drama gradually coming to grips with the problems of character, action and speech which arise from the activities of men in their social relations rather than as seen under the aspect of an over-arching Providence. Among other things this change brought about a new interest in narrative material, for the stories were no longer either familiar through the scriptures or predictable because of their didactic intent. Not that the didactic intent disappeared, any more than the allegorical method. But both were complicated by a new interest in the secular world and the exigencies of religious polemic. For the most part, the interludes dealing with religious issues raised by the Reformation — notably those of the 'bilious' John Bale, most of whose apparently copious output has providentially perished — are unreadable except for strictly historical reasons and unactable except in a context of theatrical research. And while Heywood's farces and Medwall's use of a sub-plot influenced later dramatists, they learned how to handle the complexities of dramatic plot from classical rather than native sources. Before turning to these, however, it is necessary to consider the contribution made to the development of drama by the growth of professionalism in this period, under the impact of royal and aristocratic patronage, among the players of interludes; for they were the direct ancestors of Shakespeare and his fellows, and we cannot too often remind ourselves that the study of drama is, or should be, an account of plays in performance.

The term interlude has been restricted here to cover *short* plays originally intended for indoor performance (though what some consider the greatest of interludes, David Lindsay's *A Satire of the Three Estates* apparently took nine hours to perform, while another famous one, Skelton's *Magnificence* is also a lengthy play in five parts). The conditions under which these plays were performed imposed, as we have seen, certain restrictions on the dramatists. They also determined conventions of acting and staging and the social function and role of the players in ways that were to prove decisive for the period that followed.

The development of professionalism is obviously connected with the social position of the professional, since the degree to which his skills develop will depend on how far those skills are esteemed and rewarded by society. The men who performed in the medieval cycle plays were amateurs, members of some trade guild, though there is reason to believe that during the long period in which this drama flourished, they developed a good deal of professional skill, aided perhaps by strolling players. A more stable and continuous tradition of professional playing is provided by the practice, going at least as far back as the mid-fifteenth century, of monarchs who kept 'players of interludes' as part of their retinue, a practice which the nobility were not slow to emulate. These performers occasionally presented pageants and spectacles for royal occasions in various places, but we are here concerned with their activity within the Tudor banqueting hall. They were part of the household and had the protection of the lord's livery, a circumstance which served them well in their disputes with the authorities, becoming the outward proof that they were not mere vagabonds.

These household troupes were usually quite small, consisting perhaps of three or four men and a boy to play the women's parts. Interludes were also performed by companies of children under court patronage; these were of course much larger groups and the plays written for them usually called for a greater number of actors. At first the adult troupes played exclusively in the household to which they were attached, but, for economic as well as other reasons, they very soon began to travel further and further afield, taking their repertory of plays to a wider public, playing in guildhall or inn, so that the drama which began in the halls of the great reached downward to humbler folk, deriving strength and vivacity from its contact with a living popular tradition; this in turn produced a number of plays written mainly for this more general audience. Most interludes were printed not so much to be read as to be performed by these travelling troupes, as the detailed information (not always accurate) as to which parts may be doubled makes clear. Thus the professional actors were in contact with all levels of society from the highest to the lowest as they continued to be in the heyday of the Elizabethan theatre; the difference was that till there was a purpose-built theatre where the people could go to see and hear the players, the players had to take their theatre to the people.

Though the troupes were small, the casts of the plays in which they acted were often extensive. Doubling of parts has been mentioned; it needs to be added that this was both very frequent and appears to have been relished for its own sake, rather than indulged in apologetically as a regrettable necessity. There was a well-established tradition of 'disguising' or masquerade and no doubt part of the audience's pleasure lay in recognizing the same actor in a variety of roles (this would not have been very difficult to do; the donning of a cloak or affixing a false beard was conventionally accepted as impenetrable disguise or total transformation, a convention which Elizabethan comedy would scarely have known how to do without). The title page of *Cambises* contains a table in which the 38 acting roles are assigned to a cast of eight players!

It is clear that under such conditions, any detailed or searching portrayal of individual character is out of the question, nor do any of the interludes call for this. Character is established in broad and vigorous terms and, where the theme calls for it, is transformed rather than developed. Thus the Worldly Man, a character in William Wager's *Enough is as Good as a Feast* (written about the time Shakespeare was born) announces himself thus:

Because I am a man indued with treasure,
Therefore a wordly man men do me call:
Indeed I have riches and money at my pleasure,
Yea, and I will have more in spite of them all.

But if depth of characterization is lacking, the interlude has other virtues, among them the many dramatic effects possible in a theatrical setting where actions of the most general('allegorical') significance can be given immediacy by direct address to an audience which is very close to the stage. Thus Worldly Man in the play just mentioned is struck down (literally) by God's Plague, having ignored warnings of divine wrath, whereupon Satan, who comes to collect the corpse, turns to the audience with these words:

All you worldly men, that in your riches do trust,
Be merry and jocund, build palaces and make lusty cheer:

Put your money to usury, let it not lie and rust,
Occupy yourselves in my laws while you be here!

He then promises them —

Yea and after death I will provide a place,
For you in my kingdom for ever to reign:
You shall fare no worse than doth mine own grace,
That is to lie burning for ever in pain —

— immediately after which he addresses the corpse of Worldly Man, still clad in its symbolic finery, in almost identical terms; the parallel is unsubtle but chillingly effective and is the direct consequence of the intimacy generated by the circumstances of performance.

Where the interludes centring on debate, such as those of Heywood and Rastell, have hardly any plot structure, underlying the secular moral interludes is the morality structure of the struggle for man's soul in an increasingly social-political setting, though in the later fifteenth century the emphasis tends to be more on the deserved damnation of the wicked rather than on grace and repentance. As characterization is typical, though increasingly filled out with observed social detail, so action tends to be symbolic and costume conventional, though once again both have their roots in social reality. Thus in John Redford's *Wit and Science*(c.1530) the hero throws off his gown in order to dance with Honest Recreation; at one level this obviously makes it easier for him to dance, but it also signifies his abandonment of Science (Knowledge), as the fact that the gown keeps slipping off when the fool Ignorance tries to wear it signifies that knowledge is not for fools (as Idleness rather unnecessarily points out).

Thus the conditions under which Tudor interludes were performed created a tradition of acting in which improvisation, flexibility, a high degree of conventionality in costume and gesture and above all, a unique blend of familiarity and formality between actors and audience were essential features. The plays that were written for performance in these conditions owed much to the traditions of medieval drama. But the great achievements of the Elizabethan theatre were preceded not only by this professional drama, but by the activities of learned amateurs in schools, universities and the Inns of Court.

Drama and Education

One of the strengths of the English drama at this time was that dramatic activity was not only prevalent throughout society, but that there was a healthy and fruitful contact between its various elements. We have seen how the greatest prelate and politician in the land amused himself and his guests with plays that combined ribaldry with a serious message and how such plays reached a broader audience through the activities of travelling troupes. Similarly, we can see the fruits of classical learning expressed in plays, originally intended to be performed by and for the edification of English schoolchildren which combined formal principles derived from the classics with the boisterous energy of the native tradition. Many of these appealed to an audience beyond that of the schools in which they originated.

In one sense virtually all literary drama at this time, with the possible exception of farces such as those of Heywood, was educational in intent or pretension. It claimed to teach a moral lesson, or convey useful knowledge in an agreeable form. But there was a much closer and more specific connection between Tudor education and at least one kind of dramatic performance. Under the impact of Renaissance humanism, the study of the Latin (and to a lesser extent Greek) classics became a very important part of the educational curriculum. It was not simply a matter of the formal study of a number of texts but the enthusiastic embracing of classical ideals of decorum, balance, clarity and dignity. The classics became touchstones by which these qualities could be judged and through intimate acquaintance with which they could be acquired. Hence the educational process set great store by the committing to memory of as many of these classical models as possible, whether it was the modern Latin of Erasmus's dialogue or the classical eloquence of Cicero's orations. In the less formal manner the admired models were the two Roman comic dramatists Plautus and Terence, especially the latter. As part of the process of getting to know their work intimately, many schoolmasters encouraged their pupils to perform these plays. These performances were sometimes repeated by royal or noble companies before audiences of foreign dignitaries (since professional players knowing no Latin were unable to do so), giving the children practical experience of performing to a wider audience and stimulating their love of the theatre. Doubtless this was one of the factors which went to the creation of the enthusiastic and informed audiences of the first public playhouse.

It was not long before the children proceeded from the performance of classical Latin plays to modern ones written on their model, first in Latin and later in the vernacular. By the time Elizabeth ascended the throne in 1558 the leading schools throughout the country had the performance of plays, Latin and English, as an integral part of their curriculum. Such plays were often open to the public, though in 1574 the Merchant Taylors forbade performances in the hall of their recently established school because they objected to 'the tumultous disordered persons repairing hither to see such plays, as by our Scholars were here lately played'. It is an objection we shall hear more than once in the history of the English theatre.

What has some claim to be called the first fully fledged English comedy extant belongs to the class of plays produced on classical lines by schoolmasters for their pupils. Nicholas Udall taught at Winchester, Eton and Westminister and it was probably while he was at Winchester in 1553 that he wrote *Ralph Roister Doister*, a light-hearted tale of a braggart's unsuccessful attempts to seduce an honest woman while her betrothed is away at sea. The most obvious evidence of classical influences is in the play's five-act structure (contrasting sharply with the loose episodic sequences of the 'native' dramatic tradition) and the adaptation of two staple figures of classical comedy, the braggart soldier (who is Englished as the hero Ralph Roister Doister) and the wily parasite who becomes his not always faithful servant, Matthew Merrygreek. But Merrygreek, who constantly involves his master in tricky situations and is given to practical joking, has obvious family resemblances to the Vice character of the medieval drama who became a popular favourite with his ready wit, his easy familiarity with the audience and his unfailing willingness to do anyone a bad turn whenever he could. Very English too is the country setting in which Udall places his characters and the names he gives them, such as Dobinet Doughty (though his fellow-servant Harpax has a classical ring to his name) Tibet Talkapace and Madge Mumblecrust. And Udall scrupulously substitutes the virtuous Dame Custance for the courtesan of Roman comedy. The most hilarious episode of the play, which Shakespeare may have remembered when he wrote the mechanicals' prologue to their play in *A Midsummer Night's Dream*, has Merrygreek completely altering the sense of Doister's love-letter to Dame Custance by reading it with the wrong punctuation — a neat combination of pedagogy and entertainment. The eventual outcome of the play, with the honest merchant Gawyn Goodluck trampling over the soldier Roister Doister and the Scrivener, may have been intended as a compliment to the rising merchant class (though the trouble with this kind of remark is that it is difficult to think of a time when the merchant class is not rising). Thus, while classical principles provide the five-act structure, scene divisions, a basis for the chief characters and unity of place and time (the latter a little shaky since the action is spread over three days), it is Udall's blending of these with the native elements that is the real strength of the play. The song in praise of Queen Mary which concludes the play is an apt reminder that the patronage of drama extended throughout society up to the court itself.

Udall may also have been the author of *Jack Juggler* (before 1562), adapted from Plautus's *Amphitruo*, a witty and ingenious farce with a well organized plot. More ambitious and more amusing is *Gammer Gurton's Needle* written about the same time as Udall's play, probably by William Stevenson and performed by the students of Christ's College, Cambridge. Once again we have the act and scene structure as well as the unities of classical drama, this time in the service of a plot which centres round the loss and subsequent discovery of Gammer Gurton's 'goodly, tossing spinner's needle', a fairly valuable item. The parasite is transformed here into the wandering Bedlam beggar Diccon (a comic ancestor of Edgar as Poor Tom in *Lear*) who claims to discover the whereabouts of the missing object by necromancy (it is finally found, where Gammer Gurton had left it, in the simpleton Hodge's half-mended breeches). From early efforts such as these, English comic drama taught itself the mysteries of a plot with a beginning, middle and end (though not always in that order), the desirability of characters having some motivation for their exits and entrances (something which a drama not committed to the ordinary world did not need), and the possibilities of dramatic dialogue which could at once be witty and refined. But it never lost touch with the broad humour and the rough-and-tumble vigour of the interlude tradition. It was precisely because that tradition was alive and kicking in all directions that it could absorb the lessons which Latin comedy at schools and universities could teach.

As the schoolmasters and dons gave classical shape and direction to English comedy in the mid-sixteenth century, so the students and their mentors at the Inns of Court 'England's third university' brought classical influences to bear on English tragedy; and to the extent that the native tradition of tragedy, to judge by what survives, was a crude and feeble counterpart of the comedy, the early tragedies written for performance before restricted audiences at the Inns were much closer to their Latin originals than the comedies. In its very nature, the cycle drama was not tragic in the true sense, though it had its moments of pathos and poignancy, while the morality tradition, which showed the sinner finally penitent and saved or unrepentant and justly punished, had no real tragic potential either. Such native tragedy as there was up to this time seems to have consisted of dramatizations of deeds of domestic violence and cruelty in a style analogous to that of today's popular press and horror films, or adaptions of classical myth or history such as John Pickering's *Horestes* (1567) which have a crude power, but whose crudity is more evident than their power. It is difficult to strike the truly tragic note when the hero is instructed, as in *Cambises* to enter 'without a gown, a sword thrust up into his side, bleeding' and speak such lines as:

> But! Alas! What shall I do? My life is finished!
> Wounded I am by sudden chance, my blood is minished.
> Gog's heart, what means might I make my life to preserve?
> Is there nought to be my help? Nor is there nought to serve?

Both *Horestes* and *Cambises* were performed some years after the members of the Inner Temple presented as part of their Christmas revels a play which was repeated at Whitehall before the Queen in the new year (1562). This was *Gorboduc*, justly considered a landmark in the development of English literary tragedy. The qualification is important, because following the lead of their model, the Roman dramatist Seneca, the authors, Thomas Norton and Thomas Sackville, banish virtually all action from the main drama. The story itself has plenty of action, including fratricide regicide and bloody revolution. But in the Senecan manner all this is related by messengers. The dialogue consists of disputes and discussions on the state of the kingdom fallen into disarray because of King Gorboduc's rash decision to divide his country between his two sons, and dumb shows which precede each act and symbolize the argument.

The authors of *Gorboduc* were both active politicians, members of Queen Elizabeth's first Parliament, and their didactic intention in this play — to warn of the consequences of a kingdom under a divided crown and urge that the queen should name her successor in her lifetime through parliament — is plain. Its importance in the history of drama lies less in its subject than in its handling of it. From Seneca, Sackville and Norton borrowed the five-act structure, chorus, messengers and a sensational plot. But they expanded the plot to deal with a serious political issue, striking a note of patriotic concern and emphasizing the significance of human choice. Above all they gave to the language of drama a new dignity and resonance. *Gorboduc* is the first English tragedy to be written in the blank verse that was to be the characteristic music of Elizabethan drama in the great decades to follow. In comparison with these later achievements, the language of *Gorboduc* sounds wooden and undramatic. To get some idea of the extent of its impact on its original audience we should perhaps compare the doggerel from *Cambises* quoted earlier with a passage such as this:

> If flattery then, which fails not to assail
> The tender minds of yet unskilful youth,

In one shall kindle, and increase disdain,
And envy in the other's heart inflame,
This fire shall waste their love, their lives, their land,
And ruthful ruin shall destroy them both.

This is language which has genuine possibilities of development, which is more than can be said of that of *Cambises* and its ilk. *Gorboduc* was to set a fashion in aristocratic and academic circles for quasi-Senecan plays, though none of the others which followed it are of much consequence. *Jocasta* (1566) by George Gascoigne and Francis Kinwelmersh is an English adaptation of an Italian adaptation of a Latin translation of Euripedes. *Gismound of Salerne* (1566) later revised as *Tancred and Gismunda* by Robert Wilmot is a five-act-long exercise in finger-wagging at the disasters which follow illicit love, while *The Misfortunes of Arthur* (1588) by Thomas Hughes (with dumb shows devised by Francis Bacon and other members of Gray's Inn) tells of Arthur's incest with his sister and death at the hands of his son Mordred in lines, many of which are translated directly out of Seneca. Elizabethan drama came of age when the native vigour of speech and love of sensational and spectacular action could be successfully combined with the dignity and decorum which classical works had taught. This had already happened the year before *The Misfortunes of Arthur*, when the public theatre had presented Christopher Marlowe's *Tamburlaine*.

3

Elizabethan Drama

When *Tamburlaine* was first performed, Queen Elizabeth had been on the throne for nearly thirty years. The first public theatre especially built for the performance of plays opened in 1576, eighteen years after she came to the throne. What is generally and rightly regarded as the golden age of English drama belongs therefore to the later part of the great queen's reign and to the opening years of her successor, James the First. The earlier Elizabethan drama, as we have seen, was taken up with the huff-snuffery of innumerable chronicle plays, worthy but tedious imitations of Seneca at the Inns of Court and schools plays which blended classical notions of form and character with native energy and homespun humour.

It is of course no accident that within ten years or so of the opening of the public theatres there occurred the greatest efflorescence of dramatic writing England has ever seen. For it was in these theatres that the many strands of theatrical tradition — religious and secular, popular and academic, courtly and rustic — were woven into a single splendid and many-coloured fabric. The process took some little time and many of the early experiments were of the nature of patchwork put together from whatever materials lay to hand. But these haphazard beginnings, by their sheer variety, created the taste which was able to recognize and applaud the many-splendoured thing when it appeared on the scene.

There were two kinds of public playhouse in England, both dating from the same time. The first is so well known that only a bald summary need be given here. Though individual theatre buildings almost certainly differed one from another, there is good reason to believe that the basic pattern of this theatre was shared by all. It took its overall polygonal shape from the bull- and bear-baiting rings so popular at the time. As in these places, there were three tiers of seats within, arranged round most of the polygon. In the centre was an open space where spectators could stand, much as they did in the yard of an inn or to watch a pageant or royal tableau. On the side opposite the entrance was the acting area. This consisted of a platform stage which came right out to the audience so that the spectators, standing and seated, surrounded the stage on three sides. At the back was a partition with two doors on each side, rather like the doors leading to the kitchen area in a Tudor mansion. These were the principal entrances and exits, though there were also trapdoors and characters sometimes came in through the audience, a well-established theatrical tradition by this time. There was also a small inner acting area at the back with hangings which could be used to reveal a set piece, such as a tomb or a laden table. Above the doors was a balcony which could be used as part of the stage space or to seat spectators; no doubt it was suggested by the minstrel galleries in Tudor halls. The acting area was open to the sky except for a half-roof over part of the platform with its ceiling painted to represent the heavens. (It was actually called the 'heavens' as the portion underneath the stage was called 'hell'). Thus the builders of this public theatre used their experience of acting in other places with a shrewd eye for packing the largest number of people into the available space. It was a secular theatre which still retained traces of its kinship to the earth and open sky which had once been the setting for the divine drama of death and judgement, heaven and hell.

Less well known is a variant of this, rather misleadingly known as the private theatres. Until 1608, performances in these were given by companies of children attached to the choir-schools of the Chapel Royal, Windsor, and St Paul's and the earliest private playhouses were probably no more than rooms which had been fitted up so that plays could be performed there by the children. The main physical differences between these and the playhouse structures just described are that the 'private' theatres were smaller, rectangular in shape, had artificial light and were completely roofed in. Later, buildings such as the one-time priory of Blackfriars were permanently adapted as indoor theatres. There was the same platform stage with the inner acting area and the upper gallery familiar from the 'public' playhouse, but no separate 'heavens' and no standing spectators. The running costs of such a theatre were higher than those of the open-air playhouse and because they could take in fewer spectators, they charged higher prices. They therefore tended to draw audiences from the more affluent sections of society, at least those elements who had the ability and the inclination to spend money on playgoing. These were mainly the court circle and those who wished to appear associated with it. No doubt the epithet 'private' was useful as a way of giving such theatres a certain air of social distinction.

John Lyly and Courtly Comedy

The children's companies appeared both at court and in the private theatres, in plays specially written for them and addressed to an audience presumed to be more elegant in their taste and readier to appreciate witty refinement and gracefully turned allusions to classical myth, especially in the form of courtly compliment, than their counterparts in the outdoor theatre. The taste for this witty comedy of compliment with a lightly sketched in background of classical-allegorical romance was both created and brought to its height of refinement by John Lyly, the first of the 'new wave' of Elizabethan dramatists. But it clearly would not have enjoyed the enormous vogue which it did if it had not fitted so easily into the culture and style of life of the Elizabethan court.

The contrast between Lyly's new career as a dedicated 'courtier' in the real court of Elizabeth, with its sycophancy, jockeying for position, its capricious rewards and its constant frustrations, and the enchanted court which he presents in so many of his plays is a poignant comment on the way in which art 'reflects' life. Lyly came from Oxford, where he had a reputation for nimbleness of wit rather than scholarly flair or industry ('a dapper and deft campanion' as an early biographer noted) and took the courtly world by storm with the prose romance which he had begun while still at Oxford, *Euphues, the Anatomy of Wit*(1578) and its sequel *Euphues and His England*(1580). Today even the element of self-parody in these, with their elaborate antithetical and triadic constructions and fantastical natural history adapted from Pliny cannot render these works other than eminently unreadable except in fairly small doses. But they became the touchstone of courtly conversation and literary style for a decade or more. Fifty years later Lyly's editor wrote, 'All our ladies were then his scholars; and that beauty in court which could not parley Euphuism, was as little regarded as she which now there speaks not French'. (French was fashionable at this time because Charles I's queen, Henrietta was a Frenchwoman). It was this style that Lyly adapted for use in the plays he wrote for presentation at Court and in the 'private' theatres by the children's companies.

From the beginning Lyly aimed at winning economic security and social position through the beneficial properties of 'court holy water' or flattering the great. Through his patron the Earl of Oxford he obtained the lease of the Blackfriars theatre in 1583 and organized the Children of the Chapel Royal and St Paul's into an acting company bearing his patron's name. But his eyes were set on the lucrative office of the Master of the Revels (the official responsible for censoring and licensing plays), and he lost no opportunity of bowing and scraping before those whom he thought could secure the appointment for him, from the Queen downwards. He never attained his aim and died poor and embittered. But it was not for want of trying. Within a decade Lyly produced eight witty romantic comedies all of them carefully planned to cater to the taste for dazzling verbal display which Euphuism had fostered and all but one an elegant essay in dramatic compliment. Except for *Mother Bombie,* a Plautine comedy which combines Latin intrigue with English buffoonery, all Lyly's plays make use of classical myths and figures. Thus *Endymion* is based partly on Lucian's dialogue between the moon and Venus while *Galathea* transfers Ovid's *Metamorphoses*(ix) to Lincolnshire. Scholars have found, or have thought they have found, allegorical allusions to specific contemporary characters and events in these plays — Endymion being the Earl of Leicester or James VI of Scotland, Midas King Philip of Spain, and so on. That such allusions may have been glanced at is not improbable. But what gives their special flavour to Lyly's plays is not exact topical reference so much as the pervasive air of elaborate courtly compliment which provides both their form and substance. In a slighter way they share the allegorical temper which produced the *Faerie Queene,* though they have nothing like the same power of transcending the immediate social and cultural context. They are Lyly's hopeful offerings to a court which expected such offerings and others as part of its ritual; they barely survive as dramatic productions in their own right.

Endymion gives a fair idea of Lyly's scope as a dramatist. It was 'played before the Queen's majesty on Candlemas Day at night (1588) by the Children of Paul's' and tells the story of a youth, Endymion, who is in love with Cynthia, the goddess of the moon. His love for her arouses the jealousy of Tellus who is herself in love with Endymion and through her wiles Endymion is bewitched into a sleep which lasts forty years. Only the chaste kiss of Cynthia can awake him. The play ends with Endymion now grey and aged, swearing eternal fealty to Cynthia (though they do not and cannot unite in wedlock) and various other characters duly paired off (except for Eumenides, Endymion's friend, who is rejected by Semele), and a general paean of praise for Cynthia and her court.

Pythagoras:	I had rather in Cynthia's court spend one hour than in Greece ten years.
Gyptes:	And I choose rather to live by the sight of Cynthia than by the possessing of all Egypt.

The central incident, towards which the whole action points, is the magical power of Cynthia's chaste majesty to restore life and inspire loyalty. Thus the very form of the play is derived from the notion of positive courtly patronage and is intended to arouse it. When the play proper has been concluded, the Epilogue continues the process of flattery into the real world of the Queen at Greenwich:

'Dread Sovereign, the malicious that seek to overthrow us with threats, do but stiffen our thoughts, and make them sturdier in storms; but if your Highness vouchsafe with favourable beams to glance upon us, we shall not only stoop, but with all humility lay both our hands and hearts at your Majesty's feet.'

The Epilogue was doubtless adapted for the private theatres but the same note of extravagant compliment and obsequious supplication would prevail, since it is built into the structure and language of the play. A much wider tonal range was possible, as we shall discover, in addressing the audience at the 'public' theatres. What redeems *Endymion* and perhaps *Alexander and Campaspe* is Lyly's ability to sustain the tone of high courtesy throughout in a language whose formal elgance draws attention to its own virtuosity so that style becomes the true subject of the drama rather than any moral intention. 'Sets of wit well played' (to adapt slightly a line from that most Lylean of Shakespearean comedies *Love's Labour's Lost*) are the true objective and both the material and the final cause of the plays — they are, that is to say, the reason why they exist and the stuff of which they are made. One example will give a taste of Lyly's world:

Tellus:	Then you love me, Endymion?
Endymion:	Or else I live not, Tellus.
Tellus:	Is it not possible for you, Endymion to dissemble?
Endymion:	Not, Tellus, unless I could make me a woman.
Tellus:	Why, is dissembling joined to their sex inseparable, as heat to fire, heaviness to earth, moisture to water, thinness to air?
Endymion:	No, but found in their sex as common as spots upon doves, moles upon faces, caterpillars upon sweet apples, cobwebs upon fair windows.
Tellus:	Do they all dissemble?
Endymion:	All but one.
Tellus:	Who is that?
Endymion:	I dare not tell; for if I should say you, then would you imagine my flattery to be extreme; if another, then would you think my love to be but indifferent.

In the mouths of young choirboys clad in splendid costumes and against the lavish backgrounds which court performances commonly afforded, this kind of dialogue probably sounded much wittier than it looks in cold print, especially to an audience which had already acquired a taste for the extravagances of Euphuism. It was certainly a new tone and accent in the language of drama and later Elizabethans, including Shakespeare, were quick to mould it to their own ends.

Lyly's comedy of wit and compliment was enormously popular and a play such as George Peele's *The Arraignment of Paris*, performed before the Queen four years before *Endymion*, exploits the same dramatic territory, except that Peele is handling the shadowy area where the world of the play dissolves into the actuality of Eliza's court. There is no other play of Peele's in quite this vein and his dramatic masterpiece is undoubtedly *The Old Wives' Tale* where popular romance, folk humour, realism and self-conscious theatrical illusionism merge together to form a compound that can still amuse and delight. We shall return to *The Old Wives' Tale*, which belongs to the last decade of the sixteenth century. The immediate concerns of the Elizabethan theatre were elsewhere, in the magniloquent supermen of Christopher Marlowe and the Senecan complexities of Thomas Kyd's revenge tragedy.

Marlowe's Mighty Line

If Lyly represents the career of the Elizabethan dramatist as courtier, infinitely hopeful and ultimately frustrated, Marlowe in his brief and blazing dramatic career puts us in touch with an altogether shadowier area of Elizabethan life. His beginnings are orthodox enough. The son of a prosperous shoemaker who eventually became mayor of Canterbury, Marlowe was born in 1564 (the same year as Shakespeare) and took up scholarships first at King's School Canterbury and later at Corpus Christi College, Cambridge. His university scholarship had been established by Matthew Parker, Archbishop of Canterbury and it could be held for three years, or six if the holder studied divinity with a view to holy orders. Marlowe held his for the full six years, graduating with an MA in 1587. This seems to have been his last salute to anything remotely resembling orthodoxy, whether in religion or in private life. He died in a tavern brawl at Deptford in his thirtieth year but contrived, in his short life, to be jailed for murder, almost certainly became involved in espionage and acquired a widespread reputation for atheism and homosexuality. Among the opinions attributed to him (admittedly by a character of dubious reputation who was later hanged) were 'that Christ was a bastard and his mother dishonest' and that 'all they that love not tobacco and boys were fools'. The Privy Council issued a warrant against him on charges of atheism and blasphemy but he was killed before he could appear to answer them.

The personality and life-style we sense even in such a drastic summary are worlds away from Lyly's. Marlowe's independence of mind and vigorous self-confidence resound in what are probably the first lines by him ever spoken in the public theatre:

From jigging veins of rhyming mother wits,

> And such conceits as clownage keeps in pay,
> We'll lead you to the stately tent of war,
> Where you shall hear the Scythian Tamburlaine
> Threatening the world with high astounding terms
> And scourging kingdoms with his conquering sword.
> View but his picture in this tragic glass,
> And then applaud his fortunes as you please.

In this prologue to *Tamburlaine*, a play whose spectacular success called for an immediate sequel which was equally popular, we are struck at once by the authoritative accent, the assertive independence of a dramatist who knows exactly what he wants to do and knows he has the resources to do it, as well as one who is quite clear as to how what he offers is different from what has come before. The 'jigging veins of rhyming mother wits' refers scornfully to the lumbering jog-trot rhythms of the popular theatre, while 'such conceits as clownage keeps in pay' mock its pointless buffoonery. In the eight lines of the prologue we can sense the movement of the play itself in miniature. As the play proceeds from the halting ineffectual verse of Mycetes to the opulent rhythms and spacious rhetoric of the hero Tamburlaine, so here too there is a transition from the thumpety-thump of the first two lines to the thunderous sweep of lines 4 — 6; these lines are themselves a perfect illustration of what Ben Jonson meant when he spoke of 'Marlowe's mighty line'.

But while the scope and splendour of Marlowe's verse is undoubtedly what first captured the attention and imagination of his audience, it would be misleading to think of *Tamburlaine* as merely a string of purple passages held together by nothing more dramatic than the continuous and therefore monotonous rise to power of a megalomaniac hero. The central figure of Tamburlaine is certainly worth our attention but we must always remember that he attains his full stature within a play-world with a colour and atmosphere of its own. We may begin by noting that the eloquence of Tamburlaine is not some incidental or accidental gift which enables him to spout mighty lines at will, but has a specific dramatic purpose. The prologue indicates this very clearly when it exactly balances the two phrases 'high astounding terms' and 'his conquering sword'. Within the world of the play Tamburlaine's eloquence stands as a continuing metaphor for his physical prowess and overwhelming energy, just as the weak-kneed language of his opponents is the dramatic embodiment of their corrupt and effete authority. Tamburlaine arrogantly declares that he himself *is* Fate, or at any rate that he controls fate:

> I hold the Fates bound fast in iron chains,
> And with my hand turn Fortune's wheel about . . .

and the play endorses his arrogance, for he dispenses life and death to all those about him. Marlowe is challenging a traditional conception of life and creating a new form of dramatic tragedy. In such popular Elizabethan works as *A Mirror for Magistrates* (of which a new edition appeared in 1587, the year *Tamburlaine* was first performed) there is implicit the notion of tragedy as 'the damnable life and deserved death' of great tyrants. Tragedy, on this view, should feature the fall

from power to adversity of a figure of high estate, the fall being due to his wickedness rather than to blind caprice. Against this notion Marlowe thrusts before us a
hero of humble origin, a Scythian shepherd, who, far from being content to follow
the occupation to which destiny has called him, proclaims himself to be the figure
of that destiny. And everything in the play, from the sounding splendour of its
language to the barbaric extravagance of its spectacle, conspires to prove him
right. As far as the first part of *Tamburlaine* is concerned (and it was the first part
whose music and spectacle swept the audience into such rapture that it demanded
a sequel), we are presented with the exploits of a hero whose ambition, single-
mindedness and power we are evidently intended to admire wholeheartedly. We
can only do so by ignoring ot minimizing the cruelty and ruthless egotism which
are present throughout, but shown rather as the inevitable excesses of a natural
prodigy than the damnable atrocities of a responsible human being. If moral
judgements are to be invoked, it is difficult to disagree with C. S. Lewis's
comment that *Tamburlaine* is founded on 'a hideous moral Spoonerism — Giant
the Jack Killer'.

The second part goes some way but not very far, to soften the blow to our moral
sensibilities. Where the first part ended with the hero at the very peak of his glory
and wedded to his chosen bride Zenocrate, the second shows us Tamburlaine
making ever wilder claims as his physical power and fortunes decline. His beloved
Zenocrate dies and the grief-tormented Tamburlaine destroys the town. Our
sympathy for his human agony is inhibited by the way in which he seeks to
alleviate it. One of his sons proves a coward and Tamburlaine kills him. Finally, he
himself, for all his godlike pretensions, comes to acknowledge the ultimate and
unending supremacy of death:

> For Tamburlaine, the scourge of God, must die.

In one sense this is the only tragic climax possible in such a play. If you create your
hero as the embodiment of superhuman energy, a force of destiny and nature
rather than a man, and invest him with a splendid and distinctive rhetoric as the
dramatic symbol of that energy, there is only one conceivable way in which such a
hero could fall (and tragedy seems to require some kind of fall). Not through *hubris*
or self-pride because the play triumphantly vindicates that; nor through the forces
opposed to him, because these are shown to be clearly no match for him. The only
force which can withstand and ultimately subdue Tamburlaine is that which he
has throughout refused to acknowledge, the fact of his own mortality. It is the one
enemy immune to his conquering sword and the high astounding terms which are
its verbal equivalent.

From this point of view *Tamburlaine* may seem an intensely traditional play,
almost medieval in its insistence on the inevitability of death and the futility of
man's pretensions. The dim ghost of such a play does seem to hover about
Marlowe's masterpiece. It is difficult to imagine that he was totally unaware of the
sense in which Tamburlaine's towering ambition was also a piece of gigantic folly.
But the actual effect of reading or seeing the play, as distinct from considering its
implications in summary, is completely different. It is not merely that we are so
overwhelmed by Tamburlaine's rhetoric that we come to accept his own valuation

of himself. Rather the very *action* of the play shows us the triumphal progress of that rhetoric. It is the 'working words' of Tamburlaine that effect his conquests, and there is a more positive side to this than overcoming the difficulty of staging large-scale battle scenes in the Elizabethan theatre. Thus the weak king Mycetes sends his envoy Theridamas to negotiate with Tamburlaine precisely because he believes (rightly) that Theridamas is more eloquent than himself ('thy words are swords'). But Tamburlaine's rhetoric is more than sufficient to win Theridamas over to him:

> Won with thy words, and conquered with thy looks,
> I yield myself, my men and horse to thee:
> To be partaker of thy good or ill,
> As long as life maintains Theridamas.

Tamburlaine's acknowledgement of this submission illustrates the exact equivalence of words and action:

> Theridamas my friend, take here my hand,
> Which is as much as if I swore by heaven,
> And called the gods to witness of my vow . . .

Similarly, the lines that a follower of Cosroe rashly speaks to his king echo in Tamburlaine's lips and mind till the phrase itself — the best-known in the entire play — becomes almost an instrument of conquest, or at least an immediate incentive towards it:

> And ride in triumph through Persepolis!
> Is it not brave to be a king, Techelles!
> Usumcasane and Theridamas,
> Is it not passing brave to be a king,
> And ride in triumph through Persepolis?

In addition to the two parts of *Tamburlaine* Marlowe wrote five plays, all of them having some relation to tragedy, though two of them, *The Massacre at Paris* and *Edward II*, purport to deal with historical events. In their very different ways, all Marlowe's central figures combine the twin impulses of self-fulfilment and self-destruction, but none of them is glorified as Tamburlaine is. *Dido, Queen of Carthage* (in which Marlowe's Cambridge contemporary Thomas Nashe also had a hand and which was acted by the Children of the Chapel) presents the death of Dido in sorrow at parting from Aeneas as both triumph and tragedy. *The Massacre at Paris* is difficult to judge because its text is short and garbled. It deals with the St Bartholomew's Eve Massacre of 1572 and subsequent events in a manner calculated to pander to the anti-Catholic hysteria of the Elizabethan audience in the post-Armada years. But in the character of the Guise, Marlowe created a figure who in various transformations was to stalk the English stage for decades. This was the Machiavellian, the dedicated amoralist who regards religion, loyalty and virtue as mere blinkers for the gullible, to be used by the worldly wise to their own advantage. Here his amoralism is combined with a spirit of all-or-nothing daredevilry:

Oft have I levelled, and at last have learned
That peril is the chiefest way to happiness.

When he reappears as the prologue to the *Jew of Malta* he is both more sinister and more grotesque.

And let them know that I am Machevill,
And weigh not men, and therefore not men's words:
Admir'd I am of those that hate me most. . . .
I count Religion but a childish toy,
And hold there is no sin but ignorance.

'[I] weigh not men, and therefore not men's words.' The world of *The Jew of Malta* is not one in which language any longer has the miraculous power to create or transform reality. Both here and in *Edward II*, reality presses, thwarting the ambitions and aspirations of the protagonists in many ways before their final defeat in death. And death itself is stripped of the dignity it has in *Tamburlaine* and even in *Dr Faustus*. The Jew, after a long and notably successful career of murder and intrigue (including the poisoning of an entire nunnery) finally ends up almost literally stewing in his own juice when, outmanoeuvered in Machiavellianism by the Christians, he falls into the boiling cauldron he has prepared for the Turkish conquerors. His reach exceeds his grasp and hellfire waits for him, but there is nothing either grand or tragic about his over-reaching. Marlowe takes the pattern of the tragic fall and shrinks the physical and emotional scope of the world in which it occurs and the stature of the protagonist so much that it is no longer tragedy but savage farce, as Eliot called it.

In *Edward II* the savagery is far more apparent than the farce. By the time Marlowe wrote it, Shakespeare had probably already written the three parts of *Henry VI*, his earliest attempt to present history in dramatic form. For all their occasional crudity, this early trilogy embodies all the concerns of the later histories — the conflict between public good and private gain, the sense of the vast anonymous people suffering and dying as the nobles struggle for power, the injuries and vendettas that reach across generations, the vision of order violated. Marlowe in his play seems deliberately to reject all these possibilities in order to focus on the relations between the king, his favourites and his enemies and the power struggle which culminates in the rise and fall of Mortimer. What we remember most vividly in the play is the degradation, torture and horrifying end of Edward. There can be no dignity in a death which comes as a result of a red-hot poker being inserted in the anus, nor any moral to be drawn, unless Marlowe is challenging us to see a hideous aptness in this punishment for a homosexuality which is flaunted throughout. Here is Marlowe at his most unorthodox, savagely mocking the notion that any kind of justice, poetic or otherwise, is to be found in the world of rabid sensuality and naked writhing for power which he depicts with such remorseless naturalism.

The order in which Marlowe's other plays followed *Tamburlaine* is uncertain and it is tempting to see a gradual disillusionment with human possibilities in the progress from that world-embracing vision to the grim and squalid scene of a king

dying in a foetid dungeon. But an element of disquiet about the dream of power —
military, sexual, commercial, political or intellectual — is present in all Marlowe's
plays, though most muted in Tamburlaine. It is in *Dr Faustus* that the paradoxes
and tensions in Marlowe's attitudes to orthodoxy find their most memorable
dramatic expression. The outer structure of the play is thoroughly medieval, with
Faustus as Everyman, presented with various moral choices (Marlowe even uses
the morality device of Good and Bad Angels to represent these), choosing wrongly,
sealing a bargain with the devil and receiving eternal damnation as his reward.
The opening chorus points the moral quite unequivocally. A fine piece of
dramatic foreshortening outlines the whole of Faustus' brilliant but ultimately
tragic career, ending at the point where the story just outlined is about to begin:

> And glutted now with learning's golden gifts,
> He surfeits upon cursed necromancy:
> Nothing so sweet as magic is to him,
> Which he prefers before his chiefest bliss:
> And this the man that in his study sits.

Nothing could be more pointed than the juxtaposition of 'his chiefest bliss' (the
hope of heaven) with the bleakly reductive reminder that for all his soaring ambition, it is only a *man* we see before us, as Faustus himself restlessly recalls in his
opening soliloquy:

> Yet art thou still but Faustus, and a man.

Tamburlaine had stormed through his world like a force of nature, oblivious of the
reminders all around him that 'the sweet fruition of an earthly crown' he coveted
so much was no abiding joy. Faustus is determined to transform himself into a
superhuman force whatever it costs him, and the cost is not less than everything.
The final chorus echoes the Prologue's certainty as to the meaning of the fable:

> Faustus is gone: regard his hellish fall,
> Whose fiendful fortune may exhort the wise
> Only to wonder at unlawful things:
> Whose deepness doth entice such forward wits,
> To practise more than heavenly power permits.

But between the prologue and the final chorus the words and actions of the hero
invite a variety of responses, not all of them in tune with orthodox morality. Like
Faustus, Marlowe was well versed in theology and like him discontented with the
answers it offered. He was a known associate of contemporaries with dangerously
unorthodox views. The admonitory finger-wagging of the chorus is not the spirit
in which Marlowe presents Faustus to us. It is true that what Faustus does with his
new-found power is not very impressive — it does not seem to profit a man much to
lose his own soul in order to gain hothouse grapes for a pregnant duchess or play
schoolboy pranks in the Vatican. And there is a fiendish humour in Faustus
solemnly declaring 'I think Hell's a fable' to Mephistophilis standing right beside
him. In particular, the horseplay of the sub-plot (whether it is Marlowe's work or
not) modifies severely the seriousness with which we can take Faustus's own

conjuration of devils. When all qualifications have been made, however, it remains true that Faustus in his final agonized soliloquy rises to a tragic stature that overleaps the Chorus's too-neat didactic moralizing. Marlowe knows his hero from inside in all his folly and grandeur and he has wrenched the form of the traditional Morality in order to give adequate expression to all the possibilities, tragic, comic and even ludicrous, inherent in the Faustus myth. Faustus is no more individual than Tamburlaine or the Jew. But he embodies the triumph and tragedy of individuality at a point in the history of western culture where it expresses itself in the opening up of new horizons, physical, political, intellectual and spiritual. In retrospect it seems poignantly ironic as well as deeply prophetic that the man who wished to exalt his individual potentialities to their maximum should die pleading in vain to lose that individuality in drops of water.

Later Elizabethan and Jacobean drama was to explore more deeply the possibilities and perversities of individual fulfilment, but Marlowe had already mapped that fascinating and fateful territory.

Kyd and the Tragedy of Revenge

As much of a landmark of the Elizabethan theatre as *Tamburlaine* was *The Spanish Tragedy,* the only original play known for certain to be by Thomas Kyd, who at one time shared a room with Marlowe and, probably under torture, accused him of atheism. The Senecan world of shrieking ghosts, madness, sudden death and bloody revenge which the authors of *Gorboduc* first introduced into England is combined in Kyd's great play with all the spectacular resources of the public theatre. The decorous Senecan convention of reporting rather than presenting violent action is completely abandoned and we have the whole gamut of bloody incident, from the stabbing and hanging of Horatio, to the public execution of a minor villain, Pedringano, by the common hangman (*he turnes him off* states the grimly laconic stage direction) and the spectacular climax when, after a sequence of killings, Hieronimo bites off his tongue so that no one can extort the truth from him. It is as if Kyd had deliberately chosen his dramatic style to contrast with the violence of the incidents. Where Marlowe's language was shaped to serve specific dramatic ends in each of his plays, the language of *The Spanish Tragedy,* based as it is on certain formal rhetorical figures which were codified and illustrated in manuals of rhetoric, seems designed to be incapable of anything more dramatic than the most stilted bombast. Here, for instance, is how Balthazar, the captive Portuguese prince, reflects on his indifferent success in courting Bel-imperia:

> My presents are not of sufficient cost,
> And being worthless all my labour's lost,
> Yet might she love me for my valiancy,
> Ay, but that's slandered by captivity.
> Yet might she love me to content her sire,
> Ay, but her reason masters his desire.
> Yet might she love me as her brother's friend
> Ay, but her hopes aim at some other end.

Yet might she love me to uprear her state,
Ay, but perhaps she hopes some nobler mate.
Yet might she love me as her beauty's thrall,
Ay, but I fear she cannot love at all.

And Hieronimo, discovering his son Horatio hanged and stabbed in his own orchard, expresses his grief in these lines:

O heavens, why made you night to cover sin?
By day this deed of darkness had not been.
O earth, why didst thou not in time devour
The vild (vile) profaner of this sacred bower?
O poor Horatio, what has thou misdone
To lose thy life ere life was new begun?
O wicked butcher, whatsoe'er thou wert
How couldst thou strangle virtue and desert?

At first glance it would seem that this kind of language is as limited in its range as that of Lyly. But Kyd's dramatic style has greater variety and power than these excerpts suggest. In the first place, the rhymed couplets of the extracts are not the staple of the play's language. They represent a high point of formalization in a linguistic range which includes blank verse — itself highly stylized — as well as occasional passages of sharply realistic prose, as in the scene between Pedringano and the hangman. Secondly, while Kyd's language is no more suited for subtle psychological introspection than Lyly's (or, for that matter, Marlowe's) it is capable of representing emotional states in a stylized but powerfully effective manner. To a certain extent, the sheer pleasure in rhetorical figures which the Elizabethans relished in Lyly, Kyd and the early Shakespeare was a taste which we have almost lost. But only if we are blinkered by inappropriate notions of realism in drama would we fail to respond in the theatre to lines such as those in which Hieronimo upbraids himself for his tardiness in avenging his son's murder:

See, see, oh see thy shame Hieronimo,
See here a loving father to his son:
Behold the sorrows and the sad laments
That he delivereth for his son's decease.
If love's effects so strives in lesser things,
If love enforce such moods in meaner wits,
If love express such power in poor estates:
Hieronimo, when as a raging sea,
Tost with the wind and the tide o'erturnest then
The upper billows course of waves to keep,
Whilst lesser waters labour in the deep.
Then shamest thou not Hieronimo to neglect
The sweet revenge of thy Horatio?

Hieronimo is moved to this utterance by the presence of an old man whose own son, like Horatio, has been murdered and who comes seeking justice. The incident is no more like 'real life' than the speech itself. Both are theatrical emblems which together create a powerful image of self-lacerating grief. Given an actor skilled in combining formality of speech and gesture with uninhibited, even extravagant displays of emotion, the role of Hieronimo could undoubtedly be immensely compelling. In Edward Alleyn, who created the role, as he did that of Tamburlaine, the first great tragic actor of the Elizabethan stage, Hieronimo seems to have found his ideal incarnation.

It is probably true that *The Spanish Tragedy* was the most popular stage success in the entire period from the inauguration of the public theatres to their closure in 1642. There were at least ten editions of the play during that time. Since then it has not been professionally performed at all. Both the rapturous initial reception and the subsequent total neglect are understandable, though the second is certainly undeserved. Neither the rhetorical expertise nor the theatrical virtuosity which held its original audience spellbound had any appeal for the very different audience and the very different theatre which appeared with the Restoration in 1660. But for all its occasional crudity Kyd's play is more than a museum of outdated theatrical and rhetorical fashions. Within its own terms its language has great power, variety of emotional tone and even subtlety. And it uses its paraphernalia of horrors to explore themes whose interest is by no means merely historical. The one which lies closest to the surface is concerned with the relation of private revenge to public justice and human vengeance to divine providence. These were topics widely and deeply explored in later tragedy, reaching their superb climax in *Hamlet* (a play which is regarded as being based on a lost tragedy by Kyd himself). But there is also in *The Spanish Tragedy* the more universal theme of man's place in the world and his freedom to choose his goals and actions. The sense of a fate utterly indifferent to human aspirations, moral or otherwise, and concerned only with its own implacable laws of action and counter-action literally haunts the play in the shape of the spirit of Revenge, who, with Don Andrea, forms an inner audience to the ensuing drama. In the final scene there is a series of dizzying theatrical perspectives as we, the audience, watch Andrea and Revenge, who are themselves watching the Spanish and Portuguese kings, who are watching the play which Hieronimo is producing with Lorenzo, Balthazar, Bel-imperia and himself in the main roles. The feigned deaths of this innermost play become real deaths for the 'actors'. But this multiple framing of the action which then becomes 'acting' in both senses (doing and playing) is not just a brilliant theatrical trick. Its effect is to produce in us the sense that we are ourselves looked on by the final and invisible audience of the fates with the remorseless objectivity of unsympathetic critics, and that freedom of action is a pathetic human illusion in a world of unalterable law. At the end, the mute figure of Hieronimo with his dumb and bleeding mouth stands as a savagely ironic comment on the fine flowers of rhetoric which have flourished in such profusion throughout the play. It seems as desolate an image of human helplessness as that of Faustus pleading to lose his identity and become part of mere nature without consciousness. At the very beginning of Elizabethan tragedy therefore, in the first dawn of what is usually called renaissance individualism, we have the darker side of human aspiration presented in dramatic images of unforgettable power and authority. Man's potentialities are displayed and celebrated but there is a sombre insistence on their destructive aspects; and it is those sombre accents that become increasingly insistent during the last decade of Elizabeth's reign and the opening years of the new century. Comedy too soon loses its gift for innocent ribaldry and elegant compliment and evokes a harsh and troubled laughter.

4

Varieties of Comedy

During the first four decades of the public theatre comedies outnumber tragedies by three to one. Though there were rules of comedy derived by Renaissance critics from classical and neo-classical sources playwrights, with the single and complex exception of Jonson, paid scant attention to these and many varieties of comedy flourished in rich and untidy profusion. Perhaps the categories of compliment, celebration and criticism are broad enough to encompass the variety. Needless to say no actual comedy is a pure specimen of any of these divisions — comedy more than most forms is made of a mingled yarn. It is, as always, a matter of emphasis rather than of clear-cut distinctions. Even the comedy of compliment which Lyly brought to its bright and brittle perfection, though essentially concerned with flattery had enough darker tints to prevent it being flat and flaccid. A tone of self-deprecating irony keeps Lyly's language from collapsing under the weight of endless idolization (in its absence the embittered complaints of courtly neglect which he wrote in his own person outside the framework of drama are merely pathetic in every sense). Emotions such as envy, thwarted ambition and injured pride also trouble the limpid surface of Lylean comedy. Immensely popular in his own day, Lyly's comedies catered for an enthusiasm which was reflected at one remove in the many plays, such as Jonson's *Cynthia's Revels,* in which the Queen herself was represented as the emblem of all virtue. But their true home was the court and the mainspring of many of them is metamorphosis or miraculous trans-formation of man into woman, bird or tree. The literary source of such trans-formation was, as often as not the Latin poet Ovid. Like court favour such magical change was random in its action and had the capacity to open up undreamed of vistas for those who were its objects. But it provided neither the basis for a coherent plot nor the possibility of true interaction between characters. Lyly's real contribution to comedy was that he gave it a polite language capable, in the right hands, of combining witty wordplay with genuine passion. In such plays as *Love's Labour's Lost* (where Shakespeare is indebted to Lyly for the characters of the braggart knight and the witty page among many other things), *A Midsummer Night's Dream* and in the witty lovers of Shakespearean comedy we can see the full flowering of the seed which Lyly planted.

In his last play, *Mother Bombie,* Lyly moves nearer to the concerns of popular comedy, where 'popular' would have as its opposite the term 'literary'. Typical of such concerns is George Peele's *The Old Wives' Tale* briefly mentioned earlier. Like Lyly, Peele was an Oxford man with a good classical education, so we must be wary of applying the literary-popular antithesis too rigidly. Peele made his dramatic début with the *The Arraignment of Paris,* a play of courtly compliment

51

loosely based on classical myth which was played by the Children of the Chapel before the Queen in 1583. The climax occurs when Diana presents the golden apple not to Venus, Juno or Athene but to the Queen herself

the noble phoenix of our age,
Our fair Eliza, our Zabeta fair.

For all his assiduous flattery, Peele appears to have been less successful in gaining Court favour than Lyly for all his other known plays were written for the adult companies. *The Old Wives' Tale* is a fairly sophisticated handling of unsophisticated elements. Peele takes every bit of popular lore he can lay his hands on — wandering knights, captive princesses, wicked conjurors, grateful ghosts and much more — and weaves their fantastical doings within the framework of a tale told by the wife of Clunch the smith to three serving men who have lost their way in a wood. The names of the three servants, Antic, Frolic and Fantastic are in keeping with the tale in which they appear, which makes liberal use of songs as well as such popular theatrical devices as a golden head which magically rises out of the stage and a youth transformed into an old man by day and a white bear by night. Peele, who had devised pageant shows for the city, had experience and instinct in matters of theatrical spectacle and it is his ability to combine elements from popular lore, chivalric romance, classical mythology and even topical allusion into a unified dramatic structure which makes *The Old Wives' Tale* still enchanting to watch. Though it mocks some of its sources, it does so in a spirit of festive celebration far removed from any satirical intent. Its unity is not a matter of following rules but comes from its calculated artlessness, its easy commerce with most of the available theatrical traditions. If it is parody, it creatively transforms what it parodies, finding a form flexible enough to contain its many-sided high spirits without stifling them. It is one of the most truly *enjoyable* of Elizabethan plays.

One of Peele's sources for his comedy was *Perimedes the Blacksmith*, a tale by Robert Greene. Among Greene's claims to fame is the fact that he made the first extant reference to Shakespeare as actor and playwright, calling him 'an upstart crow beautified with our feathers' — the 'our' presumably referring to those like Lyly, Nashe, Peele, Marlowe and Greene himself who had been to University and could sign themselves gentlemen. In a lifetime of thirty-four years, Greene contrived to produce a vast number of literary works, including autobiographical pamphlets, prose romances, underworld tracts and five plays, all written between 1588 and 1590. Two of these are turgid imitations of Marlowe (*Alphonsus, King of Aragon*) and Kyd (*Orlando Furioso*), while a third is a less than indifferent comedy written in collaboration with a fellow 'University wit' Thomas Lodge and called *A Looking Glass for London*. A more or less fictitious 'historical comedy' *James IV* is interesting for its portrayal of Dorothea and the proto-Machiavel Ateukin. But if this were all of Greene's dramatic output, his most important contribution to the drama would have been the fact that he provided a source for Shakespeare's *The Winter's Tale*. He earns his place as a dramatist however with a single fine comedy, *Friar Bacon and Friar Bungay*.

Greene's play may have been written to exploit the popularity of *Dr Faustus*. It too has a central character, Friar Bacon, who deals in the occult, but unlike Faustus abjures magic when he sees its fatal consequences. These include the death of two Oxford students who stab each other when they see, in a magic glass, their fathers killed in a love duel. As in *The Old Wives' Tale*, full use is made of available stage devices and properties such as magic mirrors and speaking heads. But Greene's real achievement is to create a make-believe world in which milk-maids can be wooed by princes, accept cruel love tests from their betrothed with unquestioning patience and marry into the nobility with the royal blessing. The thirteenth century England of Henry III in which the play is set has no more authenticity than the Scotland of *James IV*, but it is not historical credibility but almost its opposite which is the playwright's quarry here. Greene's own life, if we are to take his word and that of his contemporaries, was one of spectacular debauchery, punctuated by spasms of equally spectacular remorse. It was spent in the taverns and brothels of Italy, Spain and England and came to an ignominious end in London where, having deserted his wife and child and drunk and whored himself into penury, he died of a surfeit of 'pickled herrings and Rhenish wine'. The squalid reality and occasional bizarre humour of that life he put into his underworld pamphlets, embroidered with the obligatory moralizing. In *Friar Bacon and Friar Bungay* he created the idealized anti-world to the one he lived and died in, a world redolent of the freshness and fragrance of an Arcadian England. The play is a celebration of innocent love embodied in the virtuous Margaret who stands in shining contrast to all the cunning whores who flaunt their way through the cony-catching pamphlets. Its world is the world of rural festivities seen through the nostalgic eyes of metropolitan debauchery. But the nostalgia has some relation to a reality Green could have experienced as a child in his native Norwich — for communal pastimes and mainly good-humoured seasonal festivities were still a part of rural England. The very form of the play with its frequent displays of magic and marvel smacks of country fairs while its patriotism — Friar Bacon easily outshines the German magician Vandermast — is as innocent as its celebration of the triumphs of love. The challenge to the accepted social hierarchy represented by Margaret's courtship by the prince and eventual marriage to Lacy is set in a context sufficiently idealized to have any hint of real threat removed. Margaret is a jewel among women and would shine in any court. For good measure Greene ends the play with a prophecy by Friar Bacon which plays the well established game of apotheosizing the virgin Queen:

> From forth the royal garden of a king
> Shall flourish out so rich and fair a bud
> Whose brightness shall deface proud Phoebus' flower
> And overshadow Albion with her leaves.

Greene's hold on his plot in *Friar Bacon and Friar Bungay* is not quite so neatly secure as that of Peele in *The Old Wives' Tale*, but most of the time he contrives to give the action meaning and coherence by relating it to the two main figures, Margaret and Friar Bacon. The result is a comedy that for all its wild variety of incident, character and dramatic language, impresses on the stage by its overall unity, a unity compounded of powerful feeling for locality and informed nostalgia.

At the end of *Friar Bacon and Friar Bungay*, everyone sits down to a royal feast which, together with the final dance, is the usual symbol of communal harmony in the comedy of celebration, as the judgment scene is often the climax of critical comedy. A royal Shrove Tuesday feast also ends Thomas Dekker's *The Shoemaker's Holiday* first performed by the Lord Admiral's men at court during the Christmas revels of 1599. Dekker taps the same vein of nostalgia and strong local patriotism as Greene and may have borrowed the love story of Rose and Lacy from Greene's play. Dekker is typical of the newly emerged professional dramatist accustomed to churning out plays almost non-stop, most of them destined to sink without trace into the gargantuan maw of the public theatres. At least twenty-five plays were co-authored by him and he collaborated with half a dozen other writers. In his first surviving play, *Old Fortunatus* (1599) the central character expounds the genial philosophy of 'Eat, drink and be merry and let tomorrow take care of itself' which is more richly embodied in Simon Eyre, the 'merry madcap' hero of *The Shoemaker's Holiday*. Like several other dramatists, Dekker had a hand in devising civic pageants including *The Magnificent Entertainment*, intended as the city's welcome to the new king, James I. Civic pride and pride in the craft of shoemaking are very much in evidence in the play. Dekker's principal source was a collection of short stories by Thomas Deloney called *The Gentle Craft* published in 1597, and except on the title page, the play itself is designated in the original quarto as 'A pleasant Comedy of. . .The Gentle Craft'. There is a strong emphasis on the worthiness of the craft of shoemaking (the noble hero Lacy is disguised as a shoemaker and is skilled at the trade, having been trained in the craft abroad).

Dekker follows Deloney in investing Simon Eyre and his band with the attributes of comradeship, kindliness, generosity and zest for life. Indeed, Simon Eyre is more a warmhearted Lord of Misrule than a recognizable London tradesman. His language has an ebullience and energy that belong rather to carnival high spirits than to the sober routine of business. Part of Eyre's appeal is undoubtedly the promise he holds out that careless gaiety and convivial generosity can lead to, or at least be combined with the sober business of profit making and civic eminence. The detail that Eyre's rise to wealth and fame is founded on a business deal that has nothing to do with his trade is barely noticed in the bustling action, of which his lively and colourful speech is the verbal counterpart:

> Quick, snipper-snapper, away! Firk, scour thy throat, thou shalt wash it with Castilian liquor. Come, my last of the fives! Give me a can: have to thee, Hans, here, Hodge; here, Firk. Drink, you mad Greeks, and work like true Trojans, and pray for Simon Eyre the shoemaker! Here, Hans, and th'art welcome.

The paternalistic system of apprenticeship common in Elizabethan society was often harsh and repressive, but here it is idealized to the point at which work itself becomes a holiday. Apprentices' riots were often violent, destructive and savagely xenophobic. In Dekker's play they are boisterously good-humoured and good-hearted and the xenophobia is transmuted into innocuous amusement at the stage Dutch used by the disguised Lacy. Thus the comedy flatters two large sections of the London audience at once, the rising small businessman (the class from which, incidentally, most of the new dramatists came) and their prentices. The flattery is not at the expense of any other section of society but is rather designed to establish the middle class of craftsmen as a proper and honourable estate of the realm. Such criticism as there is is directed against the snobbishness of the Earl of Lincoln who scorns to have his nephew Lacy married to Rose, the daughter of London's Lord Mayor, Sir Roger Otley. Otley expresses the conventional prudent citizen's misgivings about prodigal young aristocrats:

> Too mean is my poor girl for his high birth;
> Poor citizens must not with courtiers wed,
> Who will in silks and gay apparel spend
> More in one year than I am worth by far.
> Therefore your honour need not doubt my girl.

Later in the century, when alliances between the impoverished gentry and the affluent merchant class were much sought after on both sides, a play like Philip Massinger's *A New Way to Pay Old Debts* would wholeheartedly endorse such rigid class exclusiveness and look nostalgically back to a never-never time when the social hierarchy seemed fixed and eternal. Dekker shapes his comedy so that no less a personage than the king himself sets his seal of approval on the match between Lacy and the sweet English Rose. He even gives their courtship the dignity of a serviceable if in no way memorable blank verse, as when Rose soliloquizes thus:

> Here sit thou down upon this flowery bank,
> And make a garland for thy Lacy's head.
> These pinks, these roses and these violets,
> These blushing gilliflowers, these marigolds,
> The fair embroidery of his coronet,
> Carry not half such beauty in their cheeks,
> As the sweet count'nance of my Lacy doth.
> O my most unkind father! O my stars!
> Why loured you so at my nativity,
> To make me love, yet live robbed of my love?
> Here as a thief am I imprisoned,
> For my dear Lacy's sake, within those walls
> Which by my father's cost were builded up
> For better purposes; here must I languish
> For him that does as much lament, I know,
> Mine absence, as for him I pine in woe.

If there is neither impassioned lyricism here nor the accents of genuine anguish as we hear them in Shakespeare's Juliet, the lines have a simplicity and directness which are moving both on the stage and on the page. They form an effective contrast not only to the rambustious extravagance of Eyre's larger-than-life colloquialism but also to the stale Petrarchanism in which Hammon, the suitor favoured by Rose's father but rejected by the heroine herself, conducts his courtship. In fairness though, it must be conceded that not only Dekker but Hammon himself seems to be aware that these love-conceits are thoroughly outmoded and can no longer be taken at their tarnished face value:

What, would you have me pule and pine and pray,
With 'lovely lady', 'mistress of my heart',
'Pardon your servant', and the rhymer play,
Railing on Cupid and his tyrant's dart?
Or shall I undertake some martial spoil,
Wearing your glove at tourney and at tilt,
And tell how many gallants I unhorsed?
Sweet, will this pleasure you?

The Shoemaker's Holiday contrives to have the best of both worlds, for its own plot makes use of the romantic exploits and the sentimental scenes which it mocks. Such exploits and scenes were the stock in trade of honest hacks like Thomas Heywood, author of twenty-odd surviving plays including *Four Prentices of London*. By his own account, Heywood was a super-hack even by Elizabethan standards, for he claimed to have 'an entire hand or at least a main finger' in 220 plays. Less than ten years after Dekker's play the aristocratic Francis Beaumont relentlessly mocked this type of play in *The Knight of the Burning Pestle*, to the delight of the aristocratic or would-be aristocratic audiences at the Blackfriars indoor playhouse.

But, as the very title indicates, celebration, not mockery, is the keynote of *The Shoemaker's Holiday*. Its lasting value is not as a realistic picture of daily life in Elizabethan London, which it emphatically does not provide. There are occasional poignantly realistic touches, as when Rafe the prentice returns badly wounded from the wars. But these do not seriously cloud the dramatic expression of the essentially social virtues of generosity, companionship and mutual cooperation between individuals and classes. These are combined with an enormous exuberance of spirit and appetite for life which, unless brought within the confines of communal celebration, threaten to become anarchic. The hero's progress from not-so-humble shoemaker to Lord Mayor of London presiding over a Shrove Tuesday feast is as apt a symbol of festivity contained within acceptable social bounds as the Elizabethan theatre itself; and the same voices which ranted against cakes and ale and Shrove Tuesday junketings and eventually succeeded in abolishing them by law also succeeded, within fifty years of Dekker's play, in closing the theatres themselves. By 1642 however, the theatre was no longer the representative institution of a whole society which it was in the later Elizabethan period.

A certain narrowing of range is already implicit in the third broad variety of comedy to be considered, that of critical or satirical comedy. There is something of a paradox involved here, for from one point of view critical comedy represents the dominant European tradition from classical times onwards. The purpose of comedy was supposed to be to hold a mirror up to the follies and affectations of mankind in order that the audience may laugh at such aberrations and learn to do otherwise. There was, as we have seen, another native tradition of comedy where the laughter came not from mockery but celebration, where communal merriment was seen as a source of individual well being. At its best, as in the greater comedies of Jonson, critical comedy can have as wide and universal an appeal as any other kind, but it also has its restrictive aspects. This can be seen in, among other plays, the satirical comedies produced by each of the contending parties in that short-lived and still somewhat mysterious episode in the history of Elizabethan drama commonly called the War of the Theatres.

At one level, the so-called war may be seen as a clash of temperament between two playwrights, John Marston and Ben Jonson. It may even have been a publicity stunt to drum up custom for the playhouses, or the expression of rivalry between the children's companies and the adult players. As Rosencrantz explains to Hamlet:

. . .there is, sir, an eyrie of children, little eyases, that cry out on the top of question, and are most tyranically clapped for't: these are now the fashion, and so berattle the common stages — so they call them — that many wearing rapiers are afraid of goose quills, and dare scarce come thither.

It has also been suggested that two opposing dramatic traditions, the popular and learned, were in conflict. What concerns us here however, is not the origin of the War of the Theatres but the kind of comedies produced by the combatants during the brief period (1599-1601) of struggle. The first shot was fired by John Marston with *Histriomastix,* rewritten in 1599 from an anonymous play. Here the pompous and boorish Chrysoganus is clearly intended as a satirical portrayal of Ben Jonson, who retaliated immediately with not one but two plays. *Every Man Out of his Humour* was performed in 1599 in the newly built Globe Theatre by the Chamberlain's Men (Shakespeare's company). It was not a success. In it Jonson put the unmistakable inflated and artificial diction of Marston into the mouth of the fool, Carlo Buffone. *Cynthia's Revels* was performed at the Blackfrairs theatre, presumably because after the failure of *Every Man Out,* the Chamberlain's Men were not particularly keen to appear in a new Jonson play. Here the dramatist presented himself as Crites, the honest arbiter of art and society, confirmed in that position by the Queen herself. Two plays by Marston with caricatures of Jonson followed and, according to Jonson, Marston even drew a pistol on him once. At this point the Chamberlain's Men, who may have been piqued by Jonson's change of allegiance sponsored *Satiromastix,* a joint effort by Marston and the indefatig-able Dekker. Before it could appear however, Jonson, who had evidently heard of the impending attack on him, anticipated it with *Poetaster,* performed at the Blackfriars in 1601. Here Jonson portrays himself as Horace, the honest poet attacked by ignorance and envy but vindicated by his fellow poets. He also launches a bitter attack on the Chamberlain's Men and in one scene shows Crispinus (Marston) spewing out great gobbets of pompous rhetoric as a result of swallowing an emetic prepared by Horace. With *Satiromastix,* or *The Untrussing of the Humorous Poet* performed shortly afterwards by both the Children of Pauls and the Chamberlain's Men, the War of the Theatres came to an end. The play retains Jonson as Horace and lifts another character, Captain Tucca, from *Poetaster.* Though Horace-Jonson is here subjected to such indignities as being tossed in a blanket by four ladies, there is a good deal of deference towards Jonson's erudition and wit in the play. In 1604 Marston dedicated one of his finest plays,

The Malcontent, to Jonson and in the following year collaborated with both Jonson and George Chapman in *Eastward Ho,* a play which landed the two latter dramatists in jail for its satire on James's Scottish courtiers.

None of the plays brought forth by the War of the Theatres represents the best work of their authors. But they do provide a convenient set of examples of satirical comedy, though they illustrate the limitations of this kind rather better than its strengths. We have seen that the classical tradition saw the purpose of comedy as the purging of mankind's excesses and follies, a metaphor used quite literally by Jonson in *Poetaster.* In England, there was a native tradition of satire represented by writers such as Langland and Skelton, and literary satire came to the stage through non-dramatic verse and prose, particularly the prose tracts of Nashe and Greene, the *Virgidemiarum* of Joseph Hall, Marston's own *The Scourge of Villainy* and the verse satires of John Donne. By the end of the century satire had become so scurrilous that the Archbishop of Canterbury and the Bishop of London ordered the burning of satirical works by Nashe, Hall, Harvey and Marston among others. But by this time the vogue for satire had already passed on to the stage. The obscenity, self-advertisement and personal invective which seem inevitable in any extended satire are present in ample measure in the group of plays under discussion. But more positive qualities are not entirely absent. These include a keen eye for contemporary social foibles, a good deal of theatrically effective knockabout farce and general horseplay and a dramatic idiom compounded of rhetorical figures and colloquial speech that is full of surprising twists and turns. The scurrility and wit were doubtless found especially piquant in the mouths of the 'little eyases', the boy actors for whom most of the satirical comedies were written. But even at its most effective, as in Marston's *The Malcontent* and *The Dutch Courtesan,* this kind of scabrous satirical comedy represents a diminution of the full range of corrective comedy. The full possibilities of such comedy are realized in Ben Jonson's three great plays, *Volpone, The Alchemist* and *Bartholomew Fair.*

Theory and Practice in Jonsonian Comedy

Poet and bricklayer, playwright and classical scholar, actor, duellist and soldier of fortune — Ben Jonson seems to embody in his own career something of the vigour, restlessness and many-sided activity of Elizabethan life. But he is too unique and impressive a figure to be merely representative. Lesser writers like Marston may be said to represent a phase in Elizabethan-Jacobean comedy. But Jonson, like Shakespeare, helped to create the taste of the period by combining existing elements into a new whole. He made a characteristic start to his career as actor and playwright when he collaborated with Thomas Nashe in 1597 on *The Isle of Dogs.* This satirical play, now lost, landed Jonson and two other actors in jail. It was the first of several prison sentences served by Jonson and in this he was in no way untypical of many dramatists of the period, Shakespeare excepted. His first great theatrical triumph came in the following year when the Lord Chamberlain's Men produced *Every Man in His Humour* with a cast that included Burbage, Shakespeare and the celebrated comic actor Will Kemp.

Every Man In exists in two versions, the earlier one set in Italy, the revised version in London. But even in the earlier form there is no attempt at capturing an Italian atmosphere and characters such as Cob and Tib clearly derive from the Roister Doister native tradition of comedy. But Jonson is determined to impose classical restraints on the untidy raw material and the chaotic comic energy which was his by tradition and temperament. The whole action of the play takes place within twelve hours in a single location and no 'serious' business interferes with the succession of comic episodes. Thus the alleged classical unities of time, place and action are scrupulously observed, which makes the play sound ominously academic. Nor is it reassuring to learn that the 'humour' of the title does not refer to the modern sense of the term, but to an outmoded medieval physiological theory. According to this a man's nature was supposed to be determined by the balance in his body of the four essential fluids or humours — blood, choler, phlegm and melancholy (black bile). Fortunately Jonson is too vividly aware of the oddities of Elizabethan London and relishes them too much to let a theory stand in the way of his portrayal of them. As a matter of historical fact it was not Jonson but George Chapman who introduced 'humorous' characters on to the English stage in *An Humorous Day's Mirth* first performed in 1597, a year before Jonson's comedy. For Jonson the theory of humours provides in *Every Man In* a convenient theoretical frame for characters distorted from healthy normality by some obsession — wild boasting in the case of Captain Bobadil, stupidity in Stephen's case, excessive suspicion in that of Old Knowell and so on. There is a good deal of bustling action and Jonson shows already that dexterity in juggling with different plot episodes within a single play which is used with such dazzling effect in *The Alchemist*. The didactic point of depicting deformations of personality is of course to suggest that they are corrigible, and the prologue to the revised version plainly declares the classical corrective aim, drawing attention at the same time to the aptness of the plot, characters and language to the comic form:

> . . .deeds and language such as men do use,
> And persons such as Comedy would choose;
> When she would show an image of the times,
> And sport with human follies, not with crimes;
> Except we make 'em such by loving still
> Our popular errors, when we know they're ill.
> I mean such errors, as you'll all confess,
> By laughing at them, they deserve no less;

We are duly shown how most of the humours are 'purged' as a result of the activities of Knowell's wily servant Brainworm. But the final impression we have of the play is not so much of a moralistic satire holding social aberrations up to ridicule as of a fascinating gallery of larger-than-life caricatures which puts us in mind of Dickensian grotesques. As so often in Dickens the impact of the life and energy of the characters and action is so much greater than that of the moral message. Though *Every Man In* is formally a comedy of criticism and judgment it is entirely in keeping with its spirit that its ending should be typical of celebratory comedy, when the assembled company proceed at the close to a hearty supper and a convivial evening at the residence of the amiable Justice Clement. As for 'language such as men do use' there is in this early play, as throughout Jonson's drama, a fascination with the problems and possibilities of speech and in particular there is a fine feeling for the richness and raciness of colloquial Elizabethan speech, but here too one feels that ordinary language has been amplified and transmuted rather than transcribed. Cob the Waterman launching his tirade against fasting days is a representative example of Jonson's linguistic exuberance though one extract cannot suggest the variety of forms which that exuberance takes:

A fasting day no sooner comes, but my lineage goes to rack; poor cobs, they smoke for it, they melt in passion, and your maids too know this, and yet would have me turn Hannibal, and eat my own fish and blood. (*He pulls out a red herring*). My princely coz, fear nothing. I have not the heart to devour you, an I might be made as rich as Golias. Oh, weep salt water enough now to preserve the lives of ten thousand of my kin. But I may curse none but these filthy almanacs, for an 'twere not for them, these days of persecution would ne'er be known. I'll be hanged an some fishmonger's son do not make on 'em, and puts in more fasting days than he should do, because he would utter his father's dried stockfish.

Every Man Out of his Humour performed in 1599 did not by any means repeat the success of the earlier play nor did it deserve to. The rapid sequence of constantly shifting perspectives where characters alternate between participating in the central action and commenting on it does not clarify but confuses the action and there is something frenetic and mechanical about the social types depicted, though occasionally a character like Fastidious Brisk the affected courtier or the two coxcombs Clove and Orange leap to life in a colourful turn of phrase. But *Every Man Out* does contain a passage in which Jonson delineates the genuinely humorous character and protests at the way in which 'humour' has become a catchword and a stock notion of the times, partly no doubt because of the success of his own earlier play:

So in every human body
The choler, melancholy, phlegm and blood
By reason that they flow continually
In some one part, and are not continent,
Receive the name of humours. Now thus far
It may, by metaphor, apply itself
Unto the general disposition:
As when some one peculiar quality
Doth so possess a man, that it doth draw
All his affects, his spirits, and his powers,
In their confluctions, all to run one way,
This may be truly said to be a humour.
But that a rook, in wearing a pied feather,
The cable hat-band, or the three-piled ruff,
A yard of shoe-tie, or the Switzer's knot
On his French garters, should affect a humour!
Oh, 'tis more than most ridiculous.

Jonson certainly depicted both true and false 'humours' in his comedies, but it is hardly necessary even to be aware of the theory of humours or the dramatic principles Jonson purported to derive from it in order to respond adequately to the teeming imaginative life and the moral seriousness of the three great comedies. All of these belong to the Jacobean not the Elizabethan theatre and the first in particular has something of the darkened atmosphere evoked by the later epithet. *Volpone* was acted in 1606 by Shakespeare's company, now under the patronage of James I and called the King's Men. Its locale is Venice but the Italian setting counts for a little more here than in the first version of *Every Man In*. The play revolves round Volpone, apparently on his deathbed, receiving various gifts from the greedy 'suitors' who hope to inherit his fortune. The custom of making presents to someone in the expectation of coming into wealth at his death was an Italian one, though Roman rather than Venetian. Jonson also makes some use of exotic detail and of the social distinction between Volpone, a magnifico or wealthy gentleman, and his 'parasite' Mosca. The latter can be condemned to the galleys at the end but not Volpone, who would also rather face punishment than be done down by his own servant.

But for all that, the play's preoccupations are those of Jonson's own society (and of ours), a society where the pursuit of wealth by means however devious was becoming obsessive, or so it seemed, and where the posession of material goods was rapidly replacing all other criteria of value. *Volpone* measures this frantic race for possessions (including the possession of women) against traditional norms of scorn of riches and reverence for family and personal loyalty. It deals with the deadly sins of avarice and lust and its comic design is the age-old one of the biter bit.

The satirist's reductive view of human nature is evident in the fact that all the principal characters take their names from animals most of which feed on carrion. Jonson stands the old beast-fable convention on its head; instead of investing animals with human qualities, human beings are shown taking on the appetite and ferocity of animals. The menagerie includes Mosca the flesh fly, Corvino and Corbaccio the two varieties of raven; Voltore the vulture and Volpone himself, the cunning old fox. There is also a sub-plot of sorts which deals with the humiliation of Sir Pol(itic), the talkative and fatuous Englishman abroad, by Peregrine, the sensible traveller, but this is strictly peripheral to the central action. All these are shown buzzing, sniffing and clawing at each other in their insatiable hunger for gold and there is little to choose between them, though Volpone boasts

> Yet I glory
> More in the cunning purchase of my wealth
> Than in the glad possession, since I gain
> No common way:

and Mosca distinguishes between the common or garden parasite

> those that have your bare town-art
> To know who's fit to feed 'em

and super-parasites such as himself

>   your fine elegant rascal, that can rise
> And stoop, almost together, like an arrow;
> Shoot through the air as nimbly as a star;
> Turn short as doth a swallow; and be here,
> And there, and here, and yonder, all at once;

In the end all come to an equally inglorious end.

There are at least two points in the play where Jonson forgets his own dictum that comedy should 'sport with human follies, not with crimes'. First, the attempted prostitution of his own wife by Corvino whose greed for gain exceeds even his marital possessiveness is nearer to criminality than anything we normally understand by folly. Secondly, the punishments meted out at the end are of a severity which even Jonson felt he had to account for in what purported to be a comedy. This is comedy of judgment literally with a vengeance. Mosca is flogged and sent to the galleys for life. Voltore the corrupt lawyer is disbarred and ordered into a monastery, while Corvino is sentenced to be rowed round Venice to be pelted with rotten eggs and worse, wearing a cuckold's cap with all the details of his attempt to sell his wife for Volpone's gold. As for Volpone himself, he is condemned to 'act' in reality what he only pretended to:

>   our judgment on thee
> Is that thy substance all be straight confiscate
> To the hospital of the Incurabili:
> And, since the most was gotten by imposture,
> By feigning lame, gout, palsy, and such diseases,
> Thou art to lie in prison, cramp'd with irons,
> Till thou be sick and lame indeed.

In his Dedication of the play to the Universities of Oxford and Cambridge, Jonson explains that the punishments are made harsh in order to satisfy those who attack plays for not showing vice justly and sufficiently punished — 'my special aim being to put the snaffle in their mouths, that cry out, We never punish vice in our interludes, etc.' Jonson the moralist certainly took such criticism seriously and the emphasis here is very much on vice punished rather than virtue rewarded. Contrary to comic expectation, for instance, the young hero Bonario and the virtuous heroine Celia are not united at the close. Unlike Shakespeare, Jonson is not particularly interested in romance and seemed to have lacked the ability or the inclination to depict reasonably attractive or even reasonable women. Celia and Grace Wellborn in *Bartholomew Fair* are only partial exceptions. They have nothing like the overwhelming dramatic presence of female grotesques such as the whore Dol Common or the Pig woman in *Bartholomew Fair*. In part of course this is a matter of the kind of comedy Jonson was writing. (The women in Roman comedy are invariably courtesans.) But it is clear that the portrayal of aberration, masculine as well as feminine, was more congenial to Jonson than that of normality, as well as being more suited to his satiric purpose.

To underline this we have in *Volpone* the grotesque trio of Nano the dwarf, Androgyno the hermaphrodite and Castrone the eunuch. We have no need to share the Jacobean aptitude for finding deformity funny to appreciate the dramatic point Jonson is making, namely that a man like Volpone, whose vital energy goes into getting gold rather than begetting children, neither deserves nor is capable of raising any family other than this misshapen brood. As Volpone himself says in the great speech which opens the play:

> O thou son of Sol,
> But brighter than thy father, let me kiss
> With adoration, thee, and every relic
> Of sacred treasure in this blessed room.
> Well did wise poets, by thy glorious name,
> Title that age which they would have the best;
> Thou being the best of things, and far transcending
> All style of joy in children, parents, friends,
> Or any other waking dream on earth.

Volpone's blasphemous use of the language of religion in exalting his gold combined with the visual elements of the scene (Mosca drawing aside the curtains of the inner stage to reveal the gold piled up as at an altar, Volpone kneeling and kissing the precious bane, Mosca officiating as a kind of priest at the service and so on) serves to make the moral point of the play from the outset — the perversion of man's humanity by his addiction to the pursuit of wealth. The phosphorescent beauty of Volpone's seduction speech to Celia, and his readiness to overmatch all the heedless waste and debauchery of former times for the sake of sexual stimulation is a variant of the same blasphemous inversion of values:

> See, here, a rope of pearl; and each more orient
> Than that the brave Egyptian Queen carous'd:
> Dissolve and drink 'em. See, a carbuncle
> May put out both the eyes of our St Mark;
> A diamond would have bought Lollia Paulina
> When she came in like starlight, hid with jewels
> That were the spoils of provinces; take these,
> And wear, and lose 'em:

This note of fascinated revulsion at the way lust swallows up entire fortunes 'for the poor pleasure of a bewitching minute' is one to be heard throughout Jacobean tragedy. Indeed *Volpone*, like the satirical comedies of Marston, is closer in feeling to the tragedy of the period than to the jovial city comedies of Dekker or the romantic comedies of Shakespeare (though 'romantic' is obviously far too limiting a term for the complex effect produced by, say, *Twelfth Night* or *The Merchant of Venice*; one of the reasons why Shakespeare is unique is that he, more than any other dramatist, was able to blend together almost *all* available traditions). The final line and a half of the play proper underlines its moral with grim satisfaction using the metaphor of animal appetite which runs throughout:

> Mischiefs feed
> Like beasts, till they be fat, and then they bleed.

Among Jonson's greater comedies, *Volpone* is the most insistently moralistic, but even here there is more to the total dramatic effect than the didacticism which is its theoretical justification. The verses by which Volpone tries to seduce Celia for instance display a Marlovian delight in the things of this world which to some extent runs counter to their strict moral function (though it can be argued that lines intended to seduce can hardly be other than seductive). A more serious challenge to the overt moral is provided by the obvious relish with which Jonson enters into the machinations of Volpone and especially of his parasite Mosca and all but admires the virtuosity with which they improvise and improve each occasion till the very end. (Perhaps this indulgence is an additional unacknowledged reason for the harshness of their final punishment.) Mosca's superb soliloquy at the beginning of Act III which I have already quoted from illustrates very well the self-delighting ecstasy of the artist exulting in the confidence of his own powers, a confidence which the dramatist in Jonson shares, however much the moralist may disapprove:

> I fear I shall begin to grow in love
> With my dear self, and my most prosp'rous parts,
> They do so spring and burgeon; I can feel
> A whimsy i' my blood: I know not how,
> Success hath made me wanton. I could skip
> Out of my skin now, like a subtle snake,
> I am so limber. O! your parasite
> Is a most precious thing, dropped from above,
> Not bred 'mongst clods and clot-poles, here on earth.

The words skip and dance in a rapture of self-adulation which we cannot but share, at least for the moment.

This admiration for the virtuosity of crooks and tricksters when his own moral objectives should lead him to condemn them is very much more evident in Jonson's next great comedy, *The Alchemist*, performed by the King's Men in 1610. Jonson here achieved a unique combination of strict classical formality and a feeling of spontaneous and overflowing life. He is back in his native London and the play is full of the sights, sounds and smells of the city he knew so well. The entire action is confined to a twenty-four hour period and takes place in or immediately outside a single dwelling, whose owner, a city gentleman named Lovewit, has temporarily vacated it in order to get away from an outbreak of plague, endemic in London at the time. Lovewit's butler Face, left in charge of the house, invites into it Subtle and Dol Common, respectively a quack with a smattering of alchemy and a trollop. Together they set up in business to part several gullible fools from their money by pretending to have discovered the philosopher's stone which could convert base metals into gold. The language and lore of alchemy was more familiar to Jonson's original audience than to us and the playwright makes liberal use of both throughout the play. This makes it difficult for the modern reader. Though in performance the sheer pace and variety of the action carries one along, some understanding of the basis of alchemy and of certain key alchemical ideas undoubtedly helps in appreciating the play fully. It is easy to exaggerate the extent of the knowledge required, but it is helpful to know, to begin with, that alchemy had an intellectual as well as a merely materialistic impulse behind it. The theory of alchemy derived from the Aristotelian notion that every substance was composed of varying proportions of the four elements, earth, air, water and fire, and the observed fact that one element could act on another to produce a third. This was the basis of the view that base metals could be transformed into gold, given the right materials and formula for transformation. The very difficulty of the enterprise helped to propagate the idea that only the elect, the devoted and dedicated men who pursued their goal not for sordid gain but for pure love of truth alone could hope for success. It is important to realize that in Jonson's day the pursuit of alchemy was not confined to the cranky and the credulous. Everyone, from the monarch and influential members of the Court down to the humblest peasant, believed in the existence of the philosopher's stone, though not everyone considered it lawful or even desirable to seek it. For those who did, it was a question of exactly how to find it. Jonson's play adheres very closely to the idiom and practice of alchemy, and makes savagely satirical use of many associated ideas, such as the idea that any suggestion of worldliness would endanger the success of the search. But although there is certainly a literal attack on the pursuit of alchemy in the play, Jonson's main interest is in alchemy as a metaphor for the acquisitiveness and obsessive desire to get rich quick which is so prominent a feature of Jacobean society and is not entirely absent from our own. A play on 'projection' (the technical term for the final stage of alchemical transmutation) and the activities of 'projectors', the seventeenth century word for (shady) speculators runs throughout the comedy. The activities of the trio in *The Alchemist* may well have been inspired by those of two contemporary practitioners, John Dee and Edward Kelly. Dee was a reputable scholar and scientist, which is more than can be said for Kelly, who had his ears cut off for forging money. These two were later joined by one Albert Laski. Both Dee and Kelly acquired not merely national but European reputations.

This is of interest only because it shows that for the Jacobean audience alchemy was not something that only a small minority was aware of, but an activity widely known in all ranks of society. But, like the beast fable in *Volpone*, the alchemical operations of Face and Subtle serve mainly as a means of exposing the naked greed and hypocrisy of those who are drawn to them. It would hardly be an exaggeration to say that the dramatist's real target is not the actual perpetrators of the fraud but those who are gullible or greedy enough to fall into their trap. Indeed, though Jonson never suffers fools gladly, it is not folly itself but the hypocrisy, lust and cupidity which nourish it which are the real objects of his satirical scorn. And while alchemy is the master-fraud by which 'the venture tripartite' thrives, there is practically no variety of profitable activity, legal or (preferably) otherwise, from receiving stolen goods to preparing horoscopes and giving tips on how to cheat at cards and dice which the trio do not zestfully turn their hands to. Jonson is depicting an age when the basis of power is shifting from land and social position to the possession of money, an age moreover in which there seemed to be a dizzying variety of ways in which money could be acquired provided one did not possess too scrupulous a conscience — 'the ways to enrich are many and most of them foul' as Bacon wrote, and he should have known. The victims in *The Alchemist* provide a fair cross-section of contemporary society. They include the foolish lecher Sir Epicure Mammon, the canting hypocritical Puritans, Ananias and Tribulation Wholesome and the credulous small shopkeeper Abel Drugger. All these and several others are frantically impatient to find the secret that will transform their fortunes and with that their very natures. In all of them Jonson stresses the ludicrous discrepancy between their dreams and their real selves, though there is a certain lunatic grandeur about the wild imaginings of Sir Epicure. His sexual fantasies are based on the notion that the philosopher's stone provided not only endless wealth but the elixir of life:

> I will have all my beds blown up, not stuffed;
> Down is too hard. And then, mine oval room
> Filled with such pictures as Tiberius took
> From Elephantis, and dull Aretine
> But coldly imitated. Then my glasses,
> Cut in more subtle angles, to disperse
> And multiply the figures as I walk
> Naked between my succubae. My mists
> I'll have of perfume, vapour'd 'bout the room,
> To lose ourselves in; and my baths like pits
> To fall into, from whence we will come forth
> And roll us dry in gossamer and roses.
> (Is it arrived at ruby?)

The suggestion of auto-voyeurism and the references to being lost in a mist and falling into a pit evoke distant or not so distant religious and moral values. It is almost the last time that they are so confidently appealed to in drama. But even as we sense them we are responding almost as vividly as the speaker to the sheer sensuous opulence of the vision (Mammon continues in this vein for over 30 lines). As in *Volpone* the moral point is made not by minimizing the temptation but by amplifying it and displaying it in all its feverish fascination. Jonson's imagination, using the scenes and characters of Jacobean London as its point of departure, soon leaves any kind of mere realism behind and takes off into a realm of surreal fantasy, though it is fair to add that some of the most fantastic scenes, such as the episode of Dapper and the 'Queen of the Fairies' are based on actual contemporary events. Jonson's moral vision is always steady but it is not here applied with the severity characteristic of the end of *Volpone*. All the dupes naturally end up disappointed in their expectations, but the crooks get off comparatively lightly, losing their ill-gotten gains but escaping any further punishment. In part, as I have suggested, this is due to the fact that the true satirical quarry is the victims' greed not the tricksters' villainy. I think too that there is in Jonson an element of fascination with the whole business and bombast of alchemy which imparts a tone of something like geniality to the play as compared with *Volpone*. Surly, a clear-eyed and sceptical (though, as his name suggests, not altogether balanced) critic of Subtle's alchemical pretensions, seems to become enraptured by the sheer colour, variety and sound of the ingredients of trickery much as Tamburlaine was fascinated by the sonorous phrase 'to ride in triumph through Persepolis'. 'What else are all your terms' he asks Subtle scornfully

Whereon no one o' your writers 'grees with other?
Of your elixir, your *lac virginis,*
Your stone, your medicine, and your chrysosperm,
Your sal, your sulphur, and your mercury,
Your oil of height, your tree of life, your blood,
Your marchesite, your tutie, your magnesia,
Your toad, your crow, your dragon, and your panther,
Your sun, your moon, your firmament, your adrop,
Your lato, azoch, zernich, chibrit, heautarit,
And then your red man, and your white woman,
With all your broths, your menstrues, and materials
Of piss and egg-shells, women's terms, man's blood,
Hair o' the head; burnt clouts, chalk, merds and clay,
Powder of bones, scalings of iron, glass,
And worlds of other strange ingredients
Would burst a man to name?

The intention is to condemn but the actual effect is very far from merely condemnatory. All Jonson's plays contain splendid lists, whether of jewels, items of food or cosmetics, but nowhere is his penchant for piling up item upon item into a vast and various catalogue so richly evident as in *The Alchemist;* the fact that most of the items are quite genuine only adds to the fascination. But the most important reason for his ambiguous attitude to the confidence tricksters is that like ourselves, Jonson has fallen more than half in love with their sheer virtuosity and inventiveness. Subtle and Face manoeuvre themselves out of trouble and manipulate the other characters in much the same way as Volpone and Mosca but with far more dash and resourcefulness. The hectic pace and endless liveliness of the plot are a function of the villains' ingenuity in keeping their victims from coming into contact with one another. As the various plots develop their frenzied course we begin to feel that the dazzling display cannot last, that so many balls cannot be kept up in the air for very long, that first one and then another and another must come bouncing down. Of course this finally happens and the whole amazing house of cards collapses in a heap bringing down the would-be kings and queens of fantasy, though the knaves still contrive to stay on top. The con men's efforts to save appearances are quite indistinguishable from the dramatist's exertions to keep the plot from collapsing. They are two ways of describing the same thing, which is as much to say that there is an affinity between the dramatist and the fake alchemists, as there is between the art of the theatre and that of alchemy. This affinity goes deeper than the conscious moral disapprobation which is part of the didactic purpose, cutting across it and complicating our reaction to the comic denouement. Lovewit, the master of the house who returns to sort things out in the last act, lives up to his name and rewards his butler for his quick-wittedness instead of punishing him for his knavery:

> That master
> That had received such happiness by a servant
> In such a widow and with so much wealth,
> Were very ungrateful if he would not be
> A little indulgent to that servant's wit
> And help his fortune though with some small strain
> Of his own candour.

Lovewit himself is well satisfied with his newly acquired wealth and widow and is not inclined to look too closely into either. Though the two Puritans are confirmed in their pious hypocrisy and Sir Epicure vows to turn street evangelist proclaiming the end of the world, the finale has the air of a convivial occasion not unlike that of *Every Man In*. Interestingly Surly, who has been presented as a fairly sane and critical character (not unlike the usual notion of 'morose Ben Jonson') becomes at the end little more than a disgruntled Malvolio who remains on stage instead of quitting it. And in the very last lines of the epilogue (the point at which the play-world dissolves into the real world of the audience), the play itself becomes, in Face's words, that now familiar symbol of conviviality, the communal feast:

> Yet I put myself
> On you, that are my country; and this pelf
> Which I have got, if you do quit me, rests
> To feast you often, and invite new guests.

Conviviality informs not only the title but the entire structure of Jonson's last great comedy *Bartholomew Fair*, presented at the newly opened Hope theatre on October 31, 1614 and repeated at court the following night. The play takes its name from the oldest and most celebrated of London fairs, held in Smithfield and by Jonson's time as much a summer carnival as a marketplace.

Where *The Alchemist* confined its action to a single house but added variety with a succession of related plots, *Bartholomew Fair*, while still observing the unities of time and place, does so in a more relaxed fashion. In keeping with a play which deals by and large with the underworld and the 'middling sort of people', it is written in prose, unlike the other two great comedies. With a deceptive air of casualness (since his hold on the plot is quite as sure as it is in *The Alchemist*), Jonson takes us from one part of the fair to another. We see John Littlewit's anxiety to see his puppet play (a ludicrous version of Marlowe's *Hero and Leander* transferred to Bankside) staged ,at the fair, his pregnant wife's craving for Bartholomew pork, Rabbi Zeal of the Land Busy's resolve to 'eat exceedingly' of the same 'to profess our hate and loathing of judaism'. The action consists of a series of encounters between different groups of people which enable the dramatist to contrast their motives and attitudes. Three broad groups may be distinguished and labelled for convenience judges, visitors and professionals. The first group are those who are hostile or at any rate to begin with highly critical of the fair. Chief among them is the ranting Rabbi; the group also includes the less frenzied Justice Adam Overdo, wandering in disguise looking for wrongdoing at the fair, finding motes and missing beams everywhere, and the choleric Humphrey Wasp, striving vainly to keep his charge, the doltish Bartholomew Cokes, immune from the dangers and temptations of the fair. The visitors, the second group, are invariably victims of the third, the professional cutpurses, con-men, whores and assorted villains who live by their wit and are the true natives of Bartholomew Fair. The latter group is typified by Lanthorn Leatherhead the puppet showman (who may be a skit on Inigo Jones, Jonson's collaborator and rival in the staging of Court masques), Ezekiel Edgworth the cutpurse and above all Ursula the pig woman. Their victims, apart from the fatuous Cokes himself, include Littlewit and his mother-in-law Dame Purecraft. There is a sharper line between those who lose money at the fair and those who make it than between those who ply an honest trade and those who do not. What is most noteworthy is that Jonson's attitude to the professionals is on the whole rather more favourable than it is to either of the other two groups. The reluctance to pass judgment is even more pronounced here than in *The Alchemist* for, as in *Every Man In* it is the judge himself who abdicates his office in favour of the more genial one of host and invites everyone home to supper. He tells them, and us, that 'my intents are ad correctionem, non ad destructionem; ad aedificandum, non ad diruendem' (corrective, not destructive, for building, not for ruining). In the context the phrases have no didactic sting at all.

In *Bartholomew Fair* Jonson gives free and whole-hearted expression to that extraordinary zest for life which, as with Dickens, is as much part of his comic vision as the satirical moralist's scourging of affectation and excess. The satirist is not wholly absent even here but he is very much in holiday mood. There are times when *Bartholomew Fair* faintly recalls a different comedy, Shakespeare's *As You Like It*. The fair is a kind of Arden where, in spite of or because of various pieces of knavery and deviousness, the principal characters learn something about themselves and refresh and renew their human resources. It is not surprising that Bartholomew Fair was a popular success in its day, for it presents for all its touches of satire an affectionate and expansive picture of London at play. Modern revivals have demonstrated that it is a picture still full of colour and movement today.

Jonson wrote one other fine comedy, *Epicoene or The Silent Woman* (1609), a hilarious and often farcical account of the misadventures of the noisehating Morose in search of a wife who will speak softly and seldom. It is characteristic of Jonson's mellower comic vision that it is the tolerant Truewit rather than the rule-obsessed Morose whose outlook is finally endorsed by the comedy which Dryden praised as Jonson's finest and which continued to be popular on stage for over a century after Jonson's death in 1637. There are splendid moments in his other comedies and the court masques he created in collaboration with Inigo Jones are the best of their ephemeral kind, but Jonson's claim to be the greatest comic dramatist of the age rests securely on the plays discussed above. In each of them he shows a clear understanding of the aims and methods of classical comedy and professedly follows them; in each he rather transcends those aims and methods to create a unique and unforgettable comic universe.

Marston, Middleton and Massinger

To come from Jonson to Marston is to descend to a comic world which is altogether harsher, narrower and more feverish. In an essay written forty-five years ago T.S. Eliot remarked of Marston that

> We are aware, in short, with this [*The Malcontent*] as with Marston's other plays, that we have to do with a positive, powerful and unique personality. This is an original variation of that deep discontent and rebelliousness so frequent among Elizabethan dramatists. He is, like some of the greatest of them, occupied in saying something else than appears in the literal actions and characters whom he manipulates.[1]

The discontent and rebelliousness Eliot mentions had many sources, intellectual, social and economic and is seen at its sharpest in the tragedy of the period, though it casts its dark shadow on the satirical comedy too. As for the uniqueness of Marston's personality, it is evident throughout his work. It is apparent in the erotic poem and the verse satires with which he made his literary debut, *The Metamorphosis of Pygmalion's Image and Certain Satires* (1598) and *The Scourge of Villainy* (1598-99) both written under the pseudonym of W. Kinsayder. Excess, extremity and a willed harshness give these works their characteristic flavour. To these qualities are added in the plays self-mockery and a virtuosity in handling theatrical perspectives more adroit than that of any other Jacobean dramatist. It is perhaps characteristic of the dizzying imbalance we sense in Marston that a literary career which began with the public burning of his poetry by the common hangman on the orders of the Archbishop of Canterbury should, within ten years or so, terminate with Marston taking holy orders. During this period he wrote several plays, including tragi-comedies, satirical contributions to the War of the Theatres and 'comical satires'. These divisions are fairly arbitrary and not always distinguishable one from another. Marston's art is always 'impure' in that it is intrinsically of mixed kinds. Whatever the genre or sub-genre he wrote in, his acid personality comes through in the discordant idiosyncrasy of his language. (Crispinus vomiting indigestibly turgid rhetoric was a sitting target for Jonson in *Poetaster*).

Eliot (as well as Marston himself) considered *The Wonder of Women* to be Marston's best play, but I see no reason to quarrel with the general view which gives pride of place jointly to *The Malcontent* (1603) and *The Dutch Courtesan* (1603-4). Both have been successfully revived in recent times and both act better than they read, a fact of which Marston was fully aware, for in the preface to the printed version of *The Malcontent* he writes:

> I have myself therefore set forth this comedy; but so, that my enforced absence must much rely upon the printer's discretion; but I shall entreat slight errors in orthography may be slightly overpassed, and that the unhandsome shape which this trifle in reading presents may be pardoned for

---

[1] 'John Marston' (London, 1934) in *Selected Essays* by T.S. Eliot

the pleasure it once afforded you when it was presented with the soul of lively action.

The 'unhandsome shape' is due to more than 'slight errors in orthography', though Marston is referring only to the physical appearance of the printed quarto. But there is no doubt about 'the pleasure it once afforded' to Jacobean audiences. Though the play was originally written for and performed by a children's company at Blackfriars, the most successful adult company of the day thought it worth stealing. A special 'Induction' by John Webster introduced several members of the King's Men by name discussing how the play came to be staged by them (probably in retaliation for having one of *their* successes appropriated by the children's company) and what the author intended; this was for performance at the open-air Globe theatre.

In his dedication to the play to Ben Jonson (with whom he happened to be friends at the time), Marston himself refers to 'this harsh comedy' (asperam Thaliam) and this is very much the quality of the play which is first apparent. When it was entered in the Stationer's Register on 5 July 1604 *The Malcontent* was described as 'Tragicomoedia' and it employs most of the conventions of Senecan tragedy though it lacks such expected tragic attributes as grandeur, inevitability and catastrophe. It has evident affinities with the so-called 'problem plays' of Shakespeare (*Measure for Measure, Troilus and Cressida* and *All's Well that Ends Well*) dating from the same period. With Marston it is especially difficult to separate the roles of satirist and sensationalist, the savage critic of corruption in high places and the pathological self-hater leering at his own countenance in the cesspool. The character from whom *The Malcontent* gets its name, one of a long line of self-declared misfits frequent in Jacobean drama, has often been taken as a dramatic representation of his creator. As Altofronto ('lofty browed') he is the virtuous deposed duke of Genoa, now under the corrupt rule of the usurper Pietro guided by the treacherous courtier Mendoza. But throughout most of the action Altofronto is disguised as Malevole, the bitter railer against the corruption which seethes and bubbles at court. There are several variations on the folk theme of the disguised ruler in the drama of this period. Marston used the device in another play, *The Fawn* (1605). Other examples are Middleton's *The Phoenix* (c.1604) and Shakespeare's *Measure for Measure* (1604). As Marston uses it, the double figure has the advantage of uniting the railer with the ultimate source of authority and thereby giving some sense of 'responsibility' to the ranting.

The plot of *The Malcontent* unfolds on stage with a satisfying rapidity. It concerns Mendoza's all but successful efforts to murder Pietro and assume power, the affairs carried on by Pietro's lascivious wife Aurelia with Mendoza and his rival Ferneze, and Malevole-Altofronto's final outwitting of his enemies and resumption of ducal power. Marston makes frequent use of sententious moralizing and classical allusion, perhaps as much to flatter those among his audience with intellectual pretensions as to lend weight and authority to the treatment of the themes of adultery and usurpation. The final effect is very far from anything we would wish to call Jonsonian. The persistent self-deprecation and the tone of willed near-hysteria tend to undermine the moral impact. The following is fairly typical of 'the ragged cur' Malevole, and the fact that it is part of a soliloquy in which he is supposed to be in control of his emotions underlines the precariousness of his hold on his satiric role:

> Lean thoughtfulness, a sallow meditation,
> Suck thy veins dry! Distemperance rob thy sleep!
> The heart's disquiet is revenge most deep.
> He that gets blood, the life of flesh but spills,
> But he that breaks heart's peace the dear soul kills.

But it is just this precarious balance which gives the comedy its dramatic tension. Time and time again we come upon a surprising twist or reversal when the action and language have led us to expect some disastrous outcome. Marston makes full use of the resources of the indoor theatres — formal processions, music, lights, masquing and dancing — to bring both the domestic and public themes of the play to a conclusion which stresses reconciliation rather than retribution. But it is not the sense of moral issues resolved that stays with us, rather that of a curiously ambiguous twilight world of harsh discords and violent contrasts. There is something like a note of relief in Malevole's final words as he relinquishes his role not only as railing malcontent but as restored duke:

> The rest of actors idly part,
> And as for me, I here assume my right,
> To which I hope all's pleased: to all, goodnight.

By comparison *The Dutch Courtesan* is almost genial in its atmosphere. There is a quality in this comedy which one is tempted to call sanity, though not if we come to it from, say, *The Shoemaker's Holiday*. Not that melodrama and potential tragedy are lacking here either. Marston took his story from a novella by Matteo Bandello, one of the innumerable Italian tales of intrigue which were being translated by the ream in Elizabethan England and which provided a near-inexhaustible source of plots for the drama. The main story, in which the melodrama is centred, concerns Freewill who casually passes on his former mistress, the Dutch Courtesan Franceschina, to his friend Malheureux, the self-imagined 'man of snow', in order to marry the virtuous Beatrice. Somewhat predictably, Malheureux becomes infatuated with Franceschina who attempts to use him as an instrument for her murderous revenge on Freewill. Needless to say the plot is foiled, Malheureux is cured of his foolish obsession and everything ends happily for everyone except Franceschina who is soundly scourged. There is incipient tragedy in the courtesan's predicament and a good actress can make it vivid, though Marston appears to be little interested in it. The harlot is seen as necessary to the comfortable existence of the gentry, like decent plumbing, but her sufferings are of no more consequence than the inconvenience of a blocked drain. So far *The Dutch Courtesan* is a typical comedy of judgment, making a too-easy moral point about the difference between lust and love and warning of the hazards of total abstinence in matters sexual, exemplified in the 'melancholy humour' of Malheureux. The sub-plot however is almost pure comedy of celebration, admittedly of a rather gamey sort, dealing with the antics of Cocledemoy in repeatedly outwitting the cheating vintner Mulligrub. The discomfiture of the tradesman would doubtless have delighted the fashionable young gentlemen of the Inns of Court and elsewhere who frequented the public theatres. With many of these, scorn for tradesmen went hand in hand with indebtedness to them. This is a minor theme which comes into prominence in Restoration comedy, where class antagonism is sharper and cruder.

Cocledemoy, who is described in the Dramatis Personae as 'a knavishly witty city companion' is a version of the city gallant or would-be gallant who would have been very familiar to a Jacobean audience, nearer to some than the man sitting next to them. His single-minded verbal concentration on the sexual, alimentary and excretory functions of human beings results in a rhetoric so foul-mouthed that much Restoration comic dialogue seems positively demure by comparison. But the germ's eye view of human nature which might result from such exclusiveness is redeemed by two things. It coexists in the first place with a fertility of invention and liveliness of rhythm whose final effect is the opposite of reductive:

> Why, according to the old saying. A beggar when he is lousing himself looks like a philosopher, a hard bound philosopher when he is on the stool looks like a tyrant, and a wise man, when he is in his belly act, looks like a fool. God give your worship good rest, grace and mercy. Keep your syringe straight, and your lotium unspilt.

Secondly, the very excessiveness of Cocledemoy's insistence that man is only an animal serves to remind us that he is not. The dramatic function of such insistence is to provide a contrast to the somewhat airy-fairy lyricism with which Marston invests the courtship of Freewill and Beatrice (though the other pair of lovers, Crispinella and Tysefew also offer such a contrast). In the latter pair we have Marston's version of the witty couple who jest and flirt through the whole of Restoration comedy, combining in different proportions the basic ingredients of elegant badinage and bawdy innuendo.

Thus *The Dutch Courtesan* contrives to get the best of all comic worlds. As didactic comedy it underlines the virtues of rational choice as opposed to heedless lust (Freewill's name, like that of some other characters, is symbolic in a fairly loose sense; to a Jacobean audience attuned to verbal nuances it may have suggested not only 'capable of choice' but 'experienced and liberal in sexuality'). As romantic comedy it provides a satisfying union between two sets of lovers. And as festive comedy it invites us to accept and indulge the gross and imperious appetites of the flesh. Marston has united all these in a theatrical form full of ironic cross-references and a comic pace which gains in momentum until the final scene where both plots are resolved and Cocledemoy takes his leave of the audience with the genial combination of self-deprecation, flattery and assumed scorn characteristic not only of himself but of his creator's attitude to the fashionable audience:

> We scorn to fear, and yet we fear to swell;
> We do not hope 'tis best; 'tis all, if well.

Thomas Middleton's long didactic poem, *The Wisdom of Solomon Paraphrased* appeared in 1597 when its author was only seventeen, and before he was twenty he had also published an imitation of Joseph Hall's modish satires under the title *Micro-Cynicon, Six Snarling Satires*. Though the latter attribution is not entirely certain, the two together provide a rough guide to the tone and temper of Middleton's comedies, especially if we add that the finest of them *A Chaste Maid in Cheapside* (*c.*1613) is very close to his satiric tragedy *Women Beware Women*.

Middleton's output, like that of many other playwrights of the time, was prolific, and he collaborated with several contemporaries. His partnership with William Rowley produced one of the greatest Jacobean tragedies, *The Changeling*. His characteristic strengths and limitations as a comic dramatist can be seen in two early comedies and a later one, *A Mad World, My Masters* and *A Trick to Catch the Old One*, both written around 1604-1606 for a children's company, and *A Chaste Maid in Cheapside* performed at the Swan theatre (the only extant play known to have been performed there) by an adult company formed in 1611.

A Mad World, My Masters has a hero who is typical of city comedy and a flattering version of many members of the audience. Follywit is a prodigal young gallant determined to outwit his uncle Sir Bounteous Progress and obtain his legacy in advance, although he knows he has already been named the old man's heir: 'Then, since he has no will to do me good as long as he lives, by mine own will I'll do myself good before he dies'. His success in this enterprise is equivocal, for his last ruse fails and he ends up married to his uncle's mistress, although there is some suggestion that the old man was incapable of sexual relations with her. But Follywit's disappointment is soon alleviated by Sir Bounteous's wedding gift of a thousand marks and he accepts his destiny with something more than philosophical detachment:

> By my troth, she is as good a cup of nectar as any bachelor needs to sup at.
> Tut, give me gold, it makes amends for vice;
> Maids without coin are candles without spice.

The other plot of *A Mad World* tells of the citizen Harebrain's obsessive concern to avoid becoming a cuckold (another favourite motif of Restoration comedy) and the equally determined efforts to make him one on the part of a character named Penitent Brothel. The two parts of the name neatly encapsulate the character's outlook, which is that of a lecher clinging to his lechery till it is satisfied and then promptly wallowing in remorse. In Penitent's sudden conversion it is likely that Middleton is poking fun at the many plays dealing in moralistic terms with prodigals and their near-miraculous repentance. Further parody of the heavy-handed moralizing of such plays is implied by the scene in which the disguised courtesan delivers a panegyric on marital fidelity for Harebrain's benefit while Mrs Harebrain and Penitent Brothel are in bed offstage. The climax comes when the cuckolded husband, happily deceived to the last, praises the conniving courtesan and the faithless wife in these terms:

> Two dear rare gems this hour presents me with,
> A wife that's modest, and a friend that's right.
> Idle suspect and fear, now take your flight.

It is impossible to see the audience of young men about town at a private playhouse watching such a scene in such a play performed by a troupe of young children and taking it as anything other than parody of a familiar variety of sermonizing drama.

The triumph of Witgood, the hero of *A Trick to Catch the Old One*, is less ambiguous than that of Follywit, though his objectives are similar. He gets both the girl and the money which his grasping uncle, Pecunius Lucre had taken from him. (The fact that Witgood originally lost his fortune to his uncle through dissolute living is, if anything, seen as a point in the young gallant's favour). The plot of *A Trick* is so ingenious that twenty years later Philip Massinger borrowed it for a play in a very different spirit, *A New Way to Pay Old Debts*. It recounts Witgood's efforts to persuade his uncle and his equally usurious business rival Walkadine Hoard that Witgood's former mistress is really a widow with a vast fortune. There is the typical city comedy mixture of cleverly contrived and swift-moving plot, farcical and wildly improbable incident, revealing details of contemporary manners and last-minute changes of heart so symmetrically and ploddingly represented as to suggest parody. Both Witgood and the courtesan, having achieved their ends, solemnly renounce their evil courses, though not without lingering lovingly on the details of their wickedness, retrospective in Witgood's case —

And here for ever I disclaim
The cause of youth's undoing, game,
Chiefly dice, those true outlanders,
That shake out beggars, thieves and panders,
Soul-wasting surfeits, sinful riots,
Queans' evils, doctors' diets,
      etc.

— but negatively prospective where the courtesan is concerned:

Lo, gentlemen, before you all
In true reclaimed form I fall.
Henceforth for ever I defy
The glances of a sinful eye,
Waving of fans (which some suppose
Tricks of fancy), and treading of toes,
Wringing of fingers, biting the lip
The wanton gait, the alluring trip,
      etc.

Doubtless the watching gentlemen were thoroughly familiar from the drama with the 'true reclaimed form' of the honest whore (Dekker wrote a play with this title) and from real life with the other attractions which continue for several more lines of jolly octosyllables. The level of Middleton's concern with the straightforward morality of his comedy may perhaps be gauged from the courtesan's bland assurance to her husband and the audience that 'she that knows sin knows best how to hate it'. In the end Witgood's creditors get their money and the two usurers lose nothing more than a part of their fortunes. The lovers get each other but in a rather perfunctory fashion (half a dozen lines are all Middleton gives them for their final reunion). A darker note, and one not entirely assimilated to the rest of the play comes in the treatment of the drunken lawyer Dampit, a minor character condemned in harsh terms although he is morally more or less on the same level as the other characters. 'What profit it to be a slave in this world and a devil i' th' next?' an onlooker rhetorically asks at Dampit's death. But in the main Middleton is too busy manipulating his hero manipulating the villains to place any of them against such transcendental backgrounds.

The finest of all Middleton's comedies, *A Chaste Maid in Cheapside* holds all his comic preoccupations in a satisfying rather than an uneasy dramatic tension. Perhaps because it was written for performance at a public playhouse, there is less reliance here on parody and in-jokes. The relation between sex and money forms the basis of most of Middleton's comedies and one often stands as an inverted metaphor for the other. *A Chaste Maid* is based in part on an explicit negative correlation between economic affluence and sexual impotence. On the one hand there is the wealthy couple Sir Oliver and Lady Kix publicly abusing each other for their inability to produce an heir and on the other Touchwood Senior, so prolific in paternity that he can no longer afford to live with his wife. For begetting an heir on Lady Kix he receives four hundred pounds, with a promise of more to come. Then there is Allwit who is perfectly content to live on what amounts to his wife's immoral earnings. He actively encourages his wife's affair with Sir Walter Whorehound, the Kix's heir. This arrangement produces no less than seven bastards, the last of whom is christened in the play's most resolutely realistic scene. And at the very heart of the comic action we meet the goldsmith Yellowhammer anxious to offer the valuable commodity of a virgin daughter on the marriage market to Sir Walter. When he discovers that the latter is already the father of several bastards and has had a long-standing liaison with Mrs Allwit, his sole concern is that the marriage shall still go ahead provided Sir Walter takes precautions against the pox. Allwit's complacent paean in praise of his cuckold's condition gives some idea of Middleton's clear-eyed and unsentimental view of a society where love has been corrupted into love of money, dragging down with it all human relations, even the most intimate:

> The founder's come to town. I am like a man
> Finding a table furnish'd to his hand,
> As mine is still to me, prays for the founder:
> 'Bless the right worshipful, the good founder's life'.
> I thank him, h'as maintained my house this ten years,
> Not only keeps my wife, but a keeps me
> And all my family: I am at his table;
> He gets me all my children, and pays the nurse
> Monthly, or weekly, puts me to nothing,
> Rent, nor church duties, not so much as the scavenger:
> The happiest state that ever man was born to!

This is a telling comment on the sober citizen virtues of thrift and 'providing for one's family', the more so for its cool refusal to raise its voice. The juxtaposition in the penultimate line is typical of Middleton's dramatic language which, moving easily between colourful prose and matter-of-fact and very occasionally lyrical verse, almost always gains its power from ironies of context rather than metaphorical richness or heightened intensity. It derives from an unflustered recognition of man as a creature of appetites, alimentary, sexual and economic. The unbridled satisfaction of these, regarded with indulgence in the plays written for the private theatres, is here seen as producing and perpetuating a society where all are dependent on what passes for wit and worldly wisdom and where there is little to choose in moral terms between nominal heroes and villains. (The young lovers do stand apart from the general ruck of acquisitiveness, but more as passive symbols than active agents.) Middleton has been praised for his realistic portrayal of the London scene and certainly many episodes and characters give the impression of being drawn from life. It comes as no surprise to find that Middleton was the author of at least one 'cony-catching' pamphlet, for he relies heavily on such pamphlets both for material and in general outlook, a mixture of solemn didacticism and the underlying assumption that the crooks are morally on a par with their victims. But there is in *The Chaste Maid* as in the other comedies, a Jonsonian fascination with the extravagant and exaggerated in everyday life and the wildly farcical, as in Middleton's variation on a popular theatrical device where the two lovers, presumed dead, rise from their coffins just as Touchwood senior is preaching an unctuous funeral oration for them. Even when Middleton, collaborating with Dekker, went on to write a comedy about a real-life character — Moll Frith, a notorious female cutpurse, bawd, whore and receiver — he was unconcerned except incidentally with realism. *The Roaring Girl* has a good deal of dramatic power as the portrait of a masterful and compassionate woman in a masculine world, but the evidence suggests that Middleton severely distorted or simply ignored the factual material available to him. Similarly *A Chaste Maid in Cheapside* provides an exaggerated version of the characters and driving force of the social milieu it purports to represent. It is as much a dramatic reshaping of its 'material' as Dekker's urban pastoral or Marston's snarling satires. It survives, both on the page and in occasional modern revivals, because of Middleton's sure hold on his four distinct yet interrelated plot lines, his innumerable variations of dramatic irony and above all by its consistent, often funny but occasionally savage and even sombre evocation of a group of closely observed grotesques. Almost without exception these are propelled by the appetite for gain and the desire to outsmart their rivals. Even at the end, when Yellowhammer has lost his bid to marry off his daughter to the richest suitor and she has married the man of her choice while his idiot son is wedded to a Welsh whore, he consoles himself with thoughts of money saved: 'The best is, One feast will serve them both'. If there is less 'real life' in *A Chaste Maid* than appears at first, there is plenty of dramatic vitality.

Where Middleton's moral attitude, when present at all, is usually well below the surface of the comedy, in Philip Massinger it is so intrusive that it threatens to destroy the comic world altogether. Twenty years separate *A New Way to Pay Old Debts* (1625) from the play on which it is based, Middleton's *A Trick to Catch The Old One*, and Massinger's other comedy *The City Madam* (also based on an earlier play, *Eastward Ho* by Chapman, Jonson and Marston) came ten years later. Much had happened during these years, both in the theatre and in the society which it served. The vogue for child actors had passed by the first decade of the new century but the private indoor theatres became more and more the normal pattern, drawing their audience from a section of society dominated by fashionable but impecunious young gentlemen attached, in fact or fantasy, to a court increasingly isolated from the full stream of national life. As the rift between the courtly circle and other social classes became steadily wider the private theatres came more and more to be seen as a bastion of aristocratic values rather than as the focus of national aspiration which they had been in Elizabethan times. Dramatists felt compelled to take sides in their plays as very shortly many of their immediate successors were to do on the battlefield. (We are not surprised to find that most men of the theatre supported the Royalist cause in the Civil War.) Many of these changes are reflected in Massinger's plays, as well as in some aspects of his career. Born the son of a confidential employee of the Pembroke household, Massinger had some pretensions to gentility and, in a different economic climate, might have expected to find employment himself as part of the personal entourage of a great aristocratic household, a relationship idealized in *A New Way*. But on his father's death in 1606 he left Oxford without a degree and soon found himself forced to turn to the London theatre for a living, one of many 'whose necessitous fortunes made literature their profession' to use Massinger's own words.

The well born young wastrel who is a stock figure of citizen comedy reappears as the hero of *A New Way* in a much less equivocal sense than his original, Middleton's young Witgood. Massinger's choice of name, Wellborn, is of course significant, emphasizing his hero's gentility rather than his native wit. Though he follows the main outlines of Middleton's plot, Massinger introduces us to a world which is economically upgraded but much harsher. It is a world of extortionate social-climbing landowners and their corrupt henchmen who in their rabid acquisitiveness threaten the stable order of society headed by the landed aristocracy in whom reside the virtues of courage, patriotism, magnanimity and all others. The central figure Sir Giles Overreach, whose one ambition is to see his daughter married to a member of the nobility, is based rather loosely on a contemporary monopolist, usurer and crook Sir Giles Mompesson, while Overreach's tool Justice Greedy derives from another real-life figure, Sir Francis Michell. Massinger makes no secret of his sympathies with the landed elite and it is difficult to say which he presents as more repugnant, Overreach's megalomaniac rapacity or his obsessive snobbery. To Massinger the latter is not merely a ludicrous defect of character, but as much a threat to the foundations of ordered society as the dastardly means by which Overreach plans to outwit and impoverish his opponents. The moral positives of the play are represented at the top of the social scale by Lady Allworth (who has no scruples, like her courtesan prototype in Middleton's play, about pretending to favour the young rake as her intended marriage partner in order to dupe the grasping uncle), and Lord·Lovell who eventually marries Lady Allworth. In Lord Lovell's sober statement of the need to observe social distinctions we can hear clearly enough the want-impoverished gentleman-author's plea for the respect due to his own rank, whatever his fortunes:

Nor am I of that harsh and rugged temper
As some great men are tax'd with, who imagine
They part from the respect due to their honours
If they use not all such as follow 'em,
Without distinction of their births, like slaves.
I am not so condition'd; I can make
A fitting difference between my footboy
And a gentleman by want compell'd to serve me.

Massinger's sympathy for the hereditary gentry is clearly indicated not only by such overt utterances but by the double standard which permits him to present for our approval the lying, cheating and promise-breaking by which the hero and his patrons attain their objectives while condemning these very activities in the villains. Admittedly such doings are the very stuff of intrigue comedy, but as employed by Middleton (or even Jonson), they are not used in an attempt to endorse one group of participants at the expense of others. This is quite blatantly Massinger's aim, though his uncertainty as to how far his aristocratic idealizations conform to social reality can be seen in an occasional stridency. (There is a sombre but fairly representative irony in the aristocratically minded gentleman-dramatist Massinger writing a begging letter from prison to the hard-nosed theatrical entrepreneur Philip Henslowe and calling him 'ever. . .a true loving friend to me'.) Predictably Overreach ends up without his fortunes and with his hopeful plans for his daughter's marriage shattered (with the active connivance of the daughter herself). The double calamity drives him out of his wits, but in his mad ravings he has his revenge, if not on the other characters at least on the dramatist who tried to confine him in the straitjacket of moral condemnation. For Overreach is undoubtedly the most powerful dramatic creation in the play and his dreams of power, both mad and sane, have something of the sweep of a Volpone or a Mammon with a ferocious intensity all his own:

She must part with
That humble title, and write Honourable,
Right Honourable, Marrall, my Right Honourable daughter,
If all I have, or e'er shall get, will do it.
I will have her well attended; there are ladies
Of errant knights decay'd and brought so low
That for cast clothes and meat will gladly serve her,
And 'tis my glory, though I come from the city,
To have their issue whom I have undone,
To kneel to mine as bondslaves. . . .
And therefore, I'll not have a chambermaid
That ties her shoes, or any meaner office,
But such whose fathers were Right Worshipful.
'Tis a rich man's pride.

The undistinguished but forceful blank verse which is the staple of Massinger's dramatic style rises in Overreach's final manic fury to something which has distant echoes of both Lear and Faustus, and nearer echoes of Richard III perhaps:

> No, I'll through the battalia, and, that routed, (*Flourishing his sword*)
> I'll fall to execution — ha! I am feeble:
> Some undone widow sits upon mine arm,
> And takes away the use of 't; and my sword,
> Glued to my scabbard with wrong'd orphan's tears,
> Will not be drawn. Ha! what are these? Sure, hangmen
> That come to bind my hands, and then to drag me
> Before the judgment seat; now they are new shapes,
> And do appear like Furies, with steel whips
> To scourge my ulcerous soul. Shall I then fall
> Ingloriously, and yield? No; spite of Fate,
> I will be forc'd to hell like to myself —
> Though you were legions of accursed spirits,
> Thus would I fly among you!

It is not surprising that the Romantic critics found so much to praise in Massinger's creation and that Edmund Kean, the greatest of English romantic actors, should have scored an outstanding triumph in the role of Giles Overreach. Apart from a brief eclipse during the Restoration period *A New Way to Pay Old Debts* has had an almost continuous record of successful stage presentation up to our own time. If it looks back to Jonsonian comedy of judgment and beyond that to the simplicities of morality drama, it looks forward to the cruder simplicities of late eighteenth—and early nineteenth-century melodrama with its irredeemable villains, irrepressible heroes and irreproachable heroines. It ends with wedding bells and the feast that typifies the comedy of celebration; but we hear too, the discordant ravings of the villain condemned to madness.

Edmund Kean also had a tremendous success in the leading role in Massinger's other powerful comedy *The City Madam,* which Kean revived in 1817 under the title of *Riches.* As the title hints, Massinger's target is the bourgeois women who aspire to a style of life beyond their social station. Once again the dramatist has moved his characters slightly higher up the social scale relative to his model, *Eastward Ho.* Luke Frugal, the avaricious and hypocritical central figure, is immensely wealthy and an overreacher cast in Sir Giles's mould. The play not only shows his Machiavellian schemes to acquire permanent possession of his brother's wealth utterly routed, but contrives, through him, to strip bare the ragged folly of the women's snobbish pretensions. The familiar combination of closely observed details of social life combined with a highly melodramatic plot are present once more and the play survives through the perennial fascination on the stage of the biter-bit theme rather than by the conservative social morality which Massinger relentlessly hammers home to the last line:

> . . .instruct
> Our city dames, whom wealth makes proud, to move
> In their own spheres; and willingly to confess,
> In their habits, manners, and their highest port,
> A distance 'twixt the city and the court.

Beaumont and Fletcher

Before long, the distance Massinger advocated was to be that between opposing armies. Though his idealization of the landed gentry and his emphasis on the need to preserve traditional social distinctions appealed to the more elitist audiences of the 1620s and 1630s, Massinger certainly did not flatter the court or the courtly circle as such. (Indeed in many plays, such as *The Bondman,* he attacked Court favouritism and intrigue and a passage in one of his lost plays was marked by Charles I himself with the comment 'This is too insolent and to be changed'.) The young gallants would doubtless have applauded the sympathetic portrayal of the wastrel-hero in *A New Way,* but Massinger's indulgence towards him is tempered with a conviction, however desperately held, of moral values not entirely embodied in him. The task of indiscriminately flattering the courtly or would-be courtly audience was far more effectively performed by the comedies, tragi-comedies and tragedies of Francis Beaumont and John Fletcher. Though the two are invariably mentioned together, their partnership lasted for only five years (1608-1613) after which Fletcher continued to write plays for more than ten years until his death (probably of the plague) in 1625, collaborating with, among others, Massinger himself and his older contemporary, William Shakespeare. Fifty-odd plays are attributed to the Beaumont and Fletcher canon, though the only one that has survived on the modern stage is the work of Beaumont alone, *The Knight of the Burning Pestle.* It is not typical of the kind of play associated with the pair, and it was a dismal failure when first produced in 1608. Before taking a closer look at it, it is relevant to note that both Beaumont and Fletcher came from a social rank some-what higher than that which produced the majority of Elizabethan and Jacobean dramatists. Beaumont came from an ancient Leicestershire family and was connected on his mother's side to the nobility, while Fletcher's father was Lord High Almoner (chaplain) to Queen Elizabeth and Bishop of London. Appropriately enough, the last dramatic entertainment written by Beaumont, after he had married a Kentish heiress and retired from writing for the professional theatre, was a lavish masque presented by members of the Inner Temple and Gray's Inn in February 1613, in honour of the marriage of James's daughter the princess Elizabeth to Federick, the Elector Palatine. It has all the extravagance, wildly implausible turns of story and character and display of theatrical gimmickry which mark the tragedies and tragi-comedies of Beaumont and Fletcher. The most significant thing about these is that they far surpassed Jonson and Shakespeare in popularity on the Jacobean and Caroline stage.

The *Knight of the Burning Pestle* was written by Beaumont for performance by a children's company just before he began his five-year partnership with Fletcher. It is the first full-length burlesque play in English, but it is a burlesque which has succeeded in preserving its theatrical life long after the things it burlesques have been forgotten. It parodies both the ranting rhetoric of *The Spanish Tragedy* and the ludicrous fantasizing of plays with London tradesmen as heroes of romance and high adventure, typified by such efforts as Thomas Heywood's *The Four Prentices of London.* Beaumont makes brilliant use of the play-within-the-play convention when the actors at Blackfriars are interrupted in their performance of

'The London Merchant', a parody of middle-class comedy in which the apprentice falls in love with his master's daughter, by a grocer who demands that the players 'present something notably in honour of the commons of the city' instead of one that 'still girds at citizens'. He is joined by his wife and they insist on interpolating into 'the London Merchant' their own play 'The Knight of the Burning Pestle' (grocers used pestles to pound their spices). The hero of the latter is their apprentice Rafe, who features in a series of satisfyingly impossible deeds inspired, like Don Quixote, by the romantic tales of knights and damsels he has read or heard of. (Beaumont's play appeared a year before the first part of *Don Quixote* but there are obvious affinities and he may have seen the English translation, published in 1612, in manuscript.) Beaumont goes beyond Peele in *The Old Wives' Tale* in making the grocer and his wife not merely observers framing the action but a chorus that occupies the stage (a custom much favoured by gallants and much deplored by dramatists — see the prologue to Jonson's *The Devil is an Ass* or Chapter Six of Dekker's *Gull's Hornbook*) and gives a running commentary on both plays. Thus there are at least three levels of theatrical illusion which come into changing relationship with each other, as when the couple help Rafe with money to pay his bill at the inn. The aristocratic author pokes fun not only at plays which glorified the citizenry but also at those which treated the prodigal-son theme in a didactic fashion (he has a prodigal father instead, cheerfully unrepentant and unscathed to the end), and at the middle-class taste for sentimental chivalric romance. But *The Knight of the Burning Pestle* owes more than Beaumont would perhaps have acknowledged to the earlier citizen drama it affectionately derides. The ebullience of old Merrythought, for instance, does not so much parody as echo that of Dekker's Simon Eyre —

> Yet, I thank God, I break not a wrinkle more than I had. Not a stoop, boys? Care, live with cats: I defy thee! My heart is as sound as an oak; and though I want drink to wet my whistle, I can sing,

— while the love tests which Jasper imposes on Luce are far more acceptable within a farcical context than when similar incidents are offered 'seriously' in the tragi-comedies of (chiefly) Fletcher. When *The Knight of the Burning Pestle* was revived at the Cockpit Theatre in Drury Lane in 1653 before an audience which had become narrower in social range and more sophisticated in taste, it proved a resounding success.

The decisive impact of Beaumont and Fletcher on the drama came through their tragedies and tragi-comedies which will be discussed in the next chapter. However, Fletcher's comedies of manners were also very popular with the audiences at the private theatres, and of these *The Wild Goose Chase* is as good an example as any. The theme of the wild gallant trapped into matrimony by the witty, resolute, unimpeachably and improbably virtuous heroine was to become deadeningly familiar in Restoration comedy; before Fletcher has finished with it here, he has a wooing scene between the disguised heroine and her brother as well as one in which she assumes madness. But for all its extravagance there is more dramatic life in the sex war Fletcher depicts in *The Wild Goose Chase* than in many of the tragi-comedies. In comparison to the rakes of Restoration comedy, something like innocence clings to the nonchalant amorality of the hero, for the expression of which Fletcher's sprightly verse, monotonous at length, is an admirable vehicle:

Only the wenches are not for my diet;
They are too lean and thin, their embraces brawn fallen.
Give me the plump Venetian, fat, and lusty,
That meets me soft and supple; smiles upon me,
As if a cup of full wine leap'd to kiss me;
These slight things I affect not.

Though Fletcher did nothing in the comedy of manners that the best of his Restoration successors did not do better, George Farquhar did not improve *The Wild Goose Chase* when he adapted it eighty years later as *The Inconstant.*

Brome, Shirley and the end of an era

The tradition of Jonsonian comedy survived in a pale and ghostly form in the comedies of Richard Brome, who was once Jonson's servant and later his disciple. Brome's first success, *The Lovesick Maids* was performed by the King's Men in 1629, shortly after one of Jonson's own plays had failed on the stage. His last play, *The Jovial Crew* was acted in 1641, the year before the Puritans closed the theatres. It is certainly a compliment to Brome to link him with Jonson, since he has very little of the earlier dramatist's sharp eye for human aberration and less of his linguistic gusto. Most of his surviving plays are comedies of intrigue where complexity of plot becomes almost an end in itself. Nevertheless there is enough ingenuity and delighted rendering of low life in *The Jovial Crew* to remind us of the Jonson of *Bartholomew Fair*, if not of the more savagely satirical comedies.

John Fletcher died of the plague in 1625, the same year as James I. The most considerable comic dramatist of the Caroline period (if we leave out Massinger, who is more Jacobean in temper, although *The City Madam* was written in the early 1630s) is James Shirley. An undergraduate at Oxford and Cambridge, Shirley turned to playwriting in the year of Fletcher's death, having resigned his living and the headship of a grammar school in St Albans on his conversion to Roman Catholicism. By this time there was a considerable body of English drama in print so that new dramatists, mainly university or Inns of Court men, were beginning to show the literary influence of earlier ones more obviously than before. The great folio edition of Jonson's works had been published in 1616, that of Shakespeare in 1623 and Shirley himself edited the works of Beaumont and Fletcher.

Like most of his educated contemporaries, Shirley admired Beaumont and Fletcher more than any other dramatist. In his Address to the Reader in the 1647 edition of their works, he describes their plays as 'the greatest monument of the scene that time and humanity have produced'. He imitated them, both in turgid tragedies such as *The Politician* and the simpler and more powerful *The Cardinal,* and in comedies of manners such as *The Lady of Pleasure* and *Hyde Park*. As the theatre became increasingly Court-oriented, the comedy of manners became increasingly popular. With its emphasis on class distinctions as manifested in styles of speech and dress and in the externals of social behaviour, and its assumption of the natural superiority of the courtly wit and his circle, it was to form the basis for comedy when the theatre reopened at the Restoration. Shirley, following his idols, especially Fletcher, was one of the forerunners of this type of comedy. But in *The Lady of Pleasure* there is still a trace of Jonsonian seriousness in the moral standards applied to the sexual hedonism of the central character, Aretina. Her foolishness and irresponsibility in being eager to sacrifice her husband Bornwell's fortune in order to pursue the trivial pleasures of London high society are firmly, if not entirely convincingly, condemned explicitly and by implication in her final resolve to devote herself to virtue and frugality. The emptiness and wastefulness of the fashionable circle around her are depicted for what they are, and the apparent sexual intrigue between Bornwell and the young widow Celestina takes its part in the play's moral design, rather than being present for the sake of titillation. The very shallowness of the self-elected sophisticates is a compliment to the courtly audience who, being the genuine article, would be expected to see through and laugh at the spurious imitation. Quite apart from his religion, which would have endeared him to Charles I's Catholic queen anyway, it is not surprising to find that Shirley was immensely popular at the court itself. One of his plays was performed in honour of the king's birthday and there is a contemporary statement that the king himself suggested the plot for another.

While *The Lady of Pleasure* harks back in some respects to Jonsonian comedy, *Hyde Park* is very much a play which anticipates Restoration comedy, not so much by the staple of its intrigue as by its fascination with the social foibles of various classes. The occasion of the play was the opening of Hyde Park to the public by its owner Lord Holland. The plot, such as it is, deals with the wooing of three couples drawn from various strata of society and many characters such as the decayed aristocrat and the talkative wife of the city merchant were to reappear in Restoration comedy. Though the Restoration assumption that the country was a limbo of barbarism and boredom had already made its appearance in the drama, Shirley has a sympathetic feeling for the freshness of country life, reminding us incidentally that, from our standpoint, London was still very close to the country. But the nightingale and the cuckoo we hear in Hyde Park, and the milkmaid who comes in with syllabub, take their place along with the horse races which the stage action also calls for.

Shirley died in 1666, 'overcome with affrightments, disconsolations and other miseries' suffered in the Great Fire of London according to a contemporary. Another dramatist, ten years younger, had already had no less than fifteen plays produced by the time the theatres were closed. Strict chronology therefore, demands that he too should be mentioned here. Judged on his dramatic writings alone, William Davenant is a decidedly minor figure. In the development of the English theatre, however, he has an important place, though one that is best considered in relation to the beginning of the new theatre than the end of the old one.

5

Jacobean and Caroline Tragedy

It has been suggested that in the work of the pioneer tragic dramatists of the Elizabethan theatre, Marlowe and Kyd, the major themes and preoccupations of Jacobean tragedy are already present. This is broadly true, though the atmosphere of brooding evil and melancholy which pervades the later tragedy is quite distinctive.

The terms 'Elizabethan' and 'Jacobean' are slightly misleading in this connection, as in some others, since changes in theatrical style and temper do not always obligingly coincide with the accession of monarchs. As we have seen, what we usually call 'Elizabethan drama' is the drama produced some twenty-five years after Elizabeth came to the throne. Similarly, her reign still had two years to run when that most brooding, melancholy and 'Jacobean' of tragic heroes, Hamlet, first walked the battlements of Elsinore. Plays such as *Troilus and Cressida* and Marston's *Antonio's Revenge,* where the note of cynical disillusionment commonly associated with the epithet 'Jacobean' is clearly heard, had already been performed before the century closed. The darker mood of the drama belongs, therefore, to the later 1590s.

It remains true that there was a marked development of tragedy in the reign of James I. Chapman turned from writing ponderous comedies to powerful tragedies in the first years of the new reign, and the great tragedies of Webster, Tourneur and Middleton, as well as most of Shakespeare's, were written in the first two decades of the seventeenth century. Thus, while Elizabethan drama is dominated by comedy, with the gigantic exception of Marlowe and of Kyd's single play, tragedy comes into its own in the Jacobean period; so much so that, as already noted, comedy itself is tinged with it. Indeed the fusion of the two kinds, rather than the mere presence of comic scenes in tragic plots, as in *Dr Faustus,* is one of the hallmarks of Jacobean drama.

The great tragedies of the period are distinctive and very different in their scope and effects, as we shall see shortly when we take a closer look at some of them. Nevertheless it is possible to speak of a Jacobean tragic temper in general, if perhaps occasionally superficial terms. It is clear, for instance, that the destructive and self-destructive potentialities of the amoral Machiavellian character preoccupy the Jacobean dramatist rather more than they did Marlowe or Kyd. The tragedies of the period also have a much greater sense of corruption in high places and of the morally poisonous effects of wealth and power. Both these features are doubtless connected with the disappearance of the 'Elizabethan consensus' and the growing alienation of the court from the nation as a whole. James's penchant for creating instant noblemen (he elevated forty on one memorable day) also played its part in thrusting into the consciousness of playwrights and playgoers questions about the connection between honour and nobility. The laxity of sexual morals at James's court as compared to that of Elizabeth may account in part for the increased emphasis on the traditional theme of lust's corrosive power. The growing influence of the more sophisticated private-theatre audiences led to an increasing emphasis on satirical and sometimes cynical wit which undercut tragic grandeur in the very act of presenting it. Finally, the note of doubt and despair first sounded by Kyd and Marlowe becomes increasingly louder and more insistent during the Jacobean decades. It takes its particular colouring from the 'melancholy' which is so marked a feature of literature in the early seventeenth century.

In 1621, towards the end of James I's reign, Robert Burton published his vast and vastly eccentric treatise, the *Anatomy of Melancholy*. In it he undertook to classify and describe the varieties of melancholy, their causes, symptoms and remedies. Burton's work is not merely a medical treatise, though it has been called the finest medical work written by a layman. It is also a compendium of psychology, social observation, anecdotage and much else. It is the best known of many works of the period which bear witness to contemporaneous interest in this peculiarly 'Jacobean' malady. Many things came within the scope of melancholy as the age understood it, from an obsessive preoccupation with death and the futility of human endeavour to mere fashionable pessimism or cynicism. As the latter it could take many different forms according to social position or profession, as Jaques tells us in *As You Like It* (c.1599)

> ...the scholar's melancholy, which is emulation [professional rivalry], ...the musician's, which is fantastical [artistic]. . .the courtier's, which is ambitious,. . .the lawyer's, which is politic [calculating]. . .the lady's which is nice [affectedly refined]. . .the lover's which is all these. . .

Many factors contributed to the prevalence of this temper. Though it is possible that to some small extent it was a specifically literary phenomenon, it was not merely that. The new interest in individual psychology naturally led to an interest in abnormal states, of which the various forms of melancholy were easily identifiable instances. The increased possibilities of material life which resulted from the opening up of new trade routes bringing in new commodities made the fact of death, especially in the devastating and unpredictable form of endemic plague, more appalling to contemplate. There was a growing tendency to justify and evaluate life in purely secular terms, or at any rate to take such evaluation very seriously. Death became not so much the threshold of the only Reality, as it was in the medieval view, but the termination of reality. What was involved here was not necessarily a change of belief as a change of emphasis in the way men felt about life and death. The rapid spread of venereal disease at about this time may also have contributed to the preoccupation with mortality and corruption.

Social and educational developments also fostered the growth of Jacobean melancholy. The expansion of education in the later sixteenth century had created an educated class only a very few of whom could obtain lucrative employment such as a rich church living, a sinecure at court or a profitable legal practice. The rest, and they were the swarming majority, had to claw what livelihood they could out of school-mastering or private-tutoring, or become professional writers or live by their wits. The distinction between the last two categories was by no means clear. Rich patrons of literary men were rapidly declining in numbers as the landed aristocracy from which such patrons came were themselves encountering the economic effects of galloping inflation. Indeed, inflation itself must have had its share in creating a sense of goals forever out of reach, of a world where appearance never seemed to materialize into the desired reality. It is not surprising therefore that the sense of unrecognized or unrewarded ability should deepen into a melancholy temper informing the work of many writers or sometimes express itself through a single 'melancholy' figure to whom the dramatist seems much closer than he is to his other characters; such a character, we often feel, could have written most of the drama in which he appears.

Marston and Satirical Tragedy

Our survey of individual plays may begin with two by Marston, *Antonio and Mellida* (*c.* 1599) and *Antonio's Revenge* (*c.* 1600). The second was meant to be a sequel to the first, but the differences in atmosphere and outlook between the two give an indication of the direction in which tragedy was to develop. *Antonio and Mellida* owes a great deal to *The Spanish Tragedy* (and, like Kyd's play, to Seneca) especially in the character of the father, Andrugio. In its two-part structure it recalls Marlowe's *Tamburlaine*. But Marston has no occasion to recapture Marlowe's vision of heroic energy nor has he Kyd's interest in the individual tragic predicament. It is the reality of villainy and corruption in the Italian court which engages Marston's dramatic attention. The association of Italy with corrupt statecraft, lust and poisonous intrigue which persists throughout Jacobean tragedy can be credited to Marston, though it has been pointed out that the Italy of the English tragedians is not that of the seventeenth century, Baroque and Spanish-dominated, but the earlier one of the Sforza and the Medici which was derived from historians like Guicciardini. The choice of 'Italy' was deliberate and made partly for the sake of greater outspokenness in the analysis of power politics (though it was not always guaranteed to prevent trouble with the censorship), and partly as a theatrical equivalent for a climate of attitude and opinion rather than as a realistic portrayal of an actual country. A further distancing effect is gained through the Induction, when a group of actors engage in a satirical discussion of the characters they are about to play; the fact that the actors themselves were children (the play was written for the Children of St Paul's) would have given a further 'perspective' of the action.

The central plot is concerned with an improbable version of the Romeo and Juliet story and an associated revenge intrigue. But, as has been suggested, neither represents Marston's real dramatic interest. Both are accommodations of established theatrical taste. Apart from the dark speculations on wickedness among the great which occasionally almost reach tragic intensity, there is also in the play a more scornful view of court flattery and the moral emptiness of its way of life. This is embodied chiefly in the character of Feliche, who lashes sycophancy and affectation in a manner which recalls the Marston of the verse satires. But the 'comical satire' is not particularly well integrated with the rest. *Antonio and Mellida* remains a broken-backed play. In spite of powerful satirical passages, it is neither tragedy nor satire nor yet satirical tragedy.

With *Antonio's Revenge,* Marston achieves a greater unity of tone. In bald summary, the action of the play is as ludicrous as that of any opera, a form with which it shares many features. So extravagant is some of the plotting that it has been suggested that the play is intended as a parody of earlier revenge plays, in which case its interest for us today would be purely antiquarian. I think it has more to offer than this, though particular moments, especially as portrayed by child actors, may well have had a parodic purpose intended for sophisticated theatre-goers. Some of the play's language seems straightforwardly naturalistic, some deliberate parody while some aspires to the note of serious tragedy. The induction suggests that the child actors performed in correspondingly different acting styles ranging form the natural to the stylized.

Antonio and Mellida had ended with the tyrant Duke Piero apparently reconciled to the marriage of Andrugio's son to his daughter Mellida. The later play opens with the murder of Andrugio secretly contrived by Piero and features the dead man's ghost rising to clamour for vengeance from his son and to warn his widow against marrying his murderer (more than once we are reminded of *Hamlet* though which came first is still a matter of scholarly dispute). Antonio duly kills the villanous Duke after he has been tortured and also his little son. Mellida, the Duke's daughter dies on hearing a false rumour of her lover Antonio's death, whereupon the latter retires to a life of solitary contemplation attended by a heavenly choir.

In its stagecraft *Antonio's Revenge* constitutes a little anthology of contemporary theatrical devices and conventions. It was originally presented in the small indoor theatre of St Paul's, seating perhaps a hundred spectators, but having on stage the usual two entrance doors, a 'discovery space' between them at ground level, another on the upper level flanked by two side balconies with casement windows, as well as a trap door in the main stage floor. All these areas and resources are used in the play, notably in the last two scenes, where the ghost of Andrugio appears in the central balcony, presiding over the scene on the lower stage where his victim is about to die, tongueless and therefore unable to cry for help, while musicians on the side balconies provide grim funereal music. In addition to tongueless victims and gloating ghosts, *Antonio's Revenge* also makes use of such well tried devices of the Elizabethan stage as yawning graves, bleeding bodies, severed limbs and dumb shows of funeral processions and the like. Its frequent and deliberate echoes of Shakespeare (especially *Richard III*) and other current plays reminds us that it is addressed to an audience of experienced theatregoers who would take the dramatic point of the allusions.

All this may tend to confirm the view that *Antonio's Revenge* is a shapeless hodge-podge of implausible events decked out in borrowed theatrical odds and ends. Marston's determination to make every line count, coupled with the nearest thing to a tin ear among any of the important dramatists of the time, often makes his language sound turgid and bombastic — though we must always remember that linguistic 'realism' was not the aim of tragic verse. He is also fond of coining new words or new uses of existing words. One wishes, when reading Marston, for less ore and more unloaded rifts. Antonio's account of his dream is a fair sample of Marston in full cry:

Three parts of night were swallowed in the gulf
Of ravenous time when to my slumbering powers
Two meagre ghosts made apparition.
The one's breast seemed fresh-paunched with bleeding wounds
Whose bubbling gore sprang in frighted eyes:
The other ghost assumed my father's shape;
Both cried 'Revenge!' At which my trembling joints
(Iced quite over with a frozed cold sweat)
Leaped forth the sheets. Three times I grasped at shades,
And thrice, deluded by erroneous sense,
I forced my thoughts make stand; when lo, I oped
A large bay window, through which the night
Struck terror to my soul.

But the play acts better than it reads, though few modern audiences have had a chance to decide at first hand on this point. The extravagant rhetoric must have sounded with a quite bizarre effect coming from the mouths of the 'little eyases'. Marston makes good use of the contrast between visual and rhetorical effects, as when the dance which Mellida is involved in with her rejected suitors immediately after she hears of Antonio's alleged drowning contrasts ironically with her state of mind and with her father's approval of the suitors. Music too is used to enforce ironies or make a dramatic point not explicitly made by the language. In spite of the gory action which proceeds almost non-stop from the opening stage direction — '*Enter Piero unbraced, his arms bare, smeared in blood, a poniard in one hand, bloody, and a torch in the other, Strotzo following him with a cord*' — the music at the close, with its indication of a choral conclusion based on the words 'Mellida is dead' suggests that compassion for human grief rather than fulfilled revenge is the ultimate objective. The final impression left by the play in spite of absurdities and exaggerations (which loom larger in reading than in performance) is that of a bitter recognition of wickedness in the mighty as an abiding fact of life and an affirmation of the inescapable Christian duty to survive, however removedly, in this corrupt world. In Pandulpho's words as he offers the senate's thanks for the removal of the tyrant:

We know the world, and did we know no more
We would not live to know; but since constraint
Of holy bands forceth us keep this lodge
Of dirt's corruption till dread power calls
Our soul's appearance, we will live enclosed
In holy verge of some religious order
Most constant votaries.

The moral focus of the play may be somewhat blurred, and the self-deprecating tone of Marston's ironic dedication of the printed version to 'the most honourably renowned Nobody' makes it hard to gauge the seriousness of his intention. But its despairing acknowledgement of human corruption occasionally touches the dominant chord of Jacobean tragedy, as in these lines spoken, ironically (why?) by the tyrant Piero:

> There glow no sparks of reason in the world,
> All are raked up in ashy beastliness;
> The bulk of man's as dark as Erebus,
> No branch of reason's light hangs in his trunk;
> There lives no reason to keep league withal.

It was a chord to be sounded with greater intensity, power and seriousness by Marston's immediate successors.

Honour and Politics in Chapman's Tragedy

George Chapman is closest in spirit to the earlier heroic age of Elizabethan drama. This is a slightly misleading way of putting it, for chronologically speaking, Chapman's dramatic career belongs in part to that early age. In 1598 Francis Meres praised him as among 'our best for tragedy' which implies that by that time he was a tragic dramatist of stature and reputation. But none of Chapman's tragedies from this period have survived. His reputation as a comic dramatist was also established before the end of the century. *The Blind Beggar of Alexandria* was a great success when the Admiral's Men performed it at the Rose in 1596 and another great success, *A Humorous Day's Mirth* (1597) introduced the 'comedy of humours' on the English stage.

Today neither Chapman's comedies nor the later tragedies which have survived are part of the modern repertory. Chapman is remembered, if at all, as the translator of Homer (the 'realms of gold' of Keats's famous sonnet), as the poet who concluded Marlowe's unfinished erotic poem *Hero and Leander* in a notably un-Marlovian manner, and as a shadowy contender for the role of Rival Poet in Shakespeare's sonnets. The bulk of his extant tragic achievement is represented by a group of five tragedies on political events in contemporary France and belongs to the opening years of the seventeenth century. At least one of them deserves resurrection on the modern stage.

All Chapman's tragedies are concerned with one broad theme, the relation between the individual as political subject and his sovereign. Put in these terms, the plays may sound as if they are only of historical interest, related to a critical phase of royal absolutism. But Chapman conceived of his theme in terms much wider than those we usually understand by the word 'political'. It is in *Bussy d'Ambois* (c. 1604) that the theme finds its most powerful tragic expression, and it is significant that it is the only one of his surviving tragedies to have been successful on the stage. In his non-dramatic poetry Chapman cultivated a deliberately arcane and esoteric manner, consciously writing for a chosen few. Writing for the stage he was compelled, in the nature of things, to modify this attitude, if not to abandon it altogether. In comedy, he seems to have had no scruples about giving the public exactly what they wanted in the way of farce and ribaldry; in tragedy he seems to have been a shade more classically fastidious. Though *Bussy d'Ambois* does avail itself of some standard Elizabethan theatrical gimmickry — trapdoors, secret passages, conjuring of spirits, torture, ghosts and so on — it is fairly mild compared to the magic tableaux and severed hands of Webster or the bleeding heads and blazing stars of Tourneur. A brief glance at the other four tragedies in the group will serve as a setting for a closer look at *Bussy d'Ambois*.

Bussy is the earliest of the surviving tragedies. It is separated by seven years from its sequel, *The Revenge of Bussy d'Ambois*. While *The Revenge* is perhaps deservedly neglected on stage (it contains a succession of interminable philosophical disquisitions by major and minor characters alike), it is worth mentioning as a significant variant of the Revenge convention. Chapman's hero Clermont (a character *not* based on any known historical personage) is too humane and thoughtful to rush unquestioningly into acceptance of the barbaric code of revenge imposed on him. He accepts the duty of avenging his brother's death soberly, without allowing it to derange his wits by becoming obsessed with it. Of the two people against whom he must exact revenge, he forgives one even as he kills him in a duel, and cannot bring himself to take revenge on the other because he owes him allegiance as a patron. When he learns of the death of this second 'enemy' through the machinations of the king himself, he commits suicide in preference to continued existence in a world where the fount of secular authority is thus polluted. The suicide is, as one might expect from Chapman the classicist deeply influenced by Stoic philosophy, presented as a noble act in 'the high Roman fashion' rather than as a grievous sin in Christian terms.

Between the two plays dealing with the life and death of Bussy, Chapman wrote a two-part play dealing with another figure in contemporary French politics, *The Conspiracy and Tragedy of Charles, Duke of Biron.* (1607-08) The Duke of Biron, companion at arms of Henry of Navarre and later executed for treason on Henry's orders, was one of the best known members of the French nobility in England and the similarity between his fate and that of Essex did not go unnoticed. Chapman was enough of a political realist to see that in the struggle between the aspiring subject and the absolute sovereign, the destruction of the former was inevitable, but his treatment of it has more the air of a treatise than a dramatic conflict, though this did not prevent Chapman getting into trouble with the authorities over it. The French Ambassador protested and the play was taken off, the actors jailed and Chapman took cover to avoid imprisonment himself. When it was finally printed in 1608 it was in a severely mutilated version. Its political notoriety apart, the play never really comes alive, in spite of occasional passages of sombre dignity.

The last of Chapman's French tragedies was *Chabot, Admiral of France,* written about 1611 but not published till 1639, five years after Chapman's death. Here, though the theme is once again the conflict between subject and king, the balance of sympathy is very much with the former and the king is shown as an unjust tyrant who eventually comes to repent his folly in wilfully ridding himself of such a loyal and virtuous subject. Perhaps Chapman, like many other thinking men of the time, saw the direction in which the English monarchy was moving and tried to raise a warning signal before it was too late.

It is in *Bussy d'Ambois* that Chapman's dramatic imagination is fully engaged with his theme. To Chapman, as to all the Jacobean dramatists, the court is a centre of corruption and intrigue and his hero Bussy is first presented as a poor man (which the historical Bussy was not) who has turned his back on it with stoic fortitude and contempt for worldly success. There is a hint of the Morality tradition of emblematic stage presentation in the stage direction *'Enter Bussy, poor'* which introduces the hero's opening soliloquy:

Fortune, not Reason, rules the state of things;
Reward goes backward, Honour on his head;
Who is not poor, is monstrous; only need
Gives form and worth to every human seed.

This affirmation of a necessary connection between virtue and poverty is one of the propositions which the drama sets out to test. We note first that the affirmation springs from a spirit which is anything but poor in the vehemence of its initial resolution to square itself up against the world and its gigantic confidence in the ability to do so. In true Stoic fashion Bussy continues:

Man is a torch borne in the wind; a dream
But of a shadow, summ'd with all his substance.

But the end of the soliloquy already qualifies this view of the insubstantiality of human concerns. Bussy uses the metaphor of the virtuous man as a tall ship glad of the assistance of a poor fishing boat (virtue) in negotiating the treacherous waters of state:

We must to virtue for her guide resort
Or we shall shipwreck in our safest port.

This implies not so much turning one's back on the political world as the necessity of virtue in one's dealings with it and the assurance that virtue will be sufficient protection.

As the play proceeds we realize how naive is the Stoic's belief in the omnipotence of virtue and how misplaced his confidence in his capacity to survive untainted in the foul waters of court amours and political intrigue. But it is not a total antithesis between innate virtue in the hero and irredeemable corruption in society that we are faced with. The seeds of decay are already within the hero, though unbeknown to him. The tragic action of the play arises from a tension between virtue in the sense of an ethical code or set of principles and *virtù*, the Renaissance conception of self-fulfilment. It is in this latter sense that Bussy impresses us as a dramatic character. He is conceived in the mould of the Marlovian superman and his Herculean energy, while never quite finding its verbal equivalent in 'Marlowe's mighty line', has full scope when he is embroiled in the amours and intrigues of the court. Chapman's direct source of inspiration for the play was Seneca's *Hercules Oetaeus* and there are many specific allusions to the Herculean role of Bussy. He needs very little urging by the politic Monsieur to serve the latter's faction at court. Almost immediately he engages in a duel in which three men are killed and only Bussy survives and in an affair with Tamyra, the wife of the influential courtier Montsurry. Indeed, Bussy hurls himself into court affairs, public and private, with all the mechanical momentum of a robot programmed for self-destruction, deliberately antagonizing the powerful Guise. There is a deep irony in Henry's praise of Bussy, as earlier we are given an idealized cameo of the court of Elizabeth by Henry himself, so that the violated norm is vividly present:

> . . .as courts should be, the abstracts of their kingdoms,
> In all the beauty, state, and worth they hold;
> So is hers, amply, and by her informed.
> The world is not contracted in a man
> With more proportion and expression
> Than in her court, her kingdom.

In 1604, this could only have been a nostalgic and idealized memory, but it has enough life in it in Chapman's play to underline the contrast with the actual court milieu presented; as the king himself improbably says:

> Our French court
> Is a mere mirror of confusion to it:
> The king and subject, lord and every slave,
> Dance a continual hay; our rooms of state
> Kept like our stables; no place more observed
> Than a rude market-place.

Bussy's success in such a world is an index of his moral decline. But it is also, with irreducible ambiguity, a sign of his greatness of soul, his virtù. His other writings show that Chapman embraced the usual Renaissance Neo-Platonist view of the three-fold division of mind, soul and body, with the soul as intermediary, able to elevate the human being through mind or degrade him through enslavement to bodily desires. But the tragedy is not so rigidly schematic as this. The contradiction between virtue and virtù can be reconciled only in death, in the manner of Bussy's dying. Though warned by the ghost of the friar who in life acted as go-between for them that his affair with Tamyra has been discovered and that the wrathful husband was planning his murder, Bussy grandly disregards the warning and goes to Tamyra's room where he is ambushed by his assailants. This suggests that it is not so much passion but lack of 'policy' or deviousness which brings about his downfall. Though he defeats Montsurry in single combat — another courtly skill at which he excels — he is shot in the back and dies magnanimously forgiving his murderers. Even in death it is the Stoic greatness, rather than Christian resignation or hope which animates Bussy:

> I'll not complain to earth yet, but to heaven,
> And, like a man, look upwards even in death.

He 'look(s) upwards' not to heaven's eternal justice but to his own apotheosis, which is duly commemorated by the ghost of the friar in the last lines of the play:

> Farewell, brave relics of a complete man;
> Look up and see thy spirit made a star;

Join flames with Hercules, and when thou settest
Thy radiant forehead in the firmament,
Make the vast continent, cracked with thy receipt,
Spread to a world of fire, and th'aged sky
Cheer with new sparks of old humanity.

Behind each of Chapman's political heroes — and they, especially Bussy, give the plays most of their dramatic power — we have a tragic awareness of the necessity and the impossibility of combining the active and the contemplative life, of virtù and virtue. We see a Renaissance ideal exalted with associations from classical patterns of heroism hurtling almost wilfully towards its choosen doom. The images that stay in the mind are those of a flame burning itself out and the restless energy of the ocean, metaphors which Chapman frequently uses, and above all that of the falling star. Bussy's last words sound like an epitaph to all those 'aspiring minds' of whom Essex was the most celebrated and whose company included such figures as Marlowe and Raleigh who burnt themselves out in their ceaseless desire to 'look upward':

like a falling star
Silently glanc'd, that like a thunderbolt
Look'd to have struck and shook the firmament.

Tourneur and The Revenger's Tragedy

Where biographical details are concerned, Tourneur and Webster are two of the shadowiest among the Jacobean dramatists, although we do know a little more about Tourneur than about Webster. Tourneur was born in about 1575 and served as a soldier and courier in the Low Countries. In the early years of the seventeenth century he was working as a dramatist in London and in 1612 wrote an elegy on the death of Prince Henry. He was imprisoned briefly in 1617. In 1625 he accompanied Sir Edward Cecil on a disastrous expedition to Cadiz. Tourneur fell ill on the voyage and died at Kinsale in Ireland where he was put ashore.

Of the two plays associated with his name, Tourneur can be certainly credited only with the later and lesser one, *The Atheist's Tragedy*, published in 1611, with its title page announcing that it had 'in divers places often been acted'. It is one of the most schematic of Jacobean tragedies, written to illustrate, through a series of highly artificial episodes, the fate that overtakes the central character, the atheist D'Amville. D'Amville is committed to the view that a non-moral 'Nature' governs the world and that the quest for material gain for himself and his offspring, whom he considers an extension of himself and the only form of immortality available to men, is the only rational course to pursue. He does not hesitate to instigate murder to achieve his goal and attempts seduction purely for the sake of progeny. He lives to see his own son die without issue and just as he is about to bring down the axe on his victim's head, the axe slips and he brains himself, the staging of which episode must have given a few headaches to all concerned. Before his death D'Amville has just time to deliver himself of a speech in which he finally acknowledges the existence of divine justice, whose presence has never been seriously in question throughout, due to the unbearable sententiousness of most of the writing. D'Amville's final words are a sufficient sample:

But Nature is a fool. There is a power
Above her that hath overthrown the pride
Of all my projects and posterity,
For whose surviving blood
I had erected a proud monument,
And struck them dead before me: for whose deaths
I called to thee for judgment. Thou didst want
Discretion for the sentence. But yon power
That struck me knew the judgment I deserved
And gave it.

It is not merely the generally unresonant verse and the mechanicalness of much of the action — not the lack of lifelikeness, but the lack of dramatic life, the too palpable evidence of the dramatist *engineering* the action — which make *The Atheist's Tragedy* a disappointing play. The mechanical quality extends to the too symmetrical contrasts of character — the unbeliever D'Amville against the devout Christian Charlemont, the virtuous Castabella against the lustful Levidulcia and so on — and together with the general triteness of the writing makes *The Atheist's Tragedy* difficult to take seriously, though this has not of course prevented critics from trying.

It is far otherwise with *The Revenger's Tragedy* written some years earlier (1607). This is a much more satisfying play in spite of a tendency to bludgeon the audience with ironic asides (a tendency much more evident in the later play). Though there are certain structural similarities between the two plays, *The Revenger's Tragedy* is so much better that many believe it to be the work of another dramatist, perhaps Thomas Middleton.

As we have seen, Kyd first brought the drama of revenge on to the public stage with *The Spanish Tragedy,* and he found more than one treatment of the theme in the Latin tragedies of Seneca from which he drew inspiration. But the popularity of Kyd's play (it was revived with additions in the new century) as well as the numerous revenge plays of which it was the begetter (*Hamlet* being the greatest) showed that it had struck a responsive chord in the contemporary audience. I have already glanced at some of the reasons for this, but it is worth remarking on one or two others. At a time when lordships were being bought and sold the question of family honour was a touchy subject and any affront to it had to be speedily avenged. But since the law courts were congested with litigation and the law itself, as often, far behind the times, men of all classes found it more expedient to take matters into their own hands. There was also a wider political aspect to the theme of revenge (barely touched on in Kyd's play) which the study of history ancient and modern had made men aware of. This was the question of the rights and wrongs of revenge as a political act against tyrannical oppression. And finally, in a period when 'new philosophy calls all in doubt' thinking men were bound to speculate on the nature of divine vengeance and its relation to the human variety, in particular the precise moral and other implications of man being an instrument of God's revenge.

Official religious teaching was as clear and unambiguous as civil law, which forbade private vendettas. It affirmed that vengeance was the prerogative of divine providence alone — 'vengeance is mine; I will repay, saith the Lord.' But there was a powerful tradition of private revenge dating from a time when the power of the state to punish crime was neither clearly laid down nor effectual. As a result there was a tendency to regard the avenger with some sympathy, especially where the original offence had been an act of treachery, or not strictly an offence against the law, or not one that could be legally proved. This 'unofficial' sentiment of sympathy was particularly felt towards the avenger where the original crime involved murder. It is this last set of circumstances which revenge tragedy is mainly concerned with.

The Revenger's Tragedy deals with not one but a bewildering variety of revenges and counter-revenges. The first of these, and the one which provides a framework within which the others occur, is initiated in what is one of the most theatrically brilliant opening scenes in Jacobean tragedy. It shows Vindice, the revenger of the play, standing on the balcony with a skull in his hand, while on the stage below the principal personages of the court pass by in a torchlight procession. There was a long and familiar pictorial tradition in which a young man with a skull represented the necessity for youth to be mindful of death and judgment, heaven and hell, but Vindice's savage comments on each of the court figures as they pass and the story he tells makes it plain that this is no routine contemplation of the four last things:

> Duke, royal lecher! Go, grey-haired adultery,
> And thou his son, as impious steeped as he:
> And thou his bastard, true-begot in evil:
> And thou his duchess, that will do with Devil,
> Four ex'lent characters—

He then addresses the skull, which we learn is that of his dead mistress, poisoned by the old duke, 'the parched and juiceless luxur' because she refused to yield up her virginity to him. Thus at the very outset we have a powerful visual image of one of the basic contrarieties of the play — the stark, irreducible reality of the skull and the extravagant finery with which the rich and powerful attempt to hide that reality from themselves. The ensuing action tells of Vindice's revenge against the duke which reaches its grotesquely apt climax when the latter kisses the poisoned skull, now decked out in court trimmings, believing it to be a live woman coming to keep a secret assignation with him. The opposite images of skull and finery come together in a moment of incandescent irony.

In pursuit of his revenge, Vindice adopts several disguises, and at one stage undertakes the murder of one of his own fictional selves. Disguise was a stock in trade of Elizabethan and Jacobean drama and it is carried to extreme lengths in Vindice's many rapid transformations. But it is not used merely for dazzling theatrical display or to overcome plot complications. Like Mosca or Volpone, Vindice falls in love with his own virtuosity in villainy and this is his undoing. For after the final debacle he cannot resist the temptation to boast about how he and his brother planned the duke's murder — 'Twas somewhat witty carried, tho' we say it' — and is promptly sentenced to execution by the new ruler, not so much out of considerations of justice as of political prudence — 'You that would murder him would murder me'. Looked at from this point of view therefore, *The Revenger's Tragedy* resembles *The Atheist's Tragedy;* in both cases the tragedy is that of the protagonists destroying themselves through being false to their real moral nature.

But we do not have sufficient sense of Vindice as a character *apart* from his role as avenger to be moved to the sympathy we might feel for a truly tragic protagonist, and indeed Tourneur does not invite us to do so. At one point, the disguised Vindice is asked by the duke's lecherous son Lussurioso to act as a pandar to his own sister, Castiza. Vindice decides to test both his sister and his mother, convinced that they will reject his overtures on behalf of Lussurioso with contempt and disgust. Castiza does so, but his mother Gratiana is tempted. Vindice's reaction when he realizes this shows no trace of filial feeling or any conflict between love and moral condemnation. Such conflict as he feels is stylized into a single aside-

I e'en quake to proceed, my spirit turns edge!
I fear she's unmothered, yet I'll venture

— and a grotesquely stylized image:

O suffering heaven, with thy invisible finger
E'en at this instant turn the precious side
Of both mine eyeballs inward, not to see myself!

In general, Tourneur's interest in character is perfunctory, as can be seen by the use he makes of the Morality convention of naming characters after abstract qualities or functions — Vindice, the avenger, Lussurioso, the lecher, Castiza, chastity, and so on. The duke and duchess are identified by their titles alone and the duchess's youngest son is simply 'Junior'.

But while a sense of individual character is lacking in the play, we have a strong and sharply dramatic awareness of conflicting motives and appetites. Tourneur borrows from Marston the Italianate court setting, but the smell of corruption is ranker and the fumes of decadent sensuality more pungent here than even in Marston. None of the characters belonging to the court — not the duke and his two sons (one illegitimate), nor the duchess and her three children — show the slightest concern for the moral duties attending political power. The sub-plot, concerning the arrest and eventual execution of the duchess's younger son, explicitly displays justice prostituted and travestied. For all these characters, political power is merely a kind of institutionalized pandarism, a ready means of satisfying their all but insatiable sexual appetites. The court is a hotbed of lust and sensuality, as the duke's bastard son Spurio makes clear in speaking of his own conception:

Faith, if the truth were known, I was begot
After some gluttonous dinner, some stirring dish
Was my first father; when deep healths went round,
And ladies' cheeks were painted red with wine

> Their tongues as short and nimble as their heels,
> Uttering words sweet and thick; and when they rose
> Were merrily disposed to fall again —
> In such a whispering and withdrawing hour,
> When base male bawds kept sentinel at stairhead,
> Was I stol'n softly.

But the corruption is seen as seeping downwards from the festering court to all ranks of society. Immediately after reflecting on how Spurio is about to make his father a cuckold Vindice has a savage vision reinforced by the imagery of the play throughout, of frantic and pervasive sexuality cloaked by night:

> Now 'tis full sea a-bed over the world,
> There's juggling of all sides; some that were maids
> E'en at sunset are now perhaps i' th' toll-book.
> This woman in immodest thin apparel
> Lets in her friend by water; here a dame
> Cunning, nails leather hinges to a door
> To avoid proclamation.
> Now cuckolds are a-coining, apace, apace, apace, apace!
> And careful sisters spin that thread i' th' night
> That does maintain them and their bawds i' th' day.

The sensuality at court is compounded by the fact that it is both thoroughly decadent and also fully aware of the reality of the moral standards it so avidly flouts. The decadence is evident from the fact that what the duke, his son and his duchess want is not the straightforward satisfaction of their physical lust, but the deflowering of virginity and the destruction of virtue. When the disguised Vindice suggests to Lussurioso that he should marry the virgin he lusts after so much (Vindice's own sister Castiza), the duke's son replies:

> Give me my bed by stealth — there's true delight;
> What breeds a loathing in't but night by night?

The duchess seduces Spurio by pointing out to him the added pleasure of cuckolding a father who has deprived him of legitimacy, while the duke is pleased when Vindice, luring him to his destruction through the poisonous skull, tells him how modest and virtuous is the lady whom he has persuaded to keep the assignation:

> In gravest looks the greatest faults seem less;
> Give me the sin that's robed in holiness.

Most explicit of all are the words of the duchess as she is about to entice Spurio to bed. 'Had not that kiss a taste of sin, 'twere sweet' says the bastard, to which the duchess roundly replies 'Why there's no pleasure sweet, but it is sinful'. And the acknowledgement of moral standards flouted could not be clearer than in the duke's words:

> It well becomes that judge to nod at crimes
> That does commit greater himself and lives.

All this may make *The Revenger's Tragedy* appear to be a deeply orthodox play, which in some respects it certainly is. Tourneur's explicit moral vision is certainly one that derives from a medieval sense of the temptations of the flesh and of the deadly sins of lust and murder. The universal doom that overtakes avengers and victims alike seems to point to the existence of a transcendental realm of value, a divine presence whose commandments may not be mocked. But there is another element in the play, and one that has already been suggested as characteristic of Jacobean tragedy. It is the admixture of what can only be called a note of comic relish which informs both plot and language at key points. This is related to, but not identical with the satirical temper. At the level of plot we find it in the near-farcical complications which result from the collision of independent intrigues, the instigators of some being the intended victims of others. The biter-bit theme which is native to the plot of critical comedy is here transferred and amplified with a vengeance, so to speak. For example, there is one scene in which Lussurioso bursts in to the bed-chamber of his stepmother the duchess. He does so in the hope of catching her in bed with the bastard Spurio. In order to catch them in the act Lussurioso has deferred his own plan of seducing Castiza. But Spurio has deferred *his* plan to bed the duchess so that he might catch Lussurioso and Castiza together. In the event Lussurioso finds the duchess in bed with her lawful husband and is arrested for attempting to assassinate the duke.

The verbal comic relish is displayed mainly, though not entirely in Vindice's increasingly frequent convulsions of self-praise at the ingenuity of his stratagems. (There is for instance Spurio's notable reaction to the news of the duke's demise: 'Old dad dead?') *The Revenger's Tragedy* is full of people patting themselves or each other on the back over the brilliance of their schemes, though from the point of view of the audience the ingenuity often seems that of the dramatist (or omniscient providence) rather than that of any individual character, even Vindice. Thus at one point Vindice is so overjoyed that he can hardly tell his brother Hippolito what has happened:

Vindice:	O sweet, rare, delectable, happy, ravishing!
Hippolito:	Why, what's the matter, brother?
Vindice:	O, 'tis able to make a man spring up and knock his forehead Against yon silver ceiling.

But the cause of all this is not so much Vindice's cleverness as the fact that the duke has asked him to bring a woman in secret to a dark and lonely part of the palace grounds, thus making Vindice's plan to kill him easier to carry out.

The total effect of this double vision is not, as sometimes happens with Marston and Webster, one of confusion. Tourneur's grasp of his material is so firm and his command of the various styles of the play so unfaltering that we enter a dramatic world which is distinctive and coherent, a world where the simple certitude of 'When the bad bleed, then is the tragedy good' is undercut but not destroyed by a more problematic sense of the relation between the divine providence that so obligingly provides thunder on request as an indication of its omniscient attention, and the activities and motives of its human agents.

Two Tragedies of Webster

Webster's contemporary reputation, like Tourneur's, rests on two plays, both of which are, unlike Tourneur's, frequently performed on the modern stage. These are *The White Devil* and *The Duchess of Malfi*. Apart from these, there are only two extant dramatic works by Webster, the masque *Monuments of Honour* and a tragicomedy containing a superb trial scene, *The Devil's Law-Case*. Webster also wrote the Induction to Marston's *The Malcontent* and probably collaborated with Dekker, and with Middleton and others on a play now lost, *Caesar's Fall*. He also contributed twenty-two sketches of 'characters' to a collection of these by Sir Thomas Overbury in 1615. This is almost all we know about John Webster. We do not even know for certain the dates of his birth or death, but his two great plays belong to the years 1612-14.

There is little interest in character in either of Tourneur's plays, and even less in the characters of women. Levidulcia and Castabella in the former and Gratiana and Castiza in the latter are little more than stylized representations of traditional (predominantly male) notions of feminine virtue and weakness. One of the most notable features of both *The White Devil* and *The Duchess of Malfi* on the other hand, is Webster's portrayal of the protagonists who, for all the very considerable difference between them, come across both on the stage and on the page as female characters with an inner life of their own rather than male stereotypes or wish fulfilments.

The notions about women which Tourneur inherited and uncritically dramatized go back a long way and are based ultimately on interpretations of Biblical texts or commentaries. Woman was essentially the weaker vessel and the prime cause of man's disobedience and fall. Her supreme virtues were her virginity (and later marital fidelity), infinite patience and total submissiveness to her lord and master. If she strayed from this narrow and clearly marked path, it could only be because of her innate weakness and lustfulness. Her beauty was, except within the framework of lawful marriage, the devil's snare to entrap the bodies and souls of unwary men. Thus the two most widely available images of woman were those of the madonna, all but virgin mother (or the dutiful daughter) and the harlot, the temptress who stood beckoning by the doorway to damnation, as real-life harlots stood beckoning outside the red-latticed whore-houses of the city.

But like much else, these stereotypes were coming under scrutiny in the early years of the seventeenth century. The example of a female monarch successfully holding her own in the dangerous world of political and religious intrigue was unlikely to leave Englishmen unimpressed. The change to Protestantism had led to a gradually increasing stress on woman as man's helpmeet rather than the repository of weakness and lust. The ideal of marriage was conceived in terms more positive than the Pauline 'it is better to marry than burn'. In 1549 the Book of Common Prayer had laid down the three reasons for marriage: children, relief of sexual desire and mutual companionship. This contrasted sharply with the Catholic view of celibacy as the ideal Christian life and Aquinas's opinion that a man would have been a better companion for Adam in all respects except that of procreation. Especially under Puritan influence (and Puritan thinking was close to the Anglican attitude on this matter at least), there was a growing understanding of women as persons in their own right, though this must not be exaggerated. The man was still supreme as husband or father, but wives had more say in family matters at a period when the distinction between family and wider issues was only just beginning to emerge, and daughters at least had the right of veto over their prospective husbands. In social and economic terms, a widow with a jointure (property accruing to her at her husband's death) was in effect an independent agent, and the marriageable widow with a comfortable fortune was a fairly familiar phenomenon, almost as familiar in real life perhaps, as in the drama. Finally, education for women had developed considerably, especially among the citizenry; it was the rule rather than the exception for wives to help their husbands in managing their business, which was usually carried on at home. The division between home and work-place, with the consequent break between 'private' and 'business' life comes only with industrialization although Protestantism certainly emphasized the importance of the family. Mrs Mulligrub in *The Dutch Courtesan*, helping to manage her husband's wine shop and referring to it as 'our vocation' is a typical figure of the period, as her own words indicate: 'In troth, a fine-faced wife in a wainscot carved seat is a worthy ornament to a tradesman's shop, and an attractive, I warrant. Her husband shall find it in the custom of his ware, I'll assure him.'

Foreign visitors often commented on the freedom of manners and discourse of women in England. But the developments indicated above were not of course, a matter of steady progression without interruption or setback. A lively controversy about the position of women had been going on for some time, one of its contemporary aspects being a focusing of attention on the 'mannish woman' (and her counterpart the 'womanish man'). In sermon, pamphlet and broadside the battle raged, but for fairly obvious reasons the drama was the best medium in which to examine the issues involved. On the stage the abstract pros and cons of the argument could be shown in action and the consequences illustrated through the interplay of conflicting characters and their destinies. And because drama by its nature speaks with many voices, playwrights could explore through the deeds and language of their characters attitudes towards a controversial issue which they might not necessarily hold or express in their own person, just as audiences who would have no second thoughts about behaving at home like Brabantio or Old Capulet could be induced to sympathize for the duration of a play with the actions of a Juliet or a Desdemona.

One of the most noteworthy features of the Jacobean drama therefore, is the emergence of female characters who, while evidently related to the current stereotypes, transcend them in a way which makes them markedly different from their counterparts in the earlier drama (though Bel-imperia in *The Spanish Tragedy* is a partial exception). In comedy we find the emergence of a witty, resourceful and independent-minded female, a type who finds her highest expression in such Shakespearean heroines as Beatrice or Rosalind. The practice of boys playing the parts of women no doubt helped in the development of this kind of character. But it is in Jacobean tragedy that women come into their own, for their assertions of individuality against the constraints of society often have fatal consequences.

The two tragedies of Webster, each named after the heroine, contain two of the most memorable figures in the whole range of Jacobean drama. Vittoria Corombona, 'the white devil', is the heroine of her play in a much more problematic sense than that in which the Duchess of Malfi is of hers. But she is conceived on a grander scale than any of the other characters, even her brother the Machiavellian Flamineo, and it is the flaming energy of her outburst against her corrupt judges that electrifies the stage and glows in the mind. As a dramatist Webster does not have much stamina, being better at single scenes than a whole play and often better at single speeches than scenes. He frequently gives the impression of being a literary rather than a strictly dramatic talent pushed into the drama by force of circumstances. In *The White Devil* there are two great scenes, the first the trial scene, and the other the final tragic catastrophe. There are great moments and great lines elsewhere, but the core of the play is there.

There are three women in the play apart from Vittoria. Her mother Cornelia appears as a figure in two tableaux vivants, first in outraged protest at her daughter's intention to become Duke Brachiano's mistress and her son's to act as go-between, then as the weeping mother lamenting over her younger son's death. Zanche, Vittoria's Moorish maid is a type of heedless sensuality and little more, while Isabella, Brachiano's duchess is a variant on the patient Grissell, the only initiative she shows being her resolution to protect her husband even while he betrays her. Vittoria herself is both a child of the corrupt court world, with its total disregard of all moral values while paying lip-service to their existence, and a countervailing force against its hypocrisy. The fact that she is guilty of the charge brought against her — betrayal of her marriage vows — is not of course irrelevant to our estimation of her, though Webster has provided enough poetic fire for a good actress to make it seem so. It has been said that Webster, by making a dishonourable woman behave as if she were honourable, has simply confused the moral issues. Vittoria is both a willing adultress and a ready conniver at and even instigator of the murder of a husband who has done her no wrong and whose only fault is that he stands in the way of her imperious desires. Webster makes all this perfectly clear, and that is precisely the point. We are not asked to condone Vittoria's behaviour in these matters. Our sympathy and admiration for her are demanded, even extorted, by three factors. First, the fearless energy with which she stands up to corruption in the centre of power, powerfully represented in the trial scene:

> Find me guilty, sever head from body:
> We'll part good friends: I scorn to hold my life
> At yours or any man's entreaty, Sir.

The depth of stinging contempt in that final 'Sir' is unmistakable. At the climax of the trial she hurls her defiance at the court in a resonant couplet:

> Know this, and let it somewhat raise your spite,
> Through darkness diamonds spread their richest light.

Vittoria is diamond-like in the radiant steadfastness of her passion (though not in the relevant point of purity), which is the second aspect of her character which engages our sympathy. The court is certainly a place of darkness in its hypocrisy, though perhaps we are to consider too that the darkness is partly that of Vittoria's own nature. Finally there is the steady regard with which Vittoria recognizes her own share of responsibility for her downfall —

O, my greatest sin lay in my blood.
Now my blood pays for it.

(Where 'blood', as often in Jacobean drama, signifies not only its literal sense and heredity but also unbridled passion), and wherein she was a victim of circumstance, a poison flower nourished by the foetid midden into which she was born —

O happy they that never saw the court,
Nor ever knew great men but by report!

Webster is rather addicted to these moral tags, but we are not, I think, intended to see them as telling the final truth about the characters, any more than we are to take Edgar's similar moralizings as encompassing the whole tragedy of *Lear*. In Webster they are the prelude to that final moment of intense clarity when an evil and meaningless life is almost transfigured by the unflinching acceptance of death. There is no strong sense in *The White Devil* of a moral order opposed to the universal wickedness and corruption, though it is invoked often enough, nearly always in contexts that underline its absence or at least its ineffectuality. Virtue exists, in a character like Isabella, but it is isolated, helpless and soon destroyed with a terrifying casualness, in a world where murders are only 'flea bitings'. In such a world there is something heroic, but absurdly heroic in facing death undaunted:

My soul like to a ship in a black storm,
Is driven, I know not whither.

These are almost the last words Vittoria utters, but it is her brother Flamineo who gives definitive expression to this heroic contempt of death. Flamineo, as has been noted, is the Machiavellian schemer, but there is something both fatalistic and curiously offhand about his villainy. When his mother protests at his decision to act as pandar to Brachiano in order to gain protection and advancement, Flamineo succinctly answers that such wickedness is a matter of economic necessity in this world, and in the terms of the play his arguments seem unanswerable:

Pray what means have you
To keep me from the galleys, or the gallows?

he enquires of his mother with sardonic urbanity, and goes on to give a little 'character' of himself which would have had an ominously familiar ring in Jacobean London, though the setting of the play is ostensibly Italy:

My father proved himself a gentleman,
Sold all's land, and like a fortunate fellow,
Died ere the money was spent. You brought me up
At Padua I confess, where I protest,
For want of means — the University judge me —

> I have been fain to heel my tutor's stockings,
> At least seven years; conspiring with a beard,
> Made me a graduate; then to the duke's service:
> I visited the court, whence I returned
> More courteous, more lecherous by far,
> But not a suit the richer. And shall I,
> Having a path so open and so free
> To my preferment, still retain your milk
> In my pale forehead?

But this seems as much a rationalization as Iago's statement of his motives for hating Othello. The 'path so open and so free' turns out to be exactly the reverse, for it seems not so much to be chosen by Flamineo (as Edmund chooses it in *King Lear* for instance) as to choose him, so to speak, for its ruinous course. The free man is enslaved by a destructive instinct which is also self-destructive and whose nature he barely comprehends. And far from being 'open' the path is full of hidden turnings, as he himself acknowledges in soliloquy:

> We are engaged to mischief and must on;
> As rivers to find out the ocean
> Flow with crook bendings beneath forced banks
> Or as we see, to aspire some mountain's top,
> The way ascends not straight, but imitates
> The subtle foldings of a winter's snake,
> So who knows policy and her true aspect,
> Shall find her ways winding and indirect.

Flamineo does not seem to have the delight in his wicked workings which quickens a Iago or a Richard III. Rather it seems as if his Machiavellianism exists only to propel him with irresistible force and rapidity towards the doom which he always seems to be dimly aware of and to embrace with a kind of exhausted ecstasy when it finally arrives:

> I do not look
> Who went before, nor who shall follow me;
> No, at myself I will begin and end.
> While we look up to heaven, we confound
> Knowledge with knowledge. Oh, I am in a mist!

And his last words are not a recognition of a moral order. There is a throwaway quality about his single brief salute to such an order — "'Tis well there was some goodness in my death' and the 'goodness' seems to be a matter of aesthetics more than of morals. Much more emphatic is the bleak acknowledgement of futility:

> This busy trade of life appears most vain,
> Since rest breeds rest, where all seek pain by pain.

The last lines of *The White Devil* seem to suggest the restoration of a new order in the young duke's words:

Let guilty men remember, their black deeds
Do lean on crutches made of slender reeds.

But the pat little rhyme carries little more conviction or authority here than similar couplets do elsewhere, and in any case the point seems to be that villains ought to choose tough trees not slender reeds to protect their villainy — a very politic warning indeed. But it is the words spoken by one of the unrepentant villains, Ludovico, immediately before that stay in the mind, with their terrible gloating pride in the human capacity for sadistic destructiveness:

> I do glory yet,
> That I can call this act my own. For my part,
> The rack, the gallows, and the torturing wheel,
> Shall be but sound sleeps to me: here's my rest;
> I limned this night-piece and it was my best.

In the latter part of the twentieth century we are unlikely to find the world of *The White Devil* dated or 'irrelevant'.

The Duchess of Malfi has a stronger sense of a transcendental moral order than the earlier play, but its existence is by no means unequivocally affirmed. The world of both plays is recognizably the same, with naked power, brazen corruption in church and state and rampant cruelty everywhere. But the Duchess stands less ambiguously in contrast to her surroundings than Vittoria and Webster shows a greater interest in her both as agent and victim. There is some danger, in concentrating exclusively on the Duchess, of making the fifth act seem a tacked-on epilogue, since the heroine is killed in Act IV. In fact however, the play has a firmer and more coherent structure than *The White Devil* (in spite of the fact that a whole year passes between Acts I and II, and there is enough time for the Duchess to have several children between Acts II and III), and the spirit of the dead woman irradiates the last act, as the ghost of Caesar haunts the latter part of Shakespeare's tragedy. The exploration of worldly greatness and its relation to moral stature which is Chapman's great theme becomes obsessive in Webster. But moral stature has a distinctly felt religious connotation in *The Duchess of Malfi*. Cariola, the Duchess's maid, says of her mistress:

> Whether the spirit of greatness or of woman
> Reign most in her I know not.

The examplars of masculine 'greatness' in the play are her brothers, the Cardinal and Duke Ferdinand. They typify the corruption of the religious and secular order which is set up as an ideal in Antonio's speech at the very beginning of the play:

> . . . a Prince's court
> Is like a common fountain, whence should flow
> Pure silver-drops in general. But if't chance
> Some curs'd example poison't near the head,
> Death and diseases through the whole land spread.

It is the 'curs'd example' of the Cardinal and the Duke which produces a society in which merit goes unrewarded and, as the Machiavellian Bosola finds out, where even the hatchet men of the establishment cannot be certain of obtaining their hoped-for gains. Bosola and the Duchess herself are the two most fascinating figures in the play, which is almost as much his tragedy as hers, though in a different way. He is presented as a malcontent like Flamineo, a ready tool for Duke Ferdinand's dark designs. His contempt of the court, as Antonio is quick to note, is not due to principled opposition, like Bussy's, but to envy at not himself having access to the sources of wealth and power:

> . . .I observe his railing
> Is not for simple love of piety:
> Indeed he rails at those things which he wants,
> Would be as lecherous, covetous, or proud,
> Bloody, or envious, as any man,
> If he had means to be so.

That this is at least partly true is shown by the readiness with which Bosola responds to Ferdinand's bribe with the grimly abrupt query: 'Whose throat must I cut?' The first two acts of the play are dominated by the presence of this enigmatic and sinister figure whose tendency to encapsulate character in grotesque vignettes affects other characters and shapes much of the dialogue. We may recall here that Webster was the author of several 'characters' in the Overbury collection, and also that he made a habit of noting down memorable lines for future use. In the earlier part of the play we feel, especially in reading, that we are being shown round a sur-realist or expressionist portrait gallery. There is a 'set-piece' quality about the speeches and the comparative rigidity of the rhythms puts something like a frame round each picture. Bosola's characterization of the Cardinal and Duke is typical in tone, method and movement:

> Could I be one of their flattering panders, I would hang on their ears like a
> horse-leech, till I were full, and then drop off.

Bosola tends to use prose for his 'railing' and verse for his weightier meditations, but the change from one to the other does not affect the quality of his epitomizing. Paradoxically though, a sense of furtive and febrile activity comes through the somewhat static portraits. The major and minor themes, if we may so call them, and the lines of the main action are clear. The minor theme is the depiction of a society where action and its rewards have no relation to each other at all, since the latter depends on the unpredictable whims of the powerful. The major theme is that of the limits of individual action and responsibility in a corrupt society, partic-ularized in the freedom of a woman to choose her own destiny. The Duchess's brothers insist that as a widow she should not marry, expressing the traditional view that the only motive for a woman's remarriage must be lust:

> Marry? They are most luxurious
> Will wed twice.

The Duchess gives them her promise that she would not, though she has already secretly chosen her steward Antonio as her prospective husband. To the extent that she utters a deliberate lie she may be considered to have compromised her integrity and thus to be a representative of her society, not a rebel against it. There are moments, especially towards the end of the play, when we are strongly aware of the connection between the heroine and her milieu, but in comparison with Vittoria it is the contrast between heroine and milieu which strikes us most forcibly. However, in deciding to try and outwit her brothers at their own game of secrecy and deception, the Duchess has not only marginally compromised her integrity, but also made certain that she remains indissolubly tied to that corrupt world. In her poignant words to Cariola

> wish me good speed
> For I am going into a wilderness,
> Where I shall find nor path, nor friendly clue
> To be my guide.

The first two acts are taken up by the first large movement of the play which has two phases. In the earlier one we have the main figures presented and Bosola and Antonio contrasted as types of the loyal and treacherous servant. Antonio is the more steadfast but in depth of moral imagination Bosola is his superior. In the later phase of the first movement Bosola, who has been set up by Ferdinand to spy on the Duchess, guesses correctly that she is pregnant. Its culmination is Ferdinand's revelation to the Cardinal of their sister's secret.

Against the cloudy and ill-defined cluster of motives and machinations which make up this part of the play, the betrothal scene between the Duchess and Antonio stands out with a luminous clarity. It has sometimes been urged that, for a Jacobean audience, the Duchess's action in proposing to a man would have been reprehensible on all counts — psychologically, as a woman should not take the initiative in such matters, socially because her action threatened the stability of the social order and morally because her motive was bound to be unbridled sexuality. Similar arguments have been adduced in relation to Desdemona's behaviour in *Othello*. In both cases the argument radically misconstrues the possible relations between drama and 'received ideas' (assuming, generously, that there was more uniformity about the latter in the seventeenth century than in our own time). As noted above, the whole question of what women ought or ought not to do, and what her 'essential' nature was, was a matter of continuing controversy at the time and the drama was the ideal form for controversy. Webster, like Middleton, seems to have been particularly interested in the issues involved. But the final answer to the objection is that the scene as written simply does not support the view of the Duchess as behaving foolishly and irresponsibly, any more than the play as a whole does. (Great tragedy does not usually work by confirming the superiority of our judgments to those of its protagonists.) In reading and especially in performance the betrothal scene stands out with intense clarity as one of the great positive moments in the drama. The mixture of resolution and what I can only call serious coquettishness with which the Duchess leads the astonished but not unwilling Antonio into marriage has an effect quite other than that of irresponsible egotism or wilful self-indulgence. The symbolic resonance of the Duchess's actions and words to her kneeling steward represent a coming together of many of the creative values of the play — tenderness, genuine feeling, mutuality, even perhaps (as

Bosola remarks, when the Duchess finally tells him her secret), reward for faithful service:

>   Sir,
> This goodly roof of yours, is too low-built,
> I cannot stand upright in't, nor discourse,
> Without I raised it higher: raise yourself,
> Of if you please, my hand to help you: so.
>
> (Raises him.)

Assuaging Antonio's fears about the destructive effects of being or appearing to be socially ambitious, she makes a clear and simple statement of how she 'values' him:

> If you will know where breathes a complete man,
> (I speak it without flattery), turn your eyes,   .
> And progress through your self.

She shows herself well aware of the subterfuges to which her choice has compelled her in a society where outward honour and 'greatness' are all:

> The misery of us, that are born great,
> We are forced to woo because none dare woo us:
> And as a tyrant doubles with his words,
> And fearfully equivocates: so we
> Are forced to express our violent passions
> In riddles and in dreams, and leave the path
> Of simple virtue, which was never made
> To seem the thing it is not.

The catastrophic consequences of her 'honest deception' are here fore-shadowed and we can appreciate, without fully endorsing, the maid Cariola's verdict on her mistress, to challenge male hegemony in this most intimate sphere of action as 'a fearful madness'. That the consequences *are* catastrophic is, in terms of the play's total impact, far more a condemnation of the society which destroys the heroine than of the heroine herself.

The Duchess's reaction to the discovery of her secret and the series of savagely vindictive ordeals inflicted on her by her brother Ferdinand form the second major movement of the play, and for many its real climax. Ferdinand's motives have been shadowy but darkly menacing from the very beginning. Even when the brothers first warn their sisters against remarriage, the Cardinal seems to feel that Ferdinand's vehemence is excessive. And it is Ferdinand who installs Bosola as a spy in the Duchess's household, not only without giving him any reason, but specifically drawing attention to the fact that he will not do so:

> Do not you ask the reason: but be satisfied,
> I say I would not.

This uncertainty is not merely an arbitrary stroke on Webster's part, for it continues right up to Ferdinand's own bafflement over his motives for ordering the killing of the Duchess. When Bosola tells him that the deed is done, Ferdinand cries out:

> I bade thee, when I was distracted of my wits
> Go kill my dearest friend, and thou hast done't.
> For let me but examine well the cause;
> What was the meanness of her match to me?
> Only I must confess I had a hope,
> Had she continu'd widow, to have gain'd
> An infinite mass of treasure by her death:

This is the first we hear of this mercenary motive on Ferdinand's part. Its palpable inadequacy is highlighted by the obsessive persistence with which he haunts his sister and the diabolical virtuosity of the series of torments which he inflicts on her. These begin with a threatening visit during which he leaves a poniard in her chamber, and continue with a dead man's hand allegedly Antonio's, thrust into the Duchess's in the dark, a tableau of Antonio and her children presented to her and a fantastic parade of madmen before her. These and similar effects doubtless account for Bernard Shaw's harsh words about 'the opacity that prevented Webster, the Tussaud laureate, from appreciating his own stupidity'. But the excessiveness of the display is Ferdinand's, not Webster's. It is of a piece with the language in which he rails against his sister after he has discovered her secret. His fevered imaginings of her copulation with 'some strong-thighed bargeman' and his insane ravings as a lycanthrope after her death (including the most chilling line in all Jacobean drama — 'strangling is a very quiet death'), all suggest the presence in Ferdinand of a powerful but unacknowledged incestuous desire; incest is a theme touched on in many Jacobean plays, and forms the central action of Ford's *'Tis Pity She's a Whore*. But it is not Ferdinand's emotions and their murky origins on which the stress falls in this part of the play, but on the Duchess's indomitable spirit, which remains unbroken under all her tortures, though she staggers on the edge of insanity. The climax comes when Bosola, posing first as a tomb maker and then as a bellman arrives with his henchman to strangle the Duchess and her children. The Duchess meets her end with a magnificent and magnificently theatrical (the phrase is not intended to be pejorative) combination of stoic pride — 'I am Duchess of Malfi still' — and Christian humility. When Cariola asks her to cry for help she answers with a clear-eyed recognition of her immediate surroundings and the world she is in — 'To whom? To our next neighbours? They are mad folks' — and turns to the executioners unafraid:

> Pull, and pull strongly, for your able strength
> Must pull down heaven upon me:
> Yet stay, heaven's gates are not so highly arch'd
> As princes' palaces: they that enter there
> Must go upon their knees.

The evident theatricality of this is very different from the theatricality of Flamineo rehearsing a mock-death or Vittoria struggling in vain before drawing themselves up to their full stature to face extinction. An effect of panic and exigency casts a faint shadow on their final moments. Here there is only a kind of emblematic dignity in the stage pictures as the heroine whose first life-enhancing gesture was to raise her steward from his knees, thereby rejecting a false hierarchy of values, acknowledges in her last the ultimate authority of the true one by going down on her own knees before it.

The impact of this scene is so powerful that the final act of the play is often considered anti-climactic. But it is a necessary reassertion of the dark world of murder and injustice, not transfigured by the Duchess's heroic example — that would be to risk sentimentality — but somehow touched by it. Our understanding of 'greatness' has been modified so that we find it natural to accept Delio's reference to 'these wretched eminent things' and a strange kind of pity even for the arch-villains fills the final scene. Bosola, who has learnt the hard way that villainy no less than virtue can go unrewarded in this world, dies affirming not the value of his life and death but that of the heroine, even though that value seems not to be sustained by anything outside the world of human choice:

> Fare you well,
> It may be pain: but no harm in me to die
> In so good a quarrel. O this gloomy world,
> In what a shadow, or deep pit of darkness
> Doth, womanish and fearful, mankind live?
> Let worthy minds ne'er stagger in distrust
> To suffer death or shame for what is just:
> Mine is another voyage.

The sudden dizzying drop from the penultimate line to the last opens up the whole enormous gulf between the morally sensitive nihilist and his vision of a heaven he cannot believe in. But it does not diminish the strength of the earlier affirmation, whose sententiousness is made bearable by the head-on collision in a single line between 'womanish' and 'mankind'. A similar collision, when Flamineo praises his sister's courage in death in *The White Devil* is very different in tone and more equivocal in its import:

> Th'art a noble sister,
> I love thee now; if woman do breed man
> She ought to teach him manhood. Fare thee well.
> Know so many glorious women that are fam'd
> For masculine virtue, have been vicious,
> Only a happier silence did betide them.
> She hath no faults, who hath the art to hide them.

In the later play the collocation of 'womanish' and 'mankind', coming after the stage events we have witnessed, cannot but compel us to reconsider the meanings which the society of the play has given to manhood, womanliness and 'mankind' itself. The deaths of the Cardinal and Ferdinand modulate into something beyond mere nihilism, though it is difficult to give a more positive name to it than, say, a grave quiescence (the pun is not seriously damaging). The note that is struck in the

Cardinal's line 'I am puzzled in a question about hell' is felt even in the assertiveness of Ferdinand's final couplet:

> Whether we fall by ambition, blood, or lust,
> Like diamonds we are cut with our own dust.

And the Cardinal's dying words move beyond the reach of Bosola's vindictive relish over his destruction, though that relish too is soon overlaid by other moral concerns:

> Look to my brother:
> He gave us these large wounds, as we were struggling
> Here i'th'rushes. And now, I pray, let me
> Be laid by, and never thought of. (*Dies*)

In their last moments Webster's villains seem to catch a faint and flickering perception of a moral order they have strenuously denied — the Cardinal's words 'How tedious is a guilty conscience' catches the ambivalence perfectly — and an insight into the tragic predicament whereby their vaunted freedom of action has turned out to be the blind momentum of unrecognized instincts and impulses. The life and death of the Duchess certainly does not dispel the darkness of Webster's world, but it shines very clearly in the moral confusion and the Grand Guignol extravagance of that world, a small, unwavering, inexplicable light.

Middleton's Tragic Realism

To come to the two great tragedies of Middleton after the superhuman heroics of Chapman and the extravagant Italianate grotesqueries of Webster's world is to enter what is in some ways a narrower, less splendid world. But if Middleton's world is smaller, it also strikes us as more recognizably our world than that of Chapman and of Webster, both in terms of the motivation of characters and the way in which they are presented before us. Like Webster, Middleton (born 1580) belongs to a younger generation than Chapman's, but a decade or so separates his two tragic masterpieces from Webster's. *Women Beware Women* was probably performed in 1621 or thereabouts, though some scholars favour a date several years earlier. *The Changeling* was written in 1622. Both plays had to wait thirty years before they were printed. The plays therefore belong to the last flickering years of James's reign. When he wrote them, Middleton already had behind him several successful city comedies in which his talent for realistic portrayal of character had found expression, together with his keen interest in the implications of the institution of marriage in contemporary society.

Indeed one of the first things we notice about *Women Beware Women* is its resemblance to Middleton's great satirical comedy *A Chaste Maid in Cheapside* in its atmosphere and concerns. It is true that the tragedy is set in Florence and has a duke and a cardinal among its principal characters while the comedy takes place in London and has no figure of higher social rank than a pox-riddled knight. But in both plays the central concern is with marriage in its social, economic and psychological aspects. The Duke in *Women Beware Women* is not the usual villainous autocrat of Jacobean comedy but a sensualist prepared to pay for his pleasure. The Cardinal, the only cardboard cutout among the chief characters, is simply a mouthpiece for orthodox pieties. While the tragedy ends in multiple deaths and the comedy in marriage, there is something deathly about the comic ending of *A Chaste Maid* (and not merely the young lovers arising out of their coffins) and the deaths in the tragedy occur as part of a wedding masque. In Middleton, as in Marston, tragedy and comedy are constantly trespassing on each other's territory.

Women Beware Women contains three of the most convincing feminine characters in all Jacobean drama — the heroine Bianca, the at first unwilling bride Isabella and above all Livia, the sensual schemer who lures both the others into their tragic predicaments. The central situations of both plots are motivated by the intrusion into personal relationships of purely mercenary considerations. Leantio is persuaded to accept a lucrative captaincy away from home so that his wife Bianca can become the Duke's mistress, an entanglement into which Livia draws her by dangling the bait of material prosperity; the incestuous relationship between Isabella and her uncle Hippolito is a direct consequence of the greed of her father, who compels Isabella to marry an imbecile on account of his vast fortune. Livia is symbolic of her milieu as the game of chess she plays is symbolic of a society where some are pushed about like pawns while others have greater freedom, though most are still constrained by sex or circumstance. In such a society it is almost inevitable that a Livia should express her femininity by developing to a fine art the manipulative skills of the bawd or procuress, for in that vocation she can obtain the rewards of befriending the wealthy and influential without permanently surrendering her own freedom of action or compromising it as Bianca has done. The nature and scope of the marriage choices confronting each of the three women illustrate Middleton's working out of the theme of woman's predicament in a male- and money-dominated society. When the play opens, Bianca is married to Leantio, a man from a lower social class. Her motive seems to be purely romantic, the rich girl's fascination with the idea of eloping with the humble suitor whom the family would surely disapprove of. Such as it is, however, it does represent an assertion of feminine initiative, though in a society where men make the running, no credit can accrue to her in terms of status by marrying beneath her. The flat, platitudinous quality of Bianca's first words as she accepts her new role contrast sharply with, for instance, those of Desdemona in a not dissimilar situation:

Kind mother, there is nothing can be wanting
To her that does enjoy all her desires.
Heaven send a quiet peace with this man's love,
And I am as rich as virtue can be poor.

There is no distinction in the language or rhythm to suggest any strong commitment to her choice, though it is true that there is a certain flatness in the steady, unsurprised, movement and language of the play as a whole. This is poetic drama of a kind generally very different from the richly metaphorical Shakespearean sort. Middleton's use of metaphor here is, so to speak, often literal. The iterated image of feeding to suggest the predatory quality of the society and of the language of trading to suggest its soulless commercialism are characteristic. But the style is perfectly suited to the demands Middleton makes of it which are chiefly that it should render the ordinary world, not very different from that of his audience and secondly that it should adequately convey the inner feelings of the characters, especially the women, within a fairly limited range. It makes the gradual transition from the fairly straightforward opening dialogue between Livia and the mother to the heavily charged exchanges over the game of chess totally convincing. And it catches the very movement of Bianca's mind as she succumbs to the visions of affluence suggested by the conducted tour of the Duke's palace given her by Guardiano. It can rise to the intensity of Bianca's outburst against the latter:

> Now bless me from a blasting! I saw that now
> Fearful of any woman's eye to look on.
> Infectious mists and mildews hang at's eyes,
> The weather of a doomsday dwells upon him.
> Yet since mine honour's leprous, why should I
> Preserve that fair that caused the leprosy?
> Come, poison all at once! Thou in whose baseness
> The bane of virtue broods, I'm bound in soul
> Eternally to curse thy smoooth-browed treachery
> That wore the fair veil of a friendly welcome,
> And I a stranger; think upon'it, 'tis worth it.

And it can accurately register the blend of irony and shocked self-awareness with which Bianca answers her mother's factually-intended question, 'You have not seen all since, sure?'

> That have I, mother,
> The monument and all: I'm so beholding
> To this kind, honest, courteous gentleman.
> You'ld little think it, mother — showed me all,
> Had me from place to place so fashionably;
> The kindness of some people, how't exceeds!
> 'Faith, I have seen that I little thought to see
> I'th' morning when I rose.

This ability to do equal justice to the ordinary surface demands of the situation and to its hidden depths and the inward perceptions of characters is one of the most remarkable features of Middleton's style. It is his particular variation on the current interest in the possibilities of language, a kind of extended punning seen at its most brilliant in the two central scenes of *The Changeling* but evident throughout both plays and intermittently in others. Here, for instance, what Bianca 'little thought to see' is the Duke's palace and its treasures, but it is also the revelation of his lust for her, and even more her growing acceptance of the situation in which this involves her. Recognizing that her scope is severely limited by a society in which women are commodities to be bought and sold, she resolves to sell herself to the highest bidder and the play presents her resolution without moral finger-pointing but rather with a grave sympathy.

The idea of woman as a commodity and marriage as an auction or market-place is even clearer in the second strand of the plot and the actions of Isabella, the woman chiefly concerned in it. She trembles on the brink of marriage to an idiot because her father has resolved to sell her to the highest bidder. From the first he thinks of her as an investment on which he is now about to realize a worthwhile profit. He calls her his 'dear' child but is quick to explain that he means 'dear to my purse', and for all his simple-mindedness, the ward is typical enough of the world of bargaining in which he moves to insist on an item-by-item examination of Isabella before he agrees to the marriage. For her part, Isabella ironically but quite seriously comforts herself with the very defect which, given a free choice, would have made her reject him — his complete witlessness, which will enable her to cuckold him with impunity:

> But that I have th' advantage of the fool
> As much as woman's heart can wish and joy at,
> What an infernal torment 'twere to be
> Thus bought and sold and turned and pried into; when alas
> The worst bit is too good for him! And the comfort is,
> H'as but a cater's place on't, and provides
> All for another's table.

That 'alas' is expertly placed to catch the nuances of Isabella's feelings and the obscene innuendo of 'the worst bit' mocks not so much the witless ward as the itemization of a human being. Isabella's predicament was common enough in the society of her day to be referred to in sermons and tracts. Her active consent to the incestuous liaison with her uncle is, like Bianca's adultery, seen both as evidence of the corruption of a money-infected society and the assertion of a woman's right to choose her way of life, if only in secret. It is casually assumed that Isabella will make her own extramarital sexual arrangements — 'she'll find leisure to make that good enough'. The tragedy lies in the fact that such assertions in such a society can only take the form of adultery, incest or procuring.

Both Bianca and Isabella are tainted by their acceptance of the values of an acquisitive society. Bianca's ardent romantic impulse coarsens into a hard-nosed materialism as she comes to reckon her well being in terms of new cloaks and velvet gowns and complains about the absence of silken quilts. Isabella, who suffers genuine anguish at the prospect of marrying the idiot ward, resigns herself with cynical practicality to improving the situation by incest, though she needs the face-saving assurance that her uncle is not her blood relative. It is Livia who is ready at hand to provide this assurance which she spins out of her fertile wit with no compunction whatever. It is in the character of Livia that the corruption of a society where people have become commodities is shown in its most acute form. Livia is so thoroughly imbued with the values of her society that she finds the business of intrigue and manipulation fascinating. She is thoroughly aware of the circumstances which lead women to break their marriage vows, as her words to her brother in defence of her niece Isabella show:

I must offend you then, if truth will do't,
And take my niece's part, and call't injustice
To force her love to one she never saw.
Maids should both see and like — all little enough:
If they love truly after that, 'tis well
Counting the time, she takes one man till death,
That's a hard task, I tell you; but one may
Enquire at three years' end amongst young wives
And mark how the game goes.

Her reply to her brother's 'objection that a man too has the same obligation of fidelity to a single partner as the woman shows a clear recognition of the one-sidedness of the institution of marriage in her society. Having cynically remarked that one woman is enough for a man, she goes on to explain why:

he tastes of many sundry dishes
That we poor wretches never lay our lips to —
As obedience, forsooth, subjection, duty, and such kickshaws,
All of our making, but served in to them;
And if we lick a finger then, sometimes,
We are not to blame; your best cooks use it.

The metaphor of food both trivializes the moral transgression and stresses the purely appetitive element in marriage. Livia herself, having 'buried two husbands' is determined to avoid the marriage trap henceforth. From one point of view therefore, she is already shown to be corrupted by her world, unlike Bianca and Isabella who are shown in the process of being corrupted. Her moral nature has been so infected that she is capable of flattering herself into the belief that it is her generosity of spirit and family loyalty which prompts her to help her brother in his incestuous affair (though there is an inevitable element of irony in her reflections here). Her comments during the game of chess with Leantio's mother are not only ironically apt to the seduction going on offstage but are a dramatic emblem of her role in the play. She presents herself as a comfortable, essentially kind-hearted old body, much like the widow herself with perhaps a touch more worldly wisdom, and more than half believes it herself. When she genuinely falls in love with Leantio, she knows enough about the ways of her world to woo him with offers of worldly wealth. But, as the lines quoted above show, Middleton never lets us judge Livia simply as the stereotype of the lusty widow who cannot control her sexual desire; she is given too much insight into the springs of feminine behaviour in her society for that.

The masque which concludes the tragedy is frankly theatrical and deliberately heightens the mundane atmosphere of the rest of the play. Its immediate occasion is the wedding ceremony of the Duke, now free to marry Bianca, since her husband has been disposed of by Hippolito. An almost mathematically apt justice is meted out as the proceedings take place. At the wedding masque prepared by Guardiano, where all the principal characters meet their end, Livia, the goddess of mercenary marriage, dies inhaling the incense that in a true masque would be offered up to

Juno, the marriage goddess. Isabella is struck down by the gold for which she has sold herself, Hippolito struck dead by Cupid's arrows. The masque maker falls into a trap of his own devising and the Duke and Bianca both die after drinking from the cup that should have betokened their wedded bliss.

A modern audience cannot perhaps take this ending seriously, since the form of the masque, with its allegorical representation of action (a favourite entertainment of the Jacobean court) is no longer a live theatrical convention. But it is not at all clear that even the Jacobean audience was expected to take the ending entirely at face value. Certainly their baroque deaths do not endow the protagonists with tragic stature except in the most external and superficial sense that they imitate the deaths of the high-born heroes of other Jacobean tragedies. But it is entirely fitting that a play which concentrates its dramatic attention on the distortions of marriage as an institution should reach its climax in a point-by-point destruction of the most spectacular social manifestation of that institution. The tragedy of *Women Beware Women* is not a matter of heroic deaths but of women trapped by a callously commercial society into lives of squalid subterfuge. Adultery, the mainspring of the action, is a moral offence and a social one, a sin against God and a threat to the stability of society because it puts in hazard all the *acceptable* social roles of women — as wives, mothers and daughters. But Middleton shows us that it is also the only means available to women in his society to assert their sense of being persons, not commodities. It is unpromising material for tragedy if one considers tragedy to be always and necessarily concerned with eternal questions of man's relation to fate, to the mysterious and inexorable in human life. But Middleton contrives to make it as starkly memorable as Ibsen. *Women Beware Women* (the title should by now be seen to be at least partly ironic) is the first great domestic tragedy in English, perhaps the only one.

If it has a rival, it must surely be Middleton's other great tragedy *The Changeling*, written in collaboration with William Rowley. The tragic focus is sharper here and while there is still an awareness of the constraints within which women have to live in a patriarchal society, the emphasis is more firmly on moral choice and its tragic consequences. In *The Changeling* too there is little sense of a hostile fate or of the destinies of nations depending on the outcome of the action. The entire play takes place in the castle of Vermandero and the madhouse run by Alibius. The latter place is the location of the sub-plot, usually credited together with the play's opening and closing scenes to William Rowley, who co-authored half a dozen plays with Middleton and is one of the most prolific collaborators in the drama of the period. It is often dismissed as uninspired hack work only marginally related to the central tragic action, but it is vitally connected to that action, as we shall see.

The heroine Beatrice has generally and perhaps rightly received most of the critical attention devoted to the play. Certainly Beatrice's awakening to a sense of moral responsibility for her actions is an essential element in the tragedy. She arrives at this awakening through an understanding of the human implications of a murder which she originally regards as a necessary if somewhat disagreeable act which must be carried out so that she may achieve her own desires. The original innocence of Beatrice has often been stressed, but if she is innocent, she is so in a very special sense, a sense best indicated perhaps by a pair of quotations from Graham Greene. The first is from *The Quiet American:* 'Innocence always calls mutely for protection when we would be so much wiser to guard ourselves against it; innocence is like a dumb leper who has lost his bell, wandering the world, meaning no harm'. In a later novel, *A Burnt-Out Case,* one of the characters says: 'God preserve us from all innocence. At least the guilty know what they are about.'[1] The source of Beatrice's dangerous innocence is the social and psychological position she occupies. As the only daughter of a wealthy widowed aristocrat, she has clearly been accustomed to having her own way over a good many matters in her life; she is very obviously a spoilt child. But she appears also to have inherited a certain wilfulness from her father. When, in the opening scene, Vermandero expresses his determination to see Beatrice married to Piracquo he says:

> He shall be bound to me,
> As fast as this tie can hold him; I'll want
> My will else.

Beatrice, who has found that her affections have suddenly shifted from Piracquo to Alsemero mutters under her breath: 'I shall want mine if you do it.' 'Will' becomes an ominously significant word in the play later on, both in its modern sense and in the specifically Elizabethan sense of sexual appetite. A hint of the second meaning is perhaps already present in the line with which de Flores, the ugly retainer who secretly desires Beatrice, ends the scene: 'Though I get nothing else, I'll have my will.'

De Flores is the agent of Beatrice's moral education and it is in that light alone that he has usually been regarded. Like Flamineo and Bosola, he is a decayed gentleman, deeply resentful of the circumstances in which he finds himself, debarred both by physical ugliness and his social position as an employee in Vermandero's household, from legitimately paying court to Beatrice. For it is his desire for Beatrice that dominates his entire existence. He recognizes quite clearly her intense loathing for him, but also the compulsion within himself to pursue her, if only to provoke her reaction of scornful contempt:

> Will't never mend, this scorn,
> One side nor other? Must I be enjoin'd
> To follow still while she flies from me? Well,
> Fates do your worst, I'll please myself with sight
> Of her, at all opportunities,
> If but to spite her anger;

He attributes her contempt for him to 'a peevish will' but in some depth of his being he is aware that the very ferocity of Beatrice's aversion to him brings it perilously close to its opposite. She herself is entirely unable to account for the virulent hatred he arouses in her.

---

[1] The quotations are used together by Laurence Lerner in an article on 'Graham Greene' in *The Critical Quarterly,* Autumn 1963

> Your pardon, sir, 'tis my infirmity;
> Nor can I other reason render you
> Than his or hers, of some particular thing
> They must abandon as a deadly poison,
> Which to a thousand other tastes were wholesome;
> Such to mine eyes is that same fellow there,
> The same that report speaks of the basilisk.

The collision between de Flores's desperate desire and Beatrice's callous 'innocence' occasions the two great scenes of the central plot. In the first, Beatrice hits on the plan of using de Flores's passion for her to make him get rid of her unwanted fiancé Alonso de Piracquo, so that the way is clear for her to marry Alsemero, her new love. After de Flores has done the deed, she plans to pay him off. When the scheme first occurs to her, her only self-reproach is that she may have spoilt its chance of success by her earlier attitude towards de Flores:

> I was to blame,
> I ha' marred so good a market with my scorn;
> 'T had been done questionless; the ugliest creature
> Creation fram'd for some use; yet to see
> I could not mark so much where it should be!

Two points in Beatrice's reflections here call for comment. The first is her bland assumption that, had she been a little more considerate towards de Flores, he would willingly have committed murder for her — ' 'T had been done questionless'. This shows exactly how much, or how little, she actually thinks about the deed involved. The second is the particular context in which she uses the idea of a purposive creation. The physical ugliness of de Flores is to Beatrice evidence that he was obviously intended for some nefarious purpose. The more thoughtful members of the Jacobean audience may have been prompted by these lines to reflect critically on the current view that deformity of body always betokened spiritual evil; it is certainly here a sign of Beatrice's unquestioning assumption that the sole purpose of another human being's existence was that he could be a tool in her hands. This readiness to manipulate other people (it shows itself tragically later in the play when she has no qualms about getting rid of her maid Diaphanta once she has served her purpose as a substitute in bed to fool Alsemero on the wedding night) links Beatrice to Livia, but whereas the social pressures behind Livia's manoeuvrings are clearly displayed, the stress in this play is very much on Beatrice's aberrant 'will'. We have no feeling that Beatrice has been constrained in her development as a woman. Though the original marriage with Piracquo was obviously arranged, there is no evidence that Beatrice was either unconsulted or unwilling unless we put great emphasis on her later reference to 'the first token my father made me send him'. The very smoothness with which Beatrice slips into marriage with Alsemero after Piracquo's murder indicates that Vermandero is not likely to have imposed his will on his daughter without regard to her own wishes in the matter.

To Beatrice, the elimination of Piracquo is not a moral consideration at all, but an aesthetic one, a matter of her skill in using dangerous substances:

Why, men of art make much of poison,
Keep one to expel another; where was my art?

It is significant that this reflection is made as an aside by Beatrice at a time when Alsemero is by her side. Though she professedly loves him, she does not choose to confide in him, which suggests that her innocence is not incompatible with a realization that Alsemero would be outraged by her plan. In any case, too exclusive a stress on Beatrice's innocence and her moral growth obscures the extent to which the tragedy is that of both Beatrice and de Flores. The title of the play is deliberately ambiguous and the ambiguities are listed rather than clarified in the closing moments when virtually all the protagonists are seen to be 'changelings' in one sense or another. Literally, the 'changeling' is Antonio in the sub-plot but clearly both Beatrice and de Flores have the highest claims to the epithet. She obviously presents something much subtler and more complicated than is even hinted at by Alsemero's sententious summary 'beauty changed to ugly whoredom' but it is equally important to see that de Flores's tragedy is also much more than the breach of social decorum which so offends Alsemero: 'servant obedience (changed) to a master sin, imperious murder'. (It is characteristic of Alsemero that he speaks only of external changes not inner ones.) De Flores's state of mind when Beatrice, for her own ulterior purpose, flatters him, is not simple self-deception. It is much nearer to that indicated in the opening lines of one of Shakespeare's sonnets:

When my love swears that she is made of truth,
I do believe her, though I know she lies.

With one part of himself he is perfectly aware that the face she now praises so extravagantly is unchanged from the time she abused it almost instinctively:

'Tis the same physnomy, to a hair and pimple,
Which she called scurvy scarce an hour ago.

But the change from abuse to praise is an intense, almost sexually pleasing delight so that the question of its truthfulness subsides in the ecstasy of listening:

    'Tis half an act of pleasure
To hear her talk thus to me.

One of the many ironies of this scene in which de Flores undertakes to do the evil deed for Beatrice is that her words to him, spoken as flattery, are borne out by the subsequent action:

Hardness becomes the visage of a man well,
It argues service, resolution, manhood.

These are precisely the qualities which de Flores shows during and after the murder in his attitude towards Beatrice. When de Flores kneels before her and begs to serve her, the moment is at one level a parody of the chivalrous knight vowing to rescue the damsel in distress; the 'service' involved is, after all, the murder of an innocent man. But at another level, as later events show, de Flores does act as a faithful, courageous and resourceful protector to his lady. His tragedy is that, given the social and psychological circumstances, it is only in the act of secret murder that these virtues can be shown; but to argue that because they are deployed for an evil purpose the virtues themselves are not real is cant. De Flores's single-minded pursuit of his own ends in this scene (he means to sleep with her as his reward) is almost as egotistic as Beatrice's own although it is faintly redeemed by his partial belief that she has had an inexplicable change of heart. 'Some women are odd feeders' he reflects, generalizing his inability to account for Beatrice's new attitude, as earlier he had solaced himself with a similar notion:

> I'll despair the less,
> Because there's daily precedent of bad faces
> Belov'd beyond all reason.

There are many details in the play which suggest that the hatred which Beatrice feels for de Flores is very close to desire and that it is through complicity in murder that she discovers this truth about herself. Her casting off of her second glove in rage because de Flores has picked up the one she intended for Alsemero, the obsessive nature of her aversion and her inability to account for it, the readiness with which she turns to flattering de Flores — all these point at least to the possibility of unacknowledged passion. The compelling force of this scene and the subsequent one which 'mirrors' it (when de Flores makes explicit the reward he claims) is partly due to the presence of this undercurrent of genuine passion underneath the driving egotism of both protagonists.

T.S. Eliot has written that 'the tragedy of Beatrice is not that she has lost Alsemero. . .; it is that she has won de Flores'. This seems to me a misleading way of putting it, though Eliot's view has been widely accepted. It would be more accurate to say, as I have suggested, that her tragedy is that in her social milieu she could 'win' de Flores only secretly and only through murder.

The scene in which de Flores comes for his reward is perhaps the greatest in English tragedy outside Shakespeare. It starts in an almost coquettish vein and Middleton is capable of introducing a touch of Jacobean grotesquerie not, as often in Webster, to send shivers up the spine but to add to our understanding of character and situation. There is an element of 'savage farce' in the flippancy with which de Flores shows Beatrice the dead man's finger with the ring still on it, as evidence that he has indeed kept his part of the bargain:

> *De Flores*: I've a token for you
> *Beatrice*:   For me?
> *De Flores*: But it was sent somewhat unwillingly, I could not get the ring
>   without the finger.

It is in de Flores's retort to Beatrice's horrified reaction that we see the essential difference in their moral awareness at this point. 'Why?' asks de Flores,

> is that more
> Than killing the whole man? I cut his heart strings.
> A greedy hand thrust in a dish at court
> In a mistake hath had as much as this.

De Flores is totally conscious of the gravity of what he has done and yet capable of dismissing it with a touch of casual black humour. Beatrice however is still concerned with externals, though there is the first hint of a regard for others in her words ' 'Tis the first token my father made me send him'. But she soon recovers her self-concern and is ready and anxious to pay de Flores off. As Christopher Ricks has shown,[1] this scene and to a lesser extent the earlier one are based on the exploitation of double meanings in a series of key words, each of which had specifically sexual connotations in the seventeenth century as well as more general meanings — blood, will, act, deed and service. The last of these is the most important. De Flores uses these words with a full awareness of their sexual sense and the strategy of this scene, and of the main action as a whole, is the progressive enforcement on Beatrice of the sexual implications of these words. Her moral education, in other words, can be seen as a linguistic one; her understanding of the full range of meanings of these crucial words is tantamount to her awareness of the moral implications of her action, not only in terms of the price she has to pay but also of realizing how deeply the sexual senses had influenced her initial decision to use de Flores as an instrument. The tragic implications of 'service' underpin the scene both in language and action, as the audience compares the earlier visual image of de Flores kneeling before Beatrice to beg 'employment' with the later one of Beatrice kneeling to beg de Flores to 'Let me go poor unto my bed with honour'.

But an account such as this does less than justice to the potentially tragic stature of de Flores which is also fully presented in the scene. It will not do to regard de Flores as simply the cold-hearted sensualist who has got the innocent beauty in his toils and is now gloating over her, like the moustache-twirling villain leering over his proud beauty in later melodrama. For while it is true that de Flores is as unshakeable as Shylock is his determination to have his prize of human flesh, it is equally evident that he is fully alive to all the moral consequences of the act, not only for Beatrice, *but for himself*. In Graham Greene's words 'the guilty know what they are about'. His flippancy masks a full awareness of the outrage he has committed on his own moral self by his crime, as his scornful reply to Beatrice's offer of the ring as his reward indicates:

'Twill hardly buy a capcase for one's conscience, though,
To keep it from the worm, as fine as 'tis.

His later words show his sense of the value of human life:

Offer gold?
The life blood of man! Is anything
Valued too precious for my recompense?

And the tone of his words to Beatrice — threat, command, appeal, all inextricably entwined — indicates real suffering which cannot be reduced simply to sexual impatience:

I have eased
You of your trouble, think on't, I'm in pain,
And must be eas'd of you; 'tis a charity,
Justice invites your blood to understand me.

[1] The Moral and Poetical Structure of *The Changeling, Essays in Criticism*, July 1960, Vol. X 290-360.

Like Flamineo, de Flores is fully aware of the part played by economic necessity in pushing a man towards crime, but unlike him never uses it as a complete excuse and never thinks of murder as anything other than a uniquely evil act. Finally, it is worth pointing out that while complicity in murder brings out the virtues already noted in de Flores, it does not essentially alter Beatrice's self-regarding behaviour. All it does is make her aware of a moral standard by which that behaviour is judged. But in practice she deliberately ignores this standard and remains callously egotistic to the end. She has no compunction about eliminating her maid Diaphanta when her existence may be a threat to her 'honour' and even goes to her death with lies ('Remember I am true unto your bed') and treachery towards de Flores ('He lies, the villain does belie me!') on her lips. By contrast, there is a singleness of mind about de Flores's last words which have a tragic poignancy heightened by the conviction of certain damnation:

Make haste, Joanna, by that token to thee,
Canst not forget, so lately put in mind;
I would not go to leave thee far behind.

To turn from the central action to the sub-plot may seem literally like going from the sublime to the ridiculous, but something needs to be said of the various levels of connection between the two parts of the play for, critical opinion to the contrary notwithstanding, they do form a coherent whole. In terms of plot, the two parts are linked by the presence in the madhouse of two refugees from Vermandero's castle who are suspected of Piracquo's murder. There is also the fairly familiar Jacobean device whereby the sub-plot tends to render physically what is figurative in the main plot. (Compare the Gloucester plot in *King Lear*). The madmen's antics are a visual image of the madness of love and de Flores's reference to 'barley-brake' reminds us of the madhouse games. Lollio, the madhouse keeper's servant, demands his 'share' in Isabella's favours in a cruder fashion than de Flores's analogous demand from Beatrice, and so on. In the dance of madmen at the wedding of Beatrice and Alsemero, the traditional purpose of the anti-masque at great weddings — to forestall actual mockery by ritualizing it and to demonstrate that the marriage was strong enough to withstand mockery[1] — is subverted by the audience's knowledge that this marriage *is* a mockery. But the most important function of the sub-plot is to confront the main plot with an individual and social class in terms of which the society of the main action is seen to be weak and decadent. In a sense, de Flores is the outsider in Vermandero's castle who represents a different social class from that of the effete aristocracy with its regard only for the external trappings of 'honour' (Beatrice's attitude finds its cruder equivalent in Alsemero's virginity test). The figure of Isabella, the madhouse keeper's wife has obvious analogies with that of Beatrice where their situations are concerned. She too is faced with a marriage in which her assent was not a prime consideration and by a husband who is as suspicious as Alsemero. She, like Beatrice is faced with the possibility of extra-marital adventure. But her moral

---

[1] See William Empson, *Some Versions of Pastoral*, Ch. II (London, 1950).

perception is simpler and more straightforward and she can see straight through the sham of the disguised madman's courtly pretensions:

> No, I have no beauty now,
> Nor never had, but what was in my garments.
> You a quick-sighted lover? Come not near me.
> Keep your caparisons, y'are aptly clad;
> I came a feigner to return stark mad.

In refusing Antonio's advances even though tempted by them, Isabella shows a moral steadfastness which, far from confirming the institution of enforced marriage, compels even the foolish Alibius to recognize the necessity for change. Indeed, in the clutter of references to change which strews the last few lines, it is only Alibius, and not any member of the aristocratic society who is capable of real change —

> I see all apparent, wife, and will change now
> Into a better husband

— although there is some uncertainty about exactly what he *has* learned. What is evident at the end of the play is that, de Flores apart, the society of Vermandero's Castle is quite incapable of moral growth. Nothing is clearer evidence of this fact than the blank incomprehension of the tragedy we have witnessed in Alsemero's ponderous last line:

> Man and his sorrow at the grave must part.

Beaumont and Fletcher: the trivialization of tragedy

Middleton is the last great tragic dramatist in English, with the partial exception of Ford. It is usual to speak of the later Caroline and Jacobean drama as a period of decline and there is no reason to quarrel with this view, provided we do not fall into a kind of inverted evolutionary trap where we see drama getting progressively worse through some inherent weakness until it dies of its own incurable sickness. There is nothing inevitable about the decline of the drama, though in retrospect some causes of it can be suggested. Perhaps the two most important are the progressive narrowing of the audience for new drama, and the growing emphasis, through the example of the court masque, on scenic extravagance and spectacular effects. Nor was the decline of the drama a neat and unbroken one, going steadily downhill all the way. In some ways Chapman, at the very beginning of the Jacobean period, may be said to be decadent in the moral confusion which enables him to take the tragic pretensions of heroes such as Byron so seriously, while at the very end of the period John Ford still has a recognizable though fiercely disputed claim to something of Webster's tragic stature, even though it is based on a single play. If we avoid thinking of the whole process as orderly and sequential however, it is fair enough to speak of a decline in Jacobean drama. It is most evident in the inability to take the tragic mode seriously any longer and the consequent blurring of focus which affects the quality of both comedy and tragedy. Nowhere is this more clearly marked than in the attempts at tragedy or something related to it associated with the Beaumont and Fletcher partnership.

As already stated, the actual collaboration between the two lasted for only five years till 1613, when Beaumont married and gave up writing plays. But the two best tragic plays (if that is what they are) associated with them are in fact genuine collaborative efforts; these are *The Maid's Tragedy* and *A King and No King*, both dating from about 1611. Although neither is performed except very rarely on the modern stage, there is no doubt about their theatrical effectiveness. For a long time Beaumont and Fletcher were more popular than either Shakespeare or Jonson. Writing after the Restoration, Dryden notes that for every play by Shakespeare or Jonson that was performed there were two by Beaumont and Fletcher. Indeed it may be said that their theatrical effectiveness is exactly what is the matter with them, for everything else is sacrificed to this objective. It may seem odd to criticize work intended for theatrical performance for succeeding too well, but most people have no difficulty in distinguishing between what moves, shocks or amuses them in the theatre without having any lasting impact and what haunts the mind and imagination long after the actual theatrical experience is over. It is something like the distinction we make between 'serious theatre' and 'entertainment', always providing we remember that 'serious theatre' can include comedy and even farce (e.g. Chaplin in *Modern Times*). By these standards both *The Maid's Tragedy* and *A King and No King* are undoubtedly entertaining but essentially trivial plays.

The Maid's Tragedy obviously purports to be a tragedy proper while *A King and No King* is Beaumont and Fletcher's most successful effort in the tragi-comic genre which they made so fashionable. The title of the first play refers to the grief and eventual death of Aspatia, who is rejected by her fiancé Amintor in favour of the faithless Evadne. But the bulk of the action does not in fact concern either Aspatia or her feelings, which remain static throughout the play. It is the marriage between Amintor and Evadne, or rather its aftermath, on which the dramatic interest is concentrated. The action unfolds in a series of sensational scenes, each effective in itself, but developing no cumulative power nor building up to a total understanding of either character or theme. Thus Aspatia's first entrance, when she speaks only three lines in reply to Melantius's good wishes on her marriage set up a state of suspense in the audience's mind:

My hard fortunes
Deserve not scorn; for I was never proud
When they were good.

On her exit the meaning of these puzzling lines is revealed to Melantius the returning hero, who learns that Amintor has been ordered to marry his sister Evadne by the king. We are kept waiting to find out the reason for the king's behaviour while Melantius and Calianax, Aspatia's father engage in a fierce quarrel at the spectacular marriage masque of Amintor and Evadne. The quarrel enables the dramatists to indulge in a language which is at once rhetorically overblown and poetically meagre, a fairly constant feature of their writing:

Would that blood,
That sea of blood, that I have lost in fight,

Were running in thy veins, that it might make thee
Apt to say less, or able to maintain,
Should'st thou say more!

But the quarrel gives no insight into the character of either participant or further understanding of the situation, nor does it lead anywhere, as the king orders a reconciliation. It is one of many situations engineered by the dramatists in order to extract theatrical mileage out of it, regardless of plausibility or coherence. Thus on the eve of the consummation of the marriage Aspatia is given an emotional splurge as she takes her leave of Amintor:

Go, and be happy in your lady's love,
May all the wrongs that you have done to me,
Be utterly forgotten in my death!
I'll trouble you no more; yet I will take
A parting kiss, and will not be denied.
You'll come, my lord, and see the virgins weep
When I am laid in earth, though you yourself
Can know no pity. . . .
So with my prayer I leave you, and must try
Some yet unpractised way to grieve and die.

But she is not to die for a good while yet, though the hint thrown out in the last line and a half gives one more agreeable twinge of suspense. Amintor's immediate reaction is equally extreme:

I did that lady wrong. Methinks, I feel
Her grief shook suddenly through all my veins.
Mine eyes run

Considering that it is his wedding night perhaps he is right to add: 'This is strange at such a time'. But his troubles last a bare ten lines before with a brisk 'Away, my idle fears!' he is ready to greet his new bride with suitable rapture:

Yonder she is, the lustre of whose eye
Can blot away the sad remembrance
Of all these things.

One scene is constantly blotting away the remembrance, sad or sensational, of another in *The Maid's Tragedy*. The lines of Amintor just quoted are a prelude to the great theatrical revelation of the play when we learn just why the king has ordered the marriage of Amintor and Evadne. The down-to-earth directness of Evadne's words here are a refreshing change from the attitudinizing of Aspatia and Amintor and may remind us of Middleton's sterner tragic realism. But attitudinizing is never far off. Even when he learns of the king's perfidy, Amintor's respect for sovereignty prevents him taking revenge, which provides the excuse for another theatrically effective scene when the king mocks Amintor by asking him intimately suggestive questions about the wedding night which the latter is compelled to equivocate over. Evadne's repentance for her participation in the king's trickery provides another 'fine scene', as does Amintor's sudden attack on her for killing the king. The same overriding concern for what will 'go' on the stage forms the basis of the opening scene of Act IV, when Amintor denies in asides what he says aloud to Calianax. The conception of honour which lies behind the play is not only outrageous, it is constantly shifting under no greater pressure than that of theatrical sensation. Aspatia appears disguised as a soldier for no other reason but to die in Amintor's arms, but not before she has revealed herself, causing Amintor to go mad with grief and kill himself, as well he might. And Evadne, who was able to taunt her husband cheerfully over his cuckoldry, is now so transformed that denunciation by him is enough to drive her towards suicide. Multiple deaths are of course a feature of Senecan tragedy which the Elizabethans took over and there are quite as many in plays by Webster and Tourneur (to say nothing of *Hamlet*) as in *The Maid's Tragedy*. But here there is no overall pattern, thematic or otherwise, that would justify their total psychological implausibility and naturalistic improbability. We cannot take them seriously at any level because the dramatists clearly do not. Tragedy has kept its outward show of passionate love and heroic sacrifice, but has been totally emptied of its inner core. At the end of *The Changeling,* the hollowness of Alsemero's final moralizing reflected a decadent aristocratic society which was judged by standards clearly present within the play. At the end of *The Maid's Tragedy,* the new ruler's last words simply perpetuate the confusion of values, or rather, the dramatists' readiness to shuffle them around like so many playing cards — king, queen, knave — which characterize the entire play.

In spite of its concern with the serious theme of incest, or rather because of it, *A King and No King* is even more trivial, less concerned with tragic issues than *The Maid's Tragedy.* An ostensible concern with serious issues — revenge, incest, honour — was an essential feature of the new genre of tragic-comedy of which Beaumont and Fletcher's *Philaster* (1611) was the hugely successful English prototype and which was evidently congenial to Fletcher's flashy talent. In his prefatory epistle to his first venture into the form, *The Faithful Shepherdess*, produced in 1610 but unsuccessful in its attempt to put tragi-comedy in a pastoral setting, Fletcher gives a significantly superficial definition of the new form, adapted from the Italian critic Giovanni Battista Guarini: 'A tragi-comedy' Fletcher writes,

> is not so called in respect of mirth and killing, but in respect it wants deaths, which is enough to make it no tragedy; but brings some near it, which is enough to make it no comedy; which must be a representation of familiar people with such kind of trouble as no life be questioned; so that a god is as lawful in this as in a tragedy, and mean people as in a comedy.

Guarini had written that tragi-comedy takes from tragedy, among other things, 'its danger but not its death.' The possibilities of the form are variously realized in such plays as *Cymbeline* and *Measure for Measure,* but *A King and No King* is little more than a display of theatrical virtuosity. Perhaps its appeal to the young law students who would have formed a good part of its original audience when the King's Men produced it at the Blackfriars lay in the detective-story element of the plot, the challenge to anticipate the correct solution of a tricky problem. Keeping the audience in the dark and producing one theatrical rabbit after another out of a hatful of coincidences and improbabilities becomes the name of the theatrical game. The title of the play itself provides a clue to the unravelling. The central situation of the seemingly incestuous passion of the hero Arbaces for Panthea is exploited for the maximum number of instances of the 'danger, not the death'. Thus Arbaces no sooner kisses Panthea than he is overcome by guilt and has her imprisoned, then repents and sends the buffoon soldier Bessus to act as proxy for him in his forbidden wooing. At its best in Jacobean drama, the mixing of the low comedy and high seriousness enlarges our understanding of the play as a whole — *Hamlet* and *The Changeling* are very different but equally successful examples. Here, the insistence on mixing high and low according to the tragi-comic formula results in coarsening the comedy and diluting the tragedy. It is impossible to find unity or coherence in a character such as Arbaces who goes from high-falutin' blank verse to ribald prose with no stronger motivation than a casually uttered 'Thou and I, Have not been merry lately'. Similarly the coarse buffoonery of Bessus merely devalues the seriousness of the incest theme without casting any fresh light on it, because high life and low plot have no connection stronger than the formula's requirement that both be present. Arbaces's vacillations between the determination to consummate his incestuous passion and then destroy himself and the resolve not to do either are theatrical in every possible sense except that in which theatre is an image of life. The prison scene in which he alternates between begging Panthea to yield to him and begging her not to, ending in his crazed resolve to rape her and then kill himself carries the 'danger not the death' formula to the edge of parody. Indeed one is strongly tempted to speculate that both the dramatists had their tongues firmly wedged in their cheeks while writing the play, and that the original audience were well aware of this. Lines like 'The King rages extremely: shall we slink away?' need tragic heroes made of sterner stuff than Arbaces to survive them. The final evasion of the issues of incest in *A King and No King* is not merely one blemish in an otherwise coherent play. It is simply the most obvious sign of the fact that the whole play is no more than an elaborate charade of problem-solving at the level of technical virtuosity. Beaumont and Fletcher here ask themselves a series of questions such as: 'How near to death can the central characters be brought without actually killing them? How effectively can high and low characters, tragic heroics and comic antics be intermingled for the sake of theatrical contrast alone? How can the maximum degree of surprise be obtained at the end, if surprise alone be made the objective? The solution they found to these questions was to set the pattern for the so-called Heroic Tragedy of the later seventeenth century. It is not surprising that Dryden found much to praise in *A King and No King*. Though they wrote in the reign of James I, Beaumont and Fletcher are in many ways not the last dramatists of the Jacobean period, but the first of the Restoration.

John Ford's 'Tis Pity She's a Whore

Ford is generally thought of as a Caroline dramatist, though his greatest play, and the only one regularly performed today (it was brilliantly adapted for the cinema recently) is difficult to date precisely and may date from any time between 1615 and 1633. Like many other dramatists of the period Ford began his career as a collaborator with Thomas Dekker and William Rowley. He came from a family of prosperous landed gentry in Devonshire and studied law at the Middle Temple when Marston was in residence there and was already a fashionable dramatist. Ford was careful to stress that his plays were the 'fruits of his leisure' to avoid the stigma of being a professional writer and wished to be regarded as a talented gentleman, a fairly typical ambition in his circle. Seven plays known to be by Ford alone have survived and of these *'Tis Pity She's a Whore* is undoubtedly the finest. Many of the others have powerful scenes and occasional passages of the elegantly elegiac dramatic writing which seems to have come so easily to Ford but in their jugglings with frozen aristocratic concepts of Love and Honour they are too close to the bombastic posturings of the heroic drama of the Restoration to have more than curiosity value for the modern reader, though *Perkin Warbeck* is an interesting experiment in the psychology of role-playing.

    'Tis Pity She's a Whore deals with the theme of incest which fascinated Jacobean dramatists and which continues to be as powerful a social taboo in our society as it was then. In our own time artists as diverse as D.H. Lawrence, Thomas Mann and John Osborne have handled the theme; in the Jacobean period, in addition to the trivial flirtation with it in *A King and No King* and its oblique but powerful undercurrent in *The Duchess of Malfi,* incest is the overt concern of the plays of such as Massinger's *The Unnatural Combat* and (in part) Shakespeare's *Pericles.* While there is some occasional uncertainty in Ford's attitude towards incest, there is no doubt about the depth of his interest in it, not so much as a pyschological concern but as a social prohibition. The central relationship between the brother and sister is not used to explore the nature of incestuous love and differentiate it from normal love between man and woman. Rather it is seen as a figure for a love that aspires to absolute commitment and absolute self-containment (like the central relationship in *Othello,* which it frequently echoes) and is therefore doomed to destruction through its inevitable collision with society and its institutions — marriage, the Church and paternal authority. In part these institutions actively confirm the taboo (through the Friar's exhortations to Giovanni) and seek to destroy its violator as Vasques, acting on behalf of the 'injured husband' Soranza eventually does. In part the tension generated within the lovers themselves by their growing awareness of the very basic nature of their transgression begins to tell on them and weaken them from within. This is truer of Annabella than Giovanni, who remains steadfast to the end, though the strain shows in his deranged language and behaviour and in his original willingness to share Annabella with her husband. Thus it is difficult to regard *'Tis Pity She's a Whore* as a thesis drama arguing the rightness or wrongness of incest. Giovanni certainly does so, but the shallowness, sophistry and even self-contradiction he displays in his arguments make it impossible to take him seriously as an intellectual defender of incest. We know from the Friar's praise of Giovanni's scholastic achievements that he has a fine intellect, but he is prone to the besetting sin of intellectual pride as well as to the mental aberration caused by his excessive and unusual passion. Some such account must certainly be offered of the so-called argument by which he seeks to enlist religion itself in favour of incest,

an enterprise visually mocked by the Friar's protesting presence before him as he speaks:

> Say that we had one father, say one womb
> (Curse to my joys!) gave both us life and birth;
> Are we not therefore each to other bound
> So much the more by nature? By the links
> Of blood, of reason? Nay, if you will have't,
> Even of religion, to be ever one,
> One soul, one flesh, one love, one heart, one *all?*

The specious plausibility of this may evoke, and may have been intended to evoke in the theatre an uncomfortable doubt about the rationality of the incest taboo. But we are surely intended to question the mental stability of a hero who moves in a few lines from an assertion of unshakeable allegiance of his passion —

> It were more ease to stop the ocean
> From floats and ebbs, than to dissuade my vows

— to a ready acceptance of the Friar's injunction to repentance:

> All this I'll do to free me from the rod
> Of vengeance; else I'll swear my fate's my god.

Ford treats the predicament of the lovers as both blameworthy and pitiable, though the accent is very much more on 'the pity of it all', the sense of tragic waste in the loss of such idealistic energy and passion as is represented by the young lovers. In comparison with Giovanni, Annabella's other suitors are seen to be grotesquely inept, morally and intellectually. One of them, Grimaldi, has no compunction about involving himself in a murder plot to get rid of his rival and, when he accidentally kills a different man, hiding behind the ample skirts of the Cardinal. Another, Bergetto, is a witless ninny who has much in common with the ward in *Women Beware Women*. The third, Soranzo, who eventually marries Annabella, not only makes no attempt to conceal his aristocratic scorn for his bourgeois father-in-law but avails himself of the usual double standard by which he can engage in an adulterous affair and then moralize on her sinfulness to the woman concerned. Taken together these characters inevitably suggest the venality and pettiness of the society which breeds them, but Ford is not particularly concerned, as Middleton and Webster certainly are, to give us the sense of a corrupt society. We are far more aware of the constricted area of choice available to Annabella and of the intensely isolated and rarefied quality of the love between brother and sister.

'Tis Pity She's a Whore has not one but several sub-plots, all of them connected to the main plot but none of them integral to it. Thus Hippolita, Soranzo's discarded mistress, plans a spectacular murder as part of the wedding masque; this misfires, and she dies cursing, teetering precariously on the edge of farce. Putana, Annabella's confidante, a much fouler mouthed version of Juliet's nurse is inveigled into revealing Annabella's guilty secret and has her eyes put out for her trouble. But her end is never made real to us because Ford forgets about her immediately after she is taken out until the very end when the Cardinal, dispensing

divine justice, orders that she should be burnt alive, and also takes the opportunity to confiscate the property of the numerous dead. Her down-to-earth coarseness serves not in any sense as a criticism of the idealized love of the protagonists nor as an ironic endorsement of it, but if anything it strengthens our conviction that their love is quite simply beyond her simple reductive generalities:

> Your brother's a man I hope, and I say still, if a young wench feel the fit upon her, let her take anybody, father or brother all is one.

It is in the sub-plot which culminates in the death of the simpleton Bergetto that *'Tis Pity* comes nearest to the buffoonery of Bessus in *A King and No King*. But where farcical and would-be tragic modes simply weaken each other in that play, Ford achieves not only a sort of parodic contrast between the deaths of Giovanni and Bergetta but also a curiously poignant blending of farcical language and real pathos. In performance the scene of Bergetto's death invariably arouses laughter, but it is a puzzled laughter, soon stifled as real feeling seeps in. This blending of the pathetic and the farcical is characteristically Jacobean, though there are hints of it in earlier drama. Although to some extent the various sub-plots are treated by Ford as independently effective *coups de theatre*, together they form a contrasting background of squalid intrigue and self-seeking for the radiant intensity of the central love relationship.

The climax of *'Tis Pity*, when Giovanni bursts in upon the banquet with Annabella's heart at his sword's point, is one of the most celebrated theatrical moments in English drama. The reaction it arouses among audiences accustomed to think of tragedy as not only serious but solemn, and above all not 'theatrical' invariably tends to suppress some of the mixed feelings which the original audience probably felt and Ford almost certainly meant to arouse. Almost all the great Jacobean tragedies, Shakespeare excepted, tend to lead up to a climax where effects of tragic 'nobility' are combined with an appeal to quite other responses in the audience — irony, the sense of the grotesque, even the sense of the absurd. Think of the final masque in *Women Beware Women*, or the end of *The Revenger's Tragedy* where one group of masquers ends up stabbing the corpses already murdered by another. The pattern of this kind of mixed effect is set at the very beginning of the period in the grotesque-tragic theatrical entertainment which concludes Kyd's *The Spanish Tragedy* where theatrical deaths are also 'real' ones and the tragic hero tears his tongue out. It is the pattern that Shakespeare followed only in *Titus Andronicus* but one found in virtually every other important tragedy of the period. Its chief feature, brilliantly illustrated by Ford in *'Tis Pity*, is that it is quite impossible to separate an allegedly 'pure tragic' element and give it primacy over the others evoked by the scene. Giovanni's gesture is undoubtedly a piece of play-acting. He wishes to 'make an entrance' and give the banqueting guests 'the shock of their lives' and he succeeds in full measure. For us the audience, the bleeding heart at the point of a sword is also a powerfully phallic emblem of the destructive inward turning passion that is at the core of the drama. It is also, in its very excessiveness, likely to provoke *some* kind of laughter, though we need to remind ourselves of the obvious fact that there are far more psychological sources of laughter than differences in its physical manifestation. But *together with all this* and inextricably a part of it is our sense of the tragic dimension of the scene, our awed admiration of the total and absolute commitment of the hero to his act. The mixture of styles in Giovanni's lines, the expansive tragic rhetoric merging into the bitterly ironic image of feasting and then modulating into deranged colloquialism at the end catches perfectly all the nuances of the theatrical spectacle:

> The glory of my deed
> Darkened the mid-day sun, made noon as night.
> You came to feast, my lords, with dainty fare;
> I came to feast too, but I digged for food
> In a much richer mine than gold or stone
> Of any value balanced; 'tis a heart
> A heart my lords, in which is mine entombed.
> Look well upon't; d'ee know't?

In reading and even more in performance, the power and scope of the greatest Jacobean tragedy is such that it alters our very notion of what tragedy is or might be, so that we are forced to re-think familiar notions about tragic flaws, pity and terror and so on. Ford's *'Tis Pity She's a Whore*, if not among the greatest, has an honourable place in the line that stretches from Kyd to Middleton; and it is the last English tragedy of any consequences for three centuries.

The theatres were closed by Act of Parliament in 1642 and remained closed for eighteen years. But, as one critic put it 'when the Puritans did succeed in closing the theatres. . .they inflicted no serious loss on posterity. They did no murder; they merely interred a corpse'.[1] Caroline drama has nothing of significance to offer comparable to that of the earlier seventeenth century. Comedy was tending increasingly in the direction of elegant gentlemanly self-admiration spiced with ribaldry that was to find definitive form in Restoration comedy, though, as already mentioned, Beaumont and Fletcher's early essays in this mode are as entertaining as all but the very best Restoration comedies. The sense of man's possibilities for good and evil on which earlier tragedy had been based was fast being eroded under the impact of more 'scientific' approaches to knowledge and the view of polit- ical activity as an autonomous sphere with little to do with morality (the 'Machiavellian' standpoint). 'Honour' becomes virtually empty of any real content and sovereignty a matter of paying lip-service to the outward forms of royalty, a tendency which finds its ultimate expression in the enormous extra- vagances of the Court masque. Neither Ford's tragedies (apart from *'Tis Pity*) nor those of Shirley have any vital relation to the great tragic tradition while Davenant has no importance whatsoever as a dramatist though his place in the development of the theatre is significant and will be discussed later. The last great tragedy of the period was acted out not in the private theatre or the public playhouse but on a scaffold (a common seventeenth-century term for a stage), outside the palace of Whitehall on 30 January,1649. A year later, at the exact mid-point of the century, it was described by a great poet in terms which recall vividly the tragic view of life

---

[1] *The Shakespearean Moment* by Patrick Cruttwell, Ch. V (London, 1954).

which the drama we have considered did so much to bring alive and which, as the poet is well aware, is lost for ever:

> That thence the Royal Actor born
> The tragic Scaffold might adorn:
>   While round the armed Bands
>   Did clap their bloody hands.
> He nothing common did or mean
> Upon that memorable Scene:
>   But with his keener Eye
>   The Axe's edge did try:
> Nor called the Gods with vulgar spite
> To vindicate his helpless Right,
>   But bow'd his comely Head
>   Down as upon a Bed.

6

The Restoration Theatre and its Drama

Theatre and Drama in the Interregnum

Officially, the theatres in England remained closed for eighteen years from 1642 till 1660, but drama led a shadowy half life during this period. In the beginning the law was strictly enforced and the leading company, the King's Men, had to dispose of its theatrical wardrobe and see the Globe Theatre pulled down. But within five years performances were being given, more or less clandestinely in the Cockpit, Fortune and Salisbury Court theatres. The original law forbidding theatrical performances lapsed in 1648 whereupon acting was resumed forthwith. This did not last long however, because in the following year a new statute put actors outside the law by classifying them as rogues and vagabonds (as they had been before the Act of 1572). The interiors of the remaining theatres, the Fortune, the Cockpit in Drury Lane and the Salisbury Court, were dismantled but the old-fashioned Red Bull remained intact and here surreptitious performances were given. Private houses, tennis courts and inns were also used for stage performances and many a government official bribed to turn a blind eye to them. The most frequent form of theatrical entertainment was the 'droll' or short comic scene extracted from plays that had been popular before the theatres were closed. One of the earliest of these was *The Merry Conceits of Bottom the Weaver* which an actor named Robert Cox had fashioned out of *A Midsummer Night's Dream*. Though such entertainments were popular, performance was not without its hazards. Some fellow actors betrayed Cox to the military authorities who arrested him during a performance. He died in prison in 1655, two years after his arrest.

The theatre was undoubtedly the most popular form of entertainment and those who had obtained their living out of it lived in perpetual hope that it would one day be permitted to exist without prohibition. William Beeston, whose father had been an actor in Shakespeare's company and who had himself been an actor, trained a juvenile company at the Salisbury Court theatre which he rebuilt. Another boys' company was set up at the Cockpit by a bookseller named John Rhodes. But the most important figure in the theatrical world during the Interregnum and the early years of the Restoration was William Davenant, Shakespeare's putative son who had been the chief composer of court masques at the court of Charles I, succeeding Ben Jonson. Davenant too suffered imprisonment at the hands of the Puritans, though for his political rather than his theatrical activities. In 1638 he succeeded Ben Jonson as Poet Laureate and in the following year he became manager of the Cockpit, continuing there until the theatre was closed. He first put on plays at his residence, transferring them to the Cockpit later, and calling them operas to evade the restriction on theatrical performances (musical performances were not prohibited). *The Siege of Rhodes* which Davenant presented in 1656 is something of a theatrical landmark, for it marked the beginning of opera in England and also the advent on the public stage of painted scenery of the kind Inigo Jones and his son-in-law John Webb used for court masques. Though by modern standards the stage on which the performance took place was small (22 feet wide, 18 feet deep, 11 feet high) it was in most essentials the physical form which was to govern theatrical presentation until the end of the nineteenth century. For the first time in the English public theatre, there was a proscenium arch, with a series of flat wings behind it and between these movable shutters in grooves. These could be joined together to depict various locales, and one scene could be set behind the shutter while another was in progress. There was a painted back cloth which could also be changed and later two doors in front of the proscenium arch. But a vestige of the old thrust stage remained in the form of a platform which extended in front of the proscenium arch. As in the private theatres of the earlier period, lighting was provided by candles and oil lamps, with coloured glass and strips of coloured silk for special effects. There was a row of 'footlights' at the front of the acting area and the auditorium was lit by candelabra. Though there was no curtain across the proscenium arch and the auditorium was not in darkness, we can see here the beginning of the tendency which reached its peak in the nineteenth century, to separate the world of the play from the world of the audience, making the connection between the two problematic rather than integral. But that development is still a long way away and as we shall see, there is a peculiarly intimate, if rather constricted, relationship between the professional theatre and the audience during the Restoration period.

It has already been suggested that as a playwright Davenant is negligible. *Love and Honour* (1634) is a tedious exercise in Fletcherian tragi-comedy and *The Wits*(c. 1633) a mildly amusing comedy of manners. Davenant's real importance is in relation to the history of the theatre for he and Thomas Killigrew between them controlled the early Restoration theatre and both of them constituted a link with its pre-Civil War antecedents. Killigrew too had grown up within the court and had been in exile with the royal family. As a lad he had revelled in the blood and thunder melodrama presented at the old Red Bull playhouse and later had several plays acted. During most of the early Restoration period Davenant and Killigrew were rival managers but it was Davenant who set his stamp on the post Restoration theatre.

Actors and Audience in the Restoration theatre

The early history of the Restoration theatre is complicated in its details but a brief outline of it is necessary if we are to understand the development of drama and appreciate the elements of change and continuity between the earlier seventeenth century and the later. Sir Henry Herbert, who had been Master of the Revels (the official in charge of the licensing of plays, theatres and acting companies) under Charles I eventually succeeded in his energetic efforts to resume this office under the new king. While Davenant was away in France seeking Charles II's permission for a licence, Herbert licensed three London companies, one under John Rhodes at the Cockpit, the other under William Beeston at the Salisbury Court and the third under Michael Mohun at the Red Bull. Unaware of this Charles granted Licences to Davenant and Killigrew and it took them most of the year 1660 to suppress the other three troupes and establish their joint monopoly. There was more trouble with a license that Charles granted to George Jolly, who had run a touring company in Germany during the Commonwealth. But Davenant and Killigrew managed to cheat Jolly out of his licence while he was on an English tour in 1662 by persuading the king that they had bought Jolly's London licence (they had in fact merely rented it). By 1664 the monopoly of Killigrew and Davenant was secure, and the 'patent' system of theatrical organization set up by them survived more or less unchanged until 1843.

To begin with Davenant and Killigrew worked togther, but they soon formed two companies, Killigrew taking most of the experienced actors as well as the sole right to perform a large number of Jacobean plays. This compelled Davenant to rely on innovation and spectacle to attract the audience, something which by temperament and experience he was eager to do anyway. In addition, the very fact that the older and more seasoned actors had gone with Killigrew made Davenant's troupe more forward looking, less tied to old traditions which were not appropriate to the architectural and social conventions of the new theatre. Though Killigrew's company, known as the King's, started nearly eight months before Davenant's (in a converted tennis court), it did not help them very much in attracting and retaining the audience. Killigrew had neither the ability nor the inclination for theatre management and his troupe was soon torn by internal dissension. When Davenant opened a new theatre in Lincoln's Inn Fields for his company, the Duke's, he had at least two great advantages. His was the first *public* theatre in England which had facilities for movable scenery. He also had, as a member of his acting company the greatest actor of the age Thomas Betterton. Betterton and his wife the actress Mary Sanderson were the first of a long line of players to portray the 'gay couple' who feature so prominently in Restoration comedy. The appearance of women on the stage is a momentous event in the history of the English drama since it had a decisive impact not only on stage presentation but also on the kind of drama that came to be written, a point which we shall return to later.

Davenant died in April 1668 and the effective management of his company passed to Betterton, assisted at first by a fellow actor named Harris and after 1677 by another actor, William Smith. The tradition of putting on splendid theatrical spectacles continued, and was greatly assisted when the Duke's company moved in November 1671 to a new building in Dorset Garden, the most splendid theatre in Restoration London, equipped with the very latest stage machinery, details of which Betterton had brought back from a visit to Paris. Opera and heroic tragedy both provided plenty of opportunities for stage spectacle on a lavish scale and the Duke's company established undisputed supremacy in this type of theatrical entertainment, to be feebly imitated or desperately parodied by their rivals, the King's. Killigrew's troupe also moved into a new building, the Theatre Royal in Bridges Street, in May 1663 but were dogged by internal tensions and ill-luck, the latter culminating in a fire which destroyed the building with all its equipment, costumes and properties in 1672. The company moved first into the theatre in Lincoln's Inn Fields vacated by the Duke's players and in 1674 to a new Theatre Royal in Drury Lane designed by Sir Christopher Wren. But bad management and bad luck continued and many performers deserted Killigrew's company. In 1682 what was left of it merged with Betterton's highly successful troupe and London had a single theatrical company for the next thirteen years. They used the Dorset Garden theatre for opera and spectacular tragedy and the one in Drury Lane for comedy and small-scale drama. Mismanagement on the part of Davenant's sons, who had let the financial control of the theatre fall into the hands of an unscrupulous lawyer named Christopher Rich, led Betterton and several fellow actors to secure a licence from William III to form a separate company playing at the deserted Lincoln's Inn Fields theatre. For the next thirteen years there were once again two theatrical troupes playing in London, with much rivalry between them. They also had to adapt themselves to a common enemy, the famous attack made on the theatre in 1698 by Jeremy Collier, *A Short View of the Immorality and Profaneness of the English Stage*. The controversy aroused by Collier's searching critique not only defined the terms in which Restoration Comedy continued to be discussed until and including our own time, but also had an important effect on the drama of the eighteenth century. Rich's company, for all his own personal bullying and ruthlessness, had managed to attract some talented actors and actresses, including Colley Cibber (the 'hero' of Pope's *Dunciad*) whose autobiography provides as fascinating an account of the late seventeenth-century theatre from the inside as Pepys's diary does from the outside. In 1708 the two companies merged once more.

From this brief account, some idea of the elements of change and continuity between the pre-Civil War theatre and its successor may be gained. As far as the physical properties of the theatre buildings were concerned, the private playhouses of the earlier period set the pattern. Like them, Restoration theatres were roofed, used artificial lighting and had a thrust stage. Unlike them, the new theatres had a proscenium arch, stage boxes and a gallery, and movable perspective scenery. The advent of actresses also meant the innovation of separate dressing rooms and the beginning of extra-theatrical relationships between performers and members of the audience. Where theatrical organization was concerned, the granting of monopolies to two 'patentees' narrowed and tightened the hold of the impresario over what was performed. Where in the earlier seventeenth century there had been at least six theatres in London, in the Restoration there were never more than two and sometimes only one, and this despite the phenomenal growth of the city's population. The 'town' whose taste the theatre managers attempted to satisfy consisted, as far as theatregoers were concerned, of a few thousand, of whom the regular theatregoers were no more than a few hundred. Catering to the rather specialized demands of this new audience, together with the monopoly over theatrical control, produced the professional actor and actress as we have known them since, tied to the theatre by a contractual relationship rather than by the more cooperative 'sharing' bond as in the early days of the public theatre. That bond was already weakening in the Jacobean and Caroline period and the Restoration only shows the confirmation and strengthening of a development which began much earlier.

Another point that emerges quite clearly is that the era of 'Restoration drama' which we usually associate with the comedy of manners is considerably longer than the historical period of the Restoration and produced a good deal of drama outside the genre of comedy, whether of manners or otherwise. These points will be taken up when we look at the drama of the period, but first it is necessary to get a clearer picture of the audience which witnessed that drama.

There is a popular notion that the audience at a Restoration theatre consisted exclusively of dissolute young men, who were the hangers-on of the Merry Monarch, aristocratic ladies who were no better than they should be and hopeful orange women on the make. There is evidence to suggest that this picture may not be entirely complete. With seat prices ranging from one to four shillings, theatre-going was not an inexpensive pastime, but it appears to have attracted many sections of society other than aristocratic idlers. The best known theatregoer of the age was neither idle nor aristocratic, and his social pretensions were affronted on more than one occasion by the presence of what he liked to regard as the lower orders. When Pepys went to see the second part of *The Siege of Rhodes* at the Duke's theatre on 27 December 1662, he was 'not so well pleased with the company at the house today, which was full of citizens — there being hardly a gallant man or woman in the house.' Five years later he noted the changed composition of the audience since his early playgoing days:

> Here a mighty company of citizens, 'prentices, and others; and it makes me observe, that when I begun first to be able to bestow a play on myself, I do not remember that I saw so many by half of the ordinary 'prentices and mean people in the pit at 2s.6d. a-piece as now.

Men like the scientist Robert Hooke and Sir Christopher Wren were regular theatregoers, as were Sir Isaac Newton and John Locke, if we are to go by the fact that they had many play-texts in their libraries. It is probably safe to conclude that the social composition of the audience during the Restoration was roughly similar to that of the private playhouses of the Jacobean and Caroline era. It had shrunk from the wide spectrum of national life which the Elizabethan public playhouses attracted, but it was by no means confined to debauched court parasites. Nor was its female membership entirely restricted to aristocrats and whores (not that the distinction was always applicable). One of the noteworthy features about Pepys's playgoing is the fact that his wife, and sometimes her maid, also went to the theatre frequently. Indeed Mrs Pepys sometimes went to the theatre by herself, with Pepy's knowledge and approval. And his diary shows that neither Pepys nor his wife was at all unusual in this.

The final point to make in relation to the Restoration audience is that it contained a core of people for whom theatregoing was not an occasional luxury but a regular recreation. This core was alert, well informed and on terms of varying intimacy with both dramatists and performers, as can be gathered from the prologues and epilogues which are an important feature of plays in this period, especially in its earlier phase. The behaviour of the audience at the theatre was, by modern standards, more like the behaviour of a football crowd and attending a performance was as much a regular *occasion* as a football match is to the fans. The prologue to a play performed in 1671 called *The Ordinary* gives an unflattering view of audience behaviour:

Some come with lusty Burgundy half-drunk,
T'eat China oranges, make love to punk;
And briskly mount a bench when th' Act is done,
And comb their much-loved periwigs to the tune
And can sit out a play of three hours long,
Minding no part of't but the dance or song.

The fact that such behaviour is singled out for censure suggests that for the most part the audience did take an intelligent interest in the drama itself. That at any rate was the view of the critic and dramatist John Dennis who looked back nostalgically at the beginning of the eighteenth century to the great days of the Restoration theatre when most of the audience 'had that due application, which is requisite for the judging of Comedy'. Whether for better or worse, the composition of the audience had certainly changed by the early eighteenth century and with it the kind of drama offered by the theatres.

What is 'Restoration Drama'?

On 29 May 1660, his thirtieth birthday, Charles II entered London in triumph, after years of exile. He died, after a reign characterized by easy selfishness and nonchalant treachery, just twenty-five years later. The historical period known as the Restoration covers the years of Charles's monarchy but the term 'Restoration drama' has a wider chronological span. Its beginnings, as we have seen, go back to Davenant's theatrical experiments in the last years of the Commonwealth, and the last dramatist of any consequence associated with the period, George Farquhar, wrote his best plays after 1700. In the first phase of Restoration drama, covering Charles II's reign and the brief and troubled interlude of James II, the best comic dramatists are George Etherege and William Wycherley. To this period also belong two less important but still noteworthy dramatists, Thomas Shadwell and Aphra Behn, the latter being the first of a number of female playwrights. William Congreve, John Vanbrugh and George Farquhar all wrote during the reign of William and Mary. John Dryden is the only considerable playwright whose work spans both phases. He wrote his first play in 1664 and died in 1700. For the purpose of this book and for reasons already indicated in the discussion on the theatre and by the brief summary given above, 'Restoration drama' will be taken to mean what was produced for the stage during the years from 1660 to 1708.

Having clarified our period it is necessary immediately to remove a fairly substantial misconception about it. For most people Restoration drama means the comedy of manners, and it is true and probably just that the only plays from the period which are still performed are some half dozen or dozen comedies. But most of the new plays of the time were not comedies of manners at all, but heroic tragedies and what were called operas — bombast with music and songs. The immediate begetter of these was Davenant, but heroic tragedy goes beyond him to the example set by Beaumont and Fletcher. They were two of the most popular play-wrights in the new theatres and inspired a vast number of plays whose very titles are now forgotten except by theatre historians, with the possible exception of Dryden's reworking of Shakespeare's *Antony and Cleopatra* in *All for Love* (not a very typical heroic tragedy anyway) and Otway's *Venice Preserved*. Most of this chapter will be concerned with the varieties of Restoration comedy, but a brief glance at heroic tragedy is of interest in itself as a curious chapter in the history of theatrical taste and will also help us to understand later developments.

Heroic Drama: Tragedy as Spectacle.

The basic conception of heroic tragedy is simple, not to say simple-minded. It consists of a hero conceived as a superman with no inside to him, rather like a comic-book Superman in fact. This hero is placed in a situation where he has to choose between Love and Honour, between the fulfilment of his private emotional life or dedicating himself to the public good. Great plays can of course be written on this theme, and one of the very greatest, Shakespeare's *Antony and Cleopatra* is largely concerned with it. But to do this, it is necessary to conceive the alternatives in serious terms, and it is clear that neither dramatist nor, for the most part, the audience did so. It is significant that all the fine talk of love and honour takes place not in the dissolute and intrigue-ridden society of Restoration London, but in far-away places among people with strange-sounding names — Venice, Morocco, Granada, the Court of the great Mogul Aurangzebe and so on. As Mrs Evelyn, the diarist's wife, appreciatively remarked about *The Conquest of Granada*, 'love is made so pure, and valour so nice, that one would imagine it designed for an Utopia rather than our stage.' The reality of life, or at any rate some recognizable version of it, was in the comedy; heroic tragedy was its wish-fulfilling counterpart, con-science money paid to heroic ideals by those for whom they had long ceased to matter. Occasionally, as in Otway's *Venice Preserv'd* there is an element of bitter satire against contemporary political conspiracy, but in a context so inflated that it loses a lot of its power. In the *Conquest of Granada*, for instance, the hero Almanzar makes his choice of allegiance in the following terms, as soon as he enters the stage between two rival factions:

> I cannot stay to ask which cause is best;
> But this is so to me, because opprest.

— whereupon he forthwith goes across to one of the factions. The language in which these high-falutin' proceedings are conducted is as stylized as the 'Wham!' and 'Zapow!' of the comic books, and, with rare exceptions, as little capable of conveying anything remotely resembling identifiable human attitudes and emotions. Up till about 1676, heroic tragedy was written in rhyme, on the French neo-classical model of Corneille. Later heroic drama employed blank verse, but with no perceptible gain in realism or psychological insight. Realism of any kind was of course the last thing the heroic dramatist aimed at. The super-hero was conceived as a grand examplar and his activities were intended to arouse not pity and terror but the rather different emotions of wonder and admiration. Rhymed verse, according to Dryden, was intended to raise the language above the level of 'ordinary converse' and this it certainly did, to such rarefied heights as are represented by the following excerpt from Muly Hamet's speech in *The Empress of Morocco,* one of the great stage successes of the day, by a Poet Laureate, Elkanah Settle.

> Condemn'd, never to see Morocco more!
> Thus am I doom'd to quit all I adore:
> As profane sinners are from altars driven,
> Banish'd the temples to be banisht heaven.
> Horror and tortures now my jailors be,
> Who paints damnation needs but copy me;
> For if mankind the pains of hell e'er knew,
> 'Tis when they lose a mistress as I do.

It is entirely in keeping with this kind of writing that the play should end with the villain impaled on spikes, for no very good reason than because they were there. A few lines from one of Pierre's speeches in *Venice Preserv'd* offer a fair sample of what was achieved in blank verse, neither the best (for that we must go to Dryden's *All for Love*) nor by any manner of means the worst:

> Rats die in holes and corners, dogs run mad;
> Man knows a braver remedy for sorrow:
> Revenge! the attribute of gods; they stamped it
> With their great image on our natures. Die!
> Consider well the cause that calls upon thee.
> And if thou'rt base enough, die then. Remember
> Thy Belvidera suffers; Belvidera!

In theme and manner the last passage has its ancestry stamped upon it. It could have come from any one of half a dozen plays by Fletcher — the same attitudinizing, the same tendency to make a 'scene' out of every speech and the same thinness of texture remind us once again of continuity rather than contrast. Indeed, for all the elaborate allusion to French example and Aristotelian writers which trick out the discussion of heroic tragedy in innumerable prefaces, dedicatory epistles (Dryden's contributions being the most elegant and intelligent), this sort of drama is best seen as exploiting Fletcherian tendencies on a scale of lavishness and elaboration possible only in the later theatre with its explicit dedication to spectacular visual devices and elaborate 'machines' for transformation and aerial flight, including vertical take-off. Though the platform stage of the Jacobean playhouse still thrust itself into the midst of the audience in its Restoration counterpart, it is the space behind the proscenium arch that becomes the gorgeous magic box of the new theatre, and it is there that heroic drama achieves it most splendid effects. Dryden is a great poet in his own right, but his achievement in *All for Love* a play that, within narrow limits, can still move us by the power of its language, is in some ways a misleading guide to the true quality of heroic drama. As has been suggested, it is difficult if not impossible to take its pretensions seriously if we consider simply the dialogue and human action. The ideals of moderation in social intercourse, cool rationality restraining emotional excess and an urbane scepticism with regard to the operations of providence in human life — ideals which we shall encounter when we turn to Restoration comedy — were those to which the age, at least in its upper metropolitan ranks, owed its true allegiance and the solemn sham by which heroic drama appears to replace them by those of superhuman self-sacrifice and deathless love were doubtless flattering to certain sections of the audience. In particular the women preferred their portrayal in heroic tragedy to the role given them in comedy as Addison dryly observed in retrospect:

> The ladies are wonderfully pleased to see a man insulting kings, or affronting the gods, in one scene, and throwing himself at the feet of his mistress in another. Let him behave insolently towards the men, and abjectly towards the fair one, and it is ten to one but he proves a favourite of the boxes. Dryden and Lee, in several of their tragedies, have practised this secret with good success.

But, however flattering to the fair ones, no audience could for long take seriously a drama in which, for instance, a noble prince commits suicide simply because he is *suspected* of seduction as happens in Lee's *Sophonisba;* notions of honour associated with the medieval Japanese aristocracy did not generally prevail in Restoration London, as even a superficial acquaintance with the politics of the period will show. The mechanical absurdities of the Love-Honour paradox are splendidly spoofed in this speech from *The Rehearsal,* a famous burlesque of heroic tragedy by Buckingham and others:

Volscius *sits down to pull on his boots. . .*
Volscius
How has my passion made me Cupid's scoff!
This hasty boot is on, the other off,
And sullen lies, with amorous design
To quit loud fame, and make that beauty mine. . .
My legs, the emblem of my various thought,
Show to what sad distraction I am brought.
Sometimes with stubborn Honour, like this boot,
My mind is guarded, and resolved to do't:
Sometimes again, that very mind, by Love
Disarmed, like this other leg does prove.
Shall I to Honour or to Love give way?
'Go on', cries Honour; tender Love says 'Nay'.
Honour aloud commands 'Pluck both boots on',
But softer Love does whisper 'Put on none'.
What shall I do? What conduct shall I find
To lead me through this twilight of my mind?
For, as bright day with black approach of night
Contending makes a doubtful puzzling light,
So does my Honour and my Love together

Puzzle me so, I can resolve for neither.
Goes out hopping, with one boot on and the other off

What did draw the crowds and what was undeniably theatrical, even in some cases 'heroic' was the splendour and fascination of the spectacle; *that* did indeed evoke 'wonder and admiration', especially to an audience starved of theatre for so long. The second scene in the second act of *Sophonisba* has the following stage-direction:

> The scene drawn, discovers a heaven of blood, two suns, spirits in battle, arrows shot to and fro in the air, cries of yielding persons: Cries of Carthage is fallen, Carthage, etc.,

In another play by Lee, the opening scene calls for a stately temple representing the newly established Christian Church, with side scenes showing the tortures of the early martyrs and at the back a richly adorned altar with Constantine kneeling before it, with a bloody cross in the air, surrounded by many angels and the sign: *In hoc signo, vinces.* Such spectacles would have had for the original audiences as much power to dazzle the eye and enthrall the mind as the early moving films for their first viewers or holograms for us today. Both Settle and Lee, especially the latter, had an undeniable talent for 'realizing' some of their major dramatic moments in terms of spectacle rather than action. They were moving towards what some writers on theatre today call 'theatre as theatre' where the non-verbal resources of the stage are seen as primary. Nothing in the poetic endowment of these men and most of the others, stood in the way of their willing involvement in this kind of theatre, though one of them, John Crowne, claims to avoid empty shows that hide emptier rhetoric:

> But he at show and great machines might aim
> Fine chairs to carry Poetry when lame,
> On ropes instead of raptures to rely,
> When the sense creeps to make the actors fly.
> These tricks upon our stage will never hit,
> Our company is for the old way of wit.

But for all that it was not Crowne, but Dryden who represented 'the old way of wit', at least in *All for Love*. Being a poet first and a dramatist next, Dryden was never really at ease with the baroque extravagances which he himself did so much to popularize through the success of such plays as the *Conquest of Granada* and *Tyrannic Love*. Some observations on his own play *The Spanish Friar* pinpoint both the strengths and limitations of the new spectacular theatre while tracing the source of Dryden's eventual dissatisfaction with it:

> But as 'tis my interest to please my audience, so 'tis my ambition to be read: that I am sure is the more lasting and nobler design: for the propriety of thoughts and words, which are the hidden beauties of a play, are but confusedly judged in the vehemence of action. All things are there beheld as in a hasty motion, where the objects only glide before the eye and disappear.

Theory and Practice in Restoration Comedy

There are at least two misconceptions about Restoration comedy. First, there is the assumption that all comedies of the period were of the same kind, and secondly the belief that writers of comedy were consistently guided by a single theory about the nature and function of comedy. The popular notion of the Restoration audience is matched by a popular picture of the typical Restoration comedy — one having a witty and amoral couple at its centre, a fatuous fop, a discarded mistress and a cuckolded citizen in the middle distance and assorted elderly lechers of both sexes in the background. The plot, dealing alternately with the pursuit of sex and the pursuit of money, is of Byzantine complexity, arousing a reaction like that of Granville Barker: 'How could an audience both be clever enough to understand the story and stupid enough to be interested by it when they did?' The proceedings are conducted with a maximum of style and a minimum of regard for moral principle, for the delight if not the edification of an aristocratic elite that had nothing better to do with its leisure than study its own dandified image in the flattering mirror of the drama.

The question of the audience has already been briefly discussed. As for the 'typical Restoration comedy' it will be clear from the necessarily brief examination below of some of the best known comedies of the time that this has been bred by ignorance out of over-simplification. The period covered by Restoration comedy spans nearly half a century, being almost as long as the heyday of the Elizabethan and Jacobean drama. It was also, as we have noted, a period of great change in styles of theatre, styles of acting and kind of audience. It would therefore be very strange indeed if a single type of comedy held the stage unchanged and unchallenged over so long a period when everything else was being transformed. No such bland homogeneity ever existed, needless to say. The Restoration comedies that have survived into the modern period do have certain broad features in common, such as an interest in the relation between love and marriage, the uses and abuses of 'affectation' (or socially determined behaviour) and the proper balance between impulse and control in human relationships. But themes such as these have been the perennial concern of comedy and the best Restoration comedies have very little more in common than modern comedies by different playwrights — Noel Coward, Joe Orton and Alan Bennett for example. We must also remember that the comedies which have survived are not a representative sample of the age's taste in comedy; *The Way of the World*, often regarded as the finest Restoration comedy and the ideal to which all comedies of the period are supposed to be obscurely aspiring, did not impress when first produced, while few people other than specialists have ever heard of *The Adventures of Five Hours*, a romantic comedy which was one of the great successes of the early Restoration stage. But there is no need to disturb the dust which has settled on the greater part of Restoration comedy to demonstrate its variety and vivacity; an unprejudiced look at the acknowledged dramatic successes is enough. Amongst the prejudices we must shed is one which would herd all the comedies together under one theory of the function of comic drama, namely that the business of comedy is to make vice seem ridiculous, so that laughter becomes a corrective agent in the business of adapting man to society. This was, of course, the Jonsonian view, and many Restoration dramatists paid solemn lip service to it, particularly during the controversy aroused by Collier's attack in 1698, when a moral stance had obvious strategic advantages. But, as in the very beginning of stage comedy in England, there was more than one variety and more than one purpose was served, deliberately or otherwise. An influential view of the function of comedy was that of Dryden's brother-in-law Edward Howard, who wrote that 'the chief end of comedy is the improvement of manners' which was to be achieved by arousing delight rather than the laughter of ridicule, while Aphra Behn was quite clear that at least one of her own plays was written for no higher purpose than that of amusement. In her preface to *The Dutch War* (1673) she writes: 'In short I think a play the best divertisement that wise men have' and belittles those

> who do discourse as formally about the rules of it, as if 'twere the grand affair of human life. This being my opinion of plays, I studied only to make this as entertaining as I could.

In addition to the view of comedy as corrective, or exemplary, or intended purely for pleasure, there was the claim, frequently made in prologues and epilogues, that it offered a realistic picture of life as it was, without flattery or sentimentalization. Vanbrugh's *The Provok'd Wife* (1697) makes a fairly standard claim in its prologue:

> 'tis the intent and business of the stage,
> To copy out the follies of the age:
> To hold to every man a faithful glass,
> And show him of what species he's an ass.

Realism is a notoriously tricky term, and it is certainly not the case, whatever the playwrights claim, that Restoration comedy offered an exact copy of the life led even by the narrow social stratum it purported to depict. For one thing, the requirements of comic plotting involve proliferations of intrigue rather more luxuriant than those that flourished even in a society which relished intrigue. For another, scholarly inquiry has demonstrated that the plots of many Restoration comedies are resolved in ways which the audience would recognize as legal impossibilities, particularly in the case of marriage contracts. It is unlikely that a playwright seriously concerned with realism would neglect actuality at such a crucial point in the play. The demands of the comic genre and of theatrical conventions would naturally exercise their shaping influences against the tendency to realism. Nevertheless it remains true that in certain important respects, Restoration comedy was realistic, particularly if we contrast it with its theatrical counterpart, heroic drama. It is fairly clear that a less stylized, more naturalistic style of acting was used in comedy. Scenery and stage properties would confirm visually the general impression of contemporary actuality, a world smaller, tidier and altogether more familiar than that evoked by the exotic splendour of 'heroic' settings. The appearance of Sir Credulous Easy to conduct his courtship mounted on an elephant in Aphra Behn's *Sir Patient Fancy* (1678) is the apparent exception that proves the rule; it would have passed almost unnoticed in, say, *The Empress of*

Morocco. Prose dialogue too, though stylized and by no means a mere transcription of everyday speech, would be 'realistic' in relation to the rhymed or blank inanities of heroic verse. The use of disguise, to add spice to intrigue or for somberer purposes, is well documented outside the stage and the Merry Monarch's penchant for disguise was enthusiastically shared by several of his subjects. The final realistic element is the recurrent *situation* (not the plot) of much comedy, featuring improvident gallants sniffing at likely fortunes, cautiously making their way between the twin terrors of syphilis and marriage and eventually contracting both. Bearing in mind these reservations, 'realism' is sometimes a useful term for describing Restoration comedy, some examples of which will be discussed in the rest of this chapter.

Etherege and The Man of Mode

All three of Etherege's plays are lively stage pieces, though only *The Man of Mode* is regularly performed today. His first, *The Comical Revenge,* or *Love in a Tub* is usually regarded as the first Restoration comedy, though many plays have a better claim to the title, if we are thinking of strict chronological accuracy. Abraham Cowley's *The Cutter of Coleman Street* (1661), Sir Robert Howard's *The Committee* (1662) and Samuel Tuke's *The Adventures of Five Hours* (1663), were all performed before Etherege's plays. Part of his success is due to the fact that in *The Comical Revenge* Etherege shrewdly catered for the taste of the audience in many different dramatic forms. The four plots which are interwoven to form the play may strike us as no more than a clumsy hotch-potch but their contemporary success was immediate and spectacular and the plots are combined with a good deal of skill. At the top of the social scale Etherege makes an excursion into the field of courtly romance, in Beaufort's wooing of Graciana. Neither the emotional relationship nor the dramatic convention within which it is realized commands more than the barest minimum of Etherege's talent, and the mélange of blank verse, rhyming couplets and prose in which these scenes thump along is his half-hearted tribute to 'serious' drama of the Fletcherian kind. Even a brief passage plainly declares its hollowness in the extraneous quality of the images and the predictable jogtrot of the rhythm:

> Beauty, what art thou, we so much admire!
> Thou art not real but a seeming fire,
> Which, like the glow-worm, only castst a light
> To them whose reason passion doth benight.
> Thou art a meteor, which but blazing dies,
> Made of such vapours as from us arise.
> Within thy guilty beams lurk cruel fates
> To peaceful families and warring states.

There is nothing intentionally comic about this 'high plot', but when Etherege gets into his stride as a comic dramatist, the play really comes alive. The second plot, which deals with the efforts of two confidence tricksters, Wheadle and Palmer, to part the foolish knight Sir Nicholas Cully ('knighted by Oliver') from his money, is clearly derived from Jonsonian city comedy though without any of Jonson's moral pretensions. It is a neatly done burlesque on the ideas of honour portrayed in the Beaufort-Graciana scenes, but since those ideas are impossible to take seriously owing to the way in which they are expressed even there, the burlesque is superfluous as ironic comment, though thoroughly enjoyable in itself. Etherege wisely reverts to prose for this and the other two plots and the dialogue has the raciness and wiry strength of Greene's conycatching pamphlets. Both plots end in a duel, a 'serious' one in the first and a burlesque in the other. Further complications are created by the intrusion of characters from this plot, in disguise, into that concerning the wooing of a rich widow by the young gallant Sir Federick Frollick. In these episodes we can detect, if we are so disposed, the germ of the Restoration comedy of manners. Sir Frederick's exchanges with Jenny the maid show him as the prototype of the careless gallant, dividing his time impartially between drinking and whoring, while the scenes between him and the Widow Rich introduce the insistent theme of the relation between love and money, the gallant's need of the latter being both complemented and crossed by the ageing widow's need for the former. The duel of wits between these two has an edge of malice which adds a dimension of clear-eyed realism to it. Critical claims to the contrary notwithstanding, Etherege has no particular moral intention here or elsewhere in the play. He is concerned to depict the game of love as it was, or could be actually played in the world he knew. Often it is a no-holds-barred game but the only lesson Etherege derives from this is that those who play it should improve their skills; it is a question of style, not morality. This kind of comedy is quite properly called the comedy of manners, but we should be careful not to confuse it with the comedy of good manners; that arrived on the English stage in the following century. The main title of *Love in a Tub* derives from the farcical fourth plot of the play. This concerns the Frenchman Defoy, condemned to the sweating-tub (the usual cure for venereal disease, and one which a fair number of the contemporary audience was likely to know at first hand) for pretending he was suffering from lover's melancholy when all he had was the pox. Pepys enjoyed this part of the play, though he was a little shamefaced about it, and even today I would guess that the knock-about energy of the farcical action would succeed on the stage. In reading a good deal of this is lost, though something of its flavour is conveyed in the number and variety of Etherege's lively stage directions. These show how fully he conceived the play in terms of the stage he was writing for, as he created the action by combining the dramatic forms that had proved their popularity. Neither the satirist's passion nor poetic inspiration nor the romantic desire for self-expression drew this indolent man-about-town to write for the stage. *Love in a Tub*, like all Etherege's plays, is inspired by nothing more than a desire to please himself and the 'town'; he evidently fulfilled this desire in ample measure.

By comparison *She Would If She Could* (1668) is a very much smaller play in every respect. Its plot is tidier, being mainly confined to the activities of Ariana and Gatty, two young women up from the country to enjoy the delights of the town and the gallants Freeman and Courtall, who manage to render the pursuit of pleasure at once tedious and smutty. There is a certain dramatic adroitness in the way in which the libertine world of the gallants is contrasted with the sleazy and unwilling domesticity of Sir Oliver and Lady Cockwood and the observation of London life in Mulberry Garden and the New Exchange is vivid and exact, but the play's greatest strength is the character of Rakehell who is a con-man in the best tradition of Jonson and Middleton. For all that, the witty exchanges are not quite witty enough and the farce seems tentative and less than full blooded, while the happy ending has neither propriety nor plausibility. Etherege himself blamed the failure of the play on stage on indifferent acting (according to Pepys), but he did not provide for the actors as bountifully as he did in his first comedy.

His third and last however, more than made amends. *The Man of Mode, or Sir Fopling Flutter* (1676) is certainly the best comedy of the early phase of the Restoration theatre. In it Etherege found the perfect vehicle for his particular dramatic talents — a keen sense of the ridiculous, a devotion to style and stylishness with an underlying suspicion of its emptiness as an end in itself, and a fascination with the complications of social intrigue. In Dorimant he created a character with the exuberance and malice of Sir Frederick Frollick, with more wit than Freeman and Courtall put together, and with an occasional capacity to understand his appetites instead of being merely a victim of them. Underneath the glittering surface of wit and courtship, there is certainly a darker side to the play. There is no need to convert Dorimant into a Volpone or a Iago to see that there is an element of acquisitiveness and power-hunger in his desire to control and possess others, a desire which is no sooner satisfied than it compulsively seeks new conquests. Etherege does not miss this dimension in his hero, one which links Dorimant to a real-life Restoration figure, John Wilmot, Earl of Rochester, who was believed to be one of the models for Dorimant and whose equally obsessional addiction to pleasure (he told Bishop Burnet he had been continuously drunk for five years) led to penitent and delirious death at thirty-three. Dorimant too seems to be motivated by Rochester's Lucretian devotion to impersonal investigation of human behaviour and his 'Epicurean' addiction to self-indulgence.

But to surround a discussion of *The Man of Mode* with an aura of classical philosophy is to put it in a context that is finally misleading. Dorimant's pursuit of pleasure does have a demonic quality about it, but only as an undercurrent. The really important classical author behind Etherege's play is neither Lucretius nor Epicurus but the Ovid of the *Art of Love*.[1] By ordinary standards of morality, Dorimant's behaviour is outrageous. He discards one mistress and takes up with another, and is prepared to put her off too without any scruples when a new object of sexual interest presents itself. It is only because he cannot have Harriet on any terms other than marriage ('without church security, there's no taking up there' as Young Bellair puts it, with a bawdy triple pun) that Dorimant finally resigns himself to marriage. Even in the act of consenting to go to the country (a fate worse than death to the town gallant), he is busy arranging further assignations with his mistress Belinda. His last words about his marriage emphasize the fact that he is chiefly concerned to guarantee his economic security. He tells Young Bellair:

[1] A point well developed in Harriet Hawkins's *Likenesses of Truth in Elizabethan and Restoration Drama* Ch.4. (Oxford 1972)

The wise will find a difference in our fate,
You wed a woman, I a good estate.

The fact that this is partly the rationalization of a sexual desire which he cannot control makes some difference, but not a great deal. It seems impossible to argue, as some critics have done, that the comedy shows us a rake reformed by the love of a good woman. If anything, the rake taints the 'good woman' with some of his own cruelty, for at the end Harriet, the heroine, roundly tells Loveit, the discarded mistress: 'Mr Dorimant has been your God Almighty long enough, 'tis time to think of another' and rubs it in by recommending that Loveit gets herself to a nunnery. Nor is it any more convincing to see *The Man of Mode* as a satire, with Dorimant held up as a horrible warning against unbridled libertinism and unscrupulous dissembling. Young Bellair is sometimes held up as an example of a positive standard of courtesy and sincerity against which Dorimant's ruthless duplicity is to be judged, but the most obvious point about Young Bellair as he appears in the play is that he simply lacks the dramatic stature of Dorimant. He has neither the wit nor the grace nor the sheer presence (it is partly, though not entirely, a matter of the size of the role) of the hero. To suggest that Young Bellair offers an adequate criterion for judging Dorimant is about as convincing as the same suggestion would be if made in respect of Bonario and Volpone, and for roughly the same reason. Furthermore, Young Bellair is most alive dramatically precisely when he is following in the hero's footsteps and deceiving his father with Harriet, just as Harriet has deception to thank for her very presence in London. The idea that the virtues of straightforward, honest passion and marital fidelity are illustrated by their satirical inversion in *The Man of Mode* simply will not stand up to the actuality of the play itself.

We are left with no alternative but to look elsewhere for the secret of the play's obvious and lasting appeal (it has been successfully revived in modern times), and we shall find it if we let ourselves be guided by our actual response to the play. For, above everything else, *The Man of Mode* impresses us by the wit and verve with which the hero and heroine go through the various moves in the game of love. The play takes its title from the ludicrous antics of the would-be wit, Sir Fopling Flutter. By strictly moral criteria, it could certainly be argued that Sir Fopling is a kinder, gentler, altogether *nicer* person than Dorimant but no one, so far as I know, has inferred from this that he represents the moral positives of the comedy. The difference between him and Dorimant is not in their moral nature, which does not concern Etherege. It lies entirely in the skill and self-awareness with which they play the game called moving in society. Sir Fopling, having no understanding of the purpose of social role-playing, merely imitates its outward forms and is therefore constantly liable to make a fool of himself. Dorimant, thoroughly aware that elegance of dress and address are only counters in the game and that dissembling and affectation are necessary curbs on the anarchic eruption of emotion which would disturb the player and put the prize out of reach, plays with the skill born of experience and the single-minded dedication of the competitor whose sole object is to win. To complain that his rejection of Loveit is heartless is as irrelevant as objecting to a tennis champion who plays only to win and does not reflect that his opponent deserves to win because he needs the championship money more or because he is a better husband and father. For we must realize that, as Etherege portrays it, this game is played not by the men alone, but by the women too. The rules are somewhat different for them, for by the prevailing double standard, a woman known to have surrendered her virginity is thereby precluded from marriage while the converse held for men. But Loveit and Belinda are perfectly aware of this when they begin the play, as indeed is Harriet. At one point Belinda herself exclaims about Dorimant 'Had you seen him use Mrs Loveit as I have done, you would never endure him more'. Our sympathy for Loveit is clearly intended to be tempered by her uncontrolled outbursts which would doubtless have been exaggerated for comic effect in performance. To put the matter at its simplest, *The Man of Mode* is concerned with the relative skills of players at the game of sex, money and marriage and the losers lose because they are unskilful. Loveit knows enough about the game to be able to arouse Dorimant's fading interest in her by making him believe she cares for Sir Fopling, but is forced to throw in her hand because she is maladroit enough to let Dorimant realize that she still cares for him (Dorimant). Conversely, Dorimant is able to gain Belinda because he can dissemble successfully. And the tension between Dorimant and Harriet is that between two master players who are taking each other's measure. 'She has left a pleasing image of herself that wanders in my soul' Dorimant reflects, immediately adding 'it must not settle there'. And a little later he realizes that he is in grave trouble for 'I love her, and dare not let her know it, I fear sh'as an ascendant o'er me and may revenge the wrongs I have done her sex'. In other words, he is losing control of the game, because the first rule is not to let the heart rule the head and the second not to wear your heart on your sleeve. The fact that Dorimant gets his come-uppance when he abjectly agrees to Harriet's terms may perhaps be seen as a blow for feminine independence, but is better understood as the defeat of a very good player by a better one. Harriet understands the rules as well as Dorimant, but is better able to apply them: 'I feel as great a change within' she remarks to herself, 'but he shall never know it'. And she thoroughly enjoys the game and has very little sympathy for the losers: 'Because some who want temper have been undone by gaming, must others who have it wholly deny themselves the pleasure of play?'

'The pleasure of play' in more than one sense of the term, is in fact what *The Man of Mode* offers in full measure, for there is a close analogy between the art of acting on the stage and of success in society. Both depend on self-awareness, the portrayal of emotion without succumbing to it and the conscious deploying of one's physical resources in order to move others while remaining essentially unmoved. This is not of course the only way in which stage acting can be regarded, any more than it is a desirable ideal of social conduct. The fact remains that it was one that peculiarly appealed to a section of Restoration society and one not entirely forgotten today. Etherege was very much a part of the world he depicted and loved most of it. He himself married a wealthy widow in whose company he seems to have spent as little time as possible, regarded being sent away from London (as ambassador to Ratisbon) an exile to outer darkness and, three months after the opening of *The Man of Mode*, became involved in a woman-hunting episode which resulted in a man being killed. We have to look elsewhere for a satirical examination of fashionable Restoration society and its pretensions.

Sex and Satire: William Wycherley

Wycherley's four plays belong to the 1670s, when the presence of actresses on stage was firmly established and comedy began to be much more specifically concerned with physical sex and cuckoldry. (It is interesting to note that this happens at a time when Pepys notes with distaste the increasing number of 'cits' in the audience.) Though earlier comedies, such as Etherege's do contain sexual allusions, these become much more frequent and pointed in the next decade. Thus when Vernish discovers the true sex of the disguised Fidelia in *The Plain Dealer* he exclaims:

> How! A very handsome woman, I'm sure, then: here are witnesses of't too, I confess — (*pulls off her peruke and feels her breasts*) ...

The Plain Dealer (1676) was Wycherley's last play and has a good deal in common with his masterpiece, *The Country Wife* (1675) which was not a popular success when first performed. Of his two earlier plays, *Love in a Wood* (1671) is a tedious comedy of intrigue with one good scene where the old lecher Gripe is 'cross-bitten' by an experienced bawd with the assistance of an experienced 'virgin' and her mother. *The Gentleman Dancing Master* (1672) is simpler, cleaner and much less funny; Wycherley tries to get more mileage out of newly returned foreign travellers and their affectations than a modern audience would find funny, though the play was not successful with its original audience either.

The satirical intent of *The Plain Dealer* is made quite clear by Wycherley in the prologue:

> But the coarse dauber of the coming scenes,
> To follow life and nature only means:
> Displays you as you are: makes his fine woman
> A mercenary jilt, and true to no man;
> His men of wit and pleasure of the age,
> Are as dull rogues as ever cumber'd stage.

In fact, the satire begins even before this in the printed version, for Wycherley prefaces the play with an elaborate dedication to Mother Bennet, a well known London bawd, in which he obliquely attacks the hypocrisy and commercialism of the fashionable female world. The play itself contrasts the hero, Manly, lately returned from heroic exploits at sea, with his friend Freeman, who happily accepts the need for dissembling while Manly is impatient of 'your decorums, supercilious forms and slavish ceremonies'. But his reaction to the discovery that his mistress Olivia has secretly married a fop and stolen his money is more devious than the behaviour of any other character in the play, for he decides to decoy his former mistress into an assignation and then rape her in revenge for her betrayal, using the faithful Fidelia as his messenger. Not satisfied with one assignation, Manly arranges another, suggesting that revenge may not be his prime motive, a suspicion which has already occurred to the devoted Fidelia:

Fidelia:	But you are sure 'tis revenge that makes you do this?
Manly:	Whist!
Fidelia:	'Tis a strange revenge indeed.

Manly's character is based on Molière's *Le Misanthrope* but the play's title can be applied to him only with the heaviest irony. His directness is nothing but a cloak for brutality. The happy ending, with Manly's long-overdue discovery that Fidelia is a girl and a virgin to boot, manifestly belongs to a different play. (This part of the plot is loosely based on Shakespeare's *Twelfth Night.*) Perhaps we are to regard Fidelia as the play's plain dealer, but the tenor of the dedicatory epistle is against this, and in any case Fidelia is little more than a walking statue of passive devotion. What comes through in the play is a fierce but unfocused satiric intensity.

It is in *The Country Wife* that Wycherley's ferocious satiric energy finds its appropriate form. He took a hint from Terence's *Eunuchus* to create Horner and borrowed a situation or two from Molière's *L'Ecole des Maris* and *L'Ecole des Femmes,* two plays written a few years earlier than Wycherley's which deal with the theme of forced marriage. But whatever he borrowed, Wycherley transformed entirely. The milieu of *The Country Wife* is one which literally surrounded the audience as it watched the play in the Theatre Royal at Drury Lane. Covent Garden, Russell Street, the Strand, the Cock at Bow Street and several other places mentioned in the play were in the same area as the theatre, while eastwards in Lombard Street was the centre of the Puritanical city. Of its fourteen scenes, all but two alternate between Horner's lodgings and Pinchwife's, localizing the extremes of sexual excess and deprivation within the play. But though the plot, dealing with the pretended eunuch's sexual conquest of both the fashionable town wives and the artless country wife, obviously has a lot to do with sexual matters, these are not what the most powerful satire of the play is aimed at. Its true target is not sexual appetite, though that is presented in all its degrading ravenousness with a Swiftian savagery, but the hypocrisy of the pretensions to 'honour' and 'reputation' which are rife among the ladies of fashion and to a lesser extent their husbands. For Wycherley, sexual behaviour in high society is not an elegant game but a frenzied barnyard scramble thinly disguised as one. The words 'honour' and 'reputation' are constantly on the lips of the fashionable figures, but the relation between the two is antithetical; where there is a reputation for honour (marital chastity) the genuine article does not exist. For all its artificiality, the Caroline conception of honour (represented by a poet like Lovelace for example) had embodied ideas of self-sacrifice, self-discipline and genuine devotion. It is difficult to argue that the upper ranks of the new society even paid lip-service to these ideals. The one commandment which was universally honoured was 'Thou shalt not be found out', but even this was applied differently for men and women. A man's reputation as a rake did him no harm either before or after marriage, while a woman's made her, and her husband, an object of ridicule. How seriously all this was to be taken in a society where the mistresses of the monarch and his merry men were figures of fashion and influence and where Nell Gwyn could plead for protection from an unruly crowd by exclaiming that she was the *Protestant* whore is another question. As Lucy, Alithea's maid, remarks:

> But what a devil is this honour! 'tis sure a disease in the head like megrim, or falling-sickness, that always hurries people away to do themselves mischief; men lose their lives by it: women, what's dearer to 'em, their love, the life of life.

The Falstaffian echoes only pinpoint the absence of any genuine ideal against which to contrast this. Both Alithea and Margery Pinchwife, the country wife, have been proposed as norms by which the falsity and animality of this world are to be judged. It is true that Alithea, whose name derives from the Greek word for 'truth', manages to see through her own folly in mistaking Sparkish's fatuous indifference for genuine tolerance and finds a satisfying marriage relationship with Harcourt. But for most of the play it is Alithea's blindness towards Sparkish that strikes us and Harcourt is too ineffectual a character for the relationship to impress us with any real positive force. As for the country wife, there is undoubtedly something appealing in the simplicity with which she sets about satisfying her natural desire whether for oranges or sex and the passion with which she defends Horner against the charge of impotence is impressive in its absurdity. But she *is* simple and absurd and Wycherley is too much the Londoner and man about town to offer these virtues as an adequate prescription for social behaviour. Naiveté of Margery's sort is not a desirable attribute, as Alithea's example shows. Her final stifled outburst does explode the sham and hypocrisy of the play world, but only momentarily, for it is followed by a swift and voluntary retreat into duplicity, involving her own reputation. 'Now, sir, I must pronounce your wife innocent, though I blush whilst I do it' says Horner to Pinchwife; he may well blush since he is lying in his teeth. For his part Pinchwife can only accept the lie:

> For my own sake fain I would all believe:
> Cuckolds, like lovers, should themselves deceive.

The country wife is less a moral norm than a victim and a sombre example. On the one hand Wycherley is tracing in her career the conditions under which marriage becomes a prison sentence for many women; Pinchwife, the experienced lecher, turns into the determined marital gaoler. On the other, we also see the process by which artless innocence and genuine devotion turn into sophisticated role-playing:

> *Mrs Pinchwife (aside)*: And I must be a country wife still too, I find; for I
> can't, like a city one, be rid of my musty husband and
> do what I list.

One is tempted to think that the title of the play contains the same bawdy pun that Hamlet makes to Ophelia in the play scene.

The Country Wife is beautifully constructed and often superbly funny. The contrast between the country wife's marriage, based on obsessional jealousy, and the Alithea-Sparkish relationship, based on total indifference, is skilfully pointed and the 'china' scene is justly famous for raising innuendo to a fine art; in this it only concentrates one of the main linguistic features of the play, appropriately enough, since the contrast between surface and meaning is what the play is all about. The central figure of Horner is less a character than a powerfully personified principle or set of related principles — rapacity, ruthlessness, erotism — all expressed in his resolute pursuit of sex. He is more like Volpone than like any other Restoration gallant. The foolishness of husbands like Sir Jasper who put 'business' (idling about the fringes of Whitehall) before everything else is mocked, as is the vacuous concern of Sparkish to be thought a true gallant, but the real venom in the play is directed against the ladies of fashion, Dainty, Fidget and Squeamish as well as against the lapsed lecher, Pinchwife. The 'china' scene is uproariously funny, but the laughter it arouses is of a peculiarly savage kind, both a celebration and an excoriation of human animality. The scene in which Pinchwife makes Margery write a letter at his dictation brings brutality very near the surface of the action, though it is frequently not far below. *The Country Wife* was particularly unpopular with the female section of the audience. Its success may point to something equivocal about Wycherley's stance as a satirist, something indicated in the woman-of-the-world knowingness with which the force of the play's intrigue is shrunk in the epilogue to the dimensions of yet another daredevil escapade. The epilogue was originally spoken by Mary Knepp, one of Pepys's favourites, who played the part of Lady Fidget. She warns the 'essenced boys both old and young' who 'A Horner's part may vainly think to play' that their enterprise is doomed to failure:

But, gallants, have a care, faith, what you do:
The world, which to no man his due will give,
You by experience know you can deceive,
And men may still believe you vigorous;
But then, we women — there's no cozening us.

Perhaps Wycherley wrote his true epilogue to *The Country Wife* in his last play. Olivia, who is shown in *The Plain Dealer* as false, boorish, drunken, lustful and a cheat, expresses her indignation at the play, especially the china scene (in protest at which she has broken all her own china) in impassioned terms: 'O believe me, 'tis a filthy play, and you may take my word for a filthy play as soon as another's.'

Romance and Reality in Congreve's Comedies.

William Congreve is usually remembered by one play, *The Way of the World* and by one scene in it, the famous 'proviso' scene between the hero and heroine at the end. But *Love for Love* has recently been revived with great success and has been more frequently performed. In many ways it is Congreve's best comedy, having an intelligible plot (conspicuously lacking in *The Way of the World*), and less straining after witty dialogue at the expense of situation and character, though the characters are derived from well established stage types. Congreve was only eighteen when Charles II died and his plays belong to the last years of the seventeenth century. The reign of William and Mary, during which all four of

Congreve's comedies were produced, was very different in its impact on society at large and the theatre in particular to that of Charles II. William himself was not particularly interested in the theatre and though Mary did patronize it, she died in 1694, a year after the production of Congreve's first two plays *The Old Bachelor* and *The Double Dealer*. The court circle was no longer a decisive element in the theatre audience. Its leading lights were either dead or had vanished into exile, like Etherege or into silence and obscurity, like Wycherley. The smutty comedy of the 1670s had provoked an increasingly hostile reaction, though we should not be too ready to assume that the middle class unanimously objected to obscenity. (The industrious Pepys certainly read pornographic literature, though secretly and with a severe attack of conscience afterwards.) But the audience for which Congreve wrote was markedly different from Wycherley's and at the end of the 1680s Thomas Shadwell, who had begun his dramatic career almost at the beginning of the Restoration, found it expedient to draw the audience's attention, in the prologue, to the absence of obscenity in his latest play *The Squire of Alsatia*.

In his lifetime, Congreve's greatest stage success was with *The Mourning Bride*, a tragedy much admired by Dr Johnson but unread and unacted today. *The Old Bachelor*, which was written when Congreve was barely twenty-three, was praised by Dryden who declared he 'had never seen such a first play'. It was a great popular success, a fact which must be attributed to the skill of the cast, even though the actress who played Belinda was eight months pregnant. Congreve himself commended the cast in his preface to the published version and doubtless an extra dimension was added by the fact that the veteran Betterton, who had acted the roles of rakish gallants in comedies twenty years earlier, now appeared as the elderly rake Heartwell, the old bachelor himself. But in spite of Dryden's praise, the play is no different from scores of run-of-the-mill Restoration comedies, with two hackneyed plots clumsily soldered together, Heartwell a watered-down version of Manly and Fondlewife borrowed from Wycherley's Pinchwife. The portrayal of the two women, Belinda and Araminta, does however give a foretaste of the sparkle which characterizes Congreve's later heroine, Millamant. But in general there is an air of studied contrivance about the play, as if Congreve is carefully following a well established formula to which he is not very deeply committed.

Congreve's next play, *The Double Dealer*, which appeared in the same year as his first, was not nearly so successful, but its failure as a play makes it more interesting than the success of *The Old Bachelor*. Dryden's praise this time put Congreve above Jonson and Fletcher, ranking him with Shakespeare:

> Heav'n that but once was prodigal before,
> To Shakespeare gave as much; she could not give him more.

Dryden goes on to pass his own laurels to the rising young dramatist. For all that, *The Double Dealer* remains an interesting play because Congreve here attempted something rather different from the routine intrigues of the rake and the routine amours of the gay couple. The title is obviously intended to recall Wycherley's *The Plain Dealer* but Congreve's play is hardly a satire, though it has something of Wycherley's chilling, hard-eyed vision of the world it depicts. The familiar romantic couple is there in the persons of Mellefont and Cynthia, but it is not they who are the focus of interest, but the villain Maskwell. Maskwell is an introspective intriguer, a comic version of Iago, insistent on analysing and explaining his duplicity:

> Why, let me see, I have the same face, the same words and accents, when I speak what I do think, and when I speak what I do not think — the very same — and dear dissimulation is the only art not to be known from nature.

The play is more about self-deception than about deceiving others. Most of the characters, including the romantic hero, suffer from illusions about themselves or their relations with those close to them. Thus Lady Touchwood's plotting to ruin Mellefont conceals a deep and secret love for him while her rage against Maskwell is not, as she claims, because he has made her betray her marriage vows but because he has not broken the Mellefont-Cynthia attachment. The persistent dilemma of the libertine — how to avoid obliging willing offerers who hold no attraction — leads Maskwell to dissemble against his will. The gallery of gulls and fops is varied and comprehensive, including the foolish Brisk, Lady Plyant whose vanity easily converts even Maskwell's most explicit denials to disguised protestations of love for her and Lord Touchwood who will 'be made a fool of by nobody but himself'. But Maskwell's sinister presence and the intensity of Lady Touchwood's passion for her nephew by marriage impart a quality to *The Double Dealer* which removes it equally from the genial inanities of *The Old Bachelor* and the savage satire of *The Country Wife*. The happy ending which concludes the play is no more convincing than that of *The Plain Dealer*. The dark and twisted figure of Maskwell remains in our mind long after he has been banished from the world of the play and brings the bedroom farce at the end close to a Joe Orton black comedy. The echoes of Iago in the play do not render it ridiculous. Far more than the mannered vacuities of Beaumont and Fletcher, *The Double Dealer* deserves to be called a tragi-comedy.

It is not surprising that the clear-eyed analysis of the roots of dissembling, ethical and psychological, was not popular. It was not what any section of the audience expected of a comedy. When Congreve came to write his third play, he had been hailed by Dryden as the man who could unite the courtly elegance of Etherege with the satirical force of 'manly Wycherley'. In *Love for Love* (1695) Congreve went back to the old formulas of the earlier Restoration comedy, as he had done in his first play. It is a more successful play than *The Double Dealer* because Congreve is working much more clearly and confidently within established limits. *Love for Love* was the play with which the new company opened at Lincoln's Inn Fields in April 1695 and commercial success was more than usually important. The prologue clearly makes the point that the play has been concocted to please everyone:

> We hope there's something that may please each taste,
> And tho' of homely fare we make the feast,
> Yet you will find variety at least.
> There's humour, which for cheerful friends we got,
> And for the thinking party, there's a plot.

We've something too, to gratify ill nature,
(If there by any here) and that is satire.
Tho' Satire scarce dares grin, 'tis grown so mild;
Or only shows its teeth, as if it smil'd.

The final couplet indicates Congreve's recognition of the change in audience expectations since Wycherley's time. But one cannot take the satirical pretensions of *Love for Love* very seriously. Scandal, the play's plain dealer, is a long way from Manly or Horner. What does emerge very clearly in the play, however, is a greater concern about the reality and ideals of marriage than anything in the earlier comedy, a concern which foreshadows Congreve's final comedy *The Way of the World*. The relationship between Valentine and Angelica is not simply that of pursuer and pursued. At the opening of the play Valentine has the rake's progress behind him, complete with debts and illegitimate child. But he moves by the end to a point at which his devotion to Angelica makes him able to renounce his fortune when he loses hopes of her. Needless to say, he gets both — we are within hailing distance of the sentimental comedy of the new century. (The brittle Etheregean comedy was beginning to be old-fashioned by the mid-1690s.) Critics have been as impressed with the metaphysical significance of Congreve's religious language as Collier was outraged by it (In *A Short View* published the following year, *Love for Love* is one of the specific targets.) All the talk of the 'religion of love' of miracles, blessings, good works and the like hardly confer spiritual significance on an affair which is conducted with the usual comic deviousness and comes to a successful culmination only because the heroine — aptly named Angelica according to some — has no scruples about deliberately lying to and cheating an old man. Simplicity and directness are no more recommended here than they are in any other comedy of the period. Of the two most straightforward characters, Miss Prue falls victim to Tattle's blandishments (though he finally falls into his own trap by marrying her in the belief that she is Angela in disguise) and sailor Ben realizes he is a non-survivor in this society and returns to sea, having narrowly escaped from Mrs Frail's clutches. But it is not necessary to make extravagant claims of intellectual depth and metaphysical exaltation to make two points about *Love for Love*. First, that though it makes use of quite conventional Restoration comic materials — cuckoldry, trick-marriages, lecherous old men, innocent country girls and so forth — it gives a new prominence to the central romantic plot; and secondly that this plot clearly has marriage in view and that the marriage in question is not seen as either an ordeal or a pretext for the hero to continue his career of philandering. It is easy to understand why *Love for Love* retained its popularity, albeit in bowdlerized form, even in the mid-nineteenth century, when Congreve was all but banished from the stage.

It is also a great pleasure to read, not least for the verbal extravaganzas (such as Jeremy's opening account of Will's coffee-house), with which it is studded. *The Way of the World* (1700) on the other hand, is both a pleasure and a headache to read. A pleasure for much of its dialogue, which is every bit as sparkling as it is reputed to be, and a headache because its plot is notoriously impossible to follow; even actors are said to have got lost in it. When Congreve wrote this play, at the very end of the century, he had taken some of Collier's strictures on his earlier efforts to heart. *The Way of the World* is a remarkably unbawdy play, considering some of its subject matter. But Congreve made a point of furnishing the man-hunting crone, Lady Wishfort, with a copy of Collier's tract for her closet. The play was not as successful as Congreve had hoped, though it was not a failure. In his preface to the published version, Congreve censured the audience for its inability 'to distinguish between the character of a Witwoud and a Truewit', and the Etheregean theme of genuine versus false refinement is certainly present. But the principal theme of the play is that of marriage, its reality and appearance and the tortuous plot, dealing with Lady Wishfort and the adulterers involved in a conflict over a legacy is central to its exploration. Congreve treats the motif of the reformed rake far more seriously then Etherege because he has a more positive view of both the hazards and possibilities of a genuine marriage. Arranged marriages were the rule rather than the exception and the governing considera-tions in marriage tended to be those of property and inheritance rather than mutual affection between the partners. It is against this background that we must see the final 'marriage bargain' between Millamant and Mirabell as well as the legacy hunting which forms the bulk of the plot. Mirabell's libertine career is not presented for our admiration and his behaviour to his former mistress contrasts sharply and favourably with that of Dorimant. Moreover, his wit does not express itself in a relentless pursuit of epigram so much as in a capacity to understand himself and others which produces that elegant yet thoughtful and psychologically convincing sententiousness of which Congreve was a master. But plausibility is not gained at the expense of liveliness, as a brief extract from Mirabell's arousal of his feelings for Millamant illustrates:

> I'll tell thee, Fainall, she once used me with that insolence, that in revenge I took her to pieces; sifted her and separated her failings; I studied 'em, and got 'em by rote, the catalogue was so large, that I was not without hopes, one day or other to hate her heartily: to which end I so used myself to think of 'em, that at length, contrary to my design and expectation, they gave me every hour less and less disturbance; till in a few days it became habitual to me, to remember 'em without being displeased. They are now grown as familiar to me as my own frailties; and in all probability in a little time longer I shall like 'em as well.

This is part of a longer speech yet there is nothing static about it. It catches the rhythm of Mirabell's thoughts perfectly, as the exchanges between Mrs Fainall and Mrs Marwood which open the second act capture the cautious sparring between them under the surface friendliness. Congreve's language in this play is true dramatic writing, expressive of character and creating atmosphere as well as unfolding situation, not a mere string of extraneous witticisms or carefully polished elegancies. All his characters, including servants and country cousins, are capable of coming upon witty remarks, but they are never unsuited to the speaker or the situation.

What is also noteworthy about the speech quoted is that it indicates the genuine-ness of Mirabell's feeling. In the same way, we learn of Millamant's love for

Mirabell when she confesses: 'Well, if Mirabell should not make a good husband, I am a lost thing — for I find I love him violently.' It is Congreve's ability to portray the violent passion underneath the brittle surface that gives the comedy its substance and lends urgency to the quest for a real basis for marriage. Mrs Fainall and Mrs Marwood are walking warnings of the perils of matrimony and Mirabell's past is certainly not an encouraging foundation. The extravagant behaviour of fashionable married couples conceals nothing but hypocrisy and indifference. The yawning abyss of habit and boredom lies before the gay couple. But Mirabell and Millamant need to come to terms with the way of the world, its artifice and the need for contriving, in order to outwit the Fainalls and the Marwoods. This is why the proviso scene, in spite of its triviality, and the fact that Congreve is using a device which had already been employed many times before, as in Dryden's *Secret Love*, has a fundamentally serious quality about it. By comparison, Dryden is both less serious and much less funny. *The Way of the World* may not be the best Restoration comedy nor even Congreve's best, but it is certainly the most serious (with the seriousness appropriate to comedy) in its investigation of the relation between passion and society, the turbulent surging of emotion and the restraining disciplines of marriage.

Seventeenth Century Comedy: The Last Phase

Congreve wrote his last play when he was thirty. His sinecures and the friendship of influential figures enabled him to live out the twenty-nine years remaining to him in reasonable financial security, although the stage itself had brought only modest rewards. His abandonment of drama may have been due to a combination of several factors. The cool reception of his last play, a possible estrangement from Anne Bracegirdle, the actress for whom Congreve wrote most of his leading female roles (delaying her entry for maximum effect), the effect of Collier's repeated attacks, a feeling that he had had his comic say with his last play — all these are likely to have influenced his decision, as well as the fact that in his later years he was in poor health. But it is very doubtful whether Congreve would have wished to write for either of the two London theatres at the beginning of the new century. Not only were fashions in comedy changing, but the theatres themselves were reduced to all kind of extra-dramatic expedients to attract an audience which seemed to be increasingly fascinated by French dancers, tumblers and jugglers and animal acts. Some idea of the state of the theatre can be gathered from the fact that the great actor Betterton, then managing the company, felt compelled to put on a sexy French ballerina between the acts during the revival of *The Way of the World* in 1701; in the same season and at the same theatre *The Country Wife* was embellished with a display of horsemanship.

The last 'Restoration' dramatists of any significance are Sir John Vanbrugh and George Farquhar. Vanbrugh is well known as the architect of Blenheim palace and his rebuttals of Collier's attack on the stage are as witty as anything he wrote for the stage. In addition to several adaptations of others' plays (the best of which is *The Confederacy*), Vanbrugh wrote only two complete plays, *The Relapse* (1696) and *The Provoked Wife* (1697). His dramatic work spans the decade from 1695 to 1705.

The Provoked Wife is a sceptical comedy about an unfeeling husband and his beautiful, neglected and tempted wife. It has two minor characters of distinction (the French maid and Rasor the valet) and a 'drag' scene, in which Garrick scored one of his greatest successes. This scene originally showed the husband Sir John Brute appearing before the magistrate in a clergyman's outfit, but was altered by Vanbrugh in 1725 to suit the religious sensibility of the new age, and in the later version Sir John appears in his wife's dress. The play's discussions of marriage are serious and occasionally sharp, but the wit is of a fairly long-winded and predictable kind.

The Relapse shows Vanbrugh's talent to greater advantage. This play is generally regarded as a satire on Cibber's *Love's Last Shift*, to which it is a sequel, but the two plays have a lot more in common than this would suggest. They were both performed by the same company and Cibber himself played the part of Lord Foppington in Vanbrugh's play, an elevation to the peerage of Sir Novelty Fashion in his own, a part which Cibber also played. Cibber's play unites, in a deliberate and hard-nosed fashion, the worldly wisdom of Etheregean comedy with the comedy of romantic sentiment which had already invaded the drama in the 1690s and was to turn into the sentimental comedy of the eighteenth century. Cibber knew exactly what he was doing when he gave Loveless, the rake-hero of the play, four acts of resourceful libertinism followed by a fifth act of horrified remorse as he realizes that the woman he has 'seduced' is his own rejected and still faithful wife. The epilogue explicitly draws attention to the fact that the hero is 'lewd for above four acts' while at the same time 'there's not one cuckold made'. The formula worked and the first night audience were in tears over the final reconciliation, when the hero breaks into rhyme. 'The greatest happiness we can hope on earth' he solemnly declaims

> And sure the nearest to the joys above
> Is the chaste rapture of a virtuous love.

Congreve remarked that *Love's Last Shift* had a great many things which were like wit that were not really wit. One of these was the character of Sir Novelty Fashion, the fop whom Vanbrugh turned into a genuine dramatic creation as Lord Foppington. His pretensions to wit and refinement and his aversion to country life are expressed in a language which is distinctively his. To Amanda's comment that reading books is more important than arranging them neatly in one's library, his rejoinder is:

> That, I must confess, I am nat altogether fond of. Far to mind the inside of a book, is to entertain one's self with the forced product of another man's brain. Naw I think a man of quality and breeding may be much better diverted with the natural sprauts of his own.

The two plots of the play bring together rather loosely the current concerns of comedy, with Foppington's younger brother outwitting him and marrying the country girl Foppington intended for himself in one, and Loveless 'relapsing' in the other into infidelity, while his long-suffering wife trembles on the brink of adultery without quite falling. Vanbrugh's scepticism about Loveless's reform is simply the obverse of Cibber's sentimentality and is treated with no more depth. His attempts at High Seriousness through the use of verse are uniformly disastrous. It is in the creation of Foppington, who is far more than an amusing fop (as his sarcastic congratulations on his younger brother's marriage show), and in the country scenes involving Sir Tunbelly Clumsy and his daughter Hoyden, that Vanbrugh's comic talent comes into its own. *The Relapse* is a genuinely distinguished Restoration comedy, 'minor' only if we set it beside the greatest plays of the period.

George Farquhar wrote or adapted eight plays, of which the last two, *The Recruiting Officer* (1706) and *The Beaux' Stratagem* (1707), are regularly revived, while one other, *The Constant Couple* (1699), is occasionally seen on the modern stage. The latter play popularized the fashion for 'breeches parts', acting roles in which handsome male characters are played by handsome women. The refined sensibility of the new age was immensely titillated by the spectacle of a young woman playing the part of a rake visiting a respectable girl in a house which he takes for a brothel, falling in love with her and being puzzled by her resistance. Two of the most popular eighteenth-century actresses, Peg Woffington and Dorothy Jordan, scored tremendous successes in the role of Sir Harry Wildair in Farquhar's play and the fashion for breeches parts, which persisted throughout the eighteenth century and into the nineteenth, was an important element in the convention by which the Principal Boy in pantomime is played by a woman. Farquhar began his dramatic career as an actor, but left the stage after accidentally wounding a fellow actor by using a real instead of a property sword in the last act of Dryden's *The Indian Emperor*.

In his last two plays (the last written in six weeks while he lay debt-ridden and ill in a lodging house), Farquhar broadened the range of seventeenth-century comedy in two ways. First, he got away from the claustrophobic atmosphere of fashionable London to the country, which he depicted as very different from the limbo of the earlier dramatists. Secondly, and as a result of this, he widened the social range of the characters and thereby necessarily enlarged the scope of comedy to include more than 'wit'. Shadwell had anticipated him to some extent in plays such as *Bury Fair*, but Farquhar is a more stylish writer and a defter dramatist. *The Recruiting Officer*, also written in haste, is based on his own recruiting experiences in Shropshire. It is not the somewhat tired routine of the rake and the disguised heroine Silvia which really gives the play its distinction (Farquhar manages to get the best of both worlds by making the virtuous Silvia act and speak like a libertine in her disguise), but the activity of the low life characters Sergeant Kite and Captain Brazen, who reminds us, not altogether to Farquhar's discredit, of some of Jonson's rogues and even Falstaff himself. In *The Beaux' Stratagem,* again based partly on Farquhar's experience in the country, a cleaned and tidied up version of the hard-headed comedy of libertine intrigue is skilfully blended with soft-hearted romantic assumptions. The predicament of the two gallants who go to the country to recoup their fortunes and fall in love with the women they try to trick again satisfies the demands of intrigue and sentimental comedy, and the comic antics when the heroes are mistaken for Jesuits as well as highwaymen keeps the slushiness which threatens sentimental comedy at bay. The initial contrast between a

London depicted as unstable and untrustworthy and a Lichfield which is solid, dependable and unchanging, is ironically undercut by the provincial characters' real nature and pursuits, as well as by the ironic parallel between the fine gentlemen and the real highwaymen for whom they are mistaken. Not the least intriguing aspect of the play is the divorce by mutual consent which comes at the end. By putting most of the arguments which he got from Milton's tract on divorce into Mrs Sullen's mouth, Farquhar certainly intended to raise some awkward questions in the minds of the genteel audience. In the eighteenth century women like Mrs Sullen had no legal means of freeing themselves from a drunken husband. Though it may appear fantastic, the divorce scene is in some ways the most serious in the play. All in all, *The Beaux' Stratagem* is one of the best comedies of the late seventeenth century. It has almost always been successful in the theatre and only preconceptions about the 'gradual decline of the comedy of manners' and 'anticipation of sentimental comedy' (both of which undoubtedly occurred but can tell us nothing in advance about a specific play) has prevented it from being recognized as such.

If it has done nothing else, this chapter should have illustrated the variety even within the best known Restoration comedies. In a close examination of the period, Shadwell would have merited some attention for his conscientious but elephantine effort to follow in Jonson's footsteps, and if his plays were at all readily available even in libraries, Southerne would certainly have found a place, especially for the savage comedy of *The Wives' Excuse.* But even if we think only of the peaks, it is clear that these dramatists are portraying a world which is recognizably our own — sceptical, class-conscious, money-haunted, at once fascinated and repelled by the body's desires and imperfections. They displayed that world in a form of theatre which continued virtually unchanged for two centuries, and they used all the resources of that theatre — its capacity to indicate specific locations, the intimate relationship between actors and audience, its deliberate realism and its conscious artifice — with a continual awareness of the kinship between play-acting and social intercourse. It is more rewarding to think of this drama in the words of a recent critic as 'the first modern comedies' than as the fag-end of a mythical golden age.

7

Sentiment and Melodrama: The Eighteenth and Nineteenth Centuries

This chapter will be one of the shortest in the book, although it covers one of the longest tracts of time. This is because the primary focus of this study is dramatic literature, the surviving texts that formed the basis for some of the theatrical performances of this period. Considered as literature these texts, with a handful of exceptions, make a very poor showing indeed, so that detailed discussion of them is scarcely necessary. But, as I have insisted throughout, it is highly misleading if not actually impossible to discuss plays out of their context in the theatre. And by a striking but not altogether strange paradox, the theatrical context of the period we are now entering is as rich and exciting as its dramatic texts are, generally speaking, turgid and lifeless. To a large extent therefore, this chapter will be taken up with contexts rather than texts, with 'background' so to speak, coming into the foreground.

To begin with, this is the period of some of the greatest acting ever seen on the English stage — a period that begins with Garrick and includes the stage careers of Mrs Siddons and John Kemble, of Edmund Kean and Henry Irving, to name only the brightest stars in the theatrical firmament. Secondly, we can still feel something of the power and presence of these great actors and actresses because this was also a period which saw the rise of periodical journalism and thereby produced some of our greatest dramatic critics — Hazlitt, the German Georg Lichtenberg, Lamb, Leigh Hunt, George Henry Lewes and George Bernard Shaw among them. We also find at this time great changes in the physical form of the theatre, changes which produced buildings and styles of presentation which survived into the twentieth century and have not yet entirely disappeared. Accompanying these changes and sometimes accounting for them is a transformation in the size and social composition of the audience, partly the result of the Industrial Revolution and the consequent phenomenal growth of London. Thus, while it is undeniable that the period boasts very few dramatists of the first rank — Goldsmith and Sheridan, Wilde and Shaw — and not many more of the second — Susannah Centilivre, Richard Steele, Dion Boucicault, Tom Taylor, T.W. Robertson, Henry Arthur Jones, Arthur Pinero — it forms nevertheless an important chapter in the history of English drama.

From Manners to Sentiment

It is of course quite inaccurate to talk about two centuries of drama, as a 'chapter'. The more closely we look at it, the less neat and tidy the theatrical history of the time appears; all that these two centuries have in common seems to be a comparative dearth of outstanding dramatists. As we have seen, the earlier hard-headed, satirical-cynical phase of Restoration comedy had already given way by the late 1690s to a softer, more superficially moralistic drama represented by Cibber's *Love's Last Shift* (though its sequel, Vanbrugh's *The Relapse,* had more of the earlier toughness) and the plays of Farquhar. There was an increasing tendency to treat the institution of marriage more respectfully and to propel the action, by however improbable a series of events, towards marital reconciliation. An immensely popular scene in Cibber's *The Careless Husband* (1704), showed Lady Easy, who discovers her erring husband asleep with the maid, gently covering his head with a scarf. He later wakes up to the reality of his situation and there follows a scene of repentance, reformation and reconciliation. These tend to be the keynote of comedy in the new century and are amply represented in the four complete plays of Richard Steele. Steele does not quite deserve the total neglect which has been his fate in the modern theatre. His first play *The Funeral* (1701) lays down the lines to be followed by comedy throughout most of the century. Its ranging of 'good' and 'bad' characters (the latter mostly those who would have been much less severely regarded in Restoration comedy) and its high-minded didacticism are typical. Steele was a professed admirer of Jeremy Collier and determined to expurgate comedy of the ribaldry and immorality which had so incensed the pious parson, and to make the play teach a moral lesson in favour of marital virtue. He even makes his villainess, Lady Brumpton, guilty of bigamy to prevent her inheriting her virtuous husband's wealth. For all that, the farcical underplot, the satire on undertakers and the law, and above all the sympathetic portrayal of certain female characters give *The Funeral* a good deal of life.

No such redeeming feature saves Steele's next play *The Lying Lovers* (1703) in which the hero Bookwit expresses his repentance for having killed a man in a drunken duel in unspeakable blank verse. One scene, in which Bookwit is welcomed to Newgate prison by the inmates, faintly anticipates *The Beggar's Opera.* For the rest, *The Lying Lovers* deserved its fate in being, in Steele's own words 'damn'd for its piety'.

Perhaps its priggishness and its predictable moralizing were too much even for the new Collier-fed middle-class audience. At any rate in his third play, *The Tender Husband* (1705) Steele made a conscious effort to preach less. But sentimentality oozes through almost every line of the final reconciliation scene, in which a monstrous underplot reaches its climax when a husband is united with a wife whose virtue he has tested by disguising his mistress as her suitor. The rest of the play is mercifully free from such complications, but *The Tender Husband* is chiefly noteworthy because it inspired two comic creations by greater dramatists later in the century — Steele's Biddy Tipkin is the source of Sheridan's Lydia Languish while Biddy's cousin Humphry Gubbin is clearly related to Goldsmith's Tony Lumpkin.

The Tender Husband, for all Steele's efforts, had no greater success than *The Lying Lovers* and Steele turned from writing for the theatre to politics and journalism. To him we owe the earliest theatrical journal in English, *The Theatre,* which appeared twice a week from 1719 to 1720. His last and most influential play did not appear till 1722, though he had been planning it for a dozen years. *The*

Conscious Lovers clearly shows how wide a gap can exist between comedy and laughter. Indeed, according to Theophilus Cibber, it was his father who had suggested the introduction of the comic figures Tom and Phillis, as he thought the play as it stood too grave for an English audience. According to Steele himself 'the whole was writ for the sake of the scene of the fourth act, wherein Mr Bevil evades the quarrel with his friend', and he went on to 'hope that it may have some effect upon the Goths and Vandals that frequent the theatres, or a more polite audience may supply their absence'. Later in the century Dr Johnson was to define comedy in his famous Dictionary as 'a dramatic representation of the lighter faults of man-kind with an intention to make vice and folly ridiculous'. Steele's view of comedy was rather different. *The Conscious Lovers* is exemplary comedy with a vengeance, or rather without a vengeance, for the hero nobly forgoes duelling and is suitably commended by his friend who has seen the light:

> *Myrtle:* Dear Bevil, your friendly conduct has convinced me that there is
> nothing manly but what is conducted by reason, and agreeable to
> the practice of virtue and justice. And yet how many have been
> sacrificed to that idol, the unreasonable opinion of men! Nay, they
> are so ridiculous in it, that they often use their swords against each
> other with dissembled anger and real fear.

Betrayed by honour, and compelled by shame,
They hazard being to preserve a name:
Nor dare inquire into the dread mistake,
Till plunged in sad eternity they wake.

The substitution of bourgeois Christian notions of prudence, cool rationality, filial devotion and respectful tolerance as against the older cavalier notion of a gentleman and his honour is thoroughgoing and utterly humourless in this play. As Fielding's Parson Adams said, in support of his view that *The Conscious Lovers* was the only play (apart from Addison's *Cato*) fit for a Christian to see, 'it contains things almost solemn enough for a sermon'. In addition to the non-duelling scene, the play's other great highlight is the reconciliation between the symbolically named merchant Sealand and his long lost daughter, the equally symbolically named Indiana. There is no intention here to arouse anything that can be recognized as the comic spirit in any form; pathos with a liberal helping of sentimen-tality is the beast in view and Steele succeeded beyond all expectation in the appeal which he put into the epilogue:

'Tis yours with breeding to refine the age,
To chasten wit, and moralize the stage,
   Ye modest, wise and good, ye fair, ye brave,
Tonight the champion of your virtues save;
Redeem from long contempt the comic name,
And judge politely for your country's fame.

The Conscious Lovers was so successful that it all but refined and moralized comedy out of existence. It pleased the new middle class by appealing equally to its taste for the respectable, the cautious and the maudlin. It was translated almost immediately and accelerated the vogue for *la comédie larmoyante,* tearful or sentimental comedy, in France and Germany. In England it spawned a host of forgotten mid-century comedies. *The Conscious Lovers* must have gladdened the heart of the ageing Jeremy Collier for it is as antiseptic as it is high-minded. It has nothing of the boisterous geniality of celebratory comedy nor the harsh but bracing satirical energy of the comedy of judgment. For these it substitutes a thin-blooded mixture of tears and happy ending and an undeviating determination to be exemplary which is its undoing, for 'exemplary comedy' is almost a contradiction in terms, at least in the theatre. John Dennis put the matter thus when he contrasted sentimental comedy with the classical comic ideal:

> How little do they know of the nature of true comedy, who believe that its proper business is to set us patterns for imitation: for all such patterns are serious things, and laughter is the life, and the very soul of comedy. 'Tis its proper business to expose persons to our view, whose views we may shun, and whose follies we may despise; and by showing us what is done upon the comic stage, to show us what ought never to be done upon the stage of the world.

The early years of the eighteenth century witnessed a frantic struggle for survival between the two licensed companies, Drury Lane and Lincolns Inn Fields, in a period after direct royal and courtly patronage of the theatre had effectively ceased. There were increasingly more desperate efforts to draw the audience into the theatre via the attractions of native and imported singers, acrobats, dancers, jugglers and the like. The afterpiece, a short farcical, comic or musical entertainment following the evening's main offering also dates from this period. This was another sign of the effort to attract a new middle-class audience whose dinner hour did not allow it to attend a full theatrical performance which usually began at five (later six) in the evening. For a long time a reduced rate of admission had been charged after the third act of the main drama was over, but the afterpiece provided a complete entertainment for the middle-class audience who could watch it in well fed comfort. Full length plays were often boiled down and served up as afterpieces.

In 1705 a new theatre built by Vanbrugh opened in the Haymarket, but its acoustics made it unsuitable for anything except opera, the vogue for which was increasing throughout the period. The first decade of the century saw the production of over 150 new plays by the two companies, but none of these expedients really succeeded in attracting a solid, regular and substantial audience to the theatres. The result of this mutually exhausting struggle for an elusive audience was the union of the theatrical companies in 1708. The twenty-odd years which followed probably form the deadest period of drama in a moribund century. In comedy its climactic success was Steele's *The Conscious Lovers.* In tragedy, the best these years can offer is Nicholas Rowe's parade of doomed and passionate females, begun in the early years of the century and continued with such contemporary successes as *Jane Shore* (1714) and *Lady Jane Grey* (1715) and the petrified triumph of Addison's *Cato* (1713). Rowe's tragedies represent a decline even from the limited achievement in 'pathetic tragedy' represented by Otway's *The Orphan*

(1680) and *Venice Preserved* (1682). They lack even the sheer theatrical exuberance of Lee and Settle's 'heroic tragedy' at its best. Rowe's greatest contribution to English drama was his edition of Shakespeare published in 1709. As for *Cato*, which ran for thirty-five nights in London (a very long time by eighteenth-century standards) and had an equally successful run at Oxford, it is very much a play written by a literary theorist for an age which had no tragic sense whatever. It is paralysingly polished in all its innumerable unrhymed couplets, of which the following excerpt from one of Cato's speeches is a sufficient example:

> Thy nobleness of soul obliges me.
> But know, young Price, that valour soars above
> What the world calls misfortune and affliction.
> These are not ills; else would they never fall
> On Heaven's first favourites, and the best of men:
> The Gods, in County, work up storms about us,
> That give mankind occasion to exert
> Their hidden strength, and throw out into practice
> Virtues, which shun the day, and lie conceal'd
> In the smooth seasons and the calms of life.

Addison was following French neo-classic notions of decorum and the unities and the result is dismal enough to satisfy the most diehard Francophobe. It serves to underline the fact that from its medieval beginnings right down to modern times the English tradition in drama has always favoured diversity rather than unity, preferring an untidy richness to a single-minded intensity, though the latter is hardly characteristic of Addison's play. Steele's praise of *Cato* for uniting 'French correctness' with 'British fire' notwithstanding, few sparks and no flames are noticeable in it today, and its contemporary success must be attributed at least partly to political reasons. Despite its great prestige Addison's play had few imitators, none of them very successful on stage. Opera and the insistence on poetic justice effectively combined to destroy any nascent tragedy in the period.

Fielding and Gay: Burlesque Theatre

In 1737, an act was passed which gave the Lord Chamberlain statutory powers to license theatres and required his approval of all plays before they could be publicly performed, a form of censorship that was elaborated in 1843 and remained in force until 1968. The only theatrical offering which has survived from this period into modern times is John Gay's *The Beggar's Opera,* produced at Lincoln's Inn Fields in 1728 by John Rich (making Gay rich and Rich gay, as the contemporary witticism had it). Gay wrote several plays all of which have sunk without trace, though *The What D'Ye Call It* is an effective burlesque of 'pathetic' tragedy. But *The Beggar's Opera* is in a class by itself, burlesquing the current craze for Italian opera but transcending its target and creating a new English dramatic form, the ballad opera. Quite apart from its recreation in the modern theatre by Brecht as *The Threepenny Opera,* Gay's work is dramatically alive in its own right, blending romantic and anti-romantic elements into a masterful dramatic whole in its portrayal of the London underworld. The edge of its political satire is somewhat blunted today but it was sharp enough when it first appeared for the censor to ban its rather disappointing sequel *Polly*. But it was not the work of Gay but the political theatre of Henry Fielding which eventually led Walpole to rush the Licensing Act of 1737 through Parliament. The early stages of Fielding's ten-year career as a dramatist are innocuous enough and he even dedicated his comedy *The Modern Husband* (1732) to Walpole. *Rape Upon Rape* (1730) later revised as *The Coffee House Politician* has been successfully converted into the musical *Lock Up Your Daughters* while *The Tragedy of Tom Thumb* (1730) revised as *The Tragedy of Tragedies* is a lively burlesque of heroic drama. Also worth mention is *The Author's Farce* (1730, revised 1734), Fielding's highly amusing variation of the 'rehearsal play' complete with a puppet show performed by human actors.

In 1731 Fielding first attacked the Government and actually put the royal family on the stage in *The Welsh Opera,* as a result of which he deemed it prudent to abandon political theatre for a few years. But in 1734, he returned to the attack on party politics in *Don Quixote in England,* after the success of which Fielding took on the management of the Haymarket Theatre and wrote for it *Pasquin* (1736) which is still aimed at the corruption of party politics as a whole, and *The Historical Register* (1736) together with its afterpiece *Eurydice Hiss'd,* which unequivocally lampooned the Walpole administration. Not content with this, Fielding also staged several anti-Walpole plays at the Haymarket. The inevitable result was the Licensing Act which, by legally permitting only two theatres in London, forced the Haymarket to close down and terminated Fielding's career as a playwright. Shaw declared that Fielding was 'the greatest practising dramatist, with the single exception of Shakespeare, produced by England between the Middle Ages and the nineteenth century' an encomium difficult to survive but one which should not obscure Fielding's limited but very real achievement as a burlesque playwright.

The Garrick Years, 1741-1776

David Garrick is best known of course as an actor, but he also has a place in the history of drama as theatre manager, adapter and dramatist. The years immediately following the Licensing Act led to the extinction of competition and the consequent stablization of the two licensed theatres, Drury Lane and Covent Garden. For nearly thirty years from 1747, Garrick was responsible for the management of Drury Lane where among other innovations he brought in concealed stage lighting and banished the audience from the stage. As an actor, Garrick achieved equal success in comedy, tragedy and farce and impressed contemporaries with the enormous expressiveness of his movements and features, compared with the more stilted and declamatory style of his elder contemporary James Quin. He is said to have modelled his portrayal of Lear on the distraction of an old man who accidentally killed his infant son, while an early biographer, Arthur Murphy, attributed Garrick's failure as Othello to the fact that blacking his face deprived it of expressiveness. Garrick also adhered to the then revolutionary practice of reacting to what other actors were saying and doing instead of relapsing into inattention between one's own speeches.

Another important contribution Garrick made was the regular and substantial representation of Shakespeare at Drury Lane. Three apiece of the most frequently performed tragedies and comedies at Drury Lane during this time were by Shakespeare, whose work represents nearly a fifth of the total Drury Lane repertoire under Garrick. This said, it has to be added that what was performed was not always what Shakespeare wrote, though Garrick's versions were not nearly as barbarous as such earlier eighteenth-century offerings as Granville's *The Jew of Venice* (1700) with Portia's German suitor, Mynheer van Gutts, or John Dennis's vulgarization of Falstaff as *The Comical Gallant* (1702). Among other emasculations Garrick put on a *Hamlet* without the grave-diggers, a *Lear* without the Fool and a *Romeo and Juliet* with a parting scene in the tomb for the lovers before dying. He also turned *The Taming of the Shrew* into *Katherine and Petruchio* and *The Winter's Tale* into *Florizel and Perdita*. But these were less the butcheries of wanton philistinism than a working professional's notions of what the public wanted, though the distinction is not always easy to maintain. Among Garrick's lesser deformations was the recastration of Wycherley's *The Country Wife* as *The Country Girl* (1766). Garrick's own plays were mainly farces, the most successful of which were *Miss in her Teens* (1747) and *Bon Ton* (1775), both derived from French originals, though the study of the homosexual Daffodil, who conceals his proclivities under the guise of a dashing ladies' man in *The Male Coquette* (1757) is probably his most interesting dramatic effort. Finally, as a theatrical manager, combining the roles of administrator, literary advisor and director, Garrick helped many contemporary dramatists to shape their work to suit audience requirements and thus kept contemporary dramatic writing, such as it was, alive. He not only improved the status of the theatre generally — 'he raised the character of his profession to a liberal art' as Burke said — but it was owing largely to him that, in the words of Arthur Murphy, in that period 'the theatre engrossed the minds of men to such a degree that there existed in England a *fourth estate,* King, Lords and Commons, and *Drury Lane playhouse'.*

Sheridan and Goldsmith

In 1776, after a long and successful career, Garrick handed over the management of Drury Lane to a younger man whose achievement as a comic dramatist is in sharp contrast to his inefficiency as a theatrical manager. Richard Brinsley Sheridan is undoubtedly the best dramatist of the second half of the eighteenth century and the author of some of the best stage comedies in English. Sheridan was born into the theatre, for both his parents wrote plays and his father was an actor. Like many Irishmen, he seemed to be born with a gift for words, for it is language above all that distinguishes his comedies, rather than originality of plot or insight into character. His first play, *The Rivals,* was put on at Covent Garden in 1775, when Sheridan was twenty-three. It was withdrawn for revision after two days and restaged in an improved version ten days later. Sheridan captures the fashionable life of eighteenth-century Bath which he had known as a boy with elegant skill, but his real distinction lies in the way he breathes life into a succession of theatrical stereotypes. Lydia Languish, the heroine who suffers from an overdose of circulating-library romance is, as mentioned above, derived from a character in Steele's *The Conscious Lovers* while the softhead squire, Bob Acres, was a familiar stage figure. Even the play's most famous character, Mrs Malaprop, had already appeared in forgotten plays by Garrick and Murphy. But Sheridan gives her and all his other borrowings their definitive dramatic incarnation. What Steele and a host of others had unsuccessfully attempted, namely to retain the sparkle of Restoration comic dialogue without its indecency, Sheridan managed so brilliantly that *The Rivals,* as well as his other great comedy *The School of Scandal* (1777) have retained their hold on the stage from his time to ours.

Perhaps the secret of Sheridan's success is his total lack of any overt moral intention. His dramatic career spans a mere four years (if we discount an adaptation of a German play written in 1799, and a pantomime of *Robinson Crusoe* in 1781) and he seems to have been intent on adapting existing modes in his own particular fashion, creating a self-contained comic world with clarity and elegance but no pretentious striving after moral depth. In the words of the Prologue to *The Rivals:*

> *(pointing to the Figure of Comedy)*: Look on her well — does she seem form'd
> to teach?
> Should you expect to hear this lady — preach?
> Is grey experience suited to her youth?
> Do solemn sentiments become that mouth?
> Bid her be grave, those lips should rebel prove
> To every theme that slanders mirth or love.
> Can our light scenes add strength to holy laws!
> Such puny patronage but hurts the cause:
> Fair virtue scorns our feeble aid to ask;
> And moral truth disdains the trickster's mask.

Paradoxically, by not striving too earnestly for moral effect, Sheridan obtains in his greatest comedy, *The School for Scandal,* the kind of moral effect attainable in polite comedy — the elegant but devastating exposure of scandal-mongering and hypocrisy which are as effective and relevant today as they were in the eighteenth century. *The School for Scandal* is sentimental comedy without sentimentality, for Sheridan here contrives to combine genuine feeling with comic detachment. The reconciliation of Sir Peter and his wife and the marriage between Charles and Maria are satisfying in their own terms because they belong to a coherently imagined and vividly realized comic world.

That realization includes many a skilful shaft directed against the maudlin assumptions of sentimental comedy. Sheridan's persistent concern with the theatre, both as art and institution produced his third comic triumph, *The Critic; A Tragedy Rehearsed* (1776) the best of the numerous offspring of Buckingham's *The Rehearsal.* In the character of Sir Fretful Plagiary, Sheridan hit off perfectly the attitudes and outlook of one of the successful exponents of sentimental comedy, Richard Cumberland author of, among other things, *The West Indian* (1771) and *The Jew* (1794). The tragic pretensions of the age are unforgettably sent up in the work of Mr Puff, but Puff, Sneer, Plagiary and Dangle, by virtue of their linguistic vivacity, escape from the narrow confines of their own society and inhabit the more spacious and timeless world of great comedy.

The first of Oliver Goldsmith's two plays, *The Good Natured Man* was staged at Covent Garden seven years before Sheridan's debut at the same theatre, but went unnoticed amidst the success at the rival Drury Lane of Hugh Kelly's now forgotten *False Delicacy*, which exemplified the kind of genteel vacuity against which both Sheridan and Goldsmith reacted. Though still occasionally revived and though the characters of Croaker and Lofty are genuine comic creations, the focus of the play is rather blurred. It is Goldsmith's other play, *She Stoops to Conquer*, performed at Covent Garden five years later on which his fame as a comic dramatist securely rests. In spite of superficial similarities of plot and the happy ending obligatory in all comedy, Goldsmith's play has little if anything in common with sentimental comedy. Its humour is often unashamedly 'low' without being ribald, and the basic comic situation of a well brought up young man who is diffident among his social equals but uninhibited in what he believes to be 'low' company is both hilarious and perceptive. *She Stoops to Conquer: or The Mistakes of a Night* was first produced at Covent Garden in 1773. (Garrick refused both Goldsmith's plays because of the latter's attack on the theatre managers in a section on the stage in his *Enquiry into the Present State of Polite Learning in Europe* published in 1759.) The play has been popular on the stage ever since. In an age in which excessive laughter was considered unbecoming, Horace Walpole has recorded how it made him and other gentlemen in the audience 'laugh very much'. It contains several implausibilities, such as the central one of a country gentleman's residence being consistently mistaken for an inn (although Goldsmith maintained that this was based on an actual incident), the inability of young Marlow to tell a well brought up girl like Kate Hardcastle from a serving maid, and the lady of the house imagining herself to be confronted by a highwayman on a common forty miles away when in fact she is kneeling before her husband in her own garden. But in performance these enhance rather than detract from the comic suspense. The characters, loosely based on the Jonsonian 'humours' pattern, have theatrical if not psychological individuality, so that we readily accept a Tony Lumpkin who is conversant with Latin, illiterate, shrewd and boneheaded together, an amalgam which faintly recalls some Shakespearean clowns. No more than *The Rivals* or *The School for Scandal* does *She Stoops to Conquer* depend for its effect on an acquaintance with the turgid and humourless sentimental comedy against which it was a not altogether wholehearted revolt. Goldsmith's dialogue does not have the sparkle of Sheridan's but it is vivacious and full of a humour that derives from character and situation rather than from any evident verbal wit.

Goldsmith and Sheridan light up the dismal scene of late eighteenth-century drama. But their example did not lead to any startling renascence of comedy. Goldsmith's caustic comments on sentimental drama remain true of a large number of plays produced at the time. 'These comedies' he wrote in an essay published in the same year as *She Stoops to Conquer*,

> have had of late great success, perhaps from their novelty, and also from their flattering every man in his favourite foible. In these plays almost all the

characters are good, and exceedingly generous; they are lavish enough of their *tin* money on the stage: and though they want humour, have abundance of sentiment and feeling. If they happen to have faults or foibles, the Spectator is taught not only to pardon, but to applaud them, in consideration of the goodness of their hearts; so that folly, instead of being ridiculed, is commended, and the comedy aims at touching our passions without the power of being truly pathetic.

Goldsmith here shrewdly hits on the manner in which sentimental comedy provided a flattering self-image of the rising middle class who readily applauded the successful union of a soft heart and a hard head. He concludes with a formula which applies to much of a drama of the period:

It is only sufficient to raise the characters a little;[1] to deck out the hero with a riband, or give the heroine a title: then to put an insipid dialogue, without character or humour, into their mouths, give them mighty good hearts, very fine cloths, furnish a new set of scenes, make a pathetic scene or two, with a sprinkling of tender melancholy conversation through the whole; and there is no doubt but all the ladies will cry and all the gentlemen applaud.

Theatres and Acting from Kemble to Kean

Although very little drama of any importance was written in the later eighteenth and early nineteenth century, there were some notable developments in theatrical presentation, organization and audience composition which affected the kinds of dramatic entertainment offered. These need to be briefly noted in order to set such 'serious drama' as there was in its proper perspective.

In 1771, Garrick engaged a young painter, J.P. de Loutherbourg, as scenic director at Drury Lane. de Loutherbourg continued there when Sheridan took over the management and was mainly responsible for the introduction of what may be called a heightened and spectacular naturalism into theatrical decor. This in its turn led to the attention to realistic detail and feeling for local colour which marked the productions of John Philip Kemble, who succeded Garrick as the brightest theatrical star towards the end of the eighteenth century and in the opening years of the nineteenth. Kemble's fame was overshadowed only by that of his sister Sarah Siddons, often regarded as the greatest actress England has produced.

The eighteenth century saw the management of the theatre pass from the hands of courtiers such as Davenant and Killigrew into those of actors like Betterton, Cibber and Garrick. With John Philip Kemble begins the line of great nineteenth-century actor-managers which includes such figures as W.C. Macready, Samuel Phelps and Henry Irving and continues into the twentieth with Frank Benson and Beerbohm Tree. Under their aegis theatrical management and performance became more disciplined, if also more autocratic. Though productions tended to be organized around the star who also held the purse strings and texts were amended to highlight his performance, many of the great actor managers conscien-

[1] i.e. to raise them to the 'middle' rank of society, as opposed to the 'low' one traditionally thought appropriate for comedy.

tiously attempted to conceive of a production as a coherent whole. Rehearsals became more regular and longer and drunkenness on stage less frequent. While the two great London theatres were gradually becoming more respectable, a whole host of lesser theatres attracting a diversity of audiences was opening up in London and the provinces, especially when the monopoly of the two major theatres on 'legitimate' drama ended in 1843.

Kemble, who came of a family of strolling players, made his London début as Hamlet in 1783. Hazlitt described him in the role as 'like a man in armour, with a determined inveteracy of purpose, in one undeviating straight line.' Hazlitt was a professed devotee of Kemble's younger contemporary Edmund Kean, but for all that he thought 'Kemble's sensible,[1] lonely Hamlet has not been surpassed'. Five years after his debut, Kemble took over the management of Drury Lane and for the next four years put on a number of important Shakespearean productions which gave full scope to his restrained and consciously dignified style of acting as well as to the grand manner which was his sister's natural bent. In 1794, Drury Lane was rebuilt and vastly enlarged and Kemble continued with his Shakespearean productions there till 1802, when he left for Covent Garden. Here too he carried on the same ambitious programme, interrupted when the theatre burnt down in 1808, but carried on from the following year until his retirement in 1817. In all, in nearly thirty years of acting and theatrical management, Kemble put on no less than twenty-seven of Shakespeare's plays, achieving his greatest fame (not unexpectedly in view of his acting style) as Coriolanus. Kemble inaugurated what was to be one of the great periods of Shakespearean production on the English stage, but the effect on the dramatic writing of the period of this bardolatry was little short of disastrous, producing turgid and unactable poetic dramas and others such as those of Sheridan Knowles and Thomas Talfourd which were successfully staged in vast theatres where boom and bombast, uttered by great actors, sounded as if they signified something. For Kemble's career spans the period when London's theatres lose their intimacy and become enormous arenas where only grand effects of acting and spectacle are possible. The new Covent Garden theatre opened in 1809 had 3,000 seats while the enlarged Drury Lane of 1794 had over 3,600. The economics of such theatres demanded an increasing emphasis on spectacle, melodrama, animal acts and other extravagances, and Kemble thrilled audiences in many a Gothic melodrama in addition to his Shakespearean portrayals. Thus the classical restraint of the Kemble acting style should be seen against a theatrical setting full of pageantry, spectacle and melodrama action.

Kemble evidently possessed an intensity of expression which went hand in hand with his mannered restraint. Nevertheless, the contrast with Edmund Kean was strong and startling to contemporary audiences. Kean made an explosive début as Shylock at Drury Lane in 1814 and although his theatrical peak lasted for little more than a decade, he was undoubtedly the 'bright particular star' of the English stage during that time. Where Kemble was tall and stately with classical good looks, Kean was short, slightly built and not particularly handsome. Kemble had striven for a steadily accumulating theatrical effect, while Kean captured his

[1] sensible — full of feeling, sensitive.

audience by irresistible bursts of feeling, using to full effect his dark and marvel-
lously expressive eyes and the fluid movement of which he was a master. The
Romantic exaltation of intensity as a supreme value finds its theatrical counterpart
in Kean's acting, the effect of which Coleridge described in a well known phrase as
'like reading Shakespeare by flashes of lightning'. Lamb, Byron, Coleridge and
Hazlitt all praised him extravagantly, Hazlitt in particular extolling him over and
over again. Kemble had excelled in the portrayal of virtue and nobility; by
contrast, villainous passion was Kean's *forte*. Iago, Richard Crookback, Shylock
and Sir Giles Overreach in *A New Way to Pay Old Debts* were his most memorable
performances. In private life too, the contrast between Kean and Kemble was
sharp. Kemble had striven, like Garrick before him and Macready and Irving
afterwards, to raise the social status of the acting profession. Kean harked back to
the older, wilder roots. He was probably an illegitimate child and may have had
the Marquis of Halifax as his father. His adult life was marked by habitual
drunkenness and several amours, culminating in an affair with an alderman's wife
that nearly wrecked his theatrical career. He collapsed on stage on 25 March 1833
while playing Iago to his son Charles's Othello with the words 'I am dying — speak
to them for me' and did in fact die two months later. Charles Kean, though
conspicuously lacking his father's histrionic ability, is notable for the series of
Shakespearean productions he staged at the Princess Theatre in the mid-nineteenth century. In these, lavishness of spectacle was combined with a passion for
archaeological accuracy of a kind which Shakespeare's own theatre had never
dreamed of. Thus, for a production of *The Winter's Tale*, a Fellow of the Royal
Geographical Society was consulted as to the flora and fauna of Bithynia, the
nearest available equivalent to the play's Bohemia, which obviously could not be
the real Bohemia, for that had no sea coast. This passion for an imagined
historical-topographical exactitude was one aspect of the realism which was gradually beginning to intrude into nineteenth-century drama along with melodramatic incident and spectacular presentation. Among other things it helped to
make the later part of the century one of the great periods of theatrical decor. On
the other hand, the growth of bardolatry inspired attempts to write high tragedy in
the Shakespearean manner which were generally lamentable.

Realism was certainly the keynote of the acting and production style of William
Charles Macready, 'the eminent tragedian' whose early career overlaps with that
of Kean but who outlasted him on the stage by nearly twenty years. Macready was
manager of both Covent Garden (1837 to 1839) and Drury Lane (1841 to 1843)
and the journals which he kept throughout his long theatrical career (from 1816 to
1851) together with the comments of contemporary critics like Leigh Hunt and
George Henry Lewes give an unparalleled insight both into the man himself and
to the state of the theatre in the mid-nineteenth century. The Victorian ideals of
domesticity, restraint, familial authority and social respectability are expressed
equally in Macready's personal life (despite his long stage career, he disliked the
theatrical profession and retired from it with relief), the sort of roles which
contemporary dramatists such as Sheridan Knowles and Talfourd provided for
him (mainly dominant father figures) and in the style of acting he brought to them.
This makes Macready sound formidably dull as an actor but contemporary

evidence overwhelmingly suggests otherwise. He attempted to blend Kean's passion and Kemble's dignity with a more familiar style of speech and gesture and scored some of his greatest triumphs in once lauded plays by Bulwer Lytton, Knowles and others. Like Kemble he attempted to realize a total conception of a role or a play and his many Shakespearean productions were marked by relative fidelity to the text and meticulous attention to detail. Dickens greatly admired his production of *Lear* where, after an exile of a hundred and fifty years (during which Nahum Tate's version of the play with a happy ending ruled the stage) the Fool was restored, even though he was played by a girl. As a manager Macready did a great deal to improve the standard of rehearsal and professional discipline and to enhance the image of the theatre in the eyes of the middle class. In 1842 he banned prostitutes from Drury Lane and thereby eliminated the well established practice of soliciting in the public rooms of the theatre. The same desire to make the theatre a respectable institution marked the eighteen years' tenure of Samuel Phelps at Sadler's Wells. Under Phelps's management, this theatre, which had been notorious for audience behaviour quite as sensational as the melodrama it specialized in, became the home of some of the finest Shakespearean productions of the period. It drew its audience from the working class as well as from the lower middle class and, if we are to believe the theatre critic Henry Morley, it was not only a thoroughly domesticated audience but one interested and literate enough to check the actors' words against their open Shakespearean texts.

The growing division between the 'respectable' theatre with its literate, predominantly middle-class audience, its addiction to Shakespeare, pseudo-Shakespearean and pseudo-classical tragedy and 'well-made' melodrama in the French manner, and the numerous working-class theatres providing what may be loosely called music-hall entertainment (including 'barn-storming' blood-and-thunder fare) was clearly visible by the time Charles Kean took over the management of the Princess's Theatre in 1850. Kean and his company were particular favourites of Queen Victoria, who had a stage specially constructed for their performances at Windsor. The respectability of the theatre in its upper levels was publicly confirmed in 1895 when Henry Irving became the first actor to receive a knighthood, an accolade for which Edward Alleyn, a great actor from the very first period of the English public theatre had striven without success.

Melodrama, Realism and High Comedy: From Robertson to Wilde

The combined attractions of melodrama and middle-class domesticity can be seen in different proportions in the work of two popular dramatists of the middle and late nineteenth century, Dion Boucicault and T.W. Robertson. Boucicault, who must have been one of the most prolific dramatists of all time (some 150 plays are credited to him) scored his first success with a contemporary comedy of manners, *London Assurance* in 1841, but soon turned to the more profitable and apparently inexhaustible vein of melodrama. *The Corsican Brothers* (1852), adapted from the elder Dumas and *The Colleen Bawn* (1859) later revised as *The Lily of Killarney,* an Irish melodrama, were two of his numerous successes. A natural gift for speakable stage dialogue (standard equipment in Irish dramatists from Farquhar to Beckett) together with a frank and delighted exploitation of all the resources of melodramatic intrigue make the best of Boucicault's plays stirring stuff on stage. Equally popular and almost equally prolific was Tom Taylor whose *The Ticket-of Leave Man* (1863), adapted from a French play, is lifted slightly above the general run of melodrama by an honest and workmanlike portrayal of criminals and their pursuers, including Hawkshaw the sleuth. Taylor's most memorable connection with the theatre lies in the fact that it was at a performance of his play *Our American Cousin* that Abraham Lincoln was assassinated.

T.W. Robertson, whose dramatic career was at its height in the late 1870s, made his contribution to nineteenth-century theatre with a series of successful contemporary social dramas of which *Society* (1865) and *Caste* (1867) are the best known. The abstract, monosyllabic titles of Robertson's later plays indicate his concern, however superficial, with a theme and not only with the mechanics of plot. In *Caste* especially Robertson makes some effort to explore social antagonisms but the surface realism of his settings and stage movement is undermined by stock characterization and stagey plotting. Nevertheless Robertson's example was influential both in 'domesticating' the drama and turning its attention to social actualities and was an inspiration for later dramatists like A.W. Pinero, Henry Arthur Jones, Bernard Shaw and even Oscar Wilde. In Pinero's *Trelawny of The 'Wells'* (1899) there is a vivid and affectionate picture of the theatrical situation in Robertson's time, with Robertson himself portrayed as Tom Wrench. Pinero's own small but distinctive achievement in the theatre is twofold. On the one hand there are the splendid farces such as *The Magistrate* (1885) and *Dandy Dick* (1887) which bear comparison with the masterpieces of Georges Feydeau, but with a closer relation between character and action than the French farceur, with his frantically speeded up acrobatic action, has time or inclination for. On the other we have Pinero's dramatic ventures into the realm of social problems in the wake of the controversy over Ibsen's plays which had just reached the London theatre. The first of Pinero's plays in this manner was *The Profligate* (1884), a story of seduction and suicide (though the first production substituted marital reconciliation for suicide) impossible to take seriously today. Even Pinero's best known 'serious' play *The Second Mrs Tanqueray* (1893) evades the issues it raises, sending its heroine, Paula Tanqueray 'the woman with a past' to a suicide that resettles the shibboleths of conventional morality so conscientiously ruffled in the earlier acts. Moral scruples may be satisfied but dramatic integrity of character is flagrantly betrayed. Only in *His House in Order* (1905), the story of a neglected wife who refuses the opportunity to take a justified revenge, does Pinero probe a real contemporary situation — that of the married woman in a male-dominated society — with sympathy and without the benefit of pious moralizing. It is not surprising that Shaw attacked Pinero for merely playing with serious issues instead of tackling them on their own terms.

The same pretensions towards serious engagement with social and moral issues with an even greater gap between aspiration and achievement is shown in the work of Pinero's contemporary, Henry Arthur Jones, whose successful melodrama *The Silver King* (1882) was extolled as 'literature' by Matthew Arnold. Jones wrote a number of plays on various aspects of religion in daily life including the inevitable five-act verse tragedy (as did Arnold himself) but in none of them did he overcome his tendency to sacrifice theme to melodramatic effect, and his most lasting achievement is in comedies of amours such as *The Liars* (1897), although his best known play, *Mrs Dane's Defence* (1900), contains a third-act trial scene which is both serious and dramatically powerful.

Oscar Wilde's four comedies all appeared within a period of four years in the last decade of the nineteenth century, though Wilde had earlier flirted with Napoleonic, Renaissance and Biblical themes in 'serious' plays. *Lady Windermere's Fan* (1892), *A Woman of No Importance* (1893) and *An Ideal Husband* (1895) were all popular in their day and are still regularly and successfully performed. In these plays the epigrammatic glitter which is Wilde's *forte* has not yet been shined and sparkled into its final brilliance and coexists uneasily with a plot structure which is the staple of Boucicault-type melodrama and 'well made play' alike. One cannot speak of a creative tension between the two because Wilde is never clear as to how seriously he takes the absurdities of the plot, though Shaw in his praise of Wilde seems to have assumed that the latter employed melodramatic devices in the same self-consciously satirical manner which Shaw himself perfected.

Wilde's gift for brilliant repartee and his delighted amusement at the frivolities of Victorian high life find their perfect form in his supreme comic masterpiece, *The Importance of Being Earnest* (1895). It is perhaps the best known and best loved of all English comedies, with the possible exception of that other great Victorian comic triumph, *Charley's Aunt* (1892). Together with the best of the Savoy operas, it is the outstanding achievement of the late nineteenth-century drama (Shaw excepted) far more impressive in its own terms than any of the period's 'serious' drama. Here at least it is clear that Wilde is playing with the well made play. Instead of attempting to conceal absurdities and coincidences, he revels in them. Improbability is elevated into a fine art with all the dazzling symmetry of a kaleidoscopic pattern. The play is too familiar to need detailed discussion and it may appear that extended analysis is grotesquely inappropriate to its precarious perfection. It is worth insisting however that that perfection is not only a matter of surface brilliance, however dazzling. *The Importance* is, paradoxically, Wilde's most 'serious' play (certainly more so than anything by Pinero or Jones), a comedy in which form and expression are at once triumphantly united and constantly commenting on each other. By deliberately touching on serious matters in a farcical context — equating mislaid babies with mislaid handbags, class distinctions with cucumber sandwiches and so on — Wilde draws attention to the impossibility of adequately treating such issues within such a framework. By so doing he highlights not only the triviality of the well made play but the irresponsibility of an audience who could consider such plays as embodiments of important issues. No doubt this is an unduly heavy-handed way of approaching a comedy where verbal wit is immediate and endlessly delightful, but it was perhaps not entirely playfully that Wilde called his masterpiece 'A Trivial Comedy for Serious People'. Those serious people who laughed at it certainly saw in it only a flatteringly idealized portrait of their own life style, and were delighted rather than dismayed by its elegant ribbing of their mores. Their awareness of the sharp and rigorous line between that and any real threat or transgression, was amply shown by Wilde's trial and imprisonment in the same year that his comedy was produced.

8

The Twentieth Century

Bernard Shaw and the 'drama of thought'

By the end of the nineteenth century the 'legitimate' English theatre had become an essentially middle-class institution, much addicted to melodrama and burlesque but willing to take a 'serious' interest in contemporary issues provided they were presented in a form which ensured that no radical questioning of hallowed assumptions was possible. But these tentative beginnings were to lead in the later years of the century to radical changes in styles of theatre and styles of drama. As far back as 1880, Ibsen had reached the English stage in *Quicksands*, better known under its later title *An Enemy of the People*, while Henry Arthur Jones collaborated in the first English version of *A Doll's House*, staged in 1884 as *Breaking A Butterfly*. In the last decade of the century Shaw noted that

> a modern manager need not produce *The Wild Duck*, but he must be very careful not to produce a play which will seem insipid and old-fashioned to playgoers who have seen *The Wild Duck*, even though they may have hissed it.

In spite of the efforts of Ibsen's English translator, William Archer and others to find the great Norwegian's dramatic preoccupations in Pinero and Jones, the real inheritor of Ibsen's legacy in England was of course Shaw himself, as he rarely tired of pointing out. But, as we shall see, it was a legacy which Shaw transformed to suit his own dramatic needs, creating for the purpose an 'Ibsen' who had little in common with the actual dramatist. Shaw's first play, *Widowers' Houses*, was produced in 1892, although he had begun writing it (after an unsuccessful career as a novelist) in 1885, the year after he joined the Fabian Society. His last, *Why She Would Not* was produced in 1957, seven years after his death. Both because of his chronological span and because of his conscious, indeed self-conscious iconoclasm, Shaw's work makes an appropriate starting point for a discussion of twentieth-century drama.

Shaw came to the theatre via critical journalism, fiction and public speaking, all of which activities he pursued as a means of propagating his views on political and social issues. To put the matter in another way, he was convinced of the importance and urgency of what he had to say and turned to the drama as an appropriate way of saying it, though the public theatre was not yet ready to hear him. While his three-year stint as theatre critic for *The Saturday Review* (1895 to 1898) certainly sharpened his sense of what was lacking in the drama of his day, his own earliest plays were written before he became a theatre critic, though he had earlier been a reviewer of art, music and literature. *Widowers' Houses* was a reworking of

177

William Archer's *Rheingold* while *Mrs Warren's Profession* was developed from *Mrs Daintry's Daughter* by the actress Janet Achurch, who was one of the first to play Ibsen on the English stage. *Widowers' Houses* was produced in 1892 by J.T. Grein, one of the pioneers of a new and less restrictive theatre in England, but *Mrs Warren's Profession* had to wait six years for a private production and was not publicly performed in England till 1925, though it was seen in America in 1905 and in Germany two years later. It inaugurated a series of disputes with the Lord Chamberlain of which Shaw was justifiably proud. Both Grein and William Archer, enthusiastic supporters of Ibsen and Shaw's earlier play, thoroughly disapproved of *Mrs Warren's Profession*. Shaw's attitude to the theatre of his day and its relation to society is expressed with his usual forthrightness in his preface (1902) to the play:'

> I have pointed out again and again that the influence of the theatre in England is growing so great that private conduct, religion, law, science, politics and morals are becoming more and more theatrical, whilst the theatre itself remains impervious to common sense, religion, science, politics, and morals. That is why I fight the theatre, not with pamphlets and sermons and treatises, but with plays; and so effective do I find the dramatic method that I have no doubt I shall at last persuade even London to take its conscience and its brains with it when it goes to the theatre, instead of leaving them at home with its prayer-book as it does at present.

Whether Shaw succeeded in this last aim is debatable. What is undeniable is that both through his plays and his dramatic criticism he helped to transform the English theatre in the first half of the twentieth century. His chosen technique was either to stand the assumptions of Victorian melodrama on their head or to develop its initial situations in a credible and realistic manner. Thus in *Mrs Warren's Profession*, Vivie's discovery of her mother's secret would have been quite acceptable to a nineteenth-century audience if it precipitated a scathing denunciation of the mother by her daughter followed by a suitable expression of repentance and reformation by the 'fallen woman'. What we actually get is a vigorous defence of her trade by Mrs Warren who points out to her daughter, among other things, that the Victorian virtues of thrift and independence are possible, at least so far as women are concerned, only in the line of business she has chosen. Shaw's view that economic need is the only determinant of prostitution is undoubtedly over-simple, and he takes care to underline the conventional morality which Mrs Warren wholeheartedly accepts although she is regretfully compelled to transgress it. 'I stick to that, it's wrong' Mrs Warren tells Vivie, 'But it's so, right or wrong; and a girl must make the best of it.' The prostitutes whom Macready so resolutely banished from the theatre have returned to occupy the centre of the stage. At the end of the play there is a final ironic reworking of the conventional happy ending (or perhaps of the conventional unhappy ending, as in *The Second Mrs Tanqueray*) in which mother and daughter are not reconciled but parted, but where Vivie is truly happy though apprehensive because she has found the freedom to lead her own life. But Shaw never lets his audience forget the economic foundations of that freedom and while the questions he raises here may no longer present themselves in quite the same form in our society, the conflict between will and environment which the play dramatizes is still able to move us because we can respond from contemporary experience to the wit and power with which it is presented.

In much the same way Shaw continues to turn current theatrical and ideological assumptions inside out in his early plays, both those such as *Widowers' Houses* which he classified as 'unpleasant' and such 'pleasant plays' as *Arms and the Man* (1894) and *Caesar and Cleopatra* (1898). *Arms and the Man*, which became the basis for a popular musical comedy *The Chocolate Soldier*, tilts at the twin targets of military glory and romantic love. The realistic attitudes and behaviour of the hotelier-turned-soldier Bluntschli are set against the impossible and unthinking idealism of Sergius and Raina which may be fairly taken as the orthodox Victorian attitude to war and heroism. The conversion of Raina and Sergius through their encounter with Bluntschli's hard-headed practicality constitutes the dramatic reversal of the play. Yet Shaw is not being wantonly paradoxical in his reference to Bluntschli's 'incurably romantic disposition'. Bluntschli's romantic involvement with Raina is the play's constant centre and the mainspring of most of the action. It is because he is sensitive to the horrors of war, in which one's friends can meet terrible deaths that Bluntschli is so concerned to be a good (that is, efficient and surviving,) soldier, and it is because true love matters so much to him that he is so determined not to be fobbed off by its tawdry and treacherous imitation. In reply to Raina's remark 'Do you know you are the first man I ever met who did not take me seriously?' Bluntschli is quite right, as the play demonstrates, to reply 'You mean, don't you, that I am the first man that has ever taken you quite seriously?'

Caesar and Cleopatra plays further variations on current notions of imperial greatness and of the epic passion of Cleopatra derived from, among other things, spectacular theatrical productions. Cleopatra's development is a simplification of Shakespeare's character, taking in the wilful and irresponsible girl at one end of the emotional scale and the practised erotic artiste at the other. She is one of a long line of Shavian female characters who stand out in sharp contrast to the pallidly virtuous or acceptably flawed women of nineteenth-century drama, and who make us understand Robert Louis Stevenson's admiring comment to William Archer about the Shavian female: 'I say, Archer, my God, what women!' In Caesar however, Shaw has created a dramatic character who, with suitable qualifications, can be compared to Shakespeare's Prince Hal. Like Hal, Caesar comes to a clear-eyed recognition of the necessary compromises and inevitable ironies involved in political action, and accepts them in a spirit which unites regret and resolution. His subordinates only spell out clumsily what he himself is already aware of. 'I, for one, will take no prisoners' one of them tells him, 'I will kill my enemies in the field; and then you can preach as much clemency as you please; I shall never have to fight them again.' Caesar's early protest against the horror of Pompey's murder widens out to a larger perception which is in the spirit of Shakespeare's Histories, though it is faintly tinged with brooding intimations of the Life Force, the single most powerful deadening influence on later Shavian drama:

To the end of history murder shall breed murder, always in the name of right and honour and peace, until the gods are tired of blood and create a race that can understand.

As *Mrs Warren's Profession* underscored the economic basis of virtue, so *Caesar and Cleopatra* lays bare that of political conquest:

Pothinus: Is it possible that Caesar, the conqueror of the world, has time to occupy himself with such a trifle as our taxes?

Casear: My friend, taxes are the chief business of a conqueror of the world.

In both cases the point is made over-simply, but in the dramatic situation and the social context of imperial flag-waving, relevantly and forcefully. Shaw was one of the first to realize that an attack on outmoded theatrical conventions was inevitably an attack on the society which accepted them, for theatrical conventions — whether of the glory of war and empire building or the social damnation of the 'fallen' woman — exist only because they mirror, if sometimes distortedly, the mores of society. From the beginning Shaw had declared himself in favour of a drama of ideas, remoulding Ibsen into a social reformer in the process and declaring that it was the only way forward in the theatre. 'The drama of pure feeling is no longer in the hands of the playwright' he asserted in the preface to *Mrs Warren's Profession*, 'it has been conquered by the musician. . .and there is, flatly, no future now for any drama except the drama of thought.' This is one of many comments by Shaw which has led those who have not seen his plays on stage to believe that they are full of talk and lacking in emotional power. That they are full of talk is true, but at its best the talk is brilliantly dramatic; that they lack emotional power is simply false, at least where the better plays are concerned. It is certainly the case that in the linked sequence of five plays collectively entitled *Back to Methuselah* (1921) which Shaw, almost in a minority of one, considered his masterpiece, the doctrinaire has taken over almost completely from the dramatist. But it is important to point out that the sequence is tedious not because it contains ideas but because the ideas themselves are simple-minded and their expression uncharacteristically lacking in force and wit. The progression from Eve's revulsion against and eventual reluctant acceptance of the necessity of copulation to the vision of a future where the body has completely disappeared leaving only pure thought has little philosophical interest and less dramatic urgency. It conveys nothing so much as a fastidious distaste for the necessary messiness of life which is the raison d'etre of the theatre as well as its medium. It reminds us of the Shaw who entered deliberately on a long and sexless married life and more pointedly of D.H. Lawrence's remark about Shaw's 'ideal or social or political entities, fleshless, bloodless and cold'. Lawrence's well known dictum about never trusting the artist, always the tale is also eminently applicable to Shaw, for his own comments on his plays in his lengthy Prefaces and elsewhere have frequently given a misleading account of their nature and impact. Shaw's extra-dramatic pronouncements are often fascinating in their own right, yet it is when his plays are most like his Prefaces, as in *Back to Methuselah*, that the plays are most tedious. The reason is not very far to seek. It consists in the very nature of the drama, which lives by effective conflict, whether of ideas, character, situation or a combination of these, and which inevitably generates passion, including the passion for truth. (The idea that thought exists in some passionless and antiseptic vacuum is as untrue in drama as it is in life.) When Shaw is too concerned to argue out a single pre-existing case and neglects to allow dramatic breathing space to 'the possible other case', his plays fail to come alive. When he does conceive his ideas in a truly dramatic (that is, dialectical) way, the ideas enliven the drama instead of suffocating it. This is true of most of the plays he wrote at the peak of his dramatic career, from the 1890s to the period of the first World War. This is the period which includes nearly twenty plays, among them *Candida* (1897), *Major Barbara* (1905), and *Pygmalion* (1913, revised for the screen in 1941). In none of these is an idea unfairly protected against critical attack or irony nor an important character regarded merely as oracular mouthpiece or expendable Aunty Sally.

Two of the most interesting plays of this period are *Man and Superman* (1905) and *Heartbreak House* (1915). Even in the Preface to *Man and Superman* there is an ironic note which qualifies the usual optimistic Shavian larkiness: 'Progress can do nothing but make the most of us all as we are, and that most would clearly not be enough even if those who are already raised out of the lowest abysses would allow the others a chance'. But the play itself belies the more sombre implications of the remark. Where *Back to Methuselah* pursues the notion of Creative Evolution with a one-eyed relentlessness that never commands our sympathy and eventually exhausts our interest, *Man and Superman* deploys the same ideas with infinitely greater wit and a self-irony totally absent form the later play. Shaw sees the female as the natural pursuer, biologically destined for the role by the Life Force for its own dark and mighty purposes, though social convention has obscured this fact. The tension between the apparent and the actual role of the woman generates a good deal of the comedy, whereas in a play like Strindberg's *The Father* the same perception is the source of a bitter exultation. In the Preface Shaw directs us to the neat moral conclusion we are to draw from the play, namely that the marriage of John Tanner and Ann Whitfield which forms the conventional romantic action of the play is in fact an instance of the Life Force fulfilling its higher ends. But the play follows no such simple and single track. John Tanner, middle-class Marxist and exponent of Shavian philosophy, is by no means as resolutely radical as he appears in the Preface, either in his own person or in his dream-incarnation as Don Juan which is an integral part of the comedy though it is often performed separately. The comic irony of the Shavian radical who is at heart a thoroughly respectably bourgeois, reduplicated when Tanner makes just this accusation against Roebuck Ramsden, is further complicated by the meshing-in of the female pursuer theme with that of the non-libertine Don Juan attempting to flee the pleasures of hell. Tanner's talk of the ruthlessness of women is no more convincing than Benedick's in *Much Ado About Nothing*. Ann Whitfield too is fortunately a more lightheartedly conceived character than the ruthless Venus-pursuing-Adonis which the Preface leads us to expect. Shaw's apparent anti-feminism conceals a profound and thoroughly conventional admiration for women. The ideas in *Man and Superman* are subjected to a gay irony of structure and expression and thereby acquire a sharper comic edge. They become an element, but not a separable one, in a lively series of verbal encounters between the wittiest romantic pair to appear on the stage since the 'gay couples' of *The Importance of Being Earnest*.

In *Heartbreak House* Shaw was deliberately attempting a dramatic exercise in what he took to be the Chekhovian style. He called it 'A fantasia in the Russian manner on English themes'. He began the play in 1913 when England was on the brink of war and finished it three years later when British military fortunes were at a very low ebb. It is not surprising therefore that the 'English themes' of the sub-title include a premonition of disaster to come and that the play ends with the bombs falling all around though there is no specific reference to war. *Heartbreak House* is much less a comedy than any of Chekhov's plays and the prevailing mood can perhaps best be described as one of prophetic resignation. Its structure is loosely allegorical with *Heartbreak House* standing for an England where the cultured upper class appears to have betrayed its social responsibility by its self-regarding devotion to aesthetic ideals. Like Tolstoy, Shaw has a profound aesthetic passion which he feels impelled to suppress or at least to chastise. This is one of the sources of dramatic tension, the other being the scepticism engendered by the war atmosphere regarding Shavian ideas of social reform and universal welfare. The loose rambling form of the play, so different from the compact structure of the Ibsenite drama is as much a sign of Shaw's scepticism as the brooding exchanges between the characters. Shaw himself said that *Heartbreak House* 'began with an atmosphere and does not contain a word that was foreseen before it was written'. No one character demands our especial attention or sympathy; though the focus sharpens on Captain Shotover as the play proceeds, Shaw, like Chekhov, is interested in a group and its interactions rather than in a single personality. The quickfire tempo of Shavian comedy is here replaced by a more leisurely pace. Even the strange drumming noise in the air is a reminiscence of the twang of the broken string in *The Cherry Orchard*. The symbolism of the house built like a ship (of state) is perhaps somewhat intrusive but it is not very much insisted on, certainly not as much as that of Ibsen's *The Master Builder*. Shaw explores the weakness in a whole series of Shavian assumptions through the progressive disillusionment of Ellie Dunn, culminating in her realization that Captain Shotover, that most Shavian of characters, derives his philosophy from a bottle. The doom from the skies which Ellie girds herself to face and which finally arrives, faintly recalls a similar strain of apocalyptic feeling in D.H. Lawrence's *Women in Love* written at about the same time. But apocalypse when it comes is not quite total. Though the capitalists Boss Mangan and Billy Dunn are destroyed and the rectory turned into rubble, the denizens of Heartbreak House still remain. It is as if Shaw could not finally abandon his optimism even in the midst of débacle and although there appear to be no grounds for it in the play's own terms Ellie at least is left at the end confidently awaiting the second coming of the bombers.

The best of Shaw's plays are thus far more than mere didactic tracts and Shaw himself was well aware of the distinction between drama and doctrine when he wrote:

To this day, your great dramatic poet is never a socialist, nor an individualist, nor a positivist, nor a materialist, nor any other sort of 'ist', though he comprehends all the 'isms', and is generally quoted and claimed by all the sections as an adherent. Social questions are too sectional, too topical, too temporal to move a man to the mighty effort which is needed to produce great poetry.

'Great peotry' Shaw neither attempted nor achieved. In deliberately devoting himself to a drama of 'social questions' he knew exactly what he was doing and accepted the risk of rapid obsolescence. But, perhaps in spite of his best efforts, he was, during his most creative period a dramatist first and a propagandist a long way afterwards; more of his plays seem likely to survive in the foreseeable future than of any other twentieth-century dramatist, not only on the stage but as reading texts for which he so meticulously prepared them.

The Irish Theatre: Yeats, Synge and O'Casey

Though Shaw announced his crusade against the late nineteenth-century theatre as one based on a return to realism, many of his best plays are realistic only in a very special sense. *Caesar and Cleopatra* and *Pygmalion* are hardly transcriptions of everyday life, any more than the farcical goings on of *You Never Can Tell* or the high comedy of a political extravaganza like *The Apple Cart*. Shaw was a dramatic realist in the wider sense of pushing the theatre of his day towards a closer concern with some of the real issues of the time, but his techniques included not only selective realism but farce, melodrama (*The Devil's Disciple*) and even burlesque verse drama, as in *The Admirable Bashville*. Shaw's dissatisfaction with the tedious surface realism of the 'well made play' and its pretensions to tell the truth about life was expressed in different ways by many others, though with incomparably greater creative power on the Continent than in England. English drama of the early twentieth century has little to offer when set beside the work of such European dramatists as Jarry, Chekhov, Strindberg and Pirandello. There are several reasons for this, the main and obvious one being that England is a country and Europe a continent.

Where drama in English is concerned, the most interesting developments occur not in London but in Ireland and in Manchester. One of the key figures in the growth of theatre in both places was the redoubtable Annie Horniman who devoted her wealth and energy to the establishment of a theatre where important and interesting new plays could be given a chance. As far back as 1894 she had been instrumental in the staging of Shaw's *Arms and the Man* and Yeats's *Land of Heart's Desire*. From 1908 to 1917 she maintained the Gaiety Theatre at Manchester and was directly responsible for the growth of the so-called 'Manchester School' of playwrights, at least two of whose plays, Harold Brighouse's *Hobson's Choice* and Stanley Houghton's *Hindle Wakes* are still performed regularly. At about the same time D.H. Laurence was writing the best early twentieth century provincial drama, though his plays had to wait for half a century to receive public performance. More importantly, the Manchester experiment led to the growth of the repertory movement which is, or was until very lately, so characteristic a feature of English theatrical life. Miss Horniman also promoted the growth of the theatre in Ireland, for in 1904 she helped the Irish

National Theatre Society to acquire the Abbey Theatre which became a focus for the new drama. The Society had begun life in 1899 as the Irish Literary Theatre (the qualifying epithet is significant), founded by W.B. Yeats, Lady Gregory and Edward Martyn, all playwrights dedicated to a poetic drama deriving from Celtic lore and legend, though Martyn's work had a greater strain of realism. Yeats's early plays like *Land of Heart's Desire* (1894) and *The Countess Cathleen* (1899) were consciously poetical exercises in the dream-laden manner of his early poems but, like his poetry, his drama moves forward to a concern with public issues in *The Hour Glass* (1903, revised 1912) and *The King's Threshold* (1903, revised 1913). Yeats wrote plays throughout his career, but came increasingly to realize that his own dramatic objectives did not coincide with those of the Irish national theatre. He became more and more interested in an elitist drama, based on ideas about the Japanese Noh theatre and directed towards an audience of the chosen few and away from the interests of an audience for whom nationalism in the narrowest sense was an urgent and primary concern. Nevertheless a play like *Purgatory*, produced at the Abbey in 1938 a few months before Yeats's death, with its haunting evocation of the Oedipus myth and its mixture of stylized representation and a stark directness of poetic utterance is more truly indicative of the possibilities of poetic drama than the flashier contemporary successes in the 'poetic' mode on the London stage, which included both Barrie's infantile fantasies and the sonorous vacuity of Stephen Phillips's *Paolo and Francesca* (1902).

Apart from Yeats the Irish theatre produced two other dramatists of importance, J.M. Synge and Sean O'Casey. Synge wrote five plays, all of them based on Irish peasant life and using a language which was a heightening of the rich idiomatic speech of the peasantry he knew at first hand. It is a speech and a way of life which served Synge equally well in the poignant tragedy of *Riders to the Sea* (1904) and the full-blooded comedy of his best known play, *The Playboy of the Western World* (1907). Though Synge wrote in prose his plays deserve consideration as poetic drama in the best sense as much as Yeats's because the prose he used is alive with resonances far beyond everyday speech and because Synge's almost surrealist imagination achieves a triumphant blending of soaring fantasy and the day-to-day transactions of peasant life. His pursuit of a reality deeper than that of the surface is evident in his insistence that the highly 'theatrical' plot of *The Playboy* is 'in its essence. . .probable given the psychic state of the locality'.

The third important Irish dramatist, Sean O'Casey, stands in a problematic relation to the Irish dramatic movement and to the Abbey Theatre in particular. Four of his plays were rejected by the Abbey and O'Casey was forty-three years old when *Shadow of a Gunman* was produced there in 1923. Like Synge's *Playboy* O'Casey's play deals with a central character whose assumed role — that of a gunman, taken on by the aspiring poet hero to impress a girl — catches up with reality when the girl suffers a real death, propelling the comic world into tragedy. In this and the two plays which followed it, *Juno and the Paycock* (1924) and *The Plough and the Stars* (1926 — probably his best play) O'Casey transformed the speech of the Irish urban poor as Synge had earlier transformed peasant speech. O'Casey's dramatic vision, with its perception of the contrast between aspiration and actuality as alternately comic and tragic, is at its keenest in *The Plough and the*

Stars, a play about slum dwellers during the Easter Rising in Dublin in 1916. The ironic juxtaposition of the directed energy of the political activists and the aimless and opportunistic hedonism of the bulk of the characters was unflattering to the Irish audience and the play caused a riot in the theatre when it was put on in Dublin in 1926 (as had happened earlier when Synge's *Playboy* was staged). But *The Plough and the Stars* is not merely a plea for purposive political action and a character like the boastful Rabelaisian Fluther Good is far more than merely a butt for comic satire. In these early plays O'Casey's sense of the complexities of living and the richness of individual character prevents him from descending into propaganda. His next play, *The Silver Tassie* (1928) was also rejected by Yeats when submittd to the Abbey, presumably because it marked a partial departure from the realistic style of the three earlier successes. This seems an odd decision when one takes Yeats's own bent as a dramatist into account. The framework of this play is as realistic as those of the others, dealing with a local football hero who comes home from the war a paralysed invalid and sees his girl friend become engaged to the man who saved his life and won a medal. In the second act however O'Casey experiments with the expressionist techniques which European dramatists like Georg Kaiser and Ernst Toller had already developed in Europe following the lead of the later plays of Strindberg. In reaction against Naturalism which assigned to the dramatist only the role of observer and recorder, Expressionism stressed his capacity to reinterpret and transform outer 'reality' in terms of his inner vision. It transferred interest away from the psychology of character to theme and setting, both character and milieu being symbolically conceived. In *The Silver Tassie* the second act is taken up by an expressionistic and passionately hostile rendering of war. The setting is a ruined monastery at the battle front dominated by a broken crucifix and a stained-glass figure of the Virgin with a howitzer between the two and barbed wire in the background. The characters have become representative types — First Soldier, Second Soldier and so on — and the dialogue largely stylized into a kind of incantatory choral chant interspersed with ballads. Although in reading the elaborate stage directions may seem intrusively symbolic and the bare repeated phrases monotonous, the scene is powerful and moving on the stage.

The rejection of *The Silver Tassie* led to O'Casey's withdrawal from the Irish theatre, certainly to the detriment of the latter, probably of both. For several years afterwards O'Casey would not permit his plays to be performed in Ireland. He moved further and further away from realism in his later plays, though he had never been a Naturalist in the sense that, say, Zola was. Fantasy is always a strong element in O'Casey's dramatic imagination, though in some of the later plays it comes dangerously close to banal whimsy. His most completely expressionist play is *Within the Gates* (1934) which leaves Dublin for London's Hyde Park and features characters labelled The Bishop, The Dreamer, and the Young Woman. Its four scenes are divided between Morning, Noon, Evening and Night and also correspond to the four seasons. More successful is *Red Roses for Me* (1943), one of several plays explicitly concerned with communism, with the strike of the Irish transport workers in 1913 as its background. The hero Ayamonn Breydon's unfolding vision of the transformed city in the Expressionistic third act develops very naturally out of the heightened naturalism with which O'Casey depicts the

Dublin slum milieu and is taken up in another mode in the dance between Finnoola and Ayamonn which follows. The language is never far away from Irish 'blarney' but exploits its extravagance without succumbing to its sentimentality:

Ayamonn: There's th' great dome o' th' Four Courts lookin' like a golden rose in a great bronze bowl! An' the river flowin' below it, a purple flood, marbled with ripples o' scarlet; watch th' seagulls glidin' over it — like restless white pearls astir on a royal breast. Our city's in th' grip o' God!

1st Man: [emotionally] Oh, hell, it's grand!

Among O'Casey's plays not directly concerned with political themes, one of the most enjoyable is the high-spirited fantasy *Cock-a-Doodle-Dandy* (1949), the author's own favourite, which dramatizes the antagonism between a puritanical priest and the Cock, typifying zest for life and vigorous sexuality. In a dramatic career of nearly forty years O'Casey wrote some twenty-five plays, the last of them three years before his death in 1964. In 1937 he wrote that 'The beauty, fire and poetry of drama have perished in the storm of fake realism'. O'Casey succeeded better than any English dramatist of the time in blending genuine realism, the inner truth about people's lives and relationships, with 'the beauty, fire and poetry of drama.'

Poetic drama in modern times

The phrase 'poetic drama', like 'comedy thriller' is apt to chill the blood; it has a daunting air of preciosity about it. The fact that verse was the staple of drama in the great age of English dramatic literature has had a rather disastrous effect on successive generations of dramatists who have written their way into oblivion shrouded in the turgidities of pseudo-Shakespearean blank verse. As far back as the Romantic poets and beyond, the ghost of a revived poetic language has haunted the drama and its manifestations have not generally been happy. In the nineteenth-century verse plays such as Sheridan Knowles's *Virginius* (1820) and even Tennyson's *Becket* (1893) clearly owe their success on stage more to the talents of Macready and Irving who played the respective title roles than to their authors. The attempted resuscitation of poetic drama in the twentieth century has been in general equally unrewarding. Some plays, like Thomas Hardy's *The Dynasts* (1903-8), were never intended for the stage, though it is probable that by the time this book appears Hardy's comic drama will have received its first professional performance. But a good many dramatists wrote for the theatre and some even had a measure of commercial success. At the beginning of the century Stephen Phillips was hailed as the bright white hope of English poetry and drama. In an age whose conception of poetic language was wistfully archaic and insulated from any contaminating concern with the ordinary business of living, it was possible to regard as great poetic tragedy Phillips's *Paolo and Francesca* (1902), a veritable echo-chamber of great tragedies with a penchant for immediate stage effect which sometimes recalls Fletcher. The empty decorative lyricism of James Elroy Flecker's *Hassan* (given a splendiferous production in 1923, eight years after the author's death) and the technically accomplished but equally empty historical dramas of Lawrence Binyon have more, but only very little more life than Phillips's dramatic efforts. The best of a not very distinguished group of poetic dramatists in England before the first world war is Gordon Bottomley whose play *King Lear's Wife* (1915) has real psychological depth and dramatic power. Bottomley might have developed into a major verse dramatist if his isolated way of life and the influence on him of writers like Rossetti had not led him to neglect contemporary life in favour of increasingly esoteric theatrical experiments in the Yeatsian manner.

Poetic drama continued to engage the energies of would-be dramatists after the first World War, but it was strictly marginal to the development of commercial theatre in England and did not achieve any popular success till after the second world war, when Christopher Fry's flashy and immensely enjoyable verse plays took the London theatre by storm. Basil Dean's spectacular production of Flecker's *Hassan* in 1923 has already been referred to. Ten years later the Group Theatre was formed to put on new plays whose technique or material made them unlikely to be accepted by West End commercial managements. Most of the Group's plays were produced by Rupert Doone who was responsible for putting on at the Westminster Theatre the political verse plays of Auden and Isherwood as well as T.S. Eliot's dramatic fragment *Sweeney Agonistes* (written in 1928, produced in 1935) and Stephen Spender's *Trial of A Judge* (1938). One of the earliest productions was Auden's *The Dance of Death* (1933), a left-wing satire on the decline of capitalist society which was followed by three plays on similar themes written in collaboration with Isherwood, *The Dog Beneath the Skin* (1935), *The Ascent of F6* (1936) and *On The Frontier* (1938). All use expressionist techniques and find their linguistic inspiration in popular forms like ballad, limerick, music-hall song and the jargon of newspaper headlines and advertising slogans, rather than in 'literary' poetry or drama. This gives the writing a raw vitality and humour which is refreshing after the more rarefied attempts at poetic drama, though *The Ascent of F6* has a portentous Freudian symbolism and literary knowingness which are hard to take. All in all these plays lack a sustained theatrical momentum and are better enjoyed in selective reading rather than in performance, which they rarely receive nowadays.

Eliot abandoned *Sweeney Agonistes* and turned to religious drama in the narrower sense for his next plays, a choral pageant called *The Rock* of which only the choruses have been printed, and *Murder in the Cathedral* (1935). In many ways this is Eliot's best play and though originally designed for staging within the precincts of Canterbury cathedral, its power to move audiences has been shown outside its original location. The long sermon by Becket which comes between his temptation and his assassination is unexpectedly dramatic in performance, its carefully cadenced prose as powerful as the poetry of the temptation scenes. The chorus of Canterbury women, expressing the everyday reality of secular life provide an effective and moving counterpoint to the inner world of Becket's anguished meditations. Only the Shavian pastiche of the four Knights' direct addresses to the audience seems out of place in what is perhaps the best poetic drama of the twentieth century, alas.

The success of *Murder in the Cathedral* is a very limited one, being largely dependent on a historical setting and characters in whose mouths poetry does not seem out of place merely because they are removed from us in time. When Eliot tackles the problem of poetic speech in relation to contemporary characters the results are less impressive. *The Family Reunion* (1939) is a bold attempt to solve two dramatic problems together, that of poetic speech and that of giving significance to the trivial structure of conventional drawing-room drama. Eliot's answer to the first is to give his characters two kinds of utterance, a flat stressed verse line only slightly removed from ordinary speech and a somewhat more formal language when the same characters act as a kind of chorus as in Greek tragedy. The result is that he gets the worst of both worlds, for the dramatic integrity of the characters as individuals is undermined without any compensating increase in their stature as choric figures. The attempt to invest the naturalistic dramatic structure with a wider significance through the introduction of the ghostly Eumenides or pursuing Furies is equally unconvincing in performance, as Eliot himself came to realize.

Eliot's first popular success as a dramatist came after the war with *The Cocktail Party* (1949). Here and in his two later plays, *The Confidential Clerk* (1953) and *The Elder Statesman* (1958) he continued his efforts, all too successfully in the last two plays, to conceal the fact that he was writing in verse and that his plays were anything other than naturalistic drama. The fact that *The Cocktail Party* is derived from the *Alcestis* of Euripides and *The Confidential Clerk* from his *Ion* has provided material for critical exegeses galore but amounts to very little in performance, or for that matter in reading. *The Cocktail Party* intermittently conveys a powerful sense of the sterility of the life it depicts and a vaguely but intensely felt vision of a transcendent order underlying ordinary existence. In one way or another all the plays explore aspects of the idea of martyrdom in relation to society first dramatized in *Murder in the Cathedral,* but Eliot's grasp of everyday life seems too remote to make the confrontation dramatically exciting, and his views on a verse drama based on contemporary speech whose rhythmic impact on the audience would be made by stealth, so to speak, are more interesting in theory than in practice. It is difficult to consider Eliot's later plays other than as the marginal productions of a great poet.

While Eliot attempted to conceal both the essentially religious nature of his dramatic preoccupations and his objective of smuggling poetry into drama and taking the audience unawares, several other would-be poetic dramatists essayed explicitly religious drama with no great impact either on readers or audiences. These included Ronald Duncan, Norman Nicholson, Ann Ridler and Charles Williams, whose nativity play *The House by the Stable* (1938) has a vigorous directness which occasionally recalls medieval drama. But verse drama had its first popular success on the stage since Stephen Phillips in the work of Christopher Fry. Fry's first play was produced in 1938 but his enormous popularity did not come till after the war with his second comedy *The Lady's Not for Burning* (1948). Instead of disguising verse as prose as Eliot had done, Fry went to the opposite extreme and flaunted an opulent poetic language that was constantly drawing attention to itself, but which in the tongues of actors who could speak verse (like John Gielgud, who appeared in the original production of *The Lady's Not for*

Burning) was a genuine if evanescent delight. Fry has an undoubted facility for quirky metaphors and a kind of showy lyricism though the dazzling language of his plays rarely has any particular appropriateness to character or situation. But as displays of linguistic fireworks, especially in settings far removed from the drab austerity of post-war England, his plays offered theatregoers a kaleidoscopic world of make-believe, where even burning at the stake and grave robbing are turned into prettiness and favour. *A Phoenix too Frequent* (1946) a lighthearted retelling in one act of a classical tale about how a mourning widow finds solace once more is one of Fry's most enjoyable plays, and an exchange like the following is a fair sample of the sort of witty word play and the elegantly appliquéd lyric touches which are his hallmark:

> *Doto.*   Was he on the ship?
> *Dynamene.*   He was the ship.
> *Doto.*   Oh. That makes it different.
> *Dynamene.*   He was the ship. He had such a deck, Doto,
>   Such a white, scrubbed deck. Such a stern prow,
>   Such a proud stern, so slim from port to starboard.
>   If ever you meet a man with such fine masts
>   Give your life to him, Doto. The figurehead
>   Bore his own features, so serene in the brow
>   And hung with a little seaweed. O Virilius,
>   My husband, you have left a wake in my soul.
>   You cut the glassy water with a diamond keel.
>   I must cry again.

Fry is at his best when he remains within the limits of his genuine talent for cutting verbal figures of eight, though like most writers he has felt the need to go beyond the boundaries of what he knows he can do well. In *A Sleep of Prisoners* (1951) he tries with some success to harness his verbal dexterity to a serious theme without letting one strangle the other, but his later efforts to straitjacket his language into a more sober style, in plays like *Curtmantle* (1961) have not been conspicuously successful. Neither Eliot, Auden nor Fry ushered in the golden age of poetic drama which from time to time seemed imminent in English theatre. Louis Macneice's *The Dark Tower* (1946) and Dylan Thomas's *Under Milk Wood* (1953), both significantly originally written for radio, are among the more durable achievements in a genre which has not engaged the keenest theatrical talents in recent years.

The Theatre Between the Wars

Among the many changes brought about by the first World War was a transformation in the economic organization of the theatre and its capacity to serve as a centre for the sort of serious drama which Shaw envisaged. At the beginning of his career, Shaw's only plays to be staged had been put on in 'private' theatre clubs to avoid entanglement with the censor and the increasing 'bourgeoisification' of the established London theatre. The possibility of a serious drama which could also pay its way still existed, if only precariously, in the years before the first World War. One of its most important expressions was the partnership between Harley Granville Barker and J.E. Vedrenne which between 1904 and 1907 presented at the Court Theatre (later the Royal Court,) several of Shaw's plays, as well as plays by European dramatists including Ibsen, Schnitzler and Hauptmann, and Barker's own plays. Barker was also influenced by another progressive movement in the English theatre. This was directed against the drastic emasculation and truncation of Shakespeare on the contemporary stage, made necessary by the kind of production in which the actor-manager amid settings of great visual splendour was the centre of attention. From 1895 to 1905 William Poel, under the auspices of the Elizabethan Stage Society, mounted a series of productions of Elizabethan plays which attempted to do justice to the text by restoring it to its original theatrical setting. Here is Shaw's comment on Poel's efforts:

> The more I see of these performances by the Elizabethan Stage Society, the more I am convinced that their method of presenting an Elizabethan play is not only the right method for that particular sort of play, but that any play performed on a platform amidst the audience gets closer home to its hearers than when it is presented as a picture framed by a proscenium.

Shaw's well known anti-Shakespeareanism should be seen against these and innumerable similar comments which show greater perception than do most nineteenth-century bardolaters. Granville Barker's outstanding productions of Shakespeare at the Savoy Theatre in the years immediately before the first World War were directly influenced by his experiences with Poel and the famous *Prefaces to Shakespeare* on which his reputation now rests grew out of these productions.

The war years saw an inevitable shrinking of the theatre's range, both physically and imaginatively. There were fewer theatrical performances and many of these were revivals of successful farces and light comedies. New plays when they appeared were little better than anti-German or jingoistic propaganda tracts. The paternalistic actor-manager system of the nineteenth century did not long survive the end of the war, being replaced by a more rigorous commercial system in which increased production costs and the hazards of theatrical investment made profitability the sole objective of West End theatrical managements. The escapist mood of the twenties found theatrical expression in a succession of musical extravaganzas and was treated with a modish and highly profitable cynicism in the satirical plays of Somerset Maugham and more harshly in Noel Coward's *The Vortex* (1924). But the cynical hedonism of the period gave way to a more sombre climate of feeling under the impact of public events such as the General Strike of 1926 and the Wall Street crash three years later. The political plays of Auden and Isherwood, a product of the little-theatre movement, are an expression of the changed outlook, as were such non-theatrical phenomena as the Popular Front and the Left Book Club. Even in the commercial theatre, the success of R.C. Sherriff's realistic study of men at war, *Journey's End* (1928), signalized the change of mood, though the play was rejected by some West End managements and achieved its eventual two-year run there via a Sunday night production by the Stage Society. The only dramatist with any claim to serious attentions who made a substantial impact on the mainstream English theatre was J.B. Priestley, though James Bridie occasionally displays a Shavian comic inventiveness in plays like *The Anatomist* and *Tobias and the Angel* (both 1930). Priestley's achievement as a dramatist seems to have been consistently underrated by critics, possibly because he has been both prolific and commercially successful. His experiments with the possibilities of the realistic play in *Dangerous Corner* (1932) and *Eden End* (1934) seem to me every bit as interesting as T.S. Eliot's and altogether more successful, though Priestley has of course no aspirations towards poetry, concealed or otherwise in these plays. When he gives full rein to his Yorkshire humour and realism in a lighter vein, the result is the splendid farce of *When We Are Married* (1938), while he is equally successful in his experiments with time in the theatre in *Time and the Conways* and *I Have Been Here Before* (both 1937). Priestley may have occasionally overstretched himself as a dramatist, but his best plays are certainly more than just 'good theatre'.

It must be conceded however that in the years before the Second World War the gap between serious drama and the increasingly rigid recipes of the commercial theatre was steadily widening. The era of state-subsidized theatre was yet to come. The growing popularity of the cinema and to a much smaller extent radio took the working-class audience away from the theatre in large numbers, so it is fair to say that by the outbreak of the war the English theatre was thoroughly middle class in terms of its purveyors, products and consumers. The alternative to it was represented by the little-theatre movement centred mainly in and around London and the two ancient university towns, together with the repertory companies in some of the larger towns, notably Liverpool and Birmingham.

The New Wave

The decade after the end of the war saw a London theatre whose brightest light was Christopher Fry. In addition to his own plays, Fry also achieved success with his adaptations of Anouilh and Giraudoux. There was also Terence Rattigan, whose dramatic career had begun in the mid 1930s and who continued to satisfy middle-class taste with well tailored and well mannered farces such as *While the Sun Shines* (first produced during the war in 1943) and to titillate without activating middle-class conscience in *The Winslow Boy* (1946). Peter Ustinov's wayward and apparently permanently precocious talent expressed itself in light, bright exercises in theatrical pastiche, written very much as showcases for his own virtuoso displays, like *The Love of Four Colonels* (1951) and *Romanoff and Juliet* (1956). These, together with such Priestley plays as *An Inspector Calls* (1945) and *The Linden Tree* (1947) were the best the London theatre had to offer until on 8 May, 1956, John Osborne's *Look Back in Anger* opened at the Royal Court Theatre to inaugurate a new period of creative activity in English drama of longer duration than most and one whose force has not even yet been quite spent.

Looking back nearly a quarter of a century later on *Look Back in Anger,* there seems no doubt that its original audiences saw in the play something which the political and social conditions of the time made them peculiarly responsive to but which is only an incidental element in the play itself. When it first appeared it was regarded primarily as a play of political and social rebellion and the journalistic label of the 'angry young man' soon came to be attached not only to the play's hero but to its author as well as to a whole band of other writers who had nothing in common with Osborne except being alive at the same time. Yet the play itself is very definitely centred on marital conflict and reconciliation, with an affair between the husband and the wife's best friend intervening. In form it is highly conventional, as Osborne himself has said, with a firm plot line, realistic settings and strong 'curtain lines'. The conclusion satisfactorily resolves the dramatic situation in psychological terms, when the emotionally crippled husband and the physically and emotionally exhausted wife together retreat into infantile erotic fantasy as a protection against the intolerable realities of adult domesticity.

Look Back in Anger was originally interpreted in social-political terms because an aspect of the central character, Jimmy Porter, answered to a dominant element in the prevailing climate of feeling. 1956 was of course the year of Suez and of Hungary, two political events which left many people in England, especially among the younger generation, embittered and disillusioned about the possibilities of individual political action within existing political institutions. The theatre critic Kenneth Tynan, whose enthusiastic support for the play did much to promote its success estimated, probably correctly, that it would appeal most strongly to those of its audience under the age of thirty. Their frustrated political radicalism, soon to be expressed in socio-political movements such as the Campaign for Nuclear Disarmament, found a theatrical focus in the embittered and explosive eloquence of Jimmy Porter.

The strictly political content of Porter's tirades is submerged in most of the play under a deluge of sub-Strindbergian diatribe against women and their alleged destructive power. Thus Jimmy's famous outburst that 'there are no good brave causes left' begins and ends with a sardonic fantasy of universal female butchery:

> *Jimmy:* Why, why, why, why do we let these women bleed us to death? Have you ever had a letter, and on it is franked 'Please Give Your Blood Generously'? Well, the Postmaster-General does that, on behalf of all the women of the world. I suppose people of our generation aren't able to die for good causes any longer. We had all that done for us, in the thirties and the forties, when we were still kids. (*In his familiar, semi-serious mood.*) There aren't any good, brave causes left. If the big bang does come, and we all get killed off, it won't be in aid of the old-fashioned, grand design. It'll just be for the Brave New-nothing-very-much-thank-you. About as pointless and inglorious as stepping in front of a bus. No, there's nothing left for it, my boy, but to let yourself be butchered by the women.

For the audience for whom the gentilities of established middle-class theatre seemed wholly removed from the world they lived in, it was Jimmy Porter's social origin as well as the uninhibited passion of his utterance as much as, perhaps even more than what he actually says which invited and received sympathetic identification. For Jimmy Porter was the first non-middle-class, provincial, anti-Establishment hero in modern British drama, if we leave out of account of O'Casey's early work. He is far and away the most powerful character in the play, but his power is entirely in the world of words, not in the world about him. Unlike in

Tamburlaine there is a vast gap here between language and the real world; power in one is a compensation for lack of power in the other, not a reflection of it. Tynan was right to speak of Osborne's language as one 'we had despaired of ever hearing again in the theatre'. But in responding to Jimmy Porter's rhetorical fire the original audience did not have the benefit of Osborne's stage direction to the effect that 'to be as vehement as he is is to be almost non-committal', nor of the rest of Osborne's non-committal Shaw-length comment on his hero. They were dazzled by the unimpeded vehemence of his speech and largely overlooked the considerable element of nostalgia for Edwardian certitudes (typified by Alison's father) which fuels his rhetorical fire, together with the unexamined assumption that working-class people are more real than others because they suffer more. Almost overnight Jimmy Porter became a figurehead for political activism (or at any rate political discussion) as well as a figure in a play.

Nostalgia for the Edwardian past informs both the theme and the structure of Osborne's next play, *The Entertainer* (1957), written for Laurence Olivier and representing an extension of range for both actor and playwright. Oliver gave a brilliant performance on stage and on film as Archie Rice, the seedy music-hall entertainer whose situation Osborne seeks to invest with a generalized allegorical significance. The play alternates between realistic scenes of Archie's domestic and marital entanglements and music-hall numbers symbolically suggesting the decline of Britain. The alternation works effectively in the theatre though the film tended to obliterate it, and the allegory is hardly ever heavy handed. Against the squalid, forlorn and yet somehow appealing opportunism of Archie is set the genuine but outdated dignity of his father, Billy Rice, an old trouper from the great days of Edwardian music-hall — 'in my day ladies didn't get out of a cab, they *descended*'. Billy's attempt, urged on by Archie, to a stage a comeback is a real and symbolic disaster, putting an end to Archie's hopes of retrieving his fortunes and pointing to the impossibility of restoring a bygone system of values and society.

As a social critic, Osborne's persistent weakness has been an inability to define and discriminate between his targets, an inability more excusable in Jimmy Porter than in his creator. This is most apparent in *The World of Paul Slickey* (1959), a free-ranging musical satire directed at the decline and fall of practically everybody and everything. As a dramatist Osborne has shown a restless search for a style to suit what he had to say but has not usually quite found it. In *Luther* (1961) he attempted 'epic' theatre in the manner of Brecht's *Galileo,* but without Brecht's urgent sense of historical change, the 'epic' paraphernalia seems a ludicrously inept form in which to convey the drama of one individual's life conceived in essentially psychological terms. But there is enough of Jimmy Porter's rhetorical energy, both in Luther's sermon and Tetzel's marketplace address to make them compelling in the theatre. Osborne has also produced a number of free adaptations of plays by other dramatists, among them Shakespeare, Ibsen and Lope de Vega, the most successful of these being a modern version of *Coriolanus* under the title *A Place Calling Itself Rome* (1973). But his most interesting and original play to date is *Inadmissible Evidence* (1964), a near-monologue in which the private and professional neuroses of a middle-aged lawyer are expressed in a series of eloquent speeches through which he conjures up characters from his life. The ineffectualness of language except as a refuge from the pressure of brute circumstance and the retreat into privacy foreshadowed in *Look Back in Anger* find in this play a brilliantly appropriate form.

The immediate effect of the success of *Look Back in Anger* (due partly to an excerpt being shown at peak viewing time on television) was to channel a significant amount of creative talent into the drama. The theatre seemed to have become once more a potentially exciting field for the young writer, for there was a new kind of audience, young, committed and enthusiastic ready to listen to him. Osborne's own play had been submitted as an entry in a competition to encourage new drama by the New English Stage Society whose headquarters was the Royal Court Theatre. Henceforth the Royal Court, and to a lesser extent Theatre Workshop under Joan Littlewood, provided a platform for a succession of new playwrights, many of whom had more commitment and enthusiasm than talent or stamina. Like Osborne himself many of them were of working-class origin, provincial rather than metropolitan and had not had a university education. They came to the drama not through an acquaintance with dramatic literature but mainly via direct experience of the theatre as actors or because they were touched by the new sense of theatrical excitement. None of this made the dramatists of the late fifties and early sixties into a school in any sense, though a radical political stance was evident in many of the plays. Some of them also showed an impatience with the theatrical realism within which *Look Back in Anger* had been content to work. What they all owed to Osborne was a new outspokenness and a new sense of dramatic possibilities beyond the clean, well-lighted space of West End theatre.

Arnold Wesker, John Arden and Harold Pinter are generally reckoned alongside John Osborne as key figures in the mid-century revival of English drama. They have nothing in common except perhaps that in their very different ways their plays imply a faith in the written word as a prime element in theatre. This is also true of the work of another dramatist, the Irishman Brendan Behan whose reputation rests principally on two plays, *The Quare Fellow* (1954) and *The Hostage* (1958). The former brilliantly conveys the claustrophobic sense of a prison community through its powerful contrast between the objectivity with which the details of hanging are treated and the passionate inwardness of the prisoners' view of life.

Wesker is a more interesting and adventurous playwright then a superficial acquaintance with his best known plays, the 'Wesker' trilogy and *Chips with Everything* would suggest. *Chicken Soup with Barley*, staged first at Coventry, like the other two plays, and then at the Royal Court in 1958, uses a straightforwardly naturalistic style to depict scenes in East End Jewish life from the days of the Fascist marches in pre-war London to the 1950s. Its main theme, that of the growing sense of political disillusionment from one generation to the next, is underpinned by a vaguely apprehended Ibsenite drama of the debility of the father descending to the son. In *Roots* (1959) the milieu shifts from London to the country and the approach is less rigidly naturalistic. The central figure, Beatie Bryant, the girl friend of Ronnie Kahn who appears in the earlier play, virtually acts as a mouthpiece for Ronnie, which is part of the play's point. She spends her time expounding to her apathetic country relations Ronnie's views on art, politics, sex and kindred topics. When Ronnie's expected arrival fails to materialize, Beatie at last finds her own voice, in a speech which on the page reads much like her language throughout the play but which on stage is an intensely moving climactic moment, especially as spoken by Joan Plowright in the original production. The final play in the trilogy, *I'm Talking About Jerusalem* (1960), traces the failure of an experiment in craft socialism of a vaguely William Morris type in a rural setting and moves in time to the defeat of the Labour government in 1956. Like the other two it is full of earnest exhortation, sometimes of a rather naive kind, but the naivete is not always that of the playwright. Wesker portrays the corroding disillusionment which gradually destroys idealism and leads to apathy, but is not unaware of the narrowness of social experience on which that idealism was originally founded. His own personal efforts as Director of Centre 42 from 1961 to 1970 to stimulate active interest in the arts within the trade-union movement were directed towards recapturing a working-class audience for serious drama; the attempt was a failure but it was not therefore demonstrably simple-minded.

While the trilogy is, broadly speaking, conceived in a naturalistic idiom, isolated scenes such as Beatie's dance in *Roots* and the 'creation' mime in *I'm Talking About Jerusalem* indicate Wesker's interest not so much in moving beyond naturalism as in combining it with non-naturalistic theatrical forms. This is shown in the revision of his one-act play *The Kitchen* (1958, revised 1961) which retains the original naturalistic milieu but pushes the action in the direction of allegory. The clearest and most effective expression of Wesker's non-naturalistic impulse occurs in the celebrated scene in *Chips With Everything* (1962) where a raid on an RAF coal store is carried out entirely without words. But eloquent language often tending towards the insistently didactic remains an important element in Wesker's later work, even when it moves well away form naturalistic confines, as in *Their Very Own and Golden City* (1966). *The Friends* (1970) seems to mark the end of the high idealistic aspirations of the sixties, not for Wesker whose themes have always been defeat and disillusionment, but for his characters, a group of people who retreat from the public world to find the genuine but limited solace of personal relationships. Wesker's language is not always equal to the demands he makes of it, but it has at its best a moving and impressive directness.

John Arden may yet prove to be the most important English dramatist of his generation. His best known play, *Sergeant Musgrave's Dance* (1959), lost the Royal Court Theatre, according to the playwright's own estimate, some ten thousand pounds. But though it never achieved commercial success, it is one of the most striking and individual plays of the new wave, utterly different in style and approach to anything that had appeared before in the modern English theatre. It is poetic drama but its poetry is not detachable from the dramatic whole. Though much of it is written in prose, it is a prose which in its context has an immense resonance, serving far more than the usual functions of dramatic prose, exposition, revelation of character and the like. Arden sub-titled *Sergeant Musgrave's Dance* 'an unhistorical parable' and the phrase alerts us to two important aspects of the play. It is set in the late Victorian period, but historical exactitude is deliberately avoided in setting, costume and above all language. The bizarre plot, dealing with a fanatical sergeant's expedition to a snowbound northern mining town on a supposed recruiting campaign which nearly turns out to be its grisly opposite has the stark simplicity of outline of a ballad. Arden does indeed use ballad-like verse to heighten the drama at critical points and the crude but vigorous colour symbolism — (red for blood, for love, for the soldiers' scarlet coats, black for the mines, the parson, the policeman, white for the encircling snow) — enhances the ballad quality. As a parable, the play clearly relates to the British military experience in Cyprus though the parallel is never explicitly enforced and the detached yet passionate dramatization of the hideous paradoxes of war has a far more general significance.

To see the play as a parable also directs our attention to the total pattern of action rather than to individual characters, though these have the substantiality and vividness appropriate to the dramatic world they inhabit and can even be moving, as in Musgrave's prayer at the end of the first act or Annie's angry lament for her dead lover:

Annie   (*in a sudden uprush*). Look, boy, there was a time *I* had a soldier, he made jokes, he sang songs and all — ah, *he* lived yes-sarnt no-sarnt three-bags-full-sergeant, but he called it one damned joke. God damn you, he was killed! Aye, and in your desert Empire — so what did *that* make?

Sparky. I don't know. . .

Annie.   It made a twisted little thing dead that nobody laughed at. A little withered clover — three in one it made. There was me, and there was him: and a baby in the ground. Bad shape. Dead.

She can say nothing more and he comforts her silently a moment.

Sergeant Musgrave's Dance has become a 'modern classic' and its author an 'established writer' (both phrases are ironically used by Arden in his 1977 preface to a volume of his plays). One result has been the relative neglect both in the theatre and by readers of some of his other early plays, two of the most interesting of which are *The Workhouse Donkey* (1963) and *Armstrong's Last Goodnight* (1964). In their very different ways both are theatrical *tours de force*. Arden called *The Workhouse Donkey* 'a vulgar melodrama' using the latter word in its original etymological sense of a play with music. The 'vulgarity' was also intended in its etymological sense, for it was part of a deliberate attempt on the playwright's part to revive what he considered a true theatre of the people, catering for the Dionysiac elements of 'noise, disorder, drunkenness, lasciviousness, nudity, generosity, corruption, fertility and ease'. Ideally, he wrote, he would have liked performances of his entertainment to last for several hours, the audience coming and going as it pleased, with printed synopses to guide them towards scenes of interest. Clearly a play conceived in such terms could not have the unity of a closely organized text, but the variety and verve of Arden's writing makes it fascinating to read. *The Workhouse Donkey* deals with backstairs political intrigue in a Northern town in a manner which can perhaps best be described as serious comic opera. It uses a mixture of ballad style verse and racy Northern colloquialism to celebrate the anarchic energies of comedy rather than to satirize political corruption. Arden's persistent refusal to take sides as well as his use of non-realistic language and techniques in a milieu of small-town politics normally associated with everyday realism makes the play difficult to take for those who expect a play about politics either to contain a definite political message, or to identify its satirical targets precisely, or both. But Charlie Butterthwaite, the central figure of *The Workhouse Donkey* is a political animal only in the sense that Falstaff is — no more, but certainly no less. Defiant to the last, his final speech, uttered just before he is carried out by the police, articulates the passion for survival which animates all comedy in quasi-Biblical language which would not shame his great Shakespearean counterpart:

> *He picks up a ring of flowers that has been garnishing the buffet and puts it on his head....* In my rejection I have spoken to this people. I will rejoice despite them. I will divide Dewsbury and mete out the valley of Bradford; Pudsey is mine, Huddersfield is mine, Rotherham also is the strength of my head, Osset is my lawgiver, Black Barnsley is my washpot, over Wakefield will I cast out my shoe, over Halifax will I triumph. Who will bring me into the strong city, who will lead me into the boundaries of Leeds? Wilt not thou, oh my deceitful people, who hast cast me off? And wilt not thou go forth with Charlie?

In all his experiments with different theatrical forms, Arden has maintained a lively interest in the expressive powers of different kinds of dramatic language. One of his most unusual and yet unexpectedly successful linguistic experiments occurs in *Armstrong's Last Goodnight,* first performed at the Glasgow Citizen's Theatre in 1964 and later by the National Theatre with Albert Finney in the central role. The play is set in early sixteenth-century Scotland and concerns an encounter between the Scottish bandit John Armstrong of Gilnockie and the suave courtier Sir David Lindsay. Once again, though loosely based on history, it is not intended as a faithful record of historical events. To quote Arden's preface: 'This play is founded upon history: but it is not to be read as an accurate chronicle.' And, as in *Sergeant Musgrave's Dance,* the historical situation is seen as having a relevance to a contemporary one, this time the Congo conflict, but a general rather than a specific relevance. To quote the preface again. 'all I have done is to suggest here and there a basic similarity of moral, rather than political, economic or racial problems.'

The theatrical form of *Armstrong's Last Goodnight* makes economical and effective use of one kind of medieval staging, that of 'mansions' or 'houses' situated simultaneously in different parts of the stage and signifying entirely separate locations (place-and-scaffold staging); here there are three, Armstrong's castle, the forest and the court, and the action moves swiftly and intelligibly between them, while reminding us of the ways in which they are connected to one another. But it is the language of the play which is its greatest distinction. Once again Arden uses a few snatches of ballad verse but the staple of the dialogue is a remarkable adaptation of sixteenth-century Scots for which Arden acknowledges as his model Arthur Miller's use of a modified seventeenth-century American English in his play about witchcraft in Massachusetts, *The Crucible.* (Miller's play too was directed at a contemporary situation, the Macarthy witchhunts). To complicate matters further Armstrong, who has a great many lines, is endowed by his creator with a speech impediment. Arden showed his skill in linguistic pastiche once again in his play about Magna Carta *Left-handed Liberty* (1965) but his task was more difficult though his success was equally great in the earlier play. In performance, the dialogue of *Armstrong's Last Goodnight* proved both generally intelligible and intensely exciting, with a well defined contrast between Lindsay and Armstrong between whom the dramatist steadfastly refuses to choose. Even in reading, a few minutes with the glossary thoughtfully provided in the printed text enables the reader to feel the power and poetry of Arden's dramatic language.

Soon after *Armstrong's Last Goodnight* Arden diverted his attention away from the large subsidized London theatrical establishments in which he felt administrative bureaucracy was increasingly coming between the playwright and the actors and between the play and the audience. He began to devote his energies to the possibility of a smaller, more intimate kind of theatre where a more direct relationship would be possible between all those participating in the theatrical event, including especially the audience. For several years he has been living in Ireland and his plays (mostly written in collaboration with his wife Margaretta d'Arcy) have been concerned with Ireland and its relations with England. They have become increasingly committed to political ends, sometimes very specific ones; *The Ballygombeen Bequest* (1972) was intended to arouse interest in a particular case of exploitation through absentee landlordism. Dissatisfaction with the situation within the theatre is inseparable in Arden from dissatisfaction with the society of which that theatre is a part. Both attitudes were exemplified when he and his wife addressed the audience from the stage just before a performance of their play *The Island of the Mighty* and tried to prevent the performance because they believed the production misrepresented the true intent of the play. Arden's progression from detachment to political commitment is very marked, but to put it in these terms is misleading. From the beginning there has always been in his plays a fierce and passionate concern with political and social issues and their relation to a humanly tolerable morality; the detachment consisted not of sitting on the fence but of doing scrupulous justice to all involved. Whatever one may think of the development of Arden's political views, his virtuosity in language and theatrical form continues undiminished, and his critical writings, in prefaces and the essays collected in *To Present the Pretence* contain some of the most intelligent and stimulating comment on the relations between the modern theatre and its public.

Harold Pinter's standing as a dramatist was so high in the late sixties and early seventies that among the innumerable books about him is one devoted specifically to his critical reputation. Yet his first play to be staged in London, *The Birthday Party* (1958), was not a success with either the critics or the public. Only one critic dissented from the general disparagement. 'Mr Pinter, on the evidence of this work' wrote Harold Hobson in the Sunday Times 'possesses the most original, disturbing and arresting talent in theatrical London.'

It was not long before that talent made its enormous impact on the theatre in London and all over the world. Pinter's next play, *The Caretaker* (1960) was both a critical and a commercial success and, together with *The Homecoming* (1965) and the one-act play *The Dumb Waiter* (1960) has become, for better or worse, ' a modern classic'. This predicament has evidently worried Pinter less than it did

Arden for he has gone on to write a very different kind of play for the same public. These later plays, *Landscape* and *Silence* (both 1969), *Old Times* (1971 and *No Man's Land* (1975) show preoccupations with time, memory and self-reflection which are latent in the earlier plays and may have emerged as themes while Pinter was working on a screenplay (never filmed) based on Proust's *A La Récherche du Temps Perdu*. They were as distinctive as the early plays but their very different themes demand and receive a correspondingly different dramatic form.

The Birthday Party may have bewildered its original audience by being associated with the so-called theatre of the Absurd, represented by writers such as Ionesco and Beckett whose plays were being staged in the little theatre of Paris in the early fifties. Today what is immediately evident in the play is its closeness to the ordinary surface of existence. On more than one occasion Pinter has expressed the view that this 'ordinary surface' is itself a quite extraordinary business (though not in these words). Where language is concerned, it is almost surreal in its inconsequentiality. The 'naturalism' of naturalistic dialogue is a highly conventional product, being based on a series of assumptions most of which are inapplicable to life itself. Among these are, for instance: the notion that people usually speak in complete grammatical sentences; that the relation between one sentence and another is logical or immediately evident; that a speaker knows at the beginning of his utterance just how it will end; that participants in a conversation always listen to each other, understand instantly the exact meaning of the speaker (unless a carefully engineered 'misunderstanding' is part of the plot) and reply coherently, relevantly and forcefully. A moment's reflection will show that ordinary conversation is rarely if ever like this. It is in fact much more like what goes on in *The Birthday Party* or *The Caretaker*.

Meg.	He must be still asleep. What time did you go out this morning, Petey?
Petey.	Same time as usual.
Meg.	Was it dark?
Peter.	No, it was light.
Meg. *(beginning to darn)*	But sometimes you go out in the morning and it's dark.
Petey.	That's in the winter.
Meg.	Oh, in winter.
Petey.	Yes, it gets light later in winter.
Meg.	Oh. *Pause.* What are you reading?
Petey.	Someone's just had a baby.
Meg.	Oh, they haven't! Who?
Petey.	Some girl.
Meg.	Who, Petey, who?
Petey.	I don't think you'd know her.
Meg.	What's her name?
Petey.	Lady Mary Splatt.
Meg.	I don't know her.

Petey.	No.
Meg.	What is it?
Petey (studying the paper).	Er — a girl.
Meg.	Not a boy?
Petey.	No.
Meg.	Oh, what a shame. I'd be sorry. I'd much rather have a little boy.
Petey.	A little girl's all right.
Meg.	I'd much rather have a little boy. (*The Birthday Party*)

People ask questions to which the answers are obvious or already known, answer questions with other questions or obliquely, obviously or not at all, and often let a chance word or stress in the conversation alter its entire direction. Chekhov was the first European dramatist to use dialogue that is realistic in this sense and Pinter owes more to him than to any other dramatist.

One element of Pinter's originality in these plays therefore, consisted simply in drawing attention to what no one in the English theatre seems to have noticed before, namely the sheer chaos and incoherence of ordinary speech. But, if this is all there is to them, these plays would be open to the charge of triviality. After all, it could be argued that drama, like all art, should be an interpretation of life, not just a transcription of it. There seems to be no valid reason why we should pay good money to sit in a theatre to listen to what we could hear every day of our lives in café, laundrette or bus stop. Furthermore, a transcription of surface realism in itself would hardly justify Hobson's epithet 'disturbing', or we should be terrified every day of our lives. What is distinctive about Pinter's realism is not so much the accurate reproduction of its surface as the insight into the vague but very real sense of guilt and unease that pervades most people's lives. We all have fears, forebodings, and secrets which we are afraid will be disclosed, and in these plays Pinter finds a superb theatrical equivalent for these. When Goldberg and McCann enter the seaside boarding house where Stanley has been quietly nursing his musical fantasies and subject him to a fusillade of questions before taking him away, we are naturally curious to find what Stanley has been guilty of, or even whether he is guilty at all, and where he is being taken. But the point of *The Birthday Party* is that we are not intended to find out, merely to be teased by the idea that we *might* find out. That is why the solemn efforts to establish symbolic meanings in the torrent of questions (ranging from 'Why did you kill your wife?' to 'Is the number 846 possible or necessary?') are both futile and perverse. If we could establish the precise point and purpose of every question, determine without doubt the nature and extent of Stanley's culpability and discover just where he is being taken, *The Birthday Party* would be a very different play, an exciting spy thriller perhaps (like *The Quiller Memorandum* for which Pinter wrote the screenplay), but not the play Pinter has contrived with such deliberate skill. Pinter refuses to give complete explanations because the sense of mystery gives a greater resonance to the play and because ultimately it is truer not only to the surface but to the unacknowledged depths of living. Indeed, to think of the playwright as knowing 'all' about his characters and their situation and wilfully withholding that knowledge from his audience is quite misleading. As Pinter himself puts it:

> The assumption that to verify what has happened and is happening presents few problems, I take to be inaccurate. A character on the stage who can present no convincing argument or information as to his past experiences, his present behaviour or his aspirations, nor give a comprehensive analysis of his motives, is as legitimate and as worthy of attention as one who, alarmingly, can do all these things. . .

The word 'alarmingly' indicates half-humorously Pinter's awareness of the artificiality of theatrical naturalism. In his first play *The Room* (1957) we feel that the sense of mystery is factitious, imposed on the characters and their milieu rather than arising compellingly out of it. But in *The Birthday Party* and *The Dumb Waiter* there is real mystery instead of contrived mystification and the drama is inconceivable without it. *The Caretaker* has its share of mystery in the uncertainty as to Davies's real name and identity, his background and the 'papers' which he allegedly left at Sidcup and which would explain everything if only they existed and we could take a look at them. But the main emphasis of the play is on the triangular relationship between Davies and the two brothers Mick and Aston and the struggle between them for control of the living space. Aston's apparent strangeness has a straightforward explanation in the fact that he has been in a psychiatric hospital where he has undergone electric shock therapy. Once again the surface haphazardness of the dialogue is not only convincing in itself but points insistently to the deep-seated insecurity which in different ways each of the characters shares. *The Homecoming* is a much more conventionally well made play with a perfectly intelligible plot concerning a married couple, Teddy and Ruth, who return to Teddy's working-class family home in London after many years in America where Teddy is a university teacher. The dramatic interest centres on the relations between the new arrivals and various members of Teddy's family, particularly Lenny and Max, the father. Father and brothers systematically gang up against Teddy and without showing any natural hostility make him feel totally shaken and insecure, unable to find any refuge in his superior education and intellect. But their attempts to browbeat Ruth into similar submission by treating her as a whore fail completely, not because she is outraged but because she acquiesces all too readily in their scheme to live off her immoral earnings, but only on terms which clearly establish her psychological supremacy as well as her economic independence. Teddy's idealized childhood memories of his home are thus rudely shattered and at the end he is left with his own marriage destroyed and himself excluded from the new circle of relationships over which his wife presides. The 'comedy of menace' (to use Irving Wardle's apt phrase for early Pinter) consists here of our sense of aggressive impulses lying just below the surface, and occasionally erupting in spasms of verbal and other violence, and of Pinter's ability, at once comic and disturbing, to suggest powerful undercurrents of sexuality through trivial incidents, such as the exchange between Lenny and Ruth about the glass of water. There is also a story of the past buried underneath the present action, concerning the dead mother being driven about on her business as a whore by her brother-in-law which wells up occasionally, hinting at the theme of domestic history repeating itself in the manner of an Ibsen play. Pinter has a remarkable capacity to forge a powerful and evocative dramatic language out of an impoverished urban working-class idiom which occasionally and unexpectedly breaks out into deliberate pastiche of Colour Supplement verbiage, as in Mick's extravaganza on interior decor to Davies in the second act of *The Caretaker*. Max's reminiscences at the beginning of Act Two of *The Homecoming* offer a more compact example:

> *Max:* Mind you, I was a generous man to her. I never left her short of a few bob. I remember one year I entered into negotiations with a top-class group of butchers with continental connections. I was going into association with them. I remember the night I came home. I kept quiet. First of all I gave Lenny a bath, then Teddy a bath, then Joey a bath. What fun we used to have in the bath, eh boys? Then I came downstairs and I made Jessie put her feet up on a pouffe — what happened to that pouffe, I haven't seen it for years — she put her feet up on the pouffe and I said to her, Jessie, I think our ship is going to come home. I'm going to treat you to a couple of items. I'm going to buy you a dress in pale corded blue silk, heavily encrusted in pearls, and for casual wear, a pair of pantaloons in lilac flowered taffeta. Then I gave her a drop of cherry brandy. I remember the boys came down, in their pyjamas, all their hair shining, their faces pink, it was before they started shaving, and they knelt down at our feet, Jessie's and mine. I tell you, it was like Christmas.

In these plays the characters use language in a variety of ways and with varying degrees of awareness, but the desire to be understood and to understand others is the very least of their motives. There has been much loose and confused comment on Pinter's plays as being concerned with the impossibility of communication. No dramatist who really believed that communication was impossible would write plays for an audience. Nor are Pinter's characters incapable of communicating because they lack the verbal resources to do so, as is the case, for instance, with the people in Edward Bond's *Saved*. As a rule they have, as suggested above, a spare and distinctive vocabulary, but they use it for purposes of their own choosing or those imposed on them by routine or apathy. As Pinter himself once said in an interview with Kenneth Tynan:

> I feel that instead of any inability to communicate, there is a deliberate evasion of communication. Communication itself between people is so frightening that rather than do that, there is a continual cross-talk, a continual talking about other things, rather than what is at the root of their relationship.

From Pinter's standpoint the so-called naturalistic play is unlifelike because people nearly always know and say what they mean and mean what they say.

In his later plays, the unwillingness to communicate leads to a situation where each personality is locked within its own past, a self-contained island with little or no contact with other such islands. There are two figures in *Landscape* (1968), each totally absorbed in solipsistic reminiscence; the constant possibility, never actually achieved, of strands of thought interweaving provides dramatic tension and points to the abiding human need for contact. Moments recalled in soliloquy have a haunting blend of the everyday and the hallucinatory, and are dwelt on with a kind of obsessiveness which suggests that the characters are trying to find 'significance' in them and not succeeding (a similar failure awaits exegetical critics). The sudden disturbance caused by unacknowledged sexual need faintly troubles the surface of recollection without tranquillity. *Silence* (1969) shows a girl and two men reflecting on their relationship, again mainly turned in on themselves. The play has a circular movement, a sense of ending where it is all going to begin again, that recalls Beckett's *Waiting for Godot*. The milieu here is less naturalistic than that of *Landscape* (the scene specifies only 'three areas; a chair in each area') and the bare somnambulistic movement of the figures on stage towards and away from each other powerfully enacts the sense of inevitable frustration. Language is no longer used, as in the earlier plays, to threaten, dominate or even evade, but to find what comfort one can in one's isolation — in Auden's words, 'each in the cell of himself is almost convinced of his freedom'. Only the audience senses the shifting patterns of relationship which arise out of the characters' intense and quietly desperate self-absorption.

Both *Landscape* and *Silence* are short plays. In the two later full-length plays, *Old Times* (1971) and *No Man's Land* (1975) Pinter explores further the relationship between past and present among characters whose physical proximity on the stage and shared experiences only enhance our awareness of the distance between them and of the vastly different versions of their experience which each muses over. While the earlier plays are concerned with space and the struggle for it — each character striving to gain and guard his patch and using language as one of his chief weapons in the battle — the later plays take a bare, neutral space (the stage?) as given and deal with time and the burdens of memory. The similarity to Beckett's later plays is evident in both language and structure and both dramatists have shown a keen interest in Proust, but Pinter has arrived by his own route — and his world has its own bleak but undeniably powerful atmosphere. Outwardly there is little action on the stage but Pinter's language, despite or rather because of its austerity, is immensely evocative on the stage. He is a master of the use of different kinds of silence in the drama. The world he creates is very much his own and instantly recognizable as such. It is well described in a few lines from T.S. Eliot's the *Four Quartets:*

And the conversation rises and slowly fades into silence
And you see behind every face the mental emptiness deepen
Leaving only the growing terror of nothing to think about;

Like Arden but with entirely different effect, Pinter too is a poetic dramatist, and it is fitting that the experience of his later plays should be aptly summed in the words of a great dramatic poet:

Descend lower, descend only
Into the world of perpetual solitude,

World not world, but that which is not world,
Internal darkness, deprivation
And destitution of all property,
Dessication of the world of sense,
Evacuation of the world of fancy,
Inoperancy of the world of spirit; . . .
. . . while the world moves
In appetency, on its metalled ways
Of time past and time future.

Joe Orton died in 1967 at the age of thirty-four in circumstances that might have occurred in one of his own plays. In him, modern English stage comedy lost one of its wildest and most unpredictable talents and one which, on the evidence of his last play, *What the Butler Saw* (1969) was still developing. Orton's first play for the theatre, *Entertaining Mr Sloane* (1964), indicated very clearly the area of comedy he was to make distinctively his own and his equally distinctive approach to it. The play is a kind of grotesque parody of *The Caretaker,* with a brother and sister each vying for the sexual favours of their lodger who, incidentally, has just murdered their father. The situation is resolved with all the tidiness of a typical drawing-room drama when brother and sister arrive at a compromise whereby they alternate as sleeping partners for Mr Sloane. The dramatization of events normally regarded as outrageous or at least disreputable in an idiom of the utmost propriety is Orton's special talent. It pushed him further and further into farce, a development to be regretted only if one (mistakenly) assumes that farce is *inherently* inferior to 'high' comedy. In Orton's case it allowed the contrast between matter and manner to become more uproariously evident. In *Loot* (1965) the corpse of the mother is shunted in and out of its coffin while the son frantically tries to find a hiding place for the proceeds of a bank raid, closely observed by a crooked police inspector. The original idea of the movable corpse may have come from an American satirical comedy of the late forties, Dalton Trumbo's *The Biggest Thief in Town,* but Orton plays a series of brilliant farcical variations on it, while the dialogue goes on its prim and mannered way, sniping at Orton's chosen targets — established authority, especially the Church and the police, intellectual pretension and conformity of every kind. Arden's recipe for Dionysiac theatre comes closest to realization in modern English drama in Orton, and never more so than in *What the Butler Saw.* Even a bare outline of the plot conveys something of the play's flavour. It deals with the complications arising out of a psychiatrist's sexual urges and those of his nymphomaniac wife and involve, among other things, transvestism, the father nearly seducing his daughter while the mother succeeds in doing so, and the son attempting blackmail on the mother with photographs of her sexual encounters. What no summary or even reading can convey is the effect of the contrast between the zany pace of the action and the beautifully contrived dialogue. Orton's comedy is the apotheosis of bad taste, the sick joke transmuted into anarchic farce. It is, however, to use an epithet that Orton himself would have detested, intellectual farce, concerned not merely to amuse but to disturb some cherished assumptions and prejudices by persistently offending against them.

Intellectual farce of a quite different kind is also the stock-in-trade of Tom Stoppard. Stoppard has had the misfortune to be subjected to some fairly heavy-handed criticism in terms of existential philosophy and the like which is in striking contrast to the lightness of touch so evident in his work even when he is most serious. He is, in his best known plays at least, the pasticheur par excellence and at his best is able to create an exhilarating blend of verbal and theatrical parody. Thus in his first stage success, *Rosencrantz and Guildenstern are Dead* (1966, revised 1967), the archetypal bit-part players find themselves occupying the centre of the stage without a play to act in. All they can do is fill out the stage time with a series of increasingly desperate word games and try in vain to cling to the far greater play in which they have their undistinguished but immortal being. The existential and other implications of their predicament are glanced at in the deftest manner. There is a skilfully contrived contrast between the travelling players and their willingness to enact any one of a number of pre-written roles to order, and the two central (?) characters stubbornly asserting, or trying to assert their free will, oblivious of their totally determined and expendable existence. If this makes the play sound like *Waiting for Godot* the resemblance is far more apparent than real. In Stoppard's play the theatrical metaphor sparks off speculations in which the cosmic is firmly subdued by the comic. 'The single assumption that makes our existence viable', the leader of the acting troupe asserts 'is that there is someone watching us.' The effect is very different from that of an almost identical utterance in *Waiting for Godot.*

Stoppard's marvellous feeling for the theatre and its possibilities as material as well as medium is well illustrated in another jeu d'esprit, *The Real Inspector Hound* (1968), where the apparently solid and usually unassailable world of that uniquely British sub-genre, the country-house detective thriller, becomes hopelessly and hilariously infiltrated by the private lives and preoccupations of two theatre critics watching one. *Jumpers* (1973) and *Travesties* (1974) are both more substantial plays, though their substance is that appropriate to comedy, not that of philo-sophical depth or subtlety of political or artistic analysis, which are *apparently* the respective concerns of the two plays. *Jumpers* does have a professional philosopher (confusingly named George Moore) as one of its main characters and the plot concerns itself with the murder of another. But it would be wrong to take Dr Moore's earnest concern with dotting every 'i' and crossing every 't' in his paper on the existence of God as evidence of a similar seriousness in the playwright. Philosophical perplexity is not an independent centre of interest here but the source of perpetual theatrical pleasure. As far as it goes the argument of the paper is respectable if not particularly distinguished or original. Stoppard certainly catches the flavour of much mid-century British political discussion, especially the impression that *Alice in Wonderland* is the only book most British analytic philos-ophers had read. But he savours ideas in much the same way as Christopher Fry savours words, relishing their nutty flavour and the sharp tang of sudden juxta-positions of idea and example or idea and incongruous action:

George: There is reason and there is cause and there is motion, each in infinite regress towards a moment of origin and a point of ultimate reference

— and one day! — as we stare into the fire at the mouth of our cave, suddenly! in an instant of grateful terror, we get it! — the one and only, sufficient unto himself, outside the action, uniquely immobile! — the Necessary Being, the First Cause, the Unmoved Mover!!
(He takes a climactic drink from his tumbler, which however contains only pencils. He puts the tumbler down, leaving a pencil in his mouth.)

The 'seriousness' of Dr Moore's ideas about God is, in relation to the total drama, no greater than that of his wife's obsession with what man's landing on the moon has done to her ideas about it, or of Sir Archibald Jumper's mysteriously close encounters with Mrs Moore behind closed curtains. The verbal liveliness is endless and the contrast between farcical action and high-class intellectual chat is irresistible. But it would be a serious injustice to a brilliant comic talent to think that 'seriousness' in the philosophical sense is what makes him a fine playwright. Similarly, in *Travesties*, Stoppard weaves the figures of Lenin, the Dadaist Tristan Tzara and James Joyce (who were all living in Zurich during the first World War) into a fantastic but true tale about an ill-fated expatriate production of *The Importance of Being Earnest* stage managed by Joyce and starring a minor British consular official as Algy. The device enables Stoppard to exploit to the full his gift for verbal and theatrical parody — Wildean epigram ('Joyce is the sort of name that causes comment round the font'), Joycean pastiche, Dadaist extravagance, music-hall, high comedy, the Theatre of the Absurd and several more. Stoppard assumes an audience familiar with modern movements in art and the terms in which it has been discussed, with Lenin and his general historical significance and with Joyce's achievement as a writer. The comic mileage he gets out of this assortment of topics is dazzling in its speed and copiousness. But Stoppard is not writing a play 'about' Lenin's place in history, or the significance of Dada or Joyce's contribution to modern literature. The true subject of *Travesties* is the perils and possibilities of theatrical form and it is for the wit and vivacity with which he informs his theme that the play should be valued (though it is not without its *longeurs*, especially in some of Lenin's speeches).

Latterly Stoppard has shown his impatience with his apparently effortless success as the intellectual performing flea of modern English drama and attempted to combine his verbal inventiveness and theatrical ingenuity with a manifestly serious concern with contemporary issues. In the television play *Professional Foul* (1976) he uses the actual and metaphorical framework of a football match to present the plight of a dissident in Czechoslovakia and in *Every Good Boy Deserves Favour* (1978), a musical play devised in collaboration with André Previn, explores the ethics and psychology of indoctrination in a Soviet mental hospital in terms of an orchestra and its conductor. *Night and Day* (1978) has for its theme the freedom of the press and the threats to it. All these, especially the first two, show that verbal high spirits, theatrical burlesque and serious and even moving drama are by no means incompatible. But we should beware of endowing the earlier comic inventions with a spurious and wholly unnecessary 'seriousness'.

In Edward Bond we have the outstanding example among established British playwrights of one who has from the beginning been committed to using the theatre as a weapon in the struggle for a better society. What makes him interesting and even important is that his best work is wholly free from the solemn sermonizing and earnest exhortation which such a description might imply. Together with Arden, Bond is the most creative follower of Brecht in the English theatre, though his plays do not need the benefit of Brechtian aesthetics to make their impact (any more than Brecht's do). Bond's plays conform to no tidy pattern except that they are all preoccupied with the issue of violence public and private, and that none of them is an ordinary naturalistic drama, with the doubtful exception of the first two, *The Pope's Wedding* (1962) and *Saved*(1965). The latter is the play which first brought Bond to public attention. It contains the notorious scene in which a baby is smeared with excrement and then deliberately and systematically stoned to death by a gang of youths, for no particular reason, just for the fun of it. There are two usual and opposite reactions to the play and this scene in particular. Either one could say that such scenes are too disgusting and degrading to be put on the stage, or one could argue that contemporary society is violent and brutal and that the artist has a duty to portray it. Bond himself (like Arden a very articulate prefatorial commentator on his own work) is attached to the second line of argument and defends it in the preface to a later play, *Lear* (1971):

I write about violence as naturally as Jane Austen wrote about manners. Violence shapes and obsesses our society, and if we do not stop being violent we have no future. People who do not want writers to write about violence want to stop them writing about us and our time. It would be immoral not to write about violence.

The real issue here is of course what is involved in the phrase 'writing about'. Is it a wholesale transcription intended simply to shock, in which case it should conform to minimal standards of factual truth and preferably be documentary rather than fictional, or does it show insight into the violence it portrays? *Saved*, it seems to me, clearly does. The violence of the stoning scene, though it comes with an effect of nauseating horror, is a natural outcome of the emotionally, mentally and physically degraded life of the characters. It is an act of communal self-expression, the only one available for characters who have never had the slightest incentive in their world to develop any feelings other than a shared listlessness spattered with sad obscenities of word and deed and breaking out in unspeakable savagery. This is made perfectly clear in the preceding scenes and the stoning scene itself is presented in a highly ritualized form (which is one of the factors which makes *Saved* only doubtfully naturalistic) though the brutality is not shirked in the least. I hope the foregoing comments will not be construed as in any way condoning such viciousness in real life, any more than sympathy for Othello in the last scene of Shakespeare's play would amount to an advocacy of strangling one's wife. Bond has not merely transcribed the brutality of the killing, he has orchestrated it so as to compel us to consider its real source. His achievement here is quite considerable, for he has managed to find an idiom which, while staying close to the real-life language of people almost without language, gives expressive force to their desolating way of life. The effect is cumulative and has to do partly with the relations between the respective pace of words and action, so that quotation cannot do it justice. Penelope Gilliatt, reviewing the original production of *Saved* in the *Observer*, aptly described Bond's language:

> ... the truth is that the prose is skilfully stylized. It uses a hard, curt unit of dialogue, a statement of panic masquerading as an attack, hardly ever more than five or six syllables to a line. People don't elaborate; they stab in the dark, the dagger turns into rubber or a wisp of fog, and the bad dream has already left them behind.

Saved is a sober, powerful and humane play about characters who are wild, inarticulate and savage. Its humanity consists of Bond's probing insistence that the roots of savagery lie in the sub-human conditions in which the characters live. He calls *Saved* 'almost irresponsibly optimistic' because at least one character, Len, manages to retain something of his humanity in the teeth of the inhuman pressures to which it has been subjected from birth.

Narrow Road to the Deep North (1968, revised as *The Bundle*, 1978), perhaps Bond's best play and *Lear* (1971) his most ambitious, explore the theme of violence in society while moving away in widely separate directions from the naturalistic framework of the earlier plays. In the former, Bond uses some of the devices of the Noh drama, setting his play in medieval Japan and pointing a contrast between the overt violence of the tyrant Shogo's rule and the hidden exploitative violence of Christian imperialist society, represented by the execution and mutilation of Shogo. The slaughter of the mission-school children by Shogo is presented in a stylized manner and its quiet horror sinks deep into one's mind as one watches it. The poet Basho is shown alternately taking ineffectual action, seeking the help of the English in supplanting Shogo and thereby replacing one kind of violence with another, and withdrawing into equally ineffectual bouts of meditation. Kiro, seeing no hope for a new society, takes the traditional Japanese way out of a worthless life — suicide by disembowelling. But the play's final image is that of the dead Kiro on the ground while beside him is the mysterious stranger who has just escaped from drowning and is ready to begin life anew.

Lear emphasizes the cyclical pattern of *Narrow Road* more strongly, where regime succeeds regime but the pattern of life remains unchanged, aggression, fear, mistrust and pervasive brutality being its hallmarks. Bond's play is dependent on Shakespeare's, but in a wholly creative sense. He makes effective use of our preconception about Shakespeare's Cordelia by making her counterpart a character just as much involved in *realpolitik* as her sisters, here called Bodice and Fontenelle. And he redoubles the horror of the blinding of Gloucester (Warrington) by giving it a touch of clinical expertise which brings to mind the 'scientific' atrocities of the concentration camps and subsequent technological advances in torture. As for Lear's redemption, there is no such thing, at least not in Christian-spiritual terms. As Lear himself says in the third act 'If I saw Christ on his cross I would spit at him'. Lear's regeneration comes when he sees the need not to regain his own power or to replace one authoritarian and oppressive regime by another, but to change the structure of society and so eliminate oppression, here represented by the wall which is the play's dominant visual image. In the end Lear dies vainly trying to break the wall down by himself. As with Brecht, the end of the play hurls the problem straight at the audience instead of neatly resolving it within the plot. Bond has never wavered in his conviction that violence and aggression are not the products of original sin or innate instinct but are solely due to what he sees as the insidious workings of an unjust society. Thus the pervasive violence of his plays is continually aimed at making the audience aware, not of the violence itself, but of ways to end it. And those ways, in his view, have less to do with character than enviroment though in the end he, like the rest of us, is faced with the character who mysteriously ceases to be a product of his environment and begins to transcend it — Len mending the broken chair, Lear scraping the wall down with his bare hands till he is shot dead.

★　★　★

There is no tidy way to end a book which tries to give some account of English drama up to our own time. To discuss all the interesting plays and playwrights of today would take a book at least a long as this one, and a mere list of names would be worse than useless. What can be suggested is that all the playwrights so far discussed have written primarily for the live theatre before television became the largest purveyor of popular drama ever known (more people probably see a single episode of *Coronation Street* than made up the original audiences of *all* the plays done in England from 1576 to 1642). Most of them grew up with radio rather than television, and all of them in their various ways have shown a consistent regard for the *word* in the theatre. The generation of dramatists who came to maturity under the influence of television have increasingly and naturally turned to television as their medium and even when they have written for the stage, they have used techniques adapted from the small screen. Another development has been the growth of fringe theatre movements in which the text of the play, where one exists, is a cooperative product growing out of discussion and rehearsal (to some extent, this is of course true of all plays, but usually there has been a text to start from; this is not always the case now). The possible relations between the word and image in television drama, the impact of television on the live drama and the growth of the fringe theatre are all fascinating and important subjects. But they belong to another book.

Chronological Table

Unless otherwise stated, the date given for plays is that of first performance. A few plays not mentioned in the text are identified by author. I am grateful to my colleague and friend Peter Thomson for letting me pillage his list 'The English Theatre — by Dates'.

THEATRICAL EVENTS (including births and deaths of dramatists).	HISTORICAL EVENTS (including events in literary history).
*c.*900 *Quem Quaeritis* trope dramatized	
*c.*932-983 Hroswitha, a German Benedictine abbess, writes six dramatic adaptations of Latin plays by Terence. The existence of a folk drama (as exemplified in surviving Mummers Plays) can be assumed. These lack of the literary sophistication of the Morality Plays that developed through the 15th century	
1264	Pope Urban IV establishes Feast of Corpus Christi.
1311	Pope Clement V effectively establishes Feast of Corpus Christi by ordering its adoption at Council of Vienne.
1376 First recorded reference to Corpus Christi plays, (Five Miracle Cycles remain — though published very late in their history: York, Towneley, Chester, N-town, Cornish (in Cornish).	
*c.*1405 *The Castle of Perseverance.*	
*c.*1462 Henry Medwall born.	
1485	Henry of Richmond crowned as Henry VII.
1490 David Lindsay born.	

*c.*1500	*Everyman*	
1505	Nicholas Udall born.	
1509		Accession of Henry VIII.
*c.*1510	Skelton's *Magnyfycence*	
1527		Death of Machiavelli. (born 1469).
1535		Henry VIII assumes supreme headship of Church.
*c.*1540	Sir David Lindsay's *Ane Satire of the Three Estaits.*	
*c.*1553	*Ralph Roister Doister, Gammer Gurton's Needle.*	
1558	Thomas Kyd born	Elizabeth I becomes queen.
1562	*Gorboduc* acted at Inner Temple	
1564	Christopher Marlowe and William Shakespeare born.	
1570		Elizabeth I 'deposed' and excommunicated by Pope.
1572	Ben Jonson born	'Act for the Punishment of Vagabonds' regularizes status of acting troupes.
1575	Children of St Paul's active as stage performers.	
1576	James Burbage builds the Theatre in Shoreditch. Children of the Chapel Royal commence performances at First Blackfriars. John Marston born.	
1579	John Fletcher born. Stephen Gosson's *School of Abuse* attacking stage plays published.	
1580	Middleton born.	
1581	Peele's *Arraignment of Paris.*	
1583	Massinger born. Queen's Men (acting company) founded.	
1584	Francis Beaumont born. Lyly's *Campaspe* and *Sappho and Phao.*	
1586	John Ford born.	Death of Sir Philip Sidney at Battle of Zutphen.
1587	? The Rose Theatre built. *Tamburlaine, The Spanish Tragedy.*	Pope proclaims crusade against England. Mary Queen of Scots executed.
1588	Lyly's *Endimion.*	The Armada. Greene's

		Perimedes the Blacksmith published.
1589	*Friar Bacon and Friar Bungay, The Jew of Malta,* lost play of *Hamlet* (? Kyd) *Mother Bombie.*	
1590	Paul's Boys cease playing. Peele's *Old Wives' Tale.*	
1591	Parts 2 & 3 of Shakespeare's *Henry VI.*	Sidney's *Astrophel and Stella.* and Spenser's *Complaints* and *Daphnaida* published.
1592	Theatres closed for nearly two years due to plague. *Dr Faustus,* and *Edward II, Comedy of Errors.*	
1593	Marlowe dies. *Richard III, Two Gentlemen of Verona.*	
1594	Kyd dies. *The Taming of the Shrew, Titus Andronicus.*	
1595	Swan Theatre built, *A Midsummer Night's Dream, Romeo and Juliet.*	Raleigh's voyage to Guiana. Death of Drake and Hawkins.
1598	*Every Man in His Humour, Much Ado About Nothing.* All London acting companies except Admiral's and Chamberlain's Men suppressed after trouble over *The Isle of Dogs,* a play by Thomas Nashe and others.	
1599	Globe Theatre built. Paul's Boys resume playing. *The Shoemaker's Holiday, Every Man Out of His Humour, Antonio and Mellida, As You Like It.* War of the Theatres commences (to 1601)	Essex returns from Ireland and is imprisoned.
1600	Fortune Theatre built. Chapel Boys begin playing at Second Blackfriars. *Antonio's Revenge, The Merry Wives of Windsor, Twelfth Night.*	East India Company founded. Prince Charles (later Charles I) born.
1601	*Satiromastix, Antony and Cleopatra, Hamlet, Cynthia's Revels.*	Rebellion and execution of Essex.
1603	Chamberlain's Men become King's Men; Admiral's Men, Prince Henry's Men; Worcester's Men, Queen Anne's Men; Children of the Chapel Royal, Children of the Revels. *Sejanus.*	James I of England becomes king on Elizabeth I's death. Plague in London.
1604	Alleyn retires. Second Blackfriars taken	Peace with Spain.

over from Chapel Boys by Children of the Queen's Revels. *Bussy d'Ambois, The Dutch Courtesan, The Malcontent, Measure for Measure, Othello.*

1605 ? Red Bull Theatre built. *A Trick to Catch the Old One, King Lear.*

Gunpowder plot. Bacon's *Advancement of Learning* published.

1606 ? Whitefriars theatre built in Great Hall of former priory. Davenant born. Death of Lyly. *Volpone, Macbeth, The Revenger's Tragedy.*

1607 ? Paul's Boys cease playing. *The Knight of the Burning Pestle.*

1608 Children of the Queen's Revels cease playing at second Blackfriars; King's Men take over. *Conspiracy* and *Tragedy of Byron, Coriolanus, Pericles.*

1609 *Epicoene, Cymbeline, The Atheist's Tragedy.*

Dekker's *Gull's Hornbook* published.

1610 *The Alchemist, The Maid's Tragedy, The Winter's Tale.*

Plantation of Ulster.

1611 *A King and No King, Catiline, A Chaste Maid in Cheapside, The Tempest.*

King James Bible and Spenser's collected works published.

1612 *The White Devil.*

Prince Henry dies. Lancashire witches hanged. Bacon's Essays (enlarged), Heywood's *Apology for Actors* published.

1613 Globe theatre burns down. Children of the Revels amalgamates with Lady Elizabeth's Men. Shakespeare retires.

Princess Elizabeth marries Frederick, Elector Palatine.

1614 Hope theatre and Second Globe built. *Bartholomew Fair, The Duchess of Malfi.*

1616 Shakespeare dies.

Publication of Folio edition of Jonson's works.

1621

Burton's *Anatomy of Melancholy* published. Andrew Marvell born.

1622 *The Changeling*. Middleton also writes *An Invention for the Lord Mayor* for the Lord Mayor's Feast and *The Triumphs of Honour and Virtue* for the Company of Grocers.

1623		Publication of First Folio Shakespeare.
1624	*A Game at Chess*	
1625	Jonson increasingly involved in Court Masques. Fletcher dies.	Death of James I, accession of Charles I.
1626	Argument between Jonson and Jones over relative importance of word and stage picture in masque. Tourneur dies.	Bacon dies.
1627	Middleton dies.	
1628	Ford's *The Lover's Melancholy*.	Assassination of Duke of Buckingham.
1631	Dryden born.	John Donne dies.
1632	*The City Madam, Hyde Park*.	
1633	*A New Way to Pay Old Debts, 'Tis Pity She's a Whore*.	Samuel Pepys born.
1634	Death of Chapman (also of Marston and Webster?)	
1635	George Etherege born.	
1637	Jonson dies.	
1640	Massinger dies. Wycherley born. Shirley succeeds Massinger as chief dramatist of King's Men.	
1642	Theatres closed by Act of Parliament.	Outbreak of Civil War; Charles I leaves London.
1649		Execution of Charles I.
1652	Thomas Otway born.	
1653	Nathaniel Lee born.	
1656	*The Siege of Rhodes* performed at Rutland House.	
1658		Cromwell dies.
1659	Actors arrested for Red Bull performance.	
1660	Introduction of actresses on stage. Royal patent granted to King's and Duke's companies (Killigrew and Davenant)	Restoration of Charles II. Pepys begins diary.
1661	Duke's Company begins acting at Lincoln's Inn Fields.	
1663	King's Company begins acting at Theatre Royal, Bridges Street.	
1664	*The Comical Revenge*. John Vanbrugh born.	
1665	Theatres closed by plague.	
1666	Theatres reopened Nov. Death of Shirley.	Great Fire of London.
1667	Theatres closed in July for Dutch war.	*Paradise Lost* published.

1668	*She Would If She Could.* Davenant dies. Betterton and Harris managers of Duke's Company.	Dryden's *An Essay of Dramatic Poesy* published.
1670	Congreve born. *The Conquest of Granada.*	
1671	Duke's Company opens at Dorset Garden Theatre. Colley Cibber born. *The Rehearsal, Love in a Wood.*	*Paradise Regained, Samson Agonistes* published.
1672	Addison and Steele born. Bridges Street Theatre burned. *Marriage A La Mode.*	
1674	King's Company opens Drury Lane Theatre.	Milton dies.
1675	*The Country Wife.*	
1676	*The Man of Mode, The Plain Dealer.*	
1677	*All for Love.*	
1682	King's and Duke of York's merged into United Company under Betterton and Smith. Death of Nell Gwyn (retired from stage at 19 in 1669).	
1685	Theatres closed for 3 months	Death of Charles II. Accession of James II. Death of Otway. John Gay born.
1688		Flight of James II.
1689		Accession of William and Mary.
1691	Etherege dies.	
1693	*The Old Bachelor, The Double Dealer.*	
1694	Theatres closed for Queen Mary's death.	Death of Queen Mary.
1695	*Love for Love.*	
1696	*Love's Last Shift, The Relapse.* Lord Chamberlain requires all plays be licensed.	
1698	Jeremy Collier publishes *A Short View of the Immorality and Profaneness of the English Stage.*	
1700	*The Way of the World. The Constant Couple.*	Dryden dies.
1701	*Sir Harry Wildair*	
1702		Death of William III. Accession of Queen Anne.
1705	*The Tender Husband.* Queen's Theatre in Haymarket opened.	
1706	*The Recruiting Officer*	

1707	Farquhar dies. Henry Fielding born. *The Beaux' Stratagem.*	Union of England and Scotland.
1708	Union of companies at Drury Lane. Downes's theatrical memoirs, *Roscius Anglicanus* published.	
1709		Samuel Johnson born. *Tatler* begins publication (till 1711).
1711	Haymarket Theatre restricted to operas.	
1714	Steele becomes governor of Drury Lane (gets royal patent in 1715)	Death of Queen Anne. Accession of George I.
1717	David Garrick born.	
1722	*The Conscious Lovers*	
1727		Death of George I, Accession of George II.
1728	*The Provoked Husband* (Cibber and Vanbrugh) *The Beggar's Opera.*	
1729	Congreve dies. Steele dies.	
1730	*Tom Thumb* (revised as *The Tragedy of Tragedies).* Oliver Goldsmith born.	
1731	George Lillo's *George Barnwell, or The London Merchant.*	
1736	Fielding's company at Haymarket. *Pasquin.*	
1737	*The Historical Register.* Walpole introduces Stage Licensing Act, eloquently opposed by Lord Chesterfield.	
1740	Cibber's *Apology* published (revised 1750, 1756).	
1741	Garrick's London début.	
1745		Jacobite rebellion. Swift dies.
1757	*The Male Coquette.* Colley Cibber dies. J.P. Kemble born.	William Blake born. Pitt prime minister.
1768	*The Good Natur'd Man.*	*Encyclopaedia Britannica* begun.
1769	Garrick's celebrations of Shakespeare's bicentenary at Stratford. Very wet.	
1771	Garrick engages de Loutherbourg as scene designer. Cumberland's *The West Indian.*	
1773	*She Stoops to Conquer.*	
1775	Unsuccessful début of Sarah Siddons as Portia. *The Rivals.*	Jane Austen and Charles Lamb born.

1776	Garrick retires. Sheridan at Drury Lane.	American Declaration of Independence.
1778	*The Critic.*	
1779	Garrick dies.	
1783	Kemble's début as Hamlet.	Crabbe's *The Village* published.
1788	Kemble manager of Drury Lane	Byron born.
1789		Fall of Bastille. Blake's *Songs of Innocence* published.
1794	Kemble opens enlarged Drury Lane with *Macbeth* (Sarah Siddons as Lady Macbeth).	
1799	Sheridan's *Pizarro.*	
1804		Napoleon emperor.
1805		Battle of Trafalgar.
1808	Covent Garden burns down.	
1809	Drury Lane burns down.	
1814	Edmund Kean's début as Shylock at Drury Lane.	
1815		Battle of Waterloo.
1816	Macready's début at Covent Garden. Sheridan dies.	Jane Austen's *Emma* and Shelley's *Alastor* published.
1817	Last appearance of Kemble. Gas lighting at Drury Lane and Covent Garden.	
1820	*Virginius.*	Accession of George IV. Cato Street conspiracy.
1821	New Haymarket Theatre opens.	Napoleon dies.
1832		First Reform Bill.
1833	Edmund Kean dies. Dramatic Copyright Act secures playwright's control over his work.	
1837	Macready manager of Covent Garden (till 1839). First London appearance of Samuel Phelps.	Accession of Queen Victoria.
1841	*London Assurance.* Macready at Drury Lane.	
1843	Theatre Regulation Act abolishes Patent monopoly. Macready ends Drury Lane management.	
1844	Phelps manager of Sadler's Wells (till 1862).	
1848	Theatrical performances at Windsor Castle	Chartist movement suppressed.

1830	Charles Kean begins management of Princess' Theatre (till 1859).	
1851	Macready's farewell performance (as Macbeth).	Great Exhibition
1860	*The Colleen Bawn*. J.M. Barrie born.	Lincoln elected US president.
1863	*The Ticket-of-Leave Man*. Stanislavsky born.	
1867	*Caste*.	Marx begins *Das Kapital*. Disraeli's Reform Act.
1871	Irving's sensational success in *The Bells*.	Paris Commune.
1878	Irving at Lyceum with Ellen Terry as leading lady. Phelps dies.	
1884	Ibsen's *The Wild Duck*. *Saints and Sinners, The Profligate*.	Gladstone's Reform Act.
1891	Independent Theatre Society founded by J.T. Grein. Shaw's *Quintessence of Ibsenism* published.	*The Adventures of Sherlock Holmes, Tess of the D'urbervilles* published.
1892	*The Countess Cathleen, Widowers' Houses*.	Keir Hardie elected first Labour MP.
1894	William Poel forms Elizabethan Stage Society. *Arms and the Man*. J.B. Priestley born.	
1895	*An Ideal Husband, The Importance of Being Earnest*. Irving knighted.	
1898	Formation of Irish Literary Theatre. *Trelawny of the 'Wells'*.	
1901	*The Admirable Crichton. Paolo and Francesca*.	Death of Queen Victoria. Accession of Edward VII.
1904	*Peter Pan, Candida, Riders to the Sea*. Barker-Vedrenne repertory at Court Theatre.	
1905	*Man and Superman*. Irving dies on stage at Bradford. Actors' Union formed.	
1907	*The Playboy of the Western World* causes riots at Abbey Theatre. Christopher Fry born. Synge dies.	
1910		Accession of George V.
1913	Barry Jackson starts Birmingham Repertory Theatre.	
1914	*Pygmalion*. Granville Barker's production of *A Midsummer Night's Dream*.	First World War begins
1916	*Heartbreak House*.	Jung's *Psychology of The Unconscious* published.

1918		End of World War I.
1921	*Back to Methuselah.* Peter Ustinov born.	
1925	Noel Coward's *Hay Fever.*	
1926	*The Plough and the Stars.*	General Strike.
1928	*The Silver Tassie. Journey's End.*	
1929	*Private Lives, The Apple Cart.* H.A. Jones dies.	Wall Street crash.
1930	Arden, Osborne and Pinter born.	
1933	*The Dance of Death, Laburnum Grove.* Joe Orton born.	
1935	*The Dog Beneath the Skin, Murder in the Cathedral.* Edward Bond born.	
1936		Spanish Civil War. Accession of George VI.
	The Ascent of F6	Left Book Club formed.
1938	*On the Frontier, Trial of a Judge, The House by the Stable.*	Munich crisis.
1939	*The Family Reunion, Johnson over Jordan.*	World War II begins.
1945	*An Inspector Calls.*	End of World War in Europe.
1946	Coward's *Peace in Our Time, A Phoenix Too Frequent, The Winslow Boy.*	Atom bomb on Hiroshima. TV regularly established on BBC. George Orwell's *1984* published.
1949	*The Cocktail Party, The Lady's Not for Burning, Cock-a-Doodle Dandy.*	
1950	*Venus Observed, Ring Round the Moon.* Shaw dies.	
1951	National Theatre foundation stone laid. *A Sleep of Prisoners, The Love of Four Colonels.*	Festival of Britain.
1952		Accession of Elizabeth II.
1953	*The Confidential Clerk.*	
1954	*Under Milk Wood* broadcast.	Commercial television begins.
1955	English version of *Waiting for Godot.*	
1956	*Romanoff and Juliet, Look Back in Anger.*	Soviet invasion of Hungary. British-Israeli attack on Suez.
1957	*The Entertainer.*	
1958	*A Taste of Honey, Chicken Soup with Barley, The Elder Statesman, The Birthday Party.*	

1959	*Sergeant Musgrave's Dance, The Room, Roots.*	
1960	*The Caretaker, The Dumb Waiter, I'm Talking About Jerusalem.*	
1961	*Luther*	
1962	*The Pope's Wedding, Chips with Everything.*	
1963	*The Workhouse Donkey.*	
1964	*Armstrong's Last Goodnight, Entertaining Mr Sloane, Inadmissible Evidence.*	
1965	*Saved, The Homecoming, Four Seasons.*	Vietnam War.
1966	*Loot.*	
1967	*Rosencrantz and Guildenstern are Dead.* Joe Orton dies.	
1968	Stage censorship abolished. *Narrow Road to the Deep North, What the Butler Saw, Landscape, The Real Inspector Hound.*	Student uprisings in Paris and USA.
1969	*Silence*	Violence in Ireland intensifies.
1970	*The Friends.* Laurence Olivier becomes first actor to be raised to peerage.	
1971	*Lear, Old Times.*	
1973	*A Place Calling Itself Rome, Jumpers, The Island of the Mighty.*	Britain joins Common Market.
1974	*Travesties.*	
1975	*No Man's Land.*	

Selective Bibliography

(For reasons of manageability only book length criticism and commentary are cited).

1   **Medieval Drama**

ed. A.C. Cawley *'Everyman' and Medieval Miracle Plays* (London, 1956).
ed. A.C. Cawley, *The Wakefield Pageant in the Towneley Cycle* (Manchester, 1958).
trans. and ed. J.S. Purvis, *The York Cycle of Mystery Plays* (London, 1953).

Criticism.

E.K. Chambers, *The Medieval Stage*, 2 vols. (Oxford, 1903).
S.J. Kahrl, *Traditions of Medieval English Drama* (London, 1974).
V.A. Kolve, *The Play Called Corpus Christi* (London, 1966).
R. Woolf, *The English Mystery Plays* (London, 1972).

2   **Tudor and Early Elizabethan Drama**

Texts

ed. J.Q. Adams, *Chief Pre-Shakespearean Dramas* (Boston, Mass., 1924)
ed. P. Happé *Tudor Interludes* (Harmondsworth, 1972).
ed. P. Happé *Four Morality Plays* (Harmondsworth, 1979).
ed. G. Wickham, *English Moral Interludes* (London, 1976).

Criticism

D.M. Bevington, *From 'Mankind' to Marlowe: Growth of Structure in the Popular Drama of Tudor England* (Cambridge, Mass., 1962).
F.S. Boas, *An Introduction to Tudor Drama* (Oxford, 1933).
T.W. Craik, *The Tudor Interlude: Stage, Costume and Acting* (Leicester, 1958).
A.P. Rossiter, *English Drama from Early Times to the Elizabethans* (London, 1950).

221

3   Elizabethan and Jacobean Drama

Texts

The principal plays of all the dramatists discussed are available in good modern editions in several well known series such as the Revels, Regents Renaissance, New Mermaids, Everyman and the Penguin English Library. Some of these series also contain several collections devoted to a single genre or chronological span within the period.

Criticism. (i)   *General.*

G.E. Bentley, *The Jacobean and Caroline Stage,* 7 vols. (Oxford, 1941-1968).
F.T. Bowers, *Elizabethan Revenge Tragedy* 1587-1642 (Princeton, N.J., 1940).
M.C. Bradbrook, *Themes and Conventions of Elizabethan Tragedy* (Cambridge, 1935).
M.C. Bradbrook, *The Growth and Structure of Elizabethan Comedy* (London, 1955).
M.C. Bradbrook, *The Rise of the Common Player* (London, 1962).
M.C. Bradbrook, *The Living Monument* (London, 1976).
N. Brooke, *Horrid Laughter in Jacobean Tragedy* (London, 1979).
ed. J.R. Brown and B. Harris, *Elizabethan Theatre* (London, 1966).
ed. J.R. Brown and B. Harris, *Jacobean Theatre* (London, 1960).
U. Ellis Fermor, *The Jacobean Drama* (London, 1936).
B. Gibbons, *Jacobean City Comedy* (London, 1968).
L.C. Knights, *Drama and Society in the Age of Jonson* (London, 1937).
ed. C. Leech and T.W. Craik, *The Revels History of Drama in English, Vol. III 1576-1613* (London, 1975).
M. Shapiro, *Children of the Revels: The Boy Companies of Shakespeare's Time and Their Plays* (New York, 1977).
C. Tomlinson, *A Study of Elizabethan and Jacobean Tragedy* (Cambridge, 1964).
L.B. Wright, *Middle-Class Culture in Elizabethan England* (repr. Ithaca, NY, 1958).

(ii) *Individual Dramatists*

Marlowe
M. Mahood, *Poetry and Humanism* (London, 1950).
W.Sanders, *The Dramatist and the Received Idea* (Cambridge, 1968)
J. Weil, *Christopher Marlowe: Merlin's Prophet* (Cambridge, 1977).
Kyd
W. Edwards, *Kyd and Early Elizabethan Tragedy* (London, 1966).
A. Freeman, *Kyd: Facts and Problems* (Oxford, 1967).

Jonson
J.B. Bamborough, *Ben Jonson* (London, 1970).
J. Barish, *Ben Jonson and the Language of Prose Comedy* (Cambridge, Mass., 1960).
J.J. Enck, *Jonson and the Comic Truth* (Madison, Wis., 1957).
E.B. Partridge, *The Broken Compass* (London, 1958).
Chapman
M. MacLure, *George Chapman, a Critical Study* (Toronto, 1966).
Marston
A. Caputi, *John Marston, Satirist* (Ithaca, NY, 1961).
A. Kernan, *The Cankered Muse* (New Haven, Conn., 1959).
Middleton
W.Empson, *Some Versions fo Pastoral* (London, 1935).
D.M. Farr, *Thomas Middleton and the Drama of Realism* (Edinburgh, 1973).
Massinger
A.H. Cruickshank, *Philip Massinger* (Oxford, 1920).
T.A. Dunn, *Philip Massinger: The Man and the Playwright* (Edinburgh, 1957).
Beaumont and Fletcher
W.W. Appleton, *Beaumont and Fletcher: A Critical Study* (Fair Lawn, NJ, 1956)
E.M. Waith, *The Pattern of Tragicomedy in Beaumont and Fletcher* (New Haven, Conn., 1952).
Webster
R. Berry, *The Art of John Webster* (Oxford, 1972).
Tourneur
P.B. Murray, *A Study of Cyril Tourneur* (Philadelphia, Pa., 1964).
Ford
C. Leech, *John Ford and the Drama of his Time* (London, 1957).
H.J. Oliver, *The Problem of John Ford* (Melbourne, 1955).

4 Restoration Drama

Texts

The texts of most of the plays discussed are available in The Regents' Restoration series. Some of them also appear in New Mermaids and in Everyman and Penguin anthologies.

Criticism (i) *General*

ed. E.L. Avery, A.H. Scouten, and W. van Lennep, *The London Stage 1660-1800 Part 1 1660-1700* (Carbondale, Ill., 1965)
ed. J.R. Brown and B. Harris, *Restoration Theatre* (London, 1965).
D. Bruce, *Topics in Restoration Comedy* (London, 1974)
B. Dobrée, *Restoration Tragedy* (Oxford, 1929).

H. Hawkins, *Likenesses of Truth in Elizabethan and Restoration Drama* (Oxford, 1972).
N. Holland, *The First Modern Comedies: The Significance of Etherege Wycherley and Congreve* (Cambridge, Mass., 1959).
P. Holland, *The Ornament of Action: Text and Performance in Restoration Comedy* (Cambridge, 1979).
L. Hotson, *The Commonwealth and Restoration Stage* (Cambridge, Mass., 1928).
R.D. Hume, *The Development of English Drama in the Late Seventeenth Century* (Oxford, 1976).
ed. H. Love, *Restoration Literature: Critical Approaches* (London, 1972).
K. Muir, *The Comedy of Manners* (London, 1970).
G.C.D. Odell, *Shakespeare — from Betterton to Irving* (2 vols. New York, 1920).

(ii) *Individual Dramatists*

Etherege
D. Underwood, *Etherege and the Seventeenth Century Comedy of Manners* (New Haven, Conn., 1957).
Wycherley
P.F. Vernon, *William Wycherley* (London, 1965).
R. Zimbardo, *Wycherley's Drama: A Link in the Development of English Satire* (New Haven, Conn., 1965).
Congreve
ed. B. Morris, *William Congreve* (London, 1972).
Vanburgh
B. Harris, *Sir John Vanbrugh* (London, 1967).
Farquhar
W. Connely, *Young George Farquhar: The Restoration Drama at Twilight* (London, 1949).

5   Eighteen Century Drama

Texts

Texts of Sheridan and Goldsmith are easily available and some of the minor plays appear in collections in the Everyman and World's Classics series as well as in individual volumes of the Regents' Restoration series.

Criticism and Commentary (i) *General*

ed. E.L. Avery, *The London Stage 1660-1800, Part 2*, 2 vols. (Carbondale, Ill., 1960).
F.W. Bateson, *English Comic Drama 1700-1750* (Oxford, 1929).
A. Sherbo, *English Sentimental Drama* (East Lansing, Mich., 1957).

(ii) *Individual Dramatists:*

Steele
J. Loftis, *Steele at Drury Lane* (Berkeley and Los Angeles, Calif., 1952)
Goldsmith
R.M. Wardle, *Oliver Goldsmith* (Laurence, Kans., and London, 1957).
Sheridan
ed. C. Brooks and R.B. Heilman, *Understanding Drama* (New York, 1948).

6 Nineteenth Century Drama

Texts.

The four volumes of *English Plays of the Nineteenth Century,* ed., M.R. Booth (Oxford 1969-1973) provide the most easily accessible texts of most of the plays. Smaller collections are the two World's Classics volumes edited by G. Rowell, *Late Victorian Plays* (London, 1968) and *Nineteenth Century Plays* (London, 1953).

Criticism and Commentary (i) *General*

H.B. Baker, *History of the London Stage* (New York, 1946).
E. Bentley, *The Playwright as Thinker* (London, 1940).
R. Brustein, *The Theatre of Revolt* (Boston, 1962).
J.W. Donohue, *Dramatic Character in the English Romantic Age* (Princeton, NJ, 1970).
ed. C. Leech and T.W. Craik, *Revels History of Drama in English Vol. VI, 1750-1880* (London, 1975).
G.H. Lewes, *On Actors and the Art of Acting* (London, 1875).
H. Morley, *Journal of a London Playgoer* (London, 1866).
G.B. Shaw, *Dramatic Opinions and Essays,* 2 vols. (London, 1906).
E.B. Watson, *Sheridan to Robertson* (Cambridge, Mass., 1926).
R. Williams, *Drama from Ibsen to Eliot* (London, 1952).

(ii) *Individual Dramatists:*

Wilde
ed. K. Beckson, *Oscar Wilde: The Critical Heritage* (London, 1971).
Shaw
E. Bentley, *Shaw: A Reconsideration* (London, 1947).

7 The Twentieth Century

Texts

Many of the later twentieth century plays discussed are available in the

Modern Plays and Master Playwrights series both published by Eyre-Methuen. Several are also available in the Penguin New English Dramatists Series. Osborne and Stoppard are available in Faber paperbacks.

Criticism and Commentary (i) *General*

M. Anderson, *Anger and Detachment: A Study of Arden, Osborne and Pinter* (London, 1976).
H. Granville Barker, *A National Theatre* (London, 1930).
J.R. Brown, *Theatre Language: A Study of Arden, Osborne and Pinter* (London, 1972).
ed. T.W. Craik, *The Revels History of Drama in English, vol. VII 1880 to the present day* (London, 1978).
A. Nicoll, *English Drama 1900-1930: The Beginnings of the Modern Period* (Cambridge, 1973).
J.L. Styan, *The Dark Comedy* (Cambridge, 1962)
J.R. Taylor, *Anger and After: A Guide to the New British Drama* (London, rev.ed. 1969).
J.R. Taylor, *The Second Wave: British Drama for the Seventies* (London, 1971).

(ii) *Individual Dramatists*

O'Casey
M. Malone, The Plays of O'Casey (London, 1969).
Osborne
R. Hayman, *Osborne* (London, 1968).
S. Trussler, *The Plays of Osborne* (London, 1969).
Wesker
R. Hayman, *Wesker* (London, 1970).
Arden
A. Hunt, *Arden: A Study of His Plays* (London, 1974)
Pinter
J.R. Taylor, *Pinter* (London, 1969).
M. Esslin, *Pinter: A Study of His Plays* (London, 1973).
Orton
J. Lahr, *Prick up Your Ears: The Biography of Joe Orton* (London, 1978).
Bond
T. Coult, *The Plays of Bond* (London, 1978).
S. Trussler, *Bond* (London, 1976).
Stoppard
C.W.E. Bigsby, *Stoppard* (London, 1976).

Index

Abbey Theatre, Dublin, 183–5
Achurch, Janet, *Mrs Daintry's Daughter*, 178
actors, as professionals, 30–31; *see also* individual
    companies
Addison, Joseph, 141, 164–6; *Cato*, 164–6
Admirable Bashville, The, 183
Admiral's Men, The (actors' company), 90
Adventures of Five Hours, The, 143, 145
Alcestis, 188
Alchemist, The, 58, 64–8
Alexander and Campaspe, 40
All for Love, 139–40, 142
All's Well that Ends Well, 71
Alleyn, Edward, 49, 174
Alphonsus, King of Aragon, 52
Amphitruo, 34
Anatomist, The, 191
Anouilh, Jean, 191
Antonio and Mellida, 87–8
Antonio's Revenge, 85–90
Antony and Cleopatra, 139
Apple Cart, The, 183
Aquinas, Thomas, 100
Archer, William, 177–9; *Rheingold*, 178
Arcy, Margaretta d' *see* Arden, John
Arden, John, 194, 196–8, 203, 204; *Armstrong's Last
    Goodnight*, 196, 198; *Left-handed Liberty*, 198;
    Sergeant Musgrave's Dance, 195–6; *To Present the
    Pretence* (essays), 198; *The Workhouse Donkey*,
    196–7; and Margaretta d'Arcy, *The Ballygombeen
    Bequest*, 198; *The Island of the Mighty*, 198
Arms and the Man, 179, 183
Armstrong's Last Goodnight, 196, 198
Arnold, Matthew, 175
Arraignment of Paris, The, 41, 51–2
As You Like It, 69, 86
Ascent of F6, The, 187
Atheist's Tragedy, The, 94–5, 97
Auden, W.H., 189; *The Dance of Death*, 187; and
    Christopher Isherwood, 187, 190; *The Ascent of F6*,
    187; *The Dog Beneath the Skin*, 187; *On the Frontier*,
    187
audiences, nature and composition of, 33, 38, 136–8,
    143, 174
Author's Farce, The, 167

Back to Methuselah, 180–81
Bacon, Francis, 36
Bale, John, 30
Ballygombeen Bequest, The, 198
Bandello, Matteo, 72
Barker, Harley Granville, 143, 190; *Prefaces to
    Shakespeare*, 190
Barrie, J.M., 184
Bartholomew Fair, 58, 62, 68–9, 83
Beaumont, Francis, *The Knight of the Burning Pestle*;
    and John Fletcher, 82–3, 124–6, 131, 139, 155; *A
    King and No King*, 124, 126–7, 130; *The Maid's
    Tragedy*, 124–6; *Philaster*, 126
Beaux' Stratagem, The, 160–61
Becket, 186
Beckett, Samuel, 174; *Waiting for Godot*, 203
Beeston, William, 133, 135

Beggar's Opera, The, 163, 166
Behan, Brendan, 194; *The Hostage*, 194; *The Quare
    Fellow*, 194
Behn, Aphra, 138, 144; *The Dutch War*, 144; *Sir
    Patient Fancy*, 144
Bennett, Alan, 143
Benson, Frank, 171
Betterton, Thomas, 135, 158, 171
Birthday Party, The, 198–201
Blackfriars theatre, 56–7, 81, 126
Blind Beggar of Alexandria, The, 90
Bon Ton, 168
Bond, Edward, 206–8; *Lear*, 207–8; *Narrow Road to
    the Deep North* (*The Bundle*), 208; *The Pope's
    Wedding*, 207; *Saved*, 202, 207
Bondman, The, 81
Bottomley, Gordon, *King Lear's Wife*, 187
Boucicault, Dion, 162, 174, 176; *The Colleen Bawn* (*The
    Lily of Killarney*), 174; *The Corsican Brothers*, 174;
    London Assurance, 174
Bracegirdle, Anne, 158
Breaking a Butterfly see *A Doll's House*
Brecht, Bertolt, 207; *Galileo*, 193; *The Threepenny
    Opera*, 166
Bridie, James, *The Anatomist*, 191; *Tobias and the Angel*,
    191
Brighouse, Harold, *Hobson's Choice*, 183
Brome, Richard, *The Jovial Crew*, 83; *The Lovesick
    Maids*, 83
Buckingham, Duke of *see* Villiers, George, Duke of
    Buckingham
Bundle, The see *Narrow Road to the Deep North*
Burbage, William, 58
Burke, Edmund, 168
Burnet, Gilbert, Bishop of Salisbury, 147
Burton, Robert, *Anatomy of Melancholy*, 86
Bury Fair, 160
Bussy d'Ambois, 90–94
Byron, George Gordon, Lord, 173

Caesar and Cleopatra, 179, 183
Caesar's Fall, 100
Calisto and Melibea, 28
Cambises, 31, 35–6
Candida, 181
Cardinal, The, 83
Careless Husband, The, 163
Caretaker, The, 198–9, 201–2
Caste, 175
Castle of Perseverance, The, 17–19, 21, 27
Cato, 164–6
Caxton, William, 25
Cecil, Sir Edward, 94
Centilivre, Susannah, 162
Chabot, Admiral of France, 91
Chamberlain's Men, The see Lord Chamberlain's Men,
    The
Changeling, The, 74, 111, 116–23, 126–7
Chaplin, Charles, *Modern Times* (film), 124
Chapman, George, 90–94, 111, 123; *The Blind Beggar
    of Alexandria*, 90; *Bussy d'Ambois*, 90–94; *Chabot,
    Admiral of France*, 91; *The Conspiracy and Tragedy
    of Charles, Duke of Biron*, 91; *An Humorous Day's
    Mirth*, 59, 90; *The Revenge of Bussy d'Ambois*, 91;

see also Marston, John
Charles I, King of England, 39, 81, 84, 133
Charles II, King of England, 131–2, 134–5, 138, 153
Charley's Aunt, 176
Chaste Maid in Cheapside, A, 74, 76–7, 111–12
Chekhov, Anton, 182–3; *The Cherry Orchard*, 182
Cherry Orchard, The, 182
Chester cycle, 5, 9–10
Chicken Soup with Barley, 194
Children of the Chapel, The (actors' company), 52
Children of St Paul's (actors' company), 87
Chips With Everything, 194–5
Chocolate Soldier, The (musical), 179; *see also Arms and the Man*
Cibber, Colley, 136, 163–4, 171; *The Careless Husband*, 168; *Love's Last Shift*, 159, 163
Cibber, Theophilus, 164
Cicero, 33
Citizen's Theatre, Glasgow, 197
City Madam, The, 77, 80
Clement V, Pope, 4
Cock-a-Doodle-Dandy, 186
Cockpit Theatre, 82, 133, 135
Cocktail Party, The, 188
Coffee House Politician, The see *Rape Upon Rape*
Coleridge, Samuel Taylor, 173
Colleen Bawn, The (The Lily of Killarney), 174
Collier, Jeremy, 163, 165; *A Short View of the Immorality and Profaneness of the English Stage*, 136, 144, 156, 158
Comical Gallant, The, 168
Comical Revenge, The, 145
Committee, The, 145
Confederacy, The, 158
Confidential Clerk, The, 188
Congreve, William, 138, 153–8; *The Double Dealer*, 154–5; *Love for Love*, 153–6; *The Mourning Bride*, 154; *The Old Bachelor*, 154–5; *The Way of the World*, 143, 153, 156–8
Conquest of Granada, The, 139, 142
Conscious Lovers, The, 163–5, 168
Conspiracy and Tragedy of Charles, Duke of Biron, The, 91
Constant Couple, The, 160
Coriolanus, 172, 193
Corneille, Pierre, 139
Coronation Street (television series), 209
Corpus Christi plays see Miracle plays
Corsican Brothers, The, 174
Countess Cathleen, The, 184
Country Girl, The, 168
Country Wife, The, 150–4, 158
Court Theatre see Royal Court Theatre
Covent Garden theatre, 167–8, 170, 172–3
Coventry miracle plays, 9
Coward, Noel, 143; *The Vortex*, 190
Cowley, Abraham, *The Cutter of Coleman Street*, 145
Cox, Robert, *The Merry Conceits of Bottom the Weaver*, 133
Critic, The; A Tragedy Rehearsed, 169
Crowne, John, 142
Crucible, The, 197
Crucifixion, The, 11–13

Cumberland, Richard, *The Jew*, 169; *The West Indian*, 169
Curtmantle, 189
Cutter of Coleman Street, The, 145
Cymbeline, 126
Cynthia's Revels, 51

Dance of Death, The, 187
Dandy Dick, 175
Dangerous Corner, 191
Dark Tower, The, 189
Davenant, Charles, 136
Davenant, Sir William, 84, 131, 133–8, 171; *Love and Honour*, 134; *The Siege of Rhodes*, 134, 137; *The Wits*, 134
Davenant, William (son of Sir William Davenant), 136
Dean, Basil, 187
Dee, John, 65
Dekker, Thomas, 54–6, 63, 100, 128; *The Gull's Hornbook*, 82; *The Honest Whore*, 75; *The Magnificent Entertainment* (pageant), 54; *Old Fortunatus*, 54; *The Shoemaker's Holiday*, 54–6, 72; *see also* Marston, John; Middleton, Thomas
Deloney, Thomas, *The Gentle Craft*, 54
Dennis, John, 138, 165; *The Comical Gallant*, 168
Devereux, Robert, Earl of Essex, 93–4
Devil's Disciple, The, 183
Devil is an Ass, The, 82
Devil's Law-Case, The, 100
Dickens, Charles, 59, 174
Dido, Queen of Carthage, 44
Dog beneath the Skin, The, 187
Doll's House, A (Breaking a Butterfly), 177
Don Quixote in England, 167
Donne, John, 58
Doone, Rupert, 187
Dorset Garden theatre, 135–6
Dr Faustus, 22, 45–7, 85
Double Dealer, The, 154–5
Drury Lane theatre see Theatre Royal, Drury Lane
Dryden, John, 69, 124, 127, 139–42, 144, 154–5; *All For Love*, 139–40, 142; *The Indian Emperor*, 160; *Secret Love*, 158; *The Spanish Friar*, 142
Duchess of Malfi, The, 100, 102, 105–11, 128
Duke's players (actors' company), 135–6
Duke's Theatre see Lincolns Inn Fields Theatre
Dumb Waiter, The, 198, 201
Duncan, Ronald, 188
Dutch Courtesan, The, 58, 70, 72, 101
Dutch War, The, 144
Dynasts, The, 186

Eastward Ho, 58, 78, 80
Eden End, 191
Edward II, 44–5
Edward VI, King of England, 28
Elckerlys, 21
Elder Statesman, The, 188
Eliot, T.S., 45, 70, 120, 187–9, 191; *The Cocktail Party*, 188; *The Confidential Clerk*, 188; *The Elder Statesman*, 188; *The Family Reunion*, 188; *Four Quartets* (poem), 203–4; *Murder in the Cathedral*,

187–8; *The Rock* (choral pageant), 187; *Sweeney Agonistes*, 187
Elizabeth I, Queen of England, 37, 50–52, 81, 85–6
Empress of Morocco, The, 140, 144–5
Endymion, 39–41
Enemy of the People, An (Quicksands), 177
Enough is as Good as a Feast, 31–2
Entertainer, The, 193
Entertaining Mr Sloane, 204
Epicoene or the Silent Woman, 69
Epicurus, 147
Erasmus, 33
Essex, Earl of *see* Devereux, Robert, Earl of Essex
Ethelwold, Bishop of Winchester, 2
Etherege, George, 138, 145–7, 154–5, 157; *The Comical Revenge*, 145; *Love in a Tub*, 146; *The Man of Mode, or Sir Fopling Flutter*, 147–50; *She Would If She Could*, 146–7
Euphues and His England, 39
Euphues, the Anatomy of Wit, 38
Euripides, 36; *Alcestis*, 188; *Ion*, 188
Eurydice Hiss'd, 167
Evelyn, Mary (née Browne; Mrs John Evelyn), 139
Every Good Boy Deserves Favour, 206
Every Man in His Humour, 58–61, 68–9
Every Man Out of his Humour, 57, 60
Everyman, 21–4, 27

Faithful Shepherdess, The, 126
Family Reunion, The, 188
Farquhar, George, 138, 158, 160–61, 163, 174; *The Beaux' Stratagem*, 160–61; *The Constant Couple*, 160; *The Inconstant*, 83; *The Recruiting Officer*, 160
Father, The, 181
Fawn, The, 71
Feydeau, Georges, 175
Fielding, Henry, 167; *The Author's Farce*, 167; *Don Quixote in England*, 167; *Eurydice Hiss'd*, 167; *The Historical Register*, 167; *The Modern Husband*, 167; *Pasquin*, 167; *Rape Upon Rape (The Coffee House Politician)*, 167; *The Tragedy of Tom Thumb (The Tragedy of Tragedies)*, 167; *The Welsh Opera*, 167
Finney, Albert, 197
Flecker, James Elroy, *Hassan*, 186–7
Fletcher, John, 82–3; *The Faithful Shepherdess*, 126; *The Wild Goose Chase*, 82–3; *see also* Beaumont, Francis
Fletcher, Richard, 81
Florizel and Perdita, 168
Ford, John, 123, 127–31; *Perkin Warbeck*, 128; *'Tis Pity She's a Whore*, 109, 128–31
Fortune theatre, 133
Four Ps, The, 28–9
Four Prentices of London, 56, 81
Friar Bacon and Friar Bungay, 52–3
Friends, The, 195
Fry, Christopher, 187–9, 191, 205; *Curtmantle*, 189; *The Lady's Not for Burning*, 188; *A Phoenix too Frequent*, 189; *A Sleep of Prisoners*, 189
Fulgens and Lucrece, 25–7
Funeral, The, 163

Gaiety Theatre, Manchester, 183

Galathea, 39
Galileo, 193
Gammer Gurton's Needle, 34
Garrick, David, 159, 162, 167–71; *Bon Ton*, 168; *The Country Girl*, 168; *Florizel and Perdita*, 168; *Katherine and Petruchio*, 168; *The Male Coquette*, 168; *Miss in her Teens*, 168
Gascoigne, George, and Francis Kinwelmersh, *Jocast*, 36
Gay, John, 166–7; *The Beggar's Opera*, 163, 166; *Polly*, 167; *The What D'Ye Call it*, 166
Gentle Craft, The, 54
Gentleman Dancing Master, The, 150
Gentleness and Nobility, 28
Gielgud, Sir John, 188
Giraudoux, Jean, 191
Gismound of Salerne see *Tancred and Gismunda*
Globe Theatre, 57, 71, 133
Goldsmith, Oliver, 162–3, 170–71; *Enquiry into the Present State of Polite Learning in Europe* (essay), 170; *The Good Natured Man*, 170; *She Stoops to Conquer; or The Mistakes of a Night*, 170–71
Good Natured Man, The, 170
Gorboduc, 35–6, 47
Granville, George, Baron Lansdowne, *The Jew of Venice*, 68
Greene, Graham, *A Burnt-Out Case*, 117; *The Quiet American*, 117
Greene, Robert, 52–4, 58, 146; *Alphonsus, King of Aragon*, 52; *Friar Bacon and Friar Bungay*, 52–3; *James IV*, 52–4; *Orlando Furioso*, 52; *Perimedes the Blacksmith*, 52; and Thomas Lodge, *A Looking Glass for London*, 52
Gregory, Augusta, Lady, 184
Grein, J.T., 178
Guarini, Giovanni Battista, 126
Guicciardini, Francesco, 87
Gull's Hornbook, The, 82
Gwyn, Nell, 152

Hall, Joseph, 74; *Virgidemiarum*, 58
Hamartigenia, 18
Hamlet, 49, 85, 95, 126–7, 168, 172
Hardy, Thomas, *The Dynasts*, 186
Harris, Joseph (?), 135
Harvey, Gabriel, 58
Hassan, 186–7
Hauptmann, Gerhart, 190
Hawkins, Harriet, *Likenesses of Truth in Elizabethan and Restoration Drama*, 147n
Haymarket Theatre, 165, 167
Hazlitt, William, 162, 172–3
Heartbreak House, 181–2
Henrietta Maria, Queen of England, 39, 84
Henry, Prince, 94
Henry III, King of England, 53
Henry VI, 45
Henry VII, King of England, 25
Herbert, Sir Henry, 134–5
Hercules Oetaeus, 92
Heywood, Joan (née Rastell), 28
Heywood, John, 28–30, 32–3; *The Four Ps*, 28–9; *Johan Johan*, 29; *The Pardoner and the Friar*, 29; *A*

Play of Love, 28; *The Play of the Weather*, 28; *Witty and Witless*, 29
Heywood, Thomas, *Four Prentices of London*, 56, 81
Hindle Wakes, 183
His House in Order, 175
Historical Register, The, 167
Histriomastix, 57
Hobson, Sir Harold, 198, 200
Hobson's Choice, 183
Homecoming, The, 198, 201–2
Honest Whore, The, 75
Hooke, Robert, 137
Horestes, 35
Horniman, Annie, 183
Hostage, The, 194
Houghton, Stanley, *Hindle Wakes*, 183
Hour Glass, The, 184
House by the Stable, The, 188
Howard, Edward, 144
Howard, Sir Robert, *The Committee*, 145
Hughes, Thomas, *The Misfortunes of Arthur*, 36
Humorous Day's Mirth, An, 59, 90
Hunt, James Henry Leigh, 162, 173
Hyde Park, 83–4

I Have Been Here Before, 191
Ibsen, Henrik, 116, 175, 177–8, 180, 190, 202; *A Doll's House (Breaking a Butterfly)*, 177; *An Enemy of the People (Quicksands)*, 177; *The Master Builder*, 182; *The Wild Duck*, 177
Ideal Husband, An, 176
I'm Talking About Jerusalem, 195
Importance of Being Earnest, The, 176, 182, 206
Inadmissible Evidence, 193–4
Inconstant, The, 83
Indian Emperor, The, 160
Inspector Calls, An, 191
Interlude of the Student and the Girl, 25
Ion, 188
Irving, Sir Henry, 162, 171, 174
Isherwood, Christopher *see* Auden, W.H.
Island of the Mighty, The, 198
Isle of Dogs, The, 58

Jack Juggler, 34
James I, King of England, 54, 61, 83, 85–6, 127
James IV, 52–4
Jane Shore, 165
Jarry, Alfred, 183
Jew, The, 169
Jew of Malta, The, 44–5
Jew of Venice, The, 68
Jocast, 36
Johan Johan, 29
Johnson, Samuel, 154, 164
Jolly, George, 135
Jones, Henry Arthur, 162, 175–7; *The Liars*, 176; *Mrs Dane's Defence*, 176; *The Silver King*, 175
Jones, Inigo, 69, 134
Jonson, Ben, on Marlowe, 42; and the 'War of the Theatres', 57; nature of his work, 70, 79; dedication to, 71; popularity of, 81, 124; and Brome, 83; as composer of masques, 133; influence of, 146–7,

160–61; *The Alchemist*, 58, 64–8; *Bartholomew Fair*, 58, 62, 68–9, 83; *Cynthia's Revels*, 51; *Epicoene or The Silent Woman*, 69; *Every Man in His Humour*, 58–61, 68–9; *Every Man Out of his Humour*, 57, 60; *The Devil is an Ass*, 82; *The Poetaster*, 57–8, 70; *Volpone*, 58, 61–7; and Thomas Nashe, *The Isle of Dogs*, 58; *see also* Marston, John
Jordan, Dorothy, 160
Journey's End, 190
Jovial Crew, The, 83
Joyce, James, 206
Jumpers, 205–6
Juno and the Paycock, 184

Kaiser, Georg, 185
Katherine and Petruchio, 168
Kean, Charles, 173–4
Kean, Edmund, 80, 162, 172–4
Keats, John, 90
Kelly, Edward, 65
Kemble, John Philip, 162, 171–4
Kemp, Will, 58
Killigrew, Thomas, 134–6, 171
King and No King, A, 124, 126–7, 130
King Lear, 34, 103–4, 122, 167–8, 174
King Lear's Wife, 187
King's Men, The (actors' company), 61, 64, 71, 83, 126, 133
King's Threshold, The, 184
Kinsayder, W. (ps.) *see* Marston, John
Kinwelmersh, Francis *see* Gascoigne, George
Kitchen, The, 195
Knepp, Mary, 153
Knight of the Burning Pestle, The, 56
Knowles, Sheridan, 172–4; *Virginius*, 186
Kolve, V.A., *The Play Called Corpus Christi*, 3n
Kyd, Thomas, 41, 85, 131; *The Spanish Tragedy*, 47–9, 81, 85, 87, 95, 101, 130

Lady Jane Grey, 165
Lady's Not for Burning, The, 188
Lady of Pleasure, The, 83–4
Lady Windermere's Fan, 176
Lamb, Charles, 162, 173
Land of Heart's Desire, 183–4
Landscape, 199, 202
Langland, William, 58; *The Vision of Piers Plowman*, 17
Laski, Albert, 65
Lawrence, D.H., 128, 180; *Women in Love*, 182
Lear, 207–8
Lee, Nathaniel, *Sophonisba*, 141–2
Left-handed Liberty, 198
Lenin, V.I., 206
Lerner, Laurence, 117n
Lewes, George Henry, 162, 173
Lewis, C.S., 43
Liars, The, 176
Lichtenberg, Georg, 162
Lily of Killarney, The see *Colleen Bawn, The*
Lincoln, Abraham, 175
Lincolns Inn Fields Theatre, 135, 165–6
Linden Tree, The, 191

Lindsay, David, *A Satire of the Three Estates*, 30
Littlewood, Joan, 194
Lock Up Your Daughters see *Rape Upon Rape*
Locke, John, 137
Lodge, Thomas *see* Greene, Robert
London Assurance, 174
Look Back in Anger, 191 – 4
Looking Glass for London, A, 52
Loot, 204
Lord Chamberlain's Men, The (actors' company), 57 – 8
Loutherbourg, J.P. de, 171
Love and Honour, 134
Love for Love, 153 – 6
Love in a Tub, 146
Love in a Wood, 150
Love of Four Colonels, The, 191
Love's Labour's Lost, 40, 51
Love's Last Shift, 159, 163
Lovelace, Richard, 151
Lovesick Maids, The, 83
Lucretius, 147
Lucian, 39
Luther, 193
Lying Lover, The, 163
Lyly, John, 39 – 41, 48, 51 – 2; *Alexander and Campaspe*, 40; *Endymion*, 39 – 41; *Euphues, the Anatomy of Wit*, 38; *Euphues and His England*, 39; *Galathea*, 39; *Mother Bombie*, 39, 51
Lytton, Edward George Earle Lytton Bulwer, first Baron Lytton, 174

Macneice, Louis, *The Dark Tower*, 189
Macready, William Charles, 171, 173, 178
Macro, Cox, 19
Mad World, My Masters, A, 74
Magistrate, The, 175
Magnificence, 30
Maid's Tragedy, The, 124 – 6
Major Barbara, 181
Malcontent, The, 58, 70 – 73
Male Coquette, The, 168
Man and Superman, 181
Man of Mode, The, or Sir Fopling Flutter, 147 – 50
Mankind, 19 – 21, 27
Mann, Thomas, 128
Marlowe, Christopher, 41 – 8, 52, 85, 94; *Dido, Queen of Carthage*, 44; *Edward II*, 44 – 5; *Dr Faustus*, 22, 45 – 7, 85; *Hero and Leander* (poem), 68, 90; *The Jew of Malta*, 44 – 5; *The Massacre at Paris*, 44; *Tamburlaine*, 36 – 7, 42 – 5, 67, 87, 93
Marriage of Wit and Wisdom, The, 28
Marston, John (*ps.* W. Kinsayder), 57, 70, 85 – 90, 97, 99; *Antonio and Mellida*, 87 – 8; *Antonio's Revenge*, 85 – 90; *The Dutch Courtesan*, 58, 70, 72, 101; *The Fawn*, 171; *Histriomastix*, 57; *The Malcontent*, 58, 70 – 73; *The Metamorphosis of Pygmalion's Image and Certain Satires* (poem), 70; *The Scourge of Villainy* (poem), 58, 70 *The Wonder of Women*, 70; and Thomas Dekker, *Satiromastix*, 57; and Ben Jonson and George Chapman, *Eastward Ho*, 58, 78, 80
Martyn, Edward, 184
Marvell, Andrew, quoted, 131 – 2

Mary I, Queen of England, 28
Mary II, Queen of England, 138, 153 – 4
Massacre at Paris, The, 44
Massinger, Philip, 77 – 81; *The Bondman*, 81; *The City Madam*, 77, 80; *A New Way to Pay Old Debts*, 55, 75, 78 – 81; *The Unnatural Combat*, 128
Master Builder, The, 182
Measure for Measure, 71, 126
Medwall, Henry, 30; *Fulgens and Lucrece*, 25 – 7; *Nature*, 27
Merchant of Venice, The, 63, 173
Merry Conceits of Bottom the Weaver, The, 133
Middleton, Thomas, 74 – 7, 79, 95, 107, 125, 131, 147; *A Chaste Maid in Cheapside*, 74, 76 – 7, 111 – 12; *A Mad World, My Masters*, 74; *Micro-Cynicon, Six Snarling Satires* (poem), 74; *The Phoenix*, 71; *A Trick to Catch the Old One*, 74 – 5, 77; *The Wisdom of Solomon Paraphrased* (poem), 73; *Women Beware Women*, 74, 111 – 6, 129 – 30; and Thomas Dekker, *The Roaring Girl*, 77; and William Rowley, *The Changeling*, 73, 111, 113, 116 – 23, 126 – 7; *see also* Webster, John
Midsummer Night's Dream, A, 34, 51, 133
Miller, Arthur, *The Crucible*, 197
Milton, John, 161; *Lycidas*, 24
Miracle plays, 3 – 16; *see also* Chester cycle; Coventry miracle plays; N-town cycle; Wakefield cycle; York cycle
Mirror for Magistrates, A, 42
Misanthrope, Le, 151
Misfortunes of Arthur, The, 36
Miss in her Teens, 168
Modern Husband, The, 167
Mohun, Michael, 135
Molière, *Le Misanthrope*, 151
Morality plays, 16 – 24; *see also* individual titles
More, Elizabeth *see* Rastell, Elizabeth
More, Sir Thomas, 27 – 8
Morley, Henry, 174
Morris, William, 195
Morton, John, Archbishop of Canterbury, 25, 27
Mother Bombie, 39, 51
Mourning Bride, The, 154
Mrs Daintry's Daughter, 178
Mrs Dane's Defence, 176
Mrs Warren's Profession, 178, 180
Much Ado About Nothing, 181
mummers' plays, 2
Murder in the Cathedral, 187 – 8
Murphy, Arthur, 167 – 9

N-town cycle, 5, 7, 10; *The Trial of Joseph and Mary*, 16; *The Woman Taken in Adultery*, 13 – 16
Narrow Road to the Deep North (The Bundle), 208
Nashe, Thomas, 52, 58; and *Dido, Queen of Carthage*, 44; *see also* Jonson, Ben
National Theatre, 197
Nature, 27
Nature of the Four Elements, The, 28
New Way to Pay Old Debts, A, 55, 75, 78 – 81
Newton, Sir Isaac, 137
Nicholson, Norman, 188
Night and Day, 206

No Man's Land, 199, 203
Noh theatre, 184
Norton, Thomas, and Thomas Sackville, *Gorboduc*, 35–6, 47

O'Casey, Sean, 184–6, 192; *Cock-a-Doodle-Dandy*, 186; *Juno and the Paycock*, 184; *The Plough and the Stars*, 184–5; *Red Roses for Me*, 185; *Shadow of a Gunman*, 184; *The Silver Tassie*, 185; *Within the Gates*, 185–6
Old Bachelor, The, 154–5
Old Fortunatus, 54
Old Times, 199, 203
Old Wives' Tale, The, 41, 51–3, 82
Olivier, Laurence, Lord, 193
On the Frontier, 187
Ordinary, The, 138
Orlando Furioso, 52
Orphan, The, 166
Orton, Joe, 143, 155, 204; *Entertaining Mr Sloane*, 204; *Loot*, 204; *What the Butler Saw*, 204
Osborne, John, 128, 191–4; *The Entertainer*, 193; *Inadmissible Evidence*, 193–4; *Look Back in Anger*, 191–4; *Luther*, 193; *A Place Calling Itself Rome*, 193; *The World of Paul Slickey*, 193
Othello, 104, 107, 128, 167, 173
Otway, Thomas, *The Orphan*, 166; *Venice Preserved*, 139–40, 166
Our American Cousin, 175
Overbury, Sir Thomas, 100
Ovid, 51; *The Art of Love*, 147; *Metamorphosis*, 39
Oxford, Earl of *see* Vere, Edward de, Earl of Oxford

Paolo and Francesca, 184, 186
Pardoner and the Friar, The, 29
Parker, Matthew, Archbishop of Canterbury, 41
Pasquin, 167
Peele, George,. 51–3; *The Arraignment of Paris*, 41, 51–2; *The Old Wives' Tale*, 41, 51–3, 82
Pepys, Elizabeth, 137
Pepys, Samuel, 136–7, 146, 150, 153–4
Pericles, 128
Perimedes the Blacksmith, 52
Perkin Warbeck, 128
Phelps, Samuel, 171, 174
Phillips, Stephen, *Paolo and Francesca*, 184, 186
Philaster, 126
Phoenix, The, 71
Phoenix too Frequent, A, 189
Pickering, John, *Horestes*, 35
Pinero, Arthur Wing, 162, 175–8; *Dandy Dick*, 175; *His House in Order*, 175; *The Magistrate*, 175; *The Profligate*, 175; *The Second Mrs Tanqueray*, 175, 178; *Trelawney of the 'Wells'*, 175
Pinter, Harold, 194, 198–202; *A la Recherche du Temps Perdu* (screenplay), 199; *The Birthday Party*, 198–201; *The Caretaker*, 198–9, 201–2; *The Dumb Waiter*, 198, 201; *The Homecoming*, 198, 201–2; *Landscape*, 199, 202; *No Man's Land*, 199; *Old Times*, 199, 203; *The Quiller Memorandum* (screenplay), 200; *The Room*, 201; *Silence*, 199, 202
Pirandello, Luigi, 183
Place Calling Itself Rome, A, 193

Plain Dealer, The, 150–51, 153–4
Plautus, 33; *Amphitruo*, 34
Play of Love, A, 28
Play of the Weather, The, 28
Playboy of the Western World, The, 184
Pliny, 39
Plough and the Stars, The, 184–5
Plowright, Joan, 195
Poel, William, 190
Poetaster, The, 57–8, 70
Politician, The, 83
Polly, 167
Pope, Alexander, *The Dunciad*, 136
Pope's Wedding, The, 207
Priestley, J.B., 190–91; *Dangerous Corner*, 191; *Eden End*, 191; *I Have Been Here Before*, 191; *An Inspector Calls*, 191; *The Linden Tree*, 191; *Time and the Conways*, 191; *When We Are Married*, 191
Princess's Theatre, 174
Professional Foul, 206
Profligate, The, 175
Proust, Marcel, 203; *A la Recherche du Temps Perdu*, 199
Provoked Wife, The, 144, 158–9
Prudentius, *Hamartigenia*, 18; *Psychomachia*, 17
Psychomachia, 17
Purgatory, 184
Pygmalion, 181, 183

Quare Fellow, The, 194
Quem Quaeritis?, 2
Quicksands see *Enemy of the People, An*
Quin, James, 167

Raleigh, Sir Walter, 94
Ralph Roister Doister, 33–4
Rape Upon Rape (*The Coffee House Politician*), 167
Rastell, Elizabeth (*née* More), 28
Rastell, Joan *see* Heywood, Joan
Rastell, John, 28, 30, 32; *Calisto and Melibea*, 28; (probable author) *Gentleness and Nobility*, 28; *The Nature of the Four Elements*, 28
Rattigan, Terence, 191; *While the Sun Shines*, 191; *The Winslow Boy*, 191
Real Inspector Hound, The, 205
'realism', 173–4
Recruiting Officer, The, 160
Red Bull theatre, 133–5
Red Roses for Me, 185
Redford, John, *Wit and Science*, 32
Regularis Concordia, 2
Rehearsal, The, 141–2, 169
Relapse, The, 158–60, 163
Revenge of Bussy d'Ambois, The, 91
Revenger's Tragedy, The, 95–99, 130
Rheingold, 178
Rhodes, John, 133, 135
Rich, Christopher, 136
Rich, John, 166
Richard III, 88, 104, 173
Ricks, Christopher, 121
Riders to the Sea, 184
Rivals, The, 168
Roaring Girl, The, 77

Robertson, T.W., 162, 175; *Caste*, 175; *Society*, 175
Rochester, Earl of *see* Wilmot, John, Earl of Rochester
Rogers, David, 8
Romanoff and Juliet, 191
Romeo and Juliet, 55, 168
Room, The, 201
Roots, 194–5
Rosencrantz and Guildenstern are Dead, 205
Rossetti, Dante Gabriel, 187
Rowe, Nicholas, 165–6; *Lady Jane Grey*, 165; *Jane Shore*, 165
Rowley, William, 128; *see also* Middleton, Thomas
Royal Court Theatre, 190–91, 194–5

Sackville, Thomas *see* Norton, Thomas
Sadler's Wells theatre, 174
St Paul's theatre, 88
Salisbury Court theatre, 133, 135
Sanderson, Mary (Mrs Thomas Betterton), 135
Satire of the Three Estates, A, 30
Satiromastix, 57
Saturday Review, The (journal) 177
Saved, 202, 207
Savoy Theatre, 190
Schnitzler, Arthur, 190
School for Scandal, The, 169
Second Mrs Tanqueray, The, 175, 178
Secret Love, 158
Seneca, 35–6, 87; *Hercules Oetaeus*, 92
Sergeant Musgrave's Dance, 195–6
Settle, Elkanah, 142; *The Empress of Morocco*, 140, 144–5
Shadow of a Gunman, 184
Shadwell, Thomas, 138, 154, 160–61; *Bury Fair*, 160; *The Squire of Alsatia*, 154
Shakespeare, William, collaborating on *Sir Thomas More*, 27; and comedy of wit, 41; and rhetoric, 48; Greene on, 52; as actor-manager, 57–8, 61, 133; influence of, 58, 186; and Fletcher, 81; publication of, 83, 166; popularity of, 124, 172–3, 190; and Davenant, 133; Garrick and, 168; History plays of, 179; Osborne and, 193; *All's Well That Ends Well*, 71; *Antony and Cleopatra*, 139; *As You Like It*, 69, 86; *Coriolanus*, 172, 193; *Cymbeline*, 126; *Hamlet*, 49, 85, 95, 126–7, 168, 172; *Henry VI*, 45; *King Lear*, 34, 103–4, 122, 167–8, 174; *Love's Labour's Lost*, 40, 51; *Measure for Measure*, 71, 126; *The Merchant of Venice*, 63, 173; *A Midsummer Night's Dream*, 34, 51, 133; *Much Ado About Nothing*, 181; *Othello*, 104, 107, 128, 167, 173; *Pericles*, 128; *Richard III*, 88, 104, 173; *Romeo and Juliet*, 55, 168; *Sonnets*, 90; *The Taming of the Shrew*, 168; *The Tempest*, 16; *Titus Andronicus*, 130; *Troilus and Cressida*, 71, 85; *Twelfth Night*, 63, 151; *The Winter's Tale*, 52, 168, 173
Shaw, George Bernard, 109, 162, 167, 175–83, 189–90; *The Admirable Bashville*, 183; *The Apple Cart*, 183; *Arms and the Man*, 179, 183; *Back to Methuselah*, 180–81; *Caesar and Cleopatra*, 179, 183; *Candida*, 181; *The Devil's Disciple*, 183; *Heartbreak House*, 181–2; *Major Barbara*, 181; *Man and Superman*, 181; *Mrs Warren's Profession*, 178, 180; *Pygmalion*, 181, 183; *Why She Would Not*, 177;

Widowers' Houses, 177, 179; *You Never Can Tell*, 183
She Stoops to Conquer; or The Mistakes of a Night, 170–71
She Would If She Could, 146–7
Sheridan, Richard Brinsley, 162–3, 169–71; *The Critic; A Tragedy Rehearsed*, 169; *The Rivals*, 168; *Robinson Crusoe* (pantomime), 169; *The School for Scandal*, 169
Sherriff, R.C., *Journey's End*, 190
Shirley, James, 83–4, 131; *The Cardinal*, 83; *Hyde Park*, 83–4; *The Lady of Pleasure*, 83–4; *The Politician*, 83
Shoemaker's Holiday, The, 54–6, 72
Siddons, Mrs Sarah, 162, 171
Siege of Rhodes, The, 134, 137
Silence, 199, 202
Silver King, The, 175
Silver Tassie, The, 185
Sir Patient Fancy, 144
Skelton, John, 58
Sleep of Prisoners, A, 189
Smith, William, 135
Society, 175
Sophonisba, 141–2
Southern, Robert, *The Mediaeval Theatre in the Round*, 19n
Southerne, Thomas, *The Wives' Excuse*, 161
Spanish Friar, The, 142
Spanish Tragedy, The, 47–9, 81, 85, 87, 95, 101, 130
Spender, Stephen, *Trial of a Judge*, 187
Spenser, Edmund, *The Faerie Queene*, 39
Squire of Alsatia, The, 154
Steele, Richard, 162–8; *The Conscious Lovers*, 163–5, 168; *The Funeral*, 163; *The Lying Lover*, 163; *The Tender Husband*, 163
Stevenson, William, (probable author) *Gammer Gurton's Needle*, 34
Strindberg, August, 183; *The Father*, 181
Sir Thomas More, 27–8
Skelton, John, *Magnificence*, 30
Stevenson, Robert Louis, 179
Stoppard, Tom, 205–6; *Every Good Boy Deserves Favour*, 206; *Jumpers*, 205–6; *Night and Day*, 206; *Professional Foul*, 206; *The Real Inspector Hound*, 205; *Rosencrantz and Guildenstern Are Dead*, 205; *Travesties*, 205–6
Sunday Times, The (newspaper), 198
Swan theatre, 74
Sweeney Agonistes, 187
Synge, John Millington, 184; *The Playboy of the Western World*, 184; *Riders to the Sea*, 184

Talfourd, Thomas, 172–3
Tamburlaine, 36–7, 42–5, 67, 87, 193
Taming of the Shrew, The, 168
Tancred and Gismunda (*Gismounde of Salerne*), 36
Tate, Nahum, 174
Taylor, Tom, 162; *Our American Cousin*, 175; *The Ticket-of-Leave Man*, 175
Tempest, The, 16
Tender Husband, The, 163
Tennyson, Alfred, Lord, *Becket*, 186

Terence, 33
Theatre, The (journal), 163
Theatre Royal, Bridges Street, 135
Theatre Royal, Drury Lane, 136, 165, 167–8, 170–4
Theatre Workshop, 194
theatres, medieval, 6–9; Elizabethan, 37–8; closure of, 131–4; early use of proscenium arch, 134; Shaw on, 190; *see also* individual theatres
Their Very Own and Golden City, 195
Thomas, Dylan, *Under Milk Wood*, 189
Threepenny Opera, The, 166
Ticket-of-Leave Man, The, 175
Time and the Conways, 191
'Tis Pity She's a Whore, 109, 128–31
Titus Andronicus, 130
Tobias and the Angel, 191
Toller, Ernst, 185
Tolstoy, Leo, 182
Tourneur, Cyril, 95–100, 126; *The Atheist's Tragedy*, 94–5, 97; *The Revenger's Tragedy*, 95–99, 130
Towneley cycle *see* Wakefield cycle
Tragedy of Tom Thumb, The (*The Tragedy of Tragedies*), 167
Travesties, 205–6
Tree, Sir Beerbohm, 171
Trelawney of the 'Wells', 175
Trial of a Judge, 187
Trial of Joseph and Mary, The, 16
Trick to Catch the Old One, A, 74–5, 77
Troilus and Cressida, 71, 85
tropes, *Regularis Concordia*, 2; *Quem Quaeritis?*, 2
Tuke, Samuel, *The Adventures of Five Hours*, 143, 145
Twelfth Night, 63, 151
Tynan, Kenneth, 193, 202
Tzara, Tristan, 206

Udall, Nicholas, (probable author) *Jack Juggler*, 34; *Ralph Roister Doister*, 33–4
Under Milk Wood, 189
Unnatural Combat, The, 128
Urban IV, Pope, 3–4
Ustinov, Peter, 191; *The Love of Four Colonels*, 191; *Romanoff and Juliet*, 191

Vanbrugh, Sir John, 138, 158–60, 165; *The Confederacy*, 158; *The Relapse*, 158–60, 163; *The Provoked Wife*, 144, 158–9
Vega, Lope de, 193
Venice Preserved, 139–40, 166
Vere, Edward de, Earl of Oxford, 39
Victoria, Queen of England, 174
Villiers, George, Duke of Buckingham, *The Rehearsal*, 141–2, 169
Virgidemiarum, 58
Volpone, 58, 61–7
Vortex, The, 190

Wager, William, *Enough is as Good as a Feast*, 31–2
Waiting for Godot, 203, 205
Wakefield cycle (Towneley cycle), 5, 7, 10, 27
Walpole, Horace, 170
Walpole, Sir Robert, 167
Wardle, Irving, 201

Way of the World, The, 143, 153, 156–8
Webb, John, 134
Webster, John, 71, 94, 99–111, 120, 126; *The Devil's Law-Case*, 100; *The Duchess of Malfi*, 100, 102, 105–11, 128; *Monuments of Honour* (masque), 100; *The White Devil*, 100, 102–5, 110; and Middleton *et al.*, *Caesar's Fall*, 100
Welsh Opera, The, 167
Wesker, Arnold, 194–5; *Chicken Soup with Barley*, 194; *Chips with Everything*, 194–5; *The Friends*, 195; *I'm Talking About Jerusalem*, 195; *The Kitchen*, 195; *Roots*, 194–5; *Their Very Own and Golden City*, 195
West Indian, The, 169
Westminster Theatre, 187
What D'Ye Call It, The, 166
What the Butler Saw, 204
When We Are Married, 191
While the Sun Shines, 191
White Devil, The, 100, 102–5, 110
Why She Would Not, 177
Widowers' Houses, 177, 179
Wild Duck, The, 177
Wild Goose Chase, The, 82–3
Wilde, Oscar, 162, 175–6; *An Ideal Husband*, 176; *The Importance of Being Earnest*, 176, 182, 206; *Lady Windermere's Fan*, 176; *A Woman of No Importance*, 176
William III, King of England, 136, 138, 153–4
Williams, Charles, *The House by the Stable*, 188
Wilmot, John, Earl of Rochester, 147
Wilmot, Robert, *Tancred and Gismunda* (*Gismound of Salerne*), 36
Winslow Boy, The 191
Winter's Tale The, 52, 168, 173
Wit, The, 134
Wit and Science, 32
Within the Gates, 185–6
Witty and Witless, 29
Wives' Excuse, The, 161
Woffington, Peg, 160
Wolsey, Thomas, 27
Woman of No Importance, A, 176
Woman Taken in Adultery, The, 13–16
women, dramatic depiction of, 100–102, 112
Women Beware Women, 74, 11–16, 129–30
Wonder of Women, The, 70
Workhouse Donkey, The, 196–7
World of Paul Slickey, The, 193
Wren, Sir Christopher, 136–7
Wycherley, William, 138, 150–6; *The Country Wife*, 150–4, 158; *The Gentleman Dancing Master*, 150; *Love in a Wood*, 150; *The Plain Dealer*, 150–51, 153–4
Wycliff, John, 16

Yeats, William Butler, 184–5; *The Countess Cathleen*, 184; *The Hour Glass*, 184; *The King's Threshold*, 184; *Land of Heart's Desire*, 183–4; *Purgatory*, 184
York cycle, 5, 8–10; *The Crucifixion*, 11–13
You Never Can Tell, 183

Zola, Emile, 185